尾田栄一郎

I get really antsy when I'm not reading a book. In other words, I'm a print addict, if you will. Just kidding. I just wanted to say that. And here comes volume 57!

-Eiichiro Oda, 2010

Eiichiro Oda began his manga career at the age of 17, when his one-shot cowboy manga **Wanted!** won second place in the coveted Tezuka manga awards. Oda went on to work as an assistant to some of the biggest manga artists in the industry, including Nobuhiro Watsuki, before winning the Hop Step Award for new artists. His pirate adventure **One Piece**, which debuted in **Weekly Shonen Jump** in 1997, quickly became one of the most popular manga in Japan.

ONE PIECE VOL. 57
PARAMOUNT WAR PART 1

SHONEN JUMP Manga Edition

This graphic novel contains material that was originally published in English in SHONEN JUMP #91–94. Artwork in the magazine may have been slightly altered from that presented here.

STORY AND ART BY EIICHIRO ODA

English Adaptation/Lance Caselman
Translation/Laabaman, HC Language Solutions, Inc.
Touch-up Art & Lettering/Vanessa Satone
Design/Sean Lee, Fawn Lau
Editor/Alexis Kirsch

Printed in the U.S.A.

Published by VIZ Media, LLC
P.O. Box 77010
San Francisco, CA 94107

10 9 8 7 6 5 4 3 2 1
First printing, June 2011

www.viz.com

PARENTAL ADVISORY
ONE PIECE is rated T for Teen and is recommended for ages 13 and up. This volume contains fantasy violence and tobacco usage.
ratings.viz.com

THE WORLD'S MOST POPULAR MANGA
www.shonenjump.com

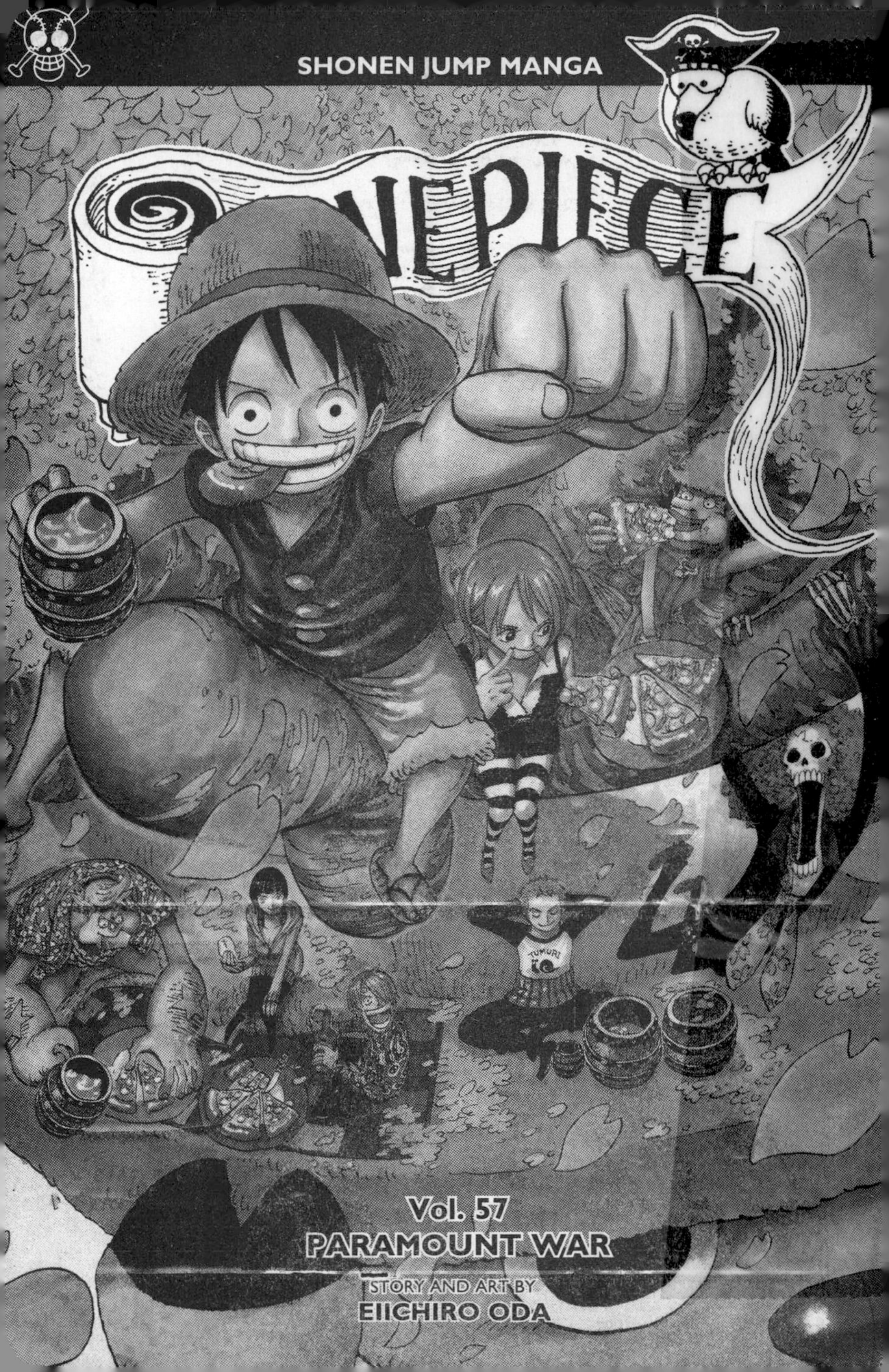
SHONEN JUMP MANGA
Vol. 57
PARAMOUNT WAR
STORY AND ART BY
EIICHIRO ODA

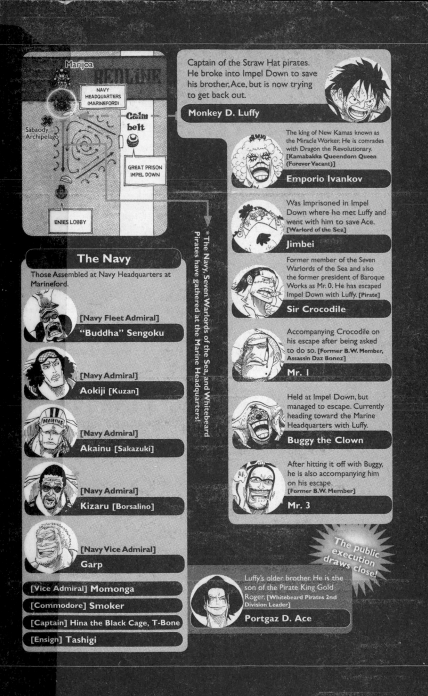

Marijoa
REDLINE
NAVY HEADQUARTERS (MARINEFORD)
Calm belt
Sabaody Archipelago
GREAT PRISON IMPEL DOWN
ENIES LOBBY

*The Navy, Seven Warlords of the Sea, and Whitebeard Pirates have gathered at the Marine Headquarters!

Captain of the Straw Hat pirates. He broke into Impel Down to save his brother, Ace, but is now trying to get back out.

Monkey D. Luffy

The king of New Kamas known as the Miracle Worker. He is comrades with Dragon the Revolutionary. [Kamabakka Queendom Queen (Forever Vacant)]

Emporio Ivankov

Was Imprisoned in Impel Down where he met Luffy and went with him to save Ace. [Warlord of the Sea]

Jimbei

Former member of the Seven Warlords of the Sea and also the former president of Baroque Works as Mr. 0. He has escaped Impel Down with Luffy. [Pirate]

Sir Crocodile

Accompanying Crocodile on his escape after being asked to do so. [Former B.W. Member, Assassin Daz Bonez]

Mr. 1

Held at Impel Down, but managed to escape. Currently heading toward the Marine Headquarters with Luffy.

Buggy the Clown

After hitting it off with Buggy, he is also accompanying him on his escape. [Former B.W. Member]

Mr. 3

The Navy

Those Assembled at Navy Headquarters at Marineford.

[Navy Fleet Admiral]

"Buddha" Sengoku

[Navy Admiral]

Aokiji [Kuzan]

[Navy Admiral]

Akainu [Sakazuki]

[Navy Admiral]

Kizaru [Borsalino]

[Navy Vice Admiral]

Garp

[Vice Admiral] **Momonga**

[Commodore] **Smoker**

[Captain] **Hina the Black Cage, T-Bone**

[Ensign] **Tashigi**

The public execution draws close!

Luffy's older brother. He is the son of the Pirate King Gold Roger. [Whitebeard Pirates 2nd Division Leader]

Portgaz D. Ace

THE STORY OF ONE PIECE

Volume 57

The Four Emperors

Whitebeard Pirates

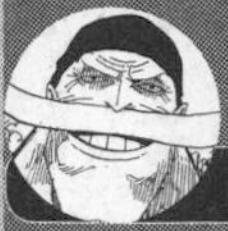

The world's strongest Pirate. He has arrived at Navy Headquarters to rescue Ace.
[Captain of Whitebeard Pirates]

Edward Newgate

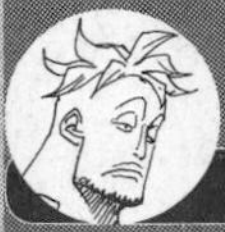

[Whitebeard Pirates 1st Division Leader]

Marco

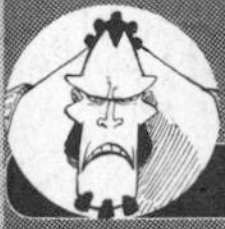

[Whitebeard Pirates 3rd Division Leader]

Jozu

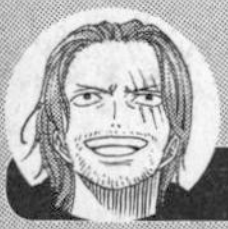

Was involved in a scuffle with Kaido in the New World.
[Captain of the Red-Haired Pirates]

"Red-Haired" Shanks

Warlords of the Sea

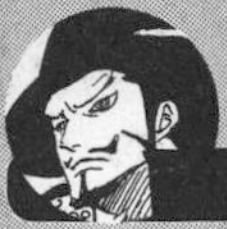

The world's most powerful swordsman. He expresses interest in Luffy and his crew.

Dracule Mihawk

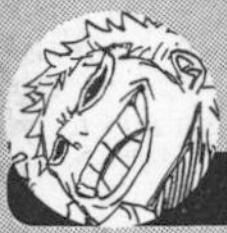

A mysterious man who believes that power is everything.

Don Quixote Doflamingo

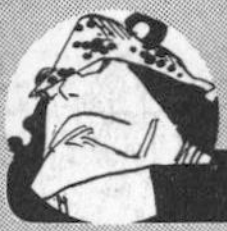

Also known as "the Tyrant." He's acted oddly when it comes to the Straw Hats.

Bartholomew Kuma

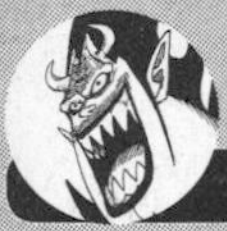

Although he already lost to Luffy once, he answers the call of battle.

Gecko Moria

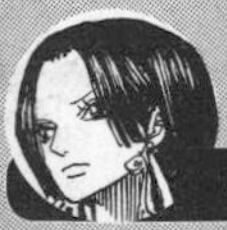

The empress of Amazon Lily and captain of the Kuja Pirates.

Boa Hancock

Luffy infiltrated the Great Prison Impel Down to rescue his brother Ace, but powerful prison guards stood in his way. Upon learning that Ace had already been escorted to the Navy Headquarters, Luffy escapes Impel Down along with many other big name pirates and chases after Ace. At the same time, Ace is taken to the execution platform and a shocking truth is revealed to the entire world: Ace is actually the biological son of the Pirate King, Gold Roger! The Navy fears the second coming of the Pirate King and is trying to take preventative measures. The Whitebeard Pirates' fleet then arrives at the Navy Headquarters, effectively sounding the signal of an all-out war!

ONE PIECE

PARAMOUNT WAR

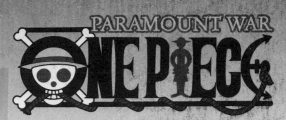

Vol. 57
Paramount War

CONTENTS

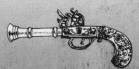

Chapter 552:
ACE AND WHITEBEARD

LIMITED COVER SERIES, NO. 15:
CHOPPER'S "I'M NOT FOOD, YOU JERKS!!"
VOL. 1: "RACCOON STEW ESCAPE"

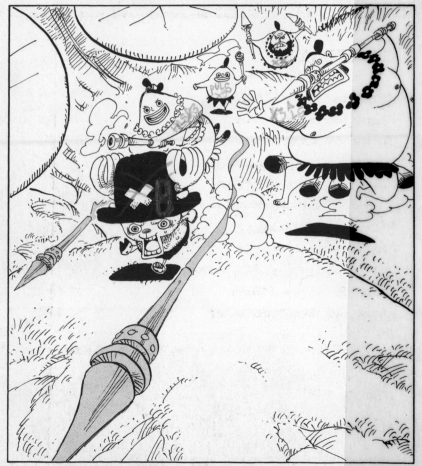

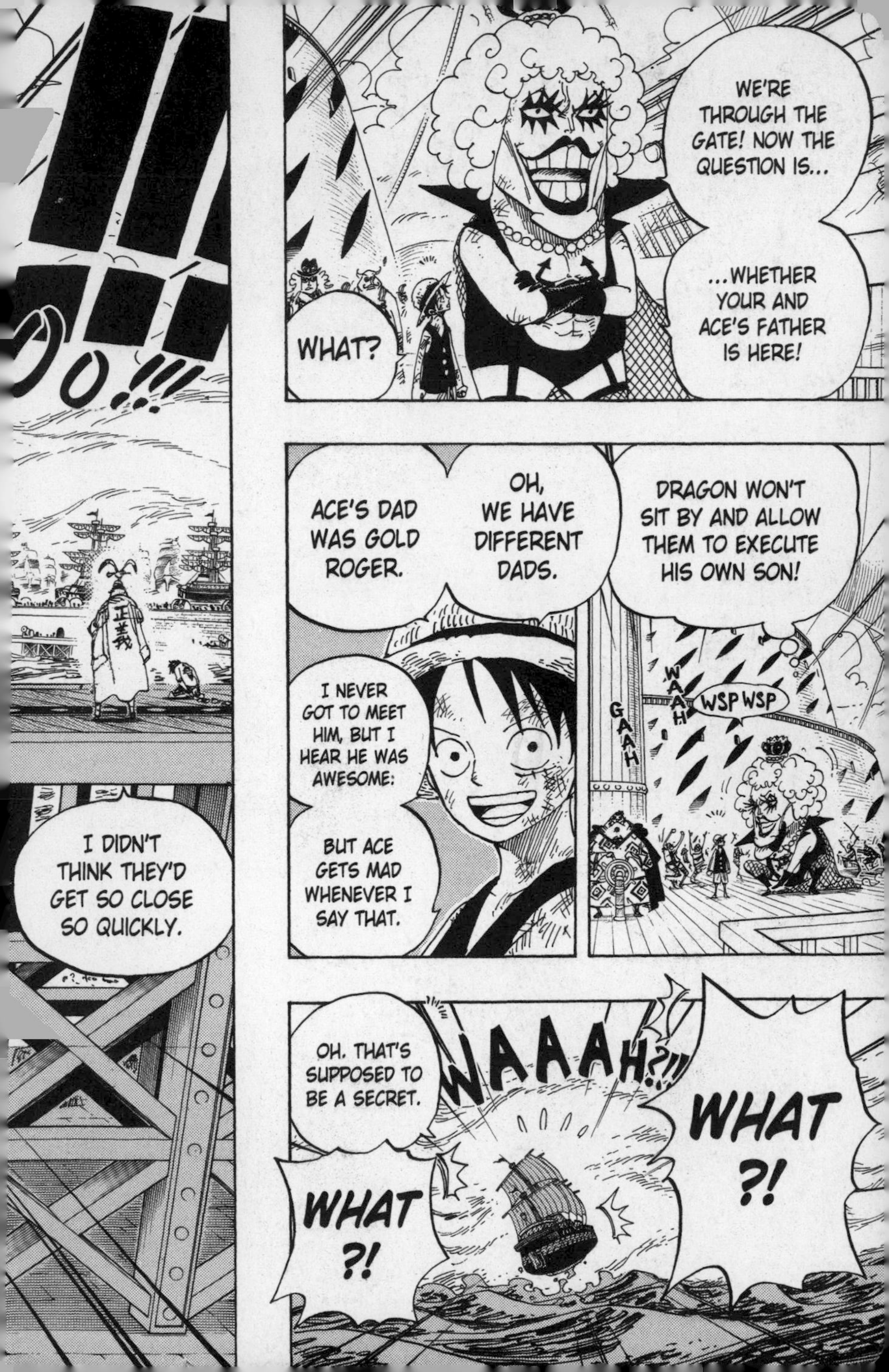
WE'RE THROUGH THE GATE! NOW THE QUESTION IS...
...WHETHER YOUR AND ACE'S FATHER IS HERE!
WHAT?
DRAGON WON'T SIT BY AND ALLOW THEM TO EXECUTE HIS OWN SON!
WSP WSP
WAAAH
GAAAH
OH, WE HAVE DIFFERENT DADS.
ACE'S DAD WAS GOLD ROGER.
I NEVER GOT TO MEET HIM, BUT I HEAR HE WAS AWESOME:
BUT ACE GETS MAD WHENEVER I SAY THAT.
OH. THAT'S SUPPOSED TO BE A SECRET.
WAAAH?!!
WHAT ?!
WHAT ?!
O..!!!
正義
I DIDN'T THINK THEY'D GET SO CLOSE SO QUICKLY.

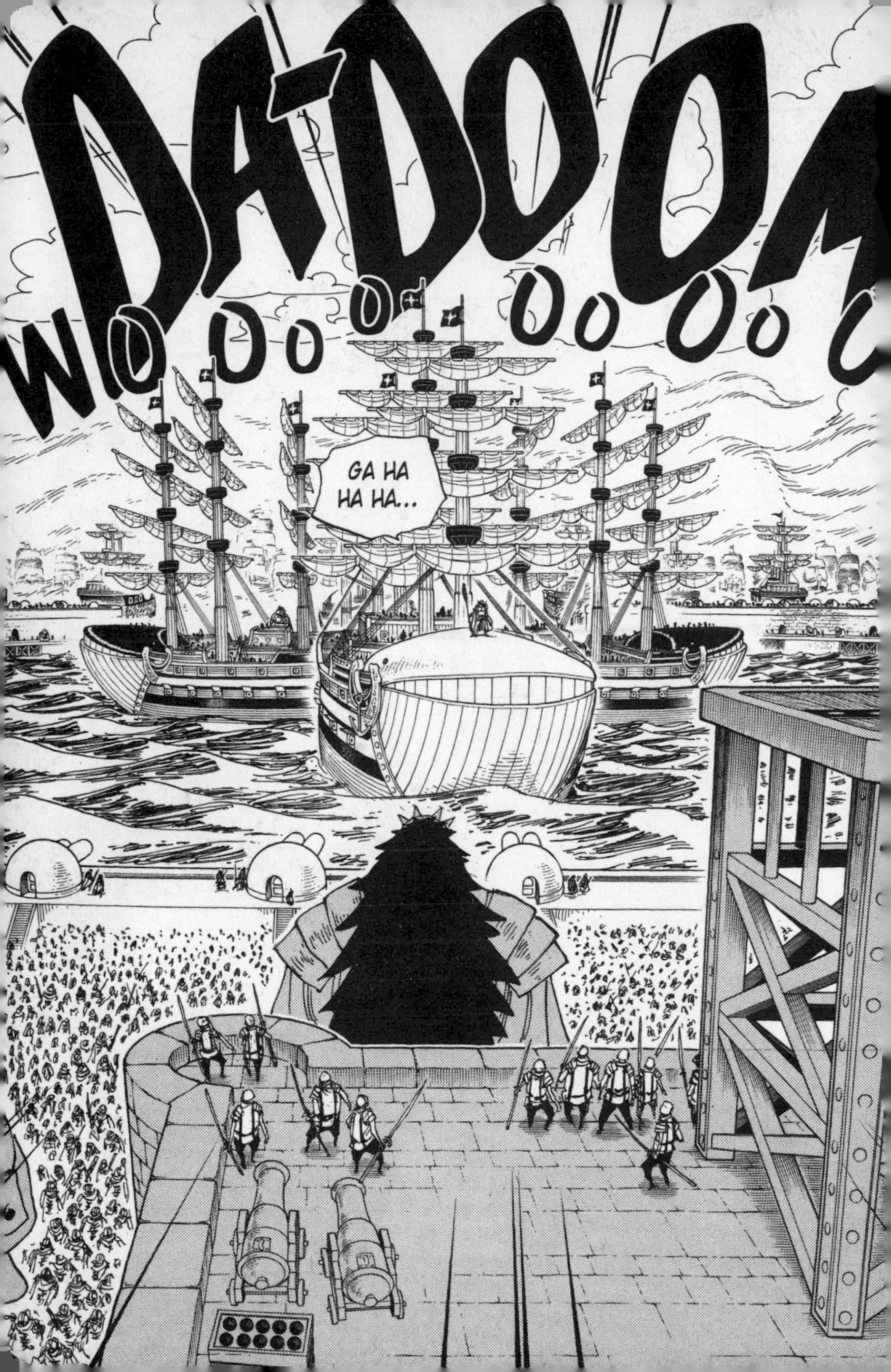
DADOOM
WOOOOOOOOOO
GA HA
HA HA...

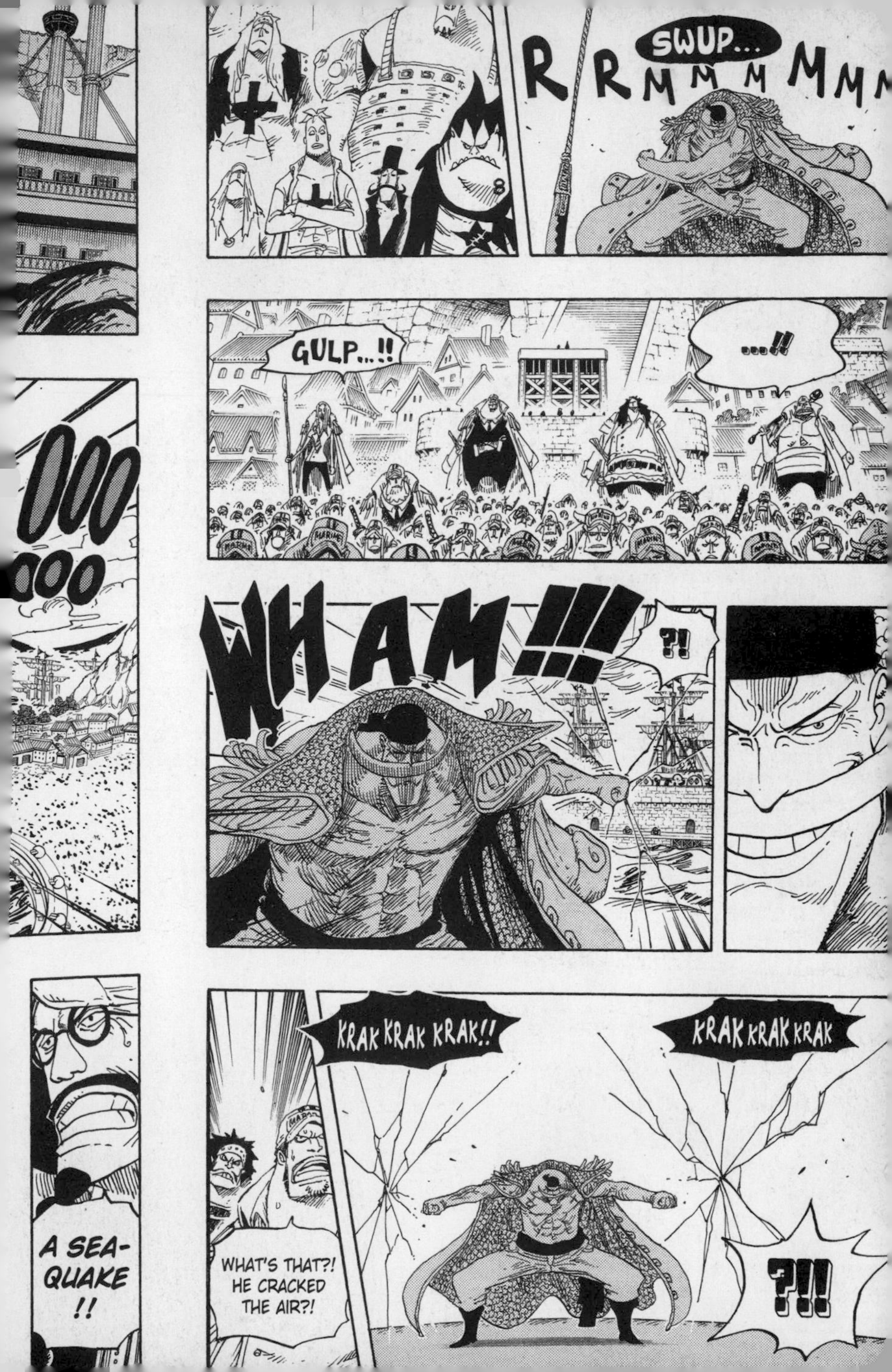
SWUP...
RRMMMMMMMM
...!!
GULP...!!
WHAM!!!
?!
KRAK KRAK KRAK
?!!
KRAK KRAK KRAK!!
WHAT'S THAT?! HE CRACKED THE AIR?!
OOOOOOO
A SEA-QUAKE!!

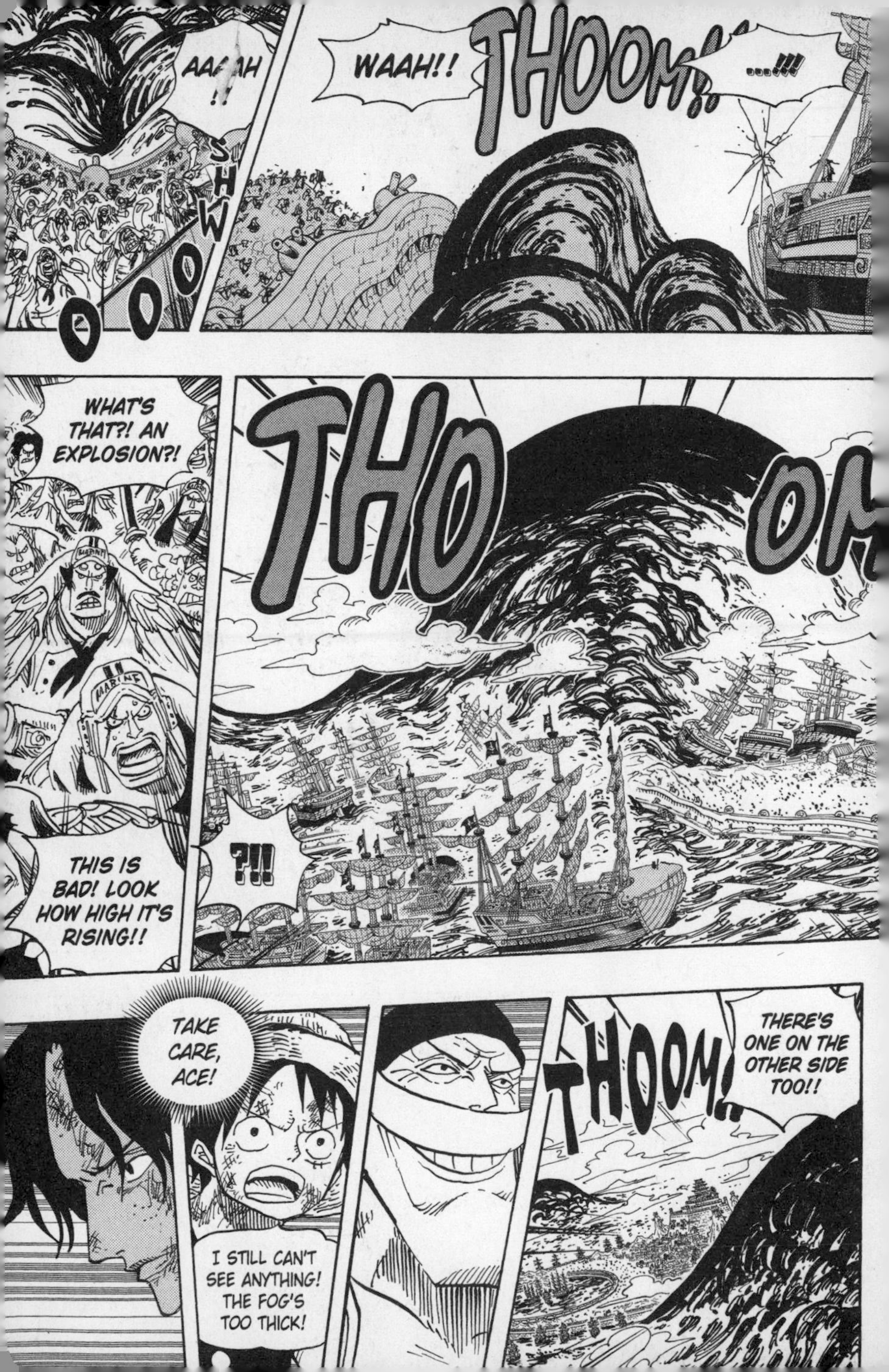
...!!!
THOOM..
WAAH!!
AAAAH!!
SHWOOOO
THOOOM
?!!
WHAT'S THAT?! AN EXPLOSION?!
THIS IS BAD! LOOK HOW HIGH IT'S RISING!!
THERE'S ONE ON THE OTHER SIDE TOO!!
THOOM..
TAKE CARE, ACE!
I STILL CAN'T SEE ANYTHING! THE FOG'S TOO THICK!

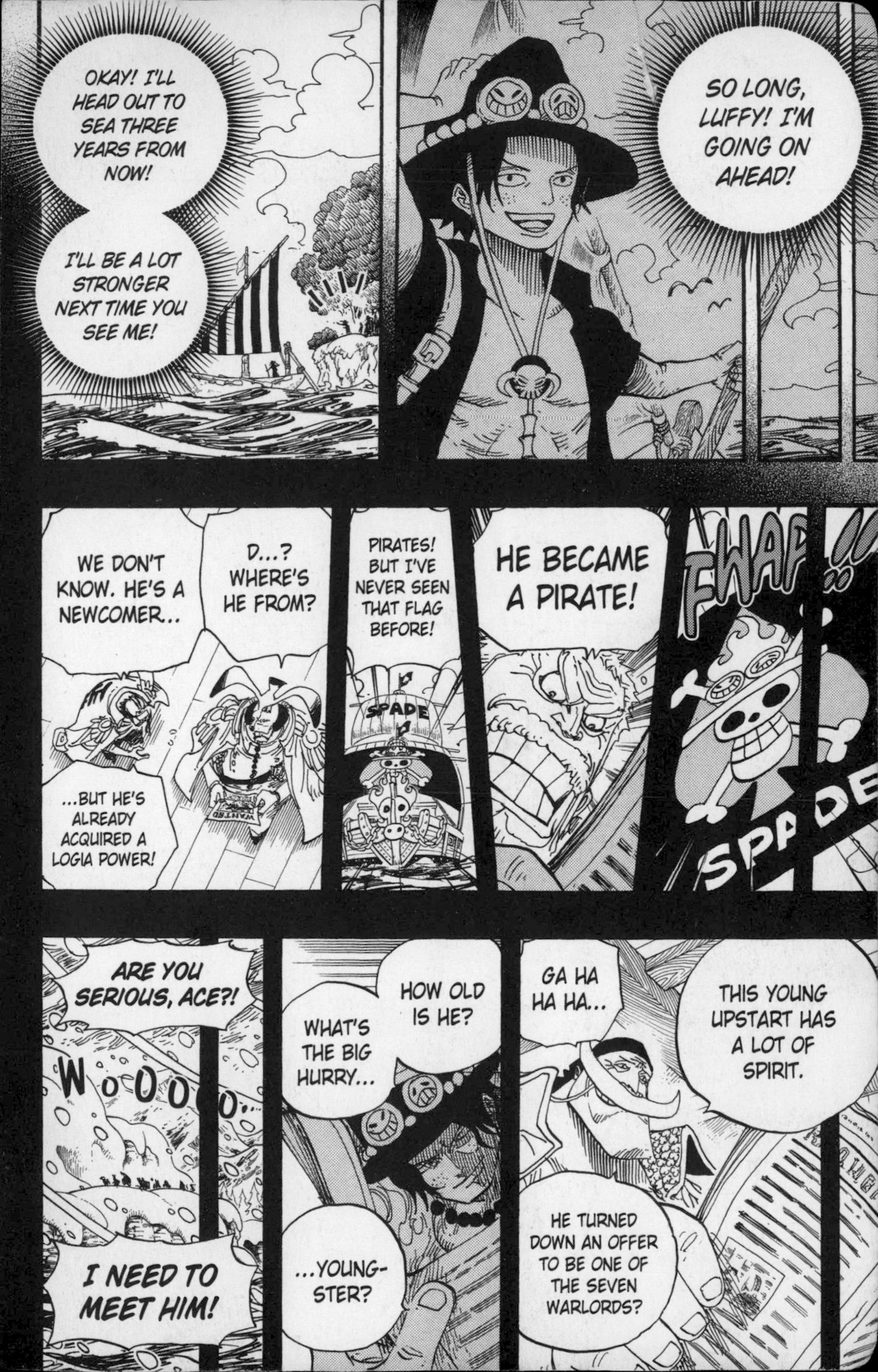
SO LONG, LUFFY! I'M GOING ON AHEAD!
OKAY! I'LL HEAD OUT TO SEA THREE YEARS FROM NOW!
I'LL BE A LOT STRONGER NEXT TIME YOU SEE ME!
FWAP!!
SPADE
HE BECAME A PIRATE!
PIRATES! BUT I'VE NEVER SEEN THAT FLAG BEFORE!
SPADE
D...? WHERE'S HE FROM?
WE DON'T KNOW. HE'S A NEWCOMER...
...BUT HE'S ALREADY ACQUIRED A LOGIA POWER!
THIS YOUNG UPSTART HAS A LOT OF SPIRIT.
GA HA HA HA...
HE TURNED DOWN AN OFFER TO BE ONE OF THE SEVEN WARLORDS?
HOW OLD IS HE?
WHAT'S THE BIG HURRY...
...YOUNG-STER?
ARE YOU SERIOUS, ACE?!
WOOOO...
I NEED TO MEET HIM!

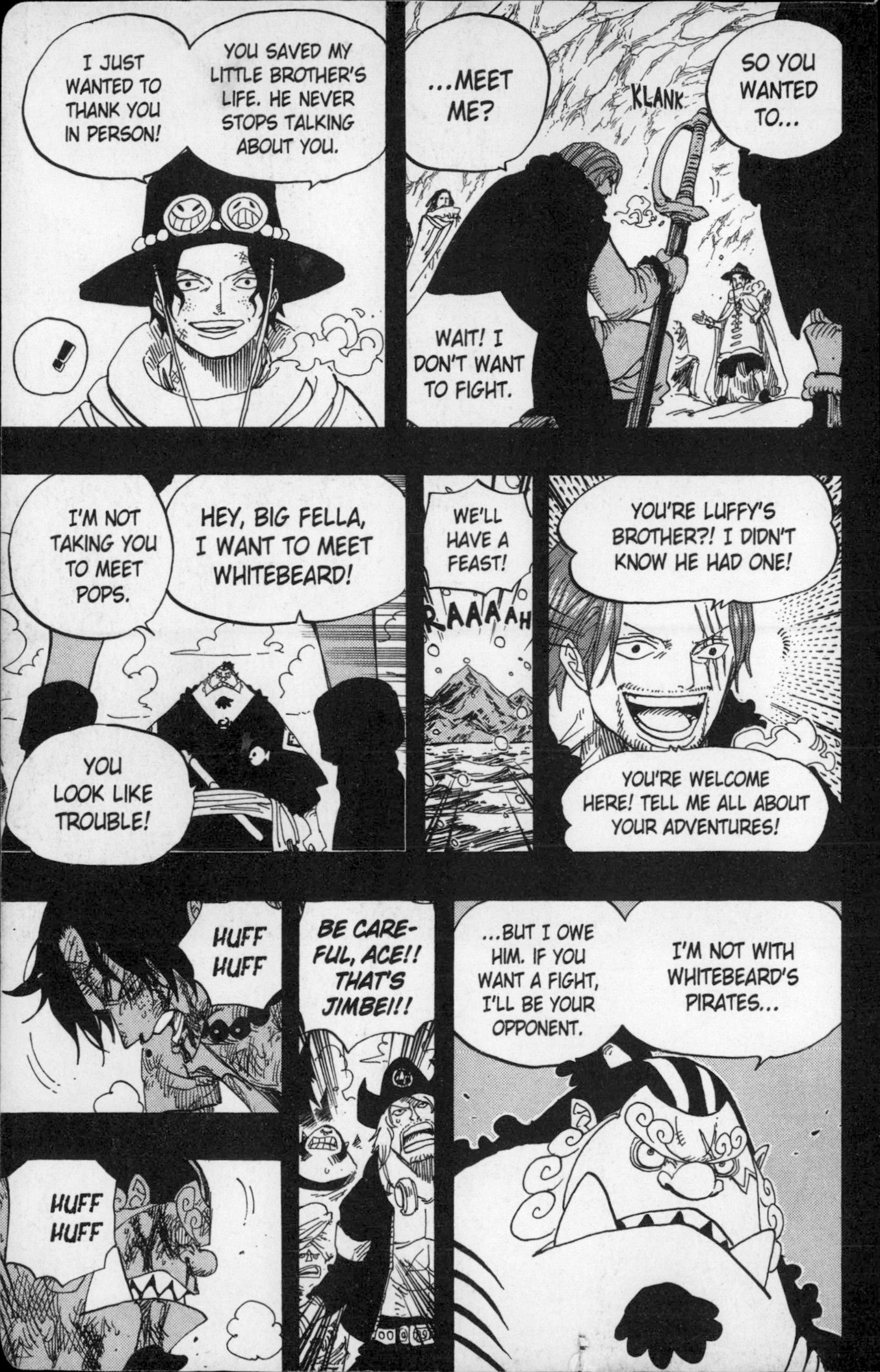
SO YOU WANTED TO...
KLANK
...MEET ME?
WAIT! I DON'T WANT TO FIGHT.
YOU SAVED MY LITTLE BROTHER'S LIFE. HE NEVER STOPS TALKING ABOUT YOU.
I JUST WANTED TO THANK YOU IN PERSON!
!
YOU'RE LUFFY'S BROTHER?! I DIDN'T KNOW HE HAD ONE!
YOU'RE WELCOME HERE! TELL ME ALL ABOUT YOUR ADVENTURES!
WE'LL HAVE A FEAST!
RAAAAH
HEY, BIG FELLA, I WANT TO MEET WHITEBEARD!
I'M NOT TAKING YOU TO MEET POPS.
YOU LOOK LIKE TROUBLE!
I'M NOT WITH WHITEBEARD'S PIRATES...
...BUT I OWE HIM. IF YOU WANT A FIGHT, I'LL BE YOUR OPPONENT.
BE CARE-FUL, ACE!! THAT'S JIMBEI!!
HUFF HUFF
HUFF HUFF

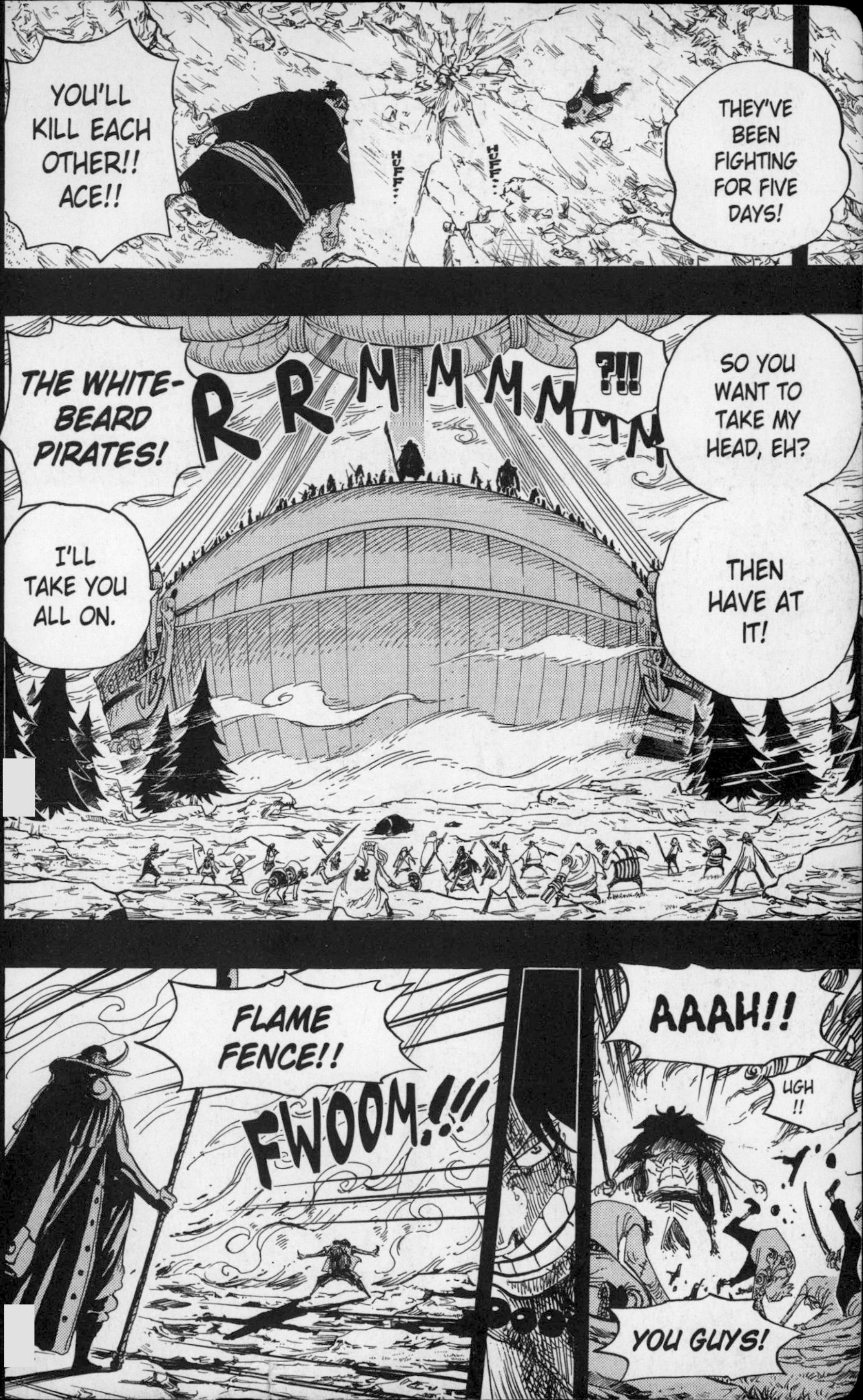
THEY'VE BEEN FIGHTING FOR FIVE DAYS!
HUFF...
HUFF...
YOU'LL KILL EACH OTHER!! ACE!!
SO YOU WANT TO TAKE MY HEAD, EH?
?!!
RRMMMMMM
THEN HAVE AT IT!
THE WHITE-BEARD PIRATES!
I'LL TAKE YOU ALL ON.
AAAH!!
UGH !!
YOU GUYS!
FLAME FENCE!!
FWOOM!!!

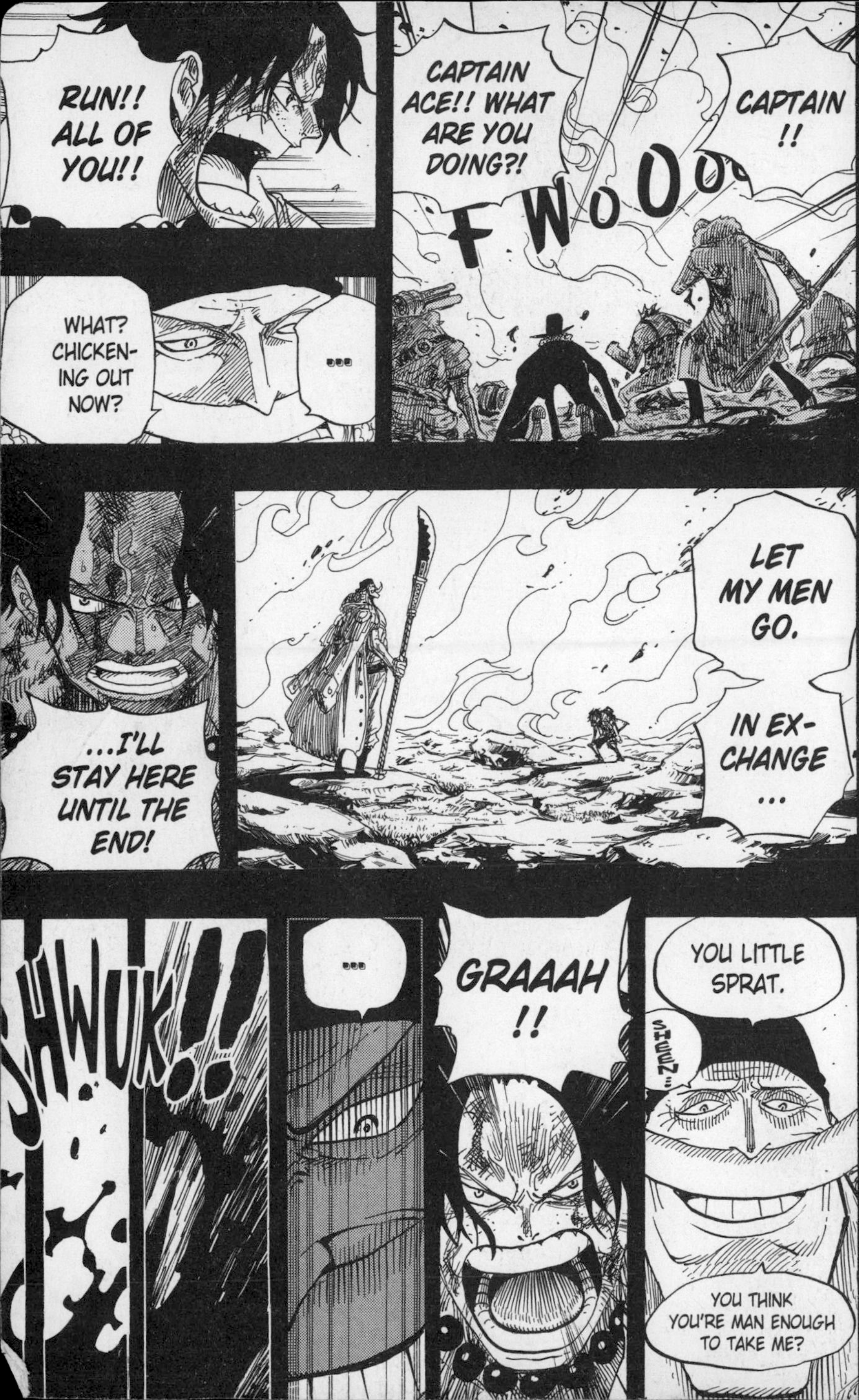
CAPTAIN !!
CAPTAIN ACE!! WHAT ARE YOU DOING?!
FWOOO
RUN!! ALL OF YOU!!
WHAT? CHICKEN-ING OUT NOW?
...
LET MY MEN GO.
IN EX-CHANGE ...
...I'LL STAY HERE UNTIL THE END!
YOU LITTLE SPRAT.
SHEEN...
YOU THINK YOU'RE MAN ENOUGH TO TAKE ME?
GRAAAH !!
...
SHWUK!!

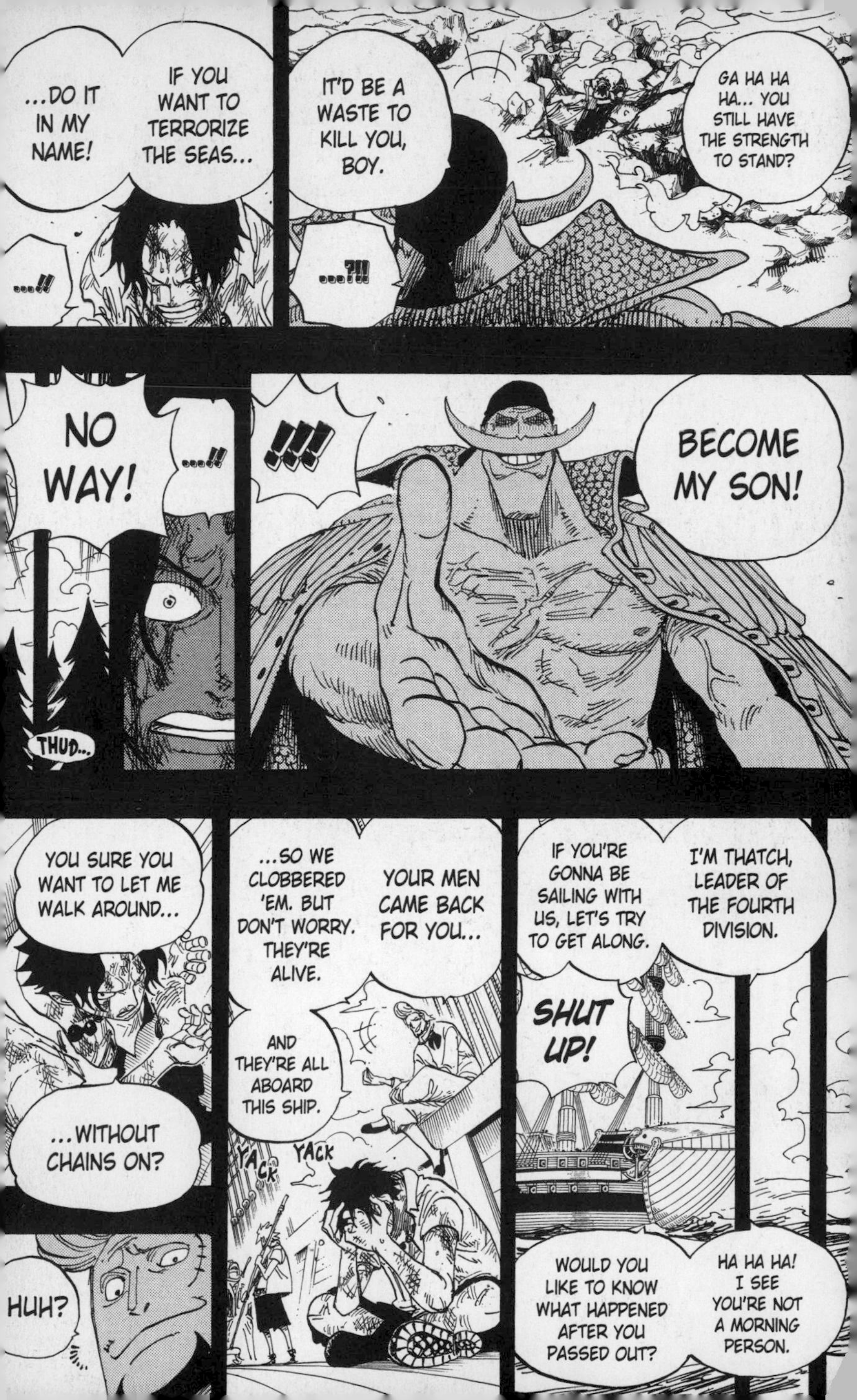
GA HA HA HA... YOU STILL HAVE THE STRENGTH TO STAND?
IT'D BE A WASTE TO KILL YOU, BOY.
...?!!
IF YOU WANT TO TERRORIZE THE SEAS...
...DO IT IN MY NAME!
...!!
BECOME MY SON!
!!!
...!!
NO WAY!
THUD...
I'M THATCH, LEADER OF THE FOURTH DIVISION.
IF YOU'RE GONNA BE SAILING WITH US, LET'S TRY TO GET ALONG.
SHUT UP!
HA HA HA! I SEE YOU'RE NOT A MORNING PERSON.
WOULD YOU LIKE TO KNOW WHAT HAPPENED AFTER YOU PASSED OUT?
YOUR MEN CAME BACK FOR YOU...
...SO WE CLOBBERED 'EM. BUT DON'T WORRY. THEY'RE ALIVE.
AND THEY'RE ALL ABOARD THIS SHIP.
YACK
YACK
YOU SURE YOU WANT TO LET ME WALK AROUND...
...WITHOUT CHAINS ON?
HUH?

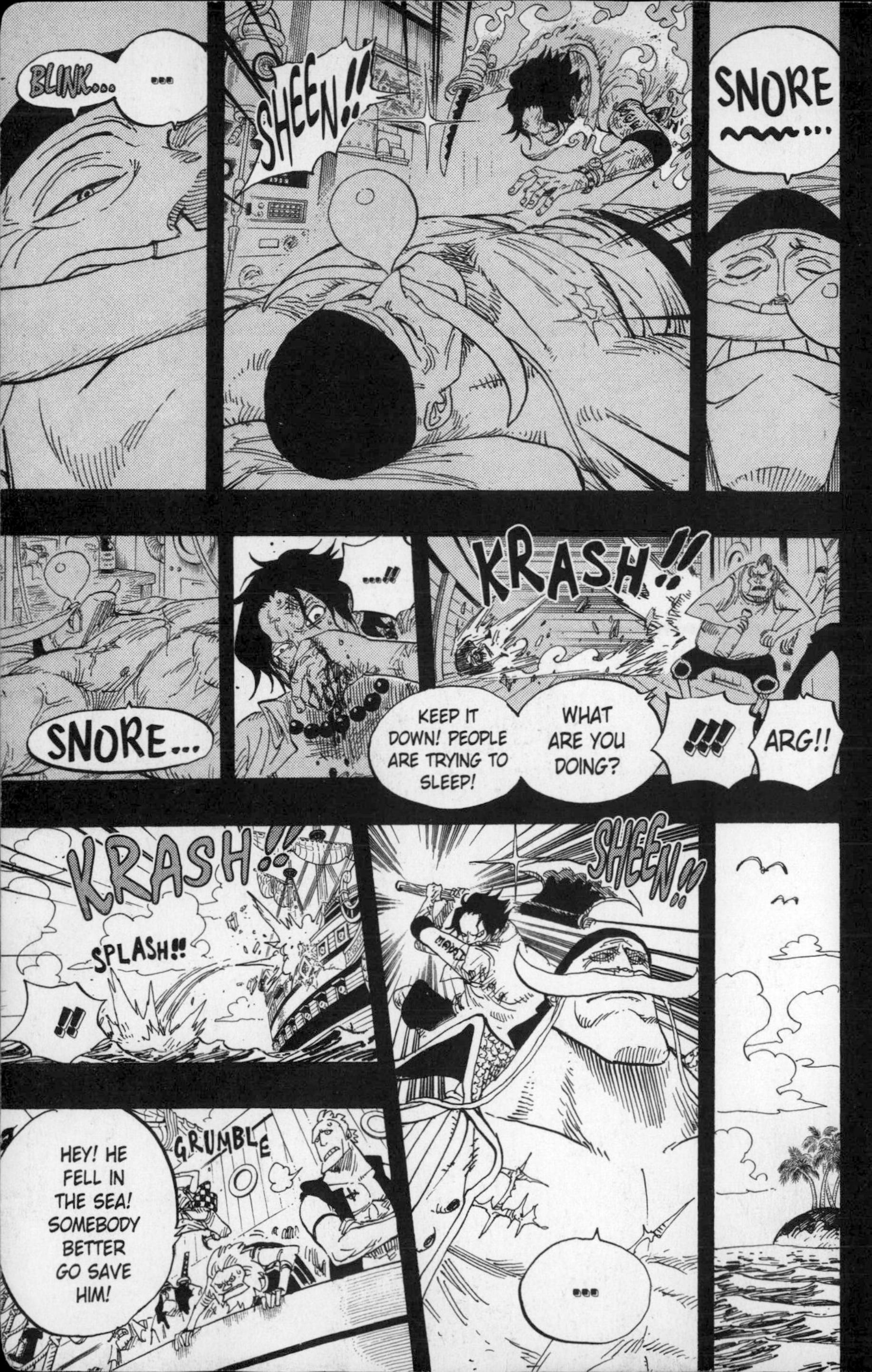
SNORE
~~~...
SHEEN!!
BLINK...
...
KRASH!!
ARG!!
!!!
WHAT ARE YOU DOING?
KEEP IT DOWN! PEOPLE ARE TRYING TO SLEEP!
...!!
SNORE...
SHEEN!!
...
KRASH!!
SPLASH!!
!!
GRUMBLE
HEY! HE FELL IN THE SEA! SOMEBODY BETTER GO SAVE HIM!
~~~

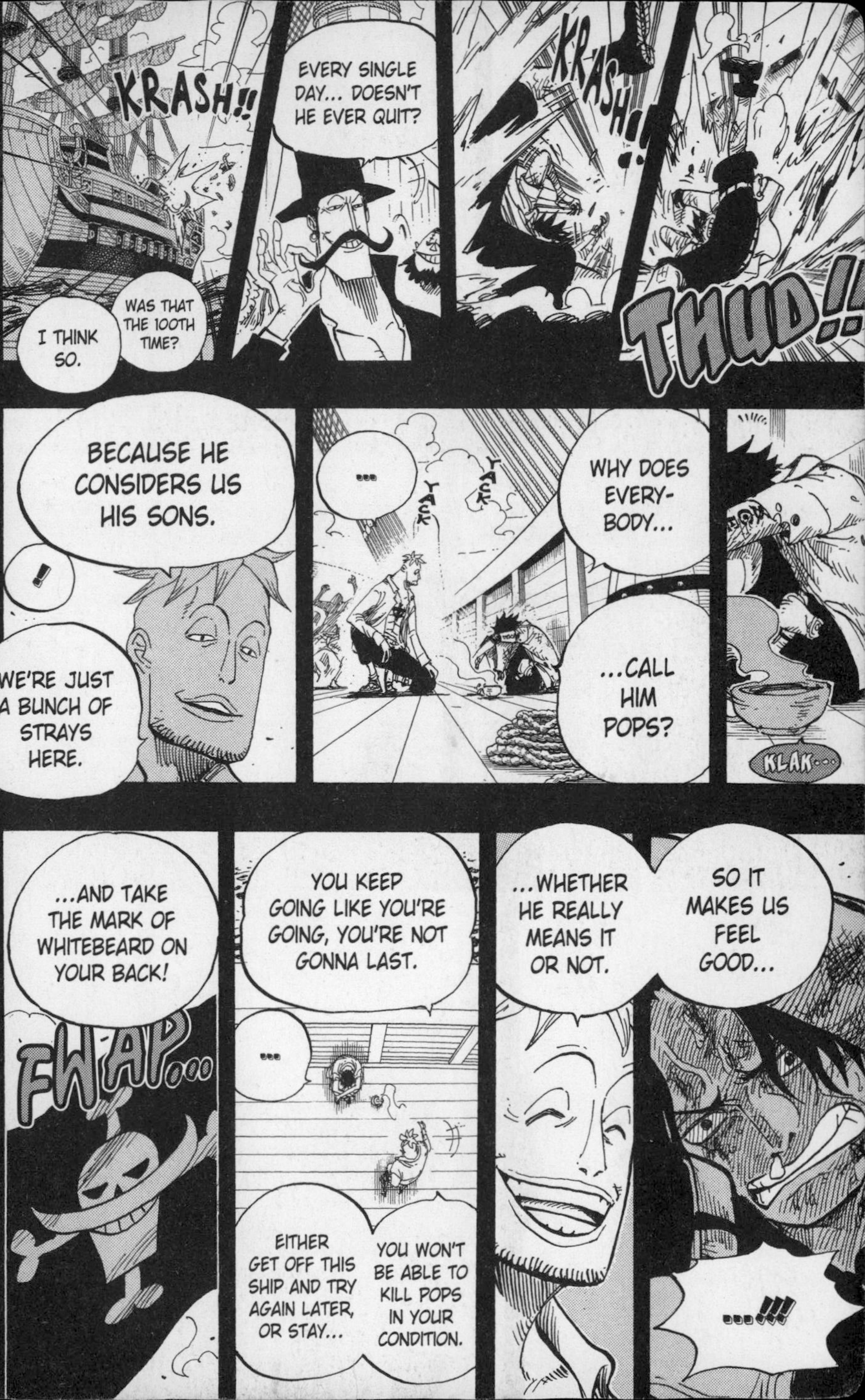
KRASH!!
THUD!!
EVERY SINGLE DAY... DOESN'T HE EVER QUIT?
KRASH!!
WAS THAT THE 100TH TIME?
I THINK SO.
KLAK...
WHY DOES EVERY-BODY...
...CALL HIM POPS?
YACK
YACK
...
BECAUSE HE CONSIDERS US HIS SONS.
!
WE'RE JUST A BUNCH OF STRAYS HERE.
SO IT MAKES US FEEL GOOD...
...!!!
...WHETHER HE REALLY MEANS IT OR NOT.
YOU KEEP GOING LIKE YOU'RE GOING, YOU'RE NOT GONNA LAST.
...
YOU WON'T BE ABLE TO KILL POPS IN YOUR CONDITION.
EITHER GET OFF THIS SHIP AND TRY AGAIN LATER, OR STAY...
...AND TAKE THE MARK OF WHITEBEARD ON YOUR BACK!
FWAP...

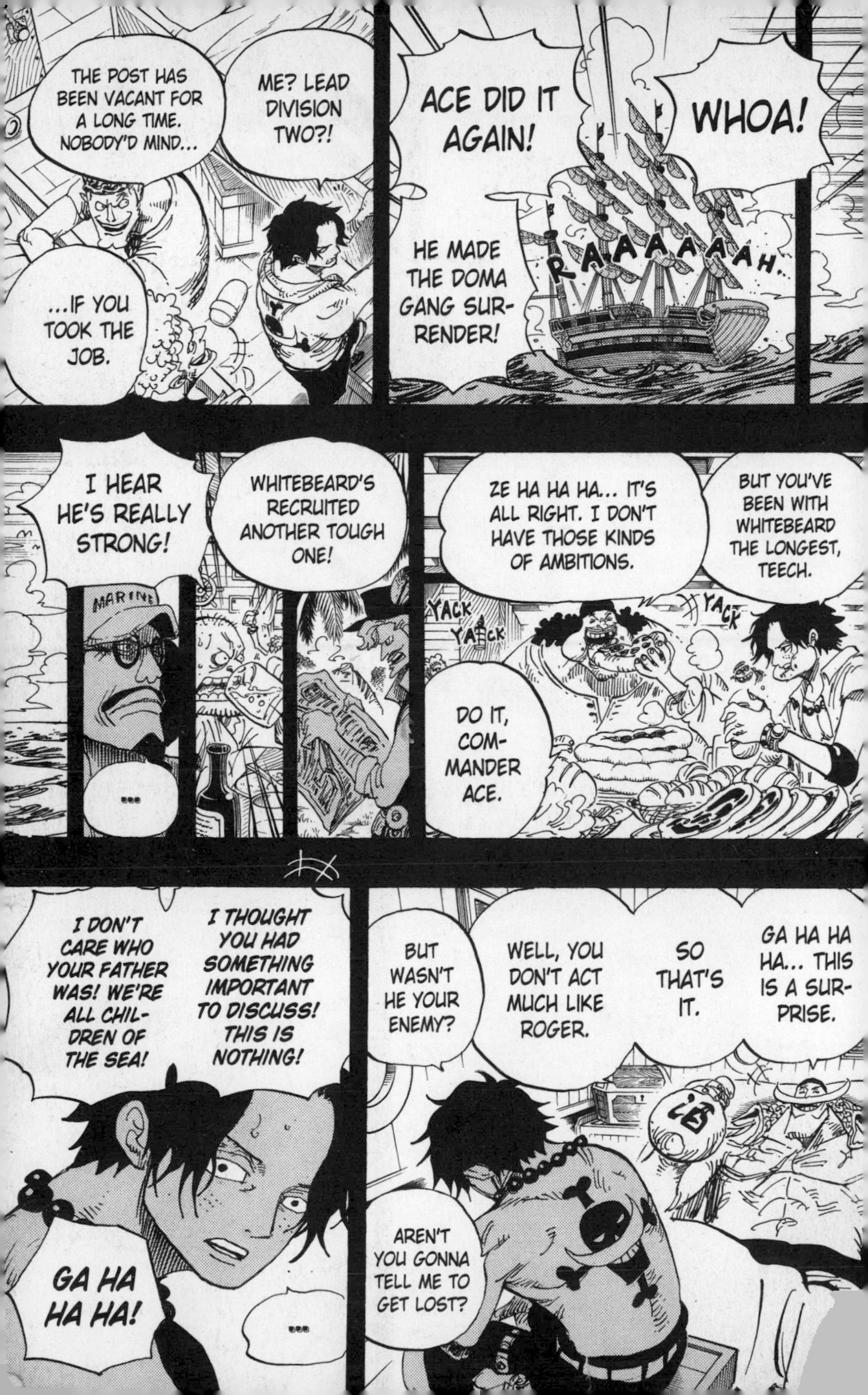
WHOA!
ACE DID IT AGAIN!
HE MADE THE DOMA GANG SURRENDER!
RAAAAAAAH..
ME? LEAD DIVISION TWO?!
THE POST HAS BEEN VACANT FOR A LONG TIME. NOBODY'D MIND...
...IF YOU TOOK THE JOB.
BUT YOU'VE BEEN WITH WHITEBEARD THE LONGEST, TEECH.
ZE HA HA HA... IT'S ALL RIGHT. I DON'T HAVE THOSE KINDS OF AMBITIONS.
YACK
YACK
YACK
DO IT, COMMANDER ACE.
WHITEBEARD'S RECRUITED ANOTHER TOUGH ONE!
I HEAR HE'S REALLY STRONG!
MARINE
...
GA HA HA HA... THIS IS A SURPRISE.
SO THAT'S IT.
WELL, YOU DON'T ACT MUCH LIKE ROGER.
BUT WASN'T HE YOUR ENEMY?
AREN'T YOU GONNA TELL ME TO GET LOST?
I THOUGHT YOU HAD SOMETHING IMPORTANT TO DISCUSS! THIS IS NOTHING!
I DON'T CARE WHO YOUR FATHER WAS! WE'RE ALL CHILDREN OF THE SEA!
GA HA HA HA!
...

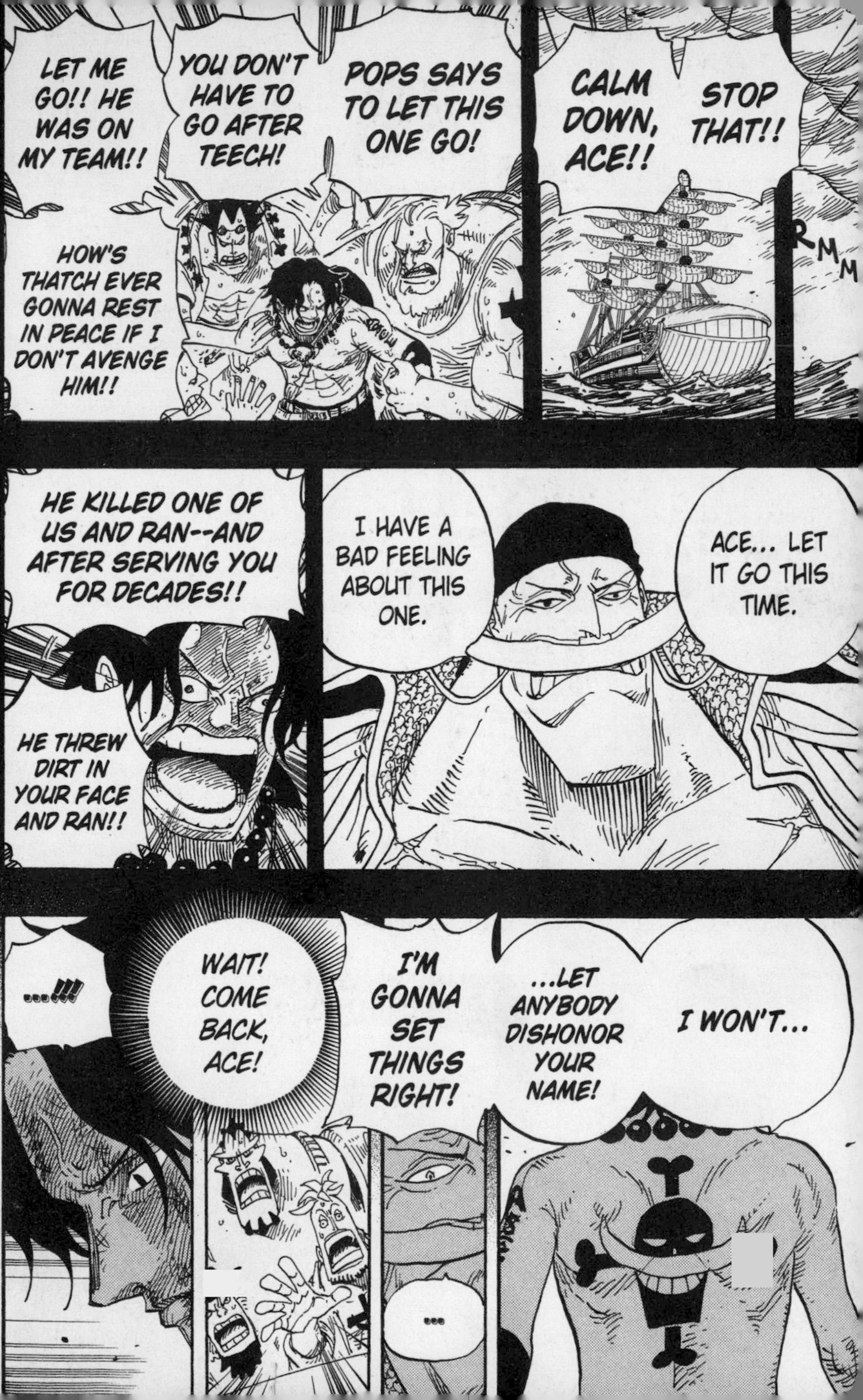
STOP THAT!!
CALM DOWN, ACE!!
RMMM
POPS SAYS TO LET THIS ONE GO!
YOU DON'T HAVE TO GO AFTER TEECH!
LET ME GO!! HE WAS ON MY TEAM!!
HOW'S THATCH EVER GONNA REST IN PEACE IF I DON'T AVENGE HIM!!
ACE... LET IT GO THIS TIME.
I HAVE A BAD FEELING ABOUT THIS ONE.
HE KILLED ONE OF US AND RAN--AND AFTER SERVING YOU FOR DECADES!!
HE THREW DIRT IN YOUR FACE AND RAN!!
I WON'T...
...LET ANYBODY DISHONOR YOUR NAME!
I'M GONNA SET THINGS RIGHT!
...
WAIT! COME BACK, ACE!
...!!!

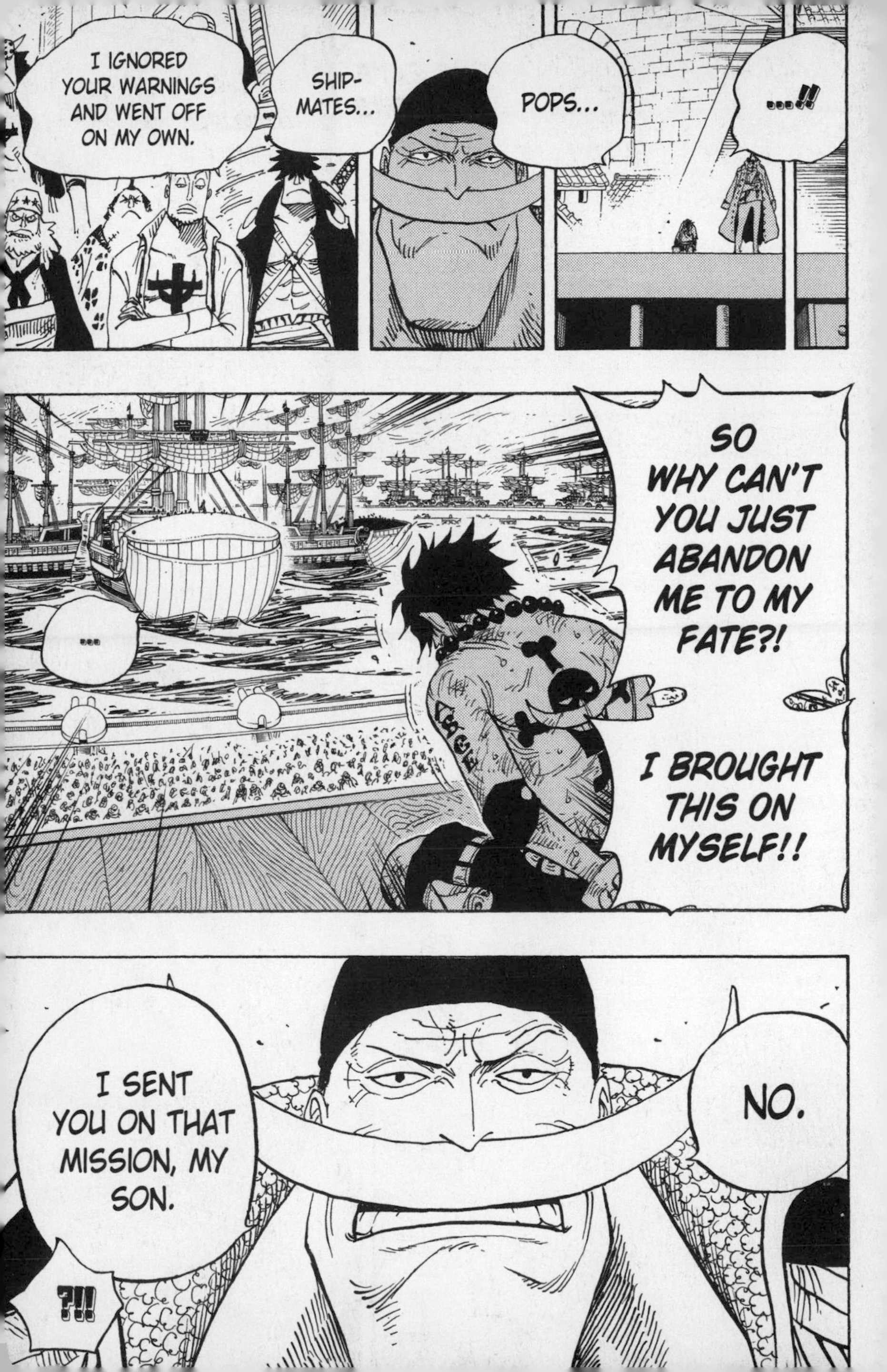
...!!
POPS...
SHIP-MATES...
I IGNORED YOUR WARNINGS AND WENT OFF ON MY OWN.
SO WHY CAN'T YOU JUST ABANDON ME TO MY FATE?!
I BROUGHT THIS ON MYSELF!!
...
NO.
I SENT YOU ON THAT MISSION, MY SON.
?!!

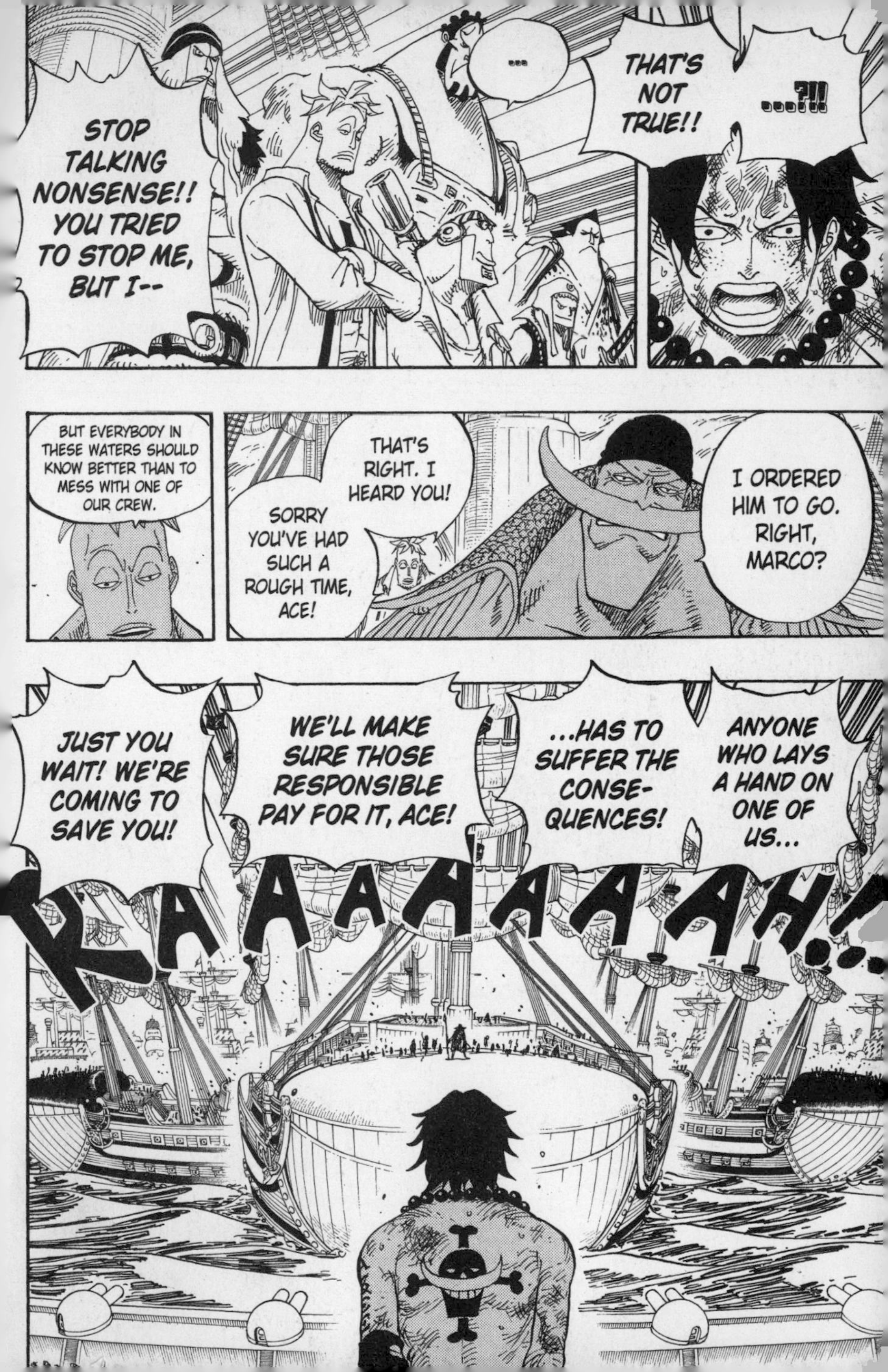
THAT'S NOT TRUE!!
...?!!
...
STOP TALKING NONSENSE!! YOU TRIED TO STOP ME, BUT I--
I ORDERED HIM TO GO. RIGHT, MARCO?
THAT'S RIGHT. I HEARD YOU!
SORRY YOU'VE HAD SUCH A ROUGH TIME, ACE!
BUT EVERYBODY IN THESE WATERS SHOULD KNOW BETTER THAN TO MESS WITH ONE OF OUR CREW.
ANYONE WHO LAYS A HAND ON ONE OF US...
...HAS TO SUFFER THE CONSE-QUENCES!
WE'LL MAKE SURE THOSE RESPONSIBLE PAY FOR IT, ACE!
JUST YOU WAIT! WE'RE COMING TO SAVE YOU!
RAAAAAAAH!!

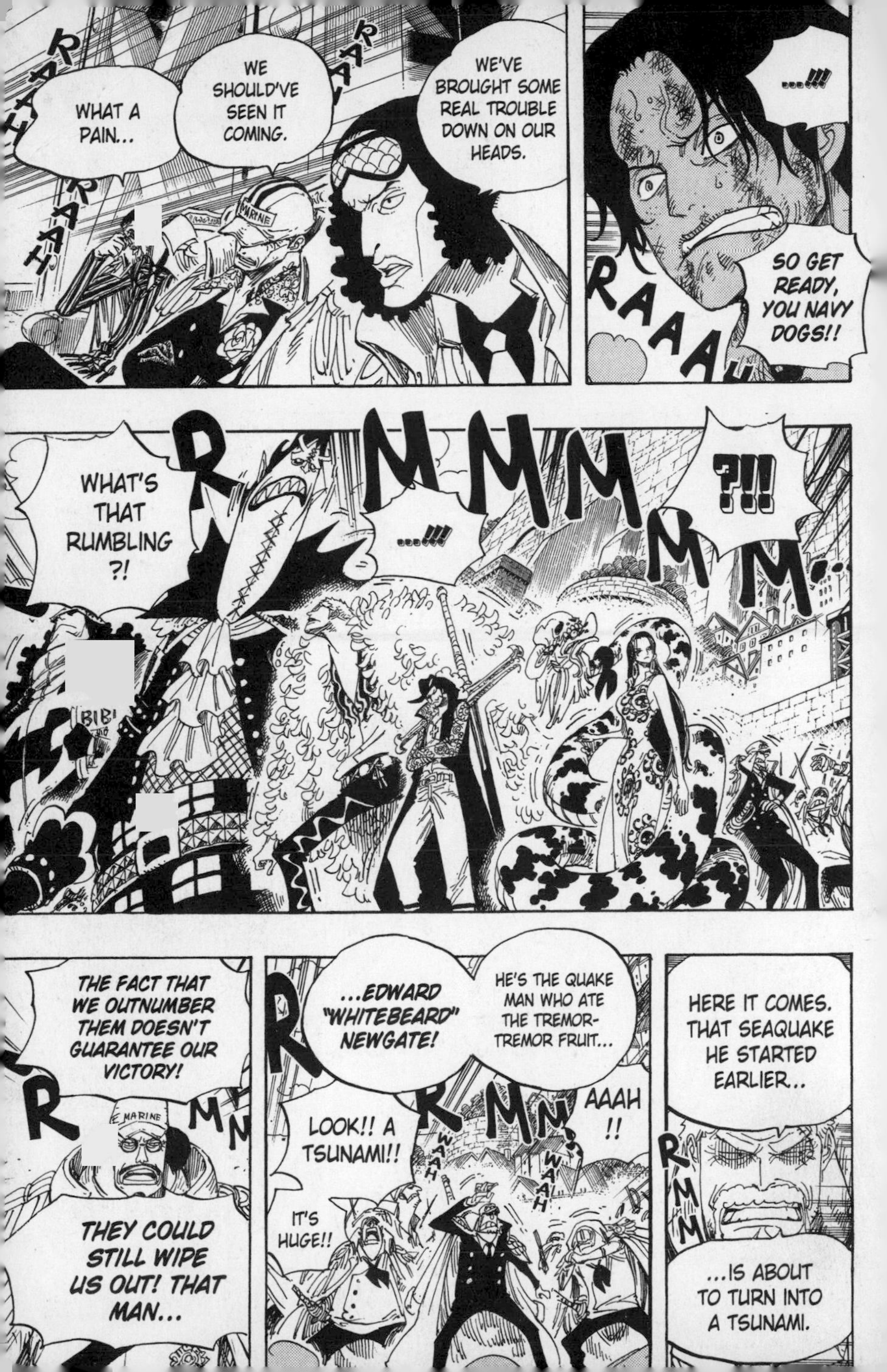
...!!!
SO GET READY, YOU NAVY DOGS!!
RAAAH
WE'VE BROUGHT SOME REAL TROUBLE DOWN ON OUR HEADS.
RAAA
WE SHOULD'VE SEEN IT COMING.
WHAT A PAIN...
RAAAH
RAAAH
?!!
RMMMMM
...!!!
WHAT'S THAT RUMBLING ?!
HERE IT COMES. THAT SEAQUAKE HE STARTED EARLIER...
RMM
...IS ABOUT TO TURN INTO A TSUNAMI.
HE'S THE QUAKE MAN WHO ATE THE TREMOR-TREMOR FRUIT...
...EDWARD "WHITEBEARD" NEWGATE!
AAAH !!
RMM
LOOK!! A TSUNAMI!!
WAAH
WAAH
IT'S HUGE!!
THE FACT THAT WE OUTNUMBER THEM DOESN'T GUARANTEE OUR VICTORY!
RMN
THEY COULD STILL WIPE US OUT! THAT MAN...

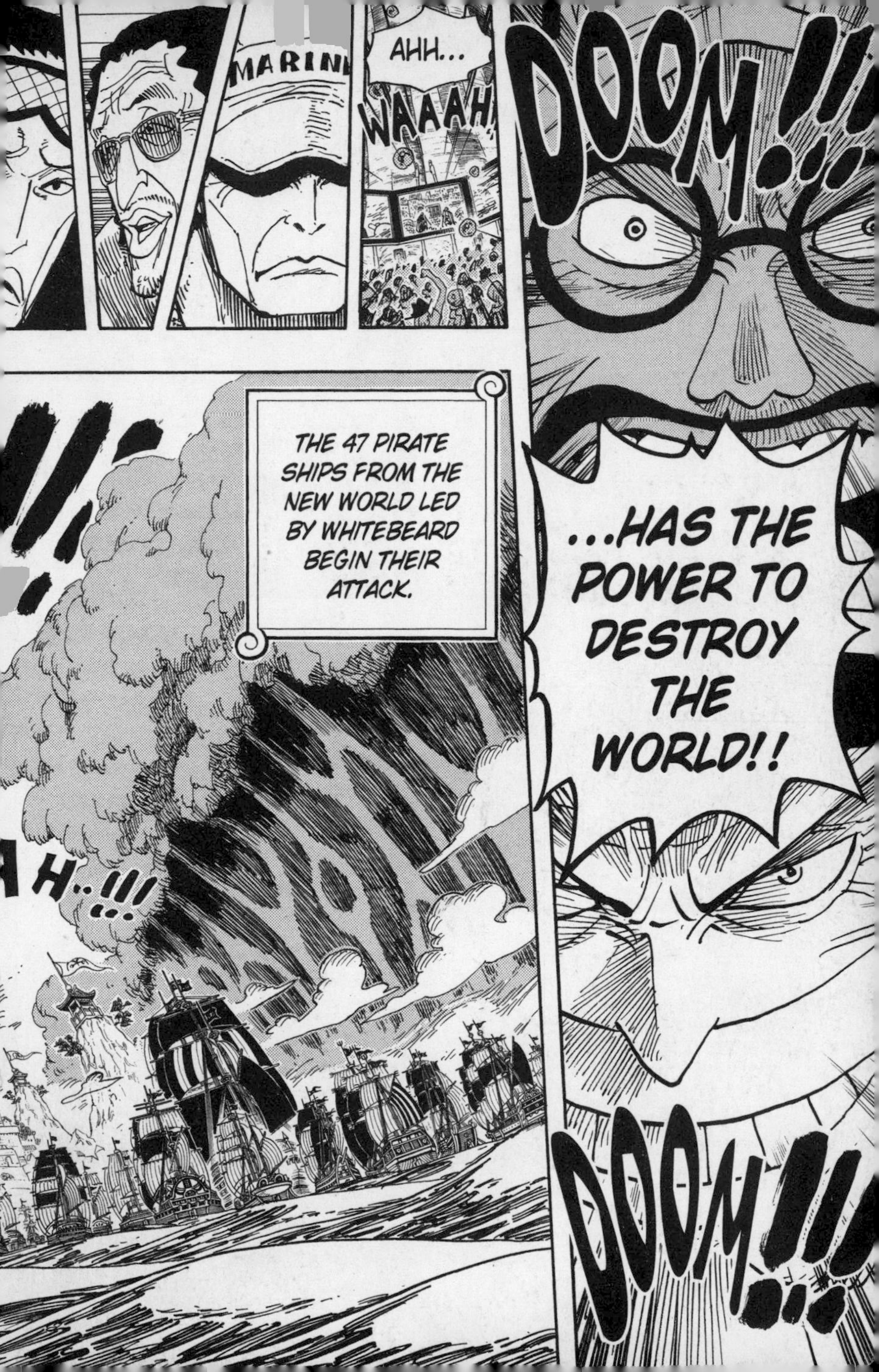
DOOM!!!
...HAS THE POWER TO DESTROY THE WORLD!!
DOOM!!!
AHH...
WAAAH
THE 47 PIRATE SHIPS FROM THE NEW WORLD LED BY WHITEBEARD BEGIN THEIR ATTACK.

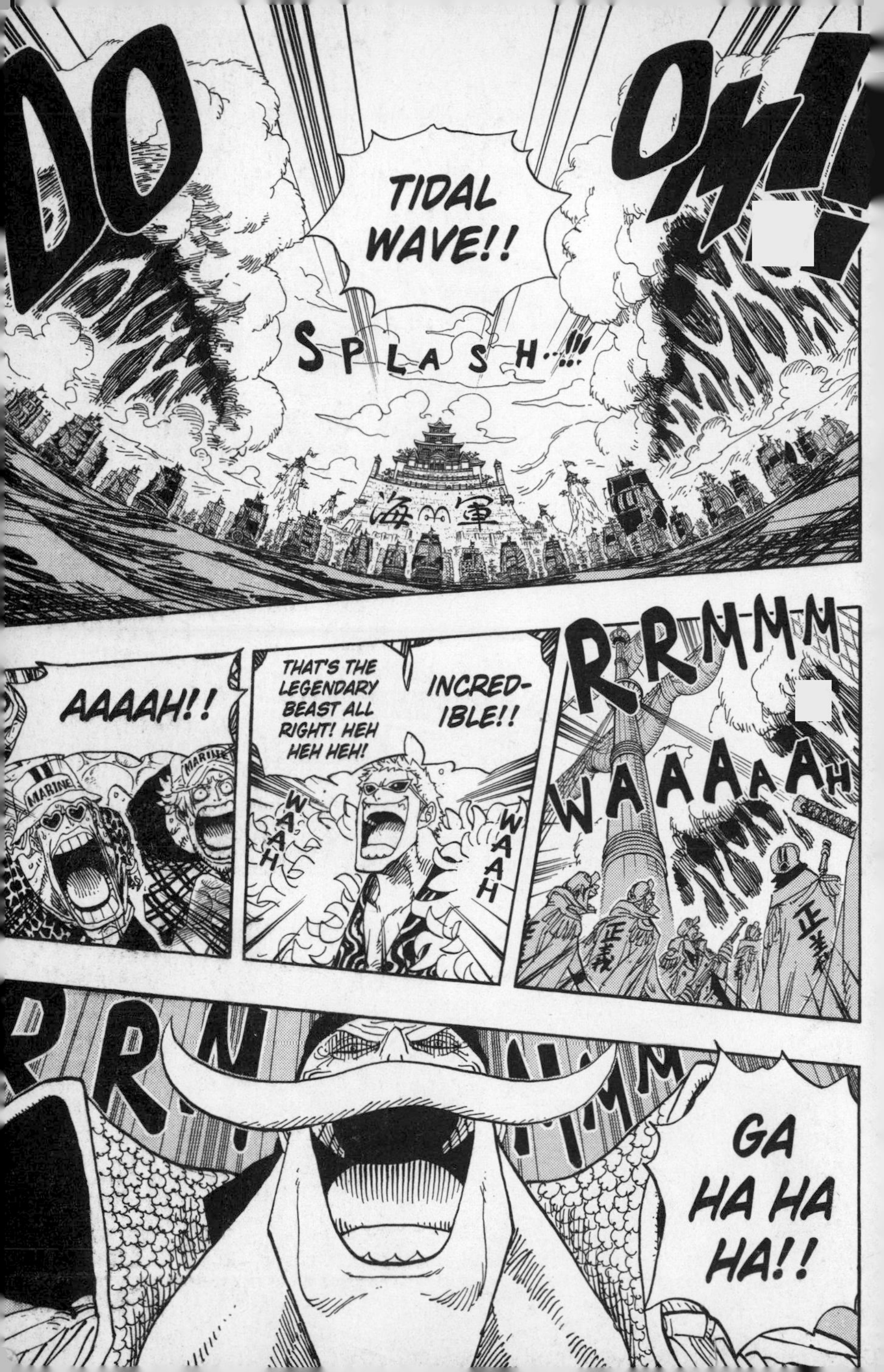
DOOM!!
TIDAL WAVE!!
SPLASH...!!!
海軍
RRMMM
WAAAAAH
INCRED-IBLE!!
THAT'S THE LEGENDARY BEAST ALL RIGHT! HEH HEH HEH HEH!
WAAAH
WAAAH
AAAAH!!
MARINE
MARINE
RRMMMM
GA HA HA HA!!

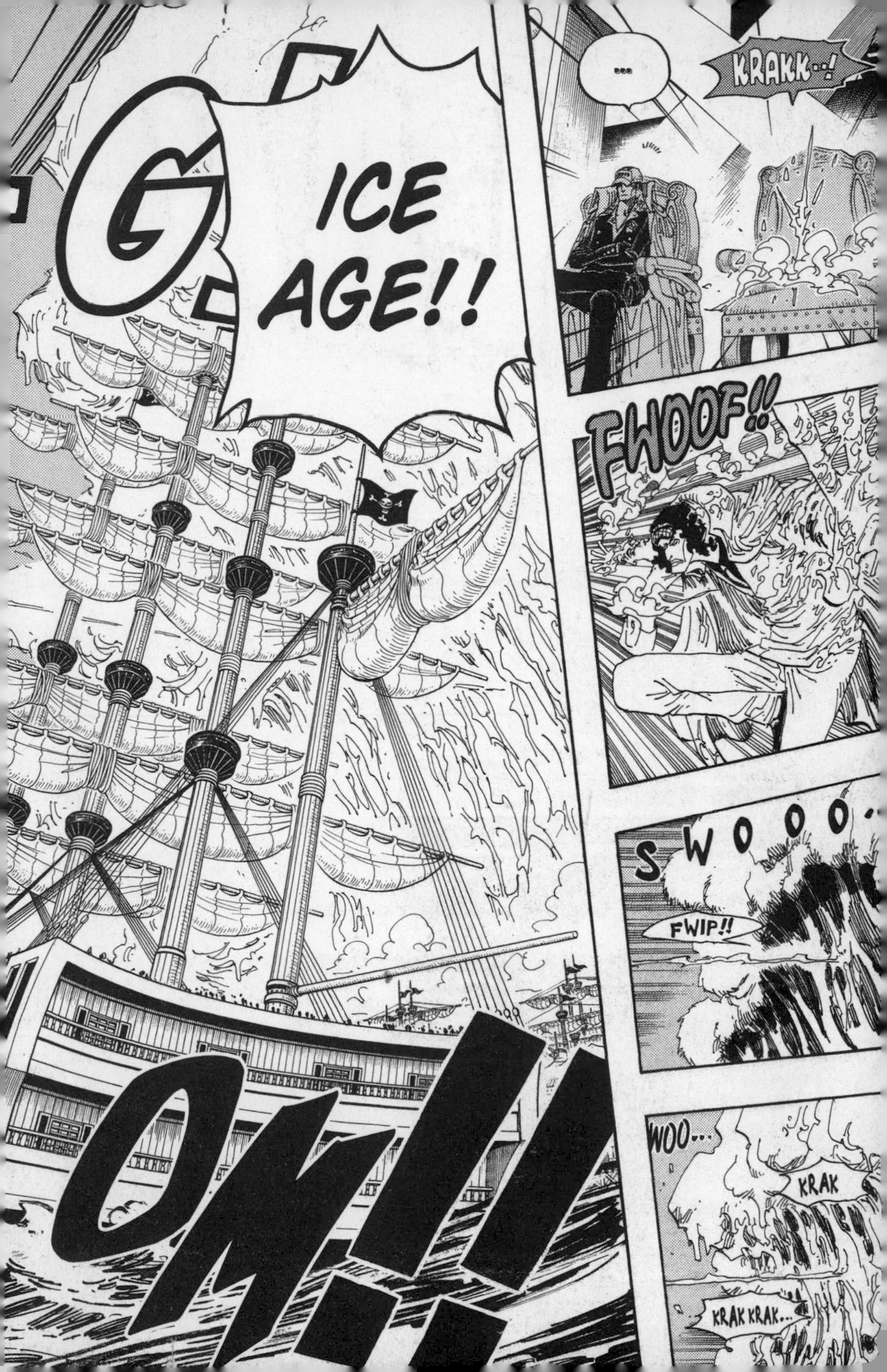
KRAKK..!
...
FWOOF!!
SWOOO...
FWIP!!
WOO...
KRAK
KRAK KRAK...
ICE AGE!!
OH!!

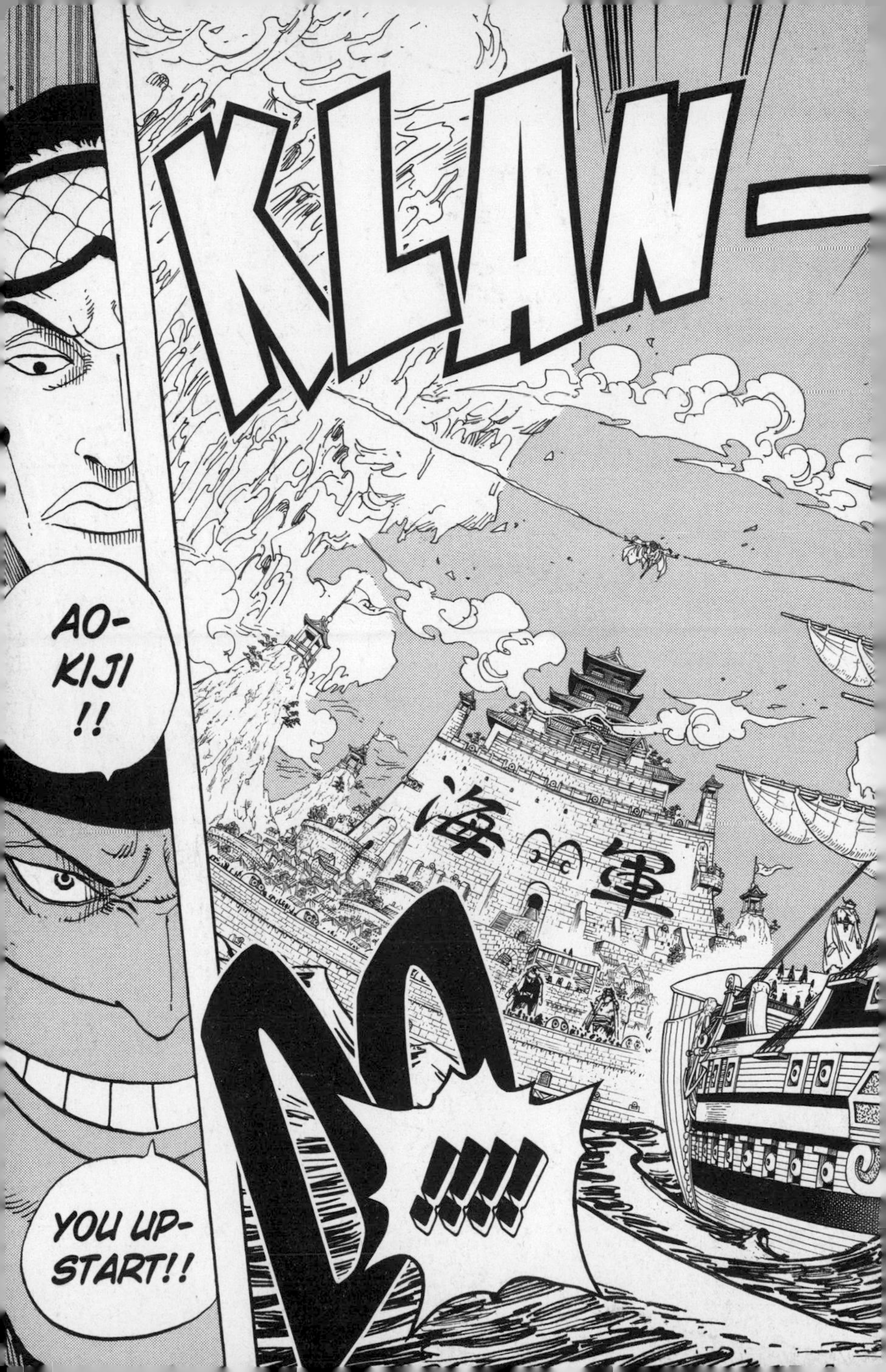
KLAN—
DO!!!!
AO-KIJI!!
YOU UP-START!!

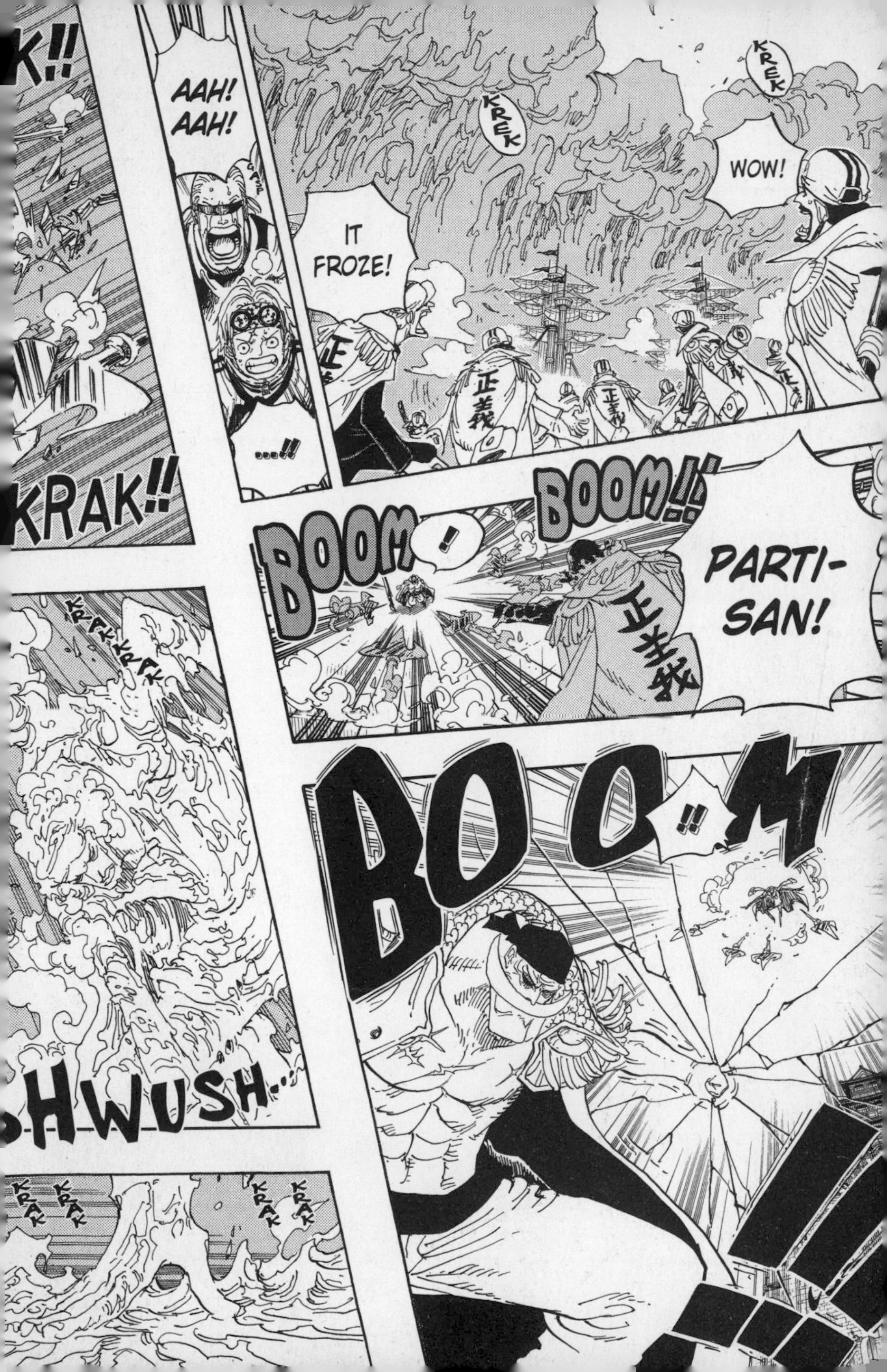
KREK
WOW!
KREK
IT FROZE!
AAH! AAH!
GASP
...!!
K!!
KRAK!!
PARTI-SAN!
BOOM!!
!
BOOM
BOOM!!
KRAK KRAK
SHWUSH...
KRAK KRAK
KRAK KRAK

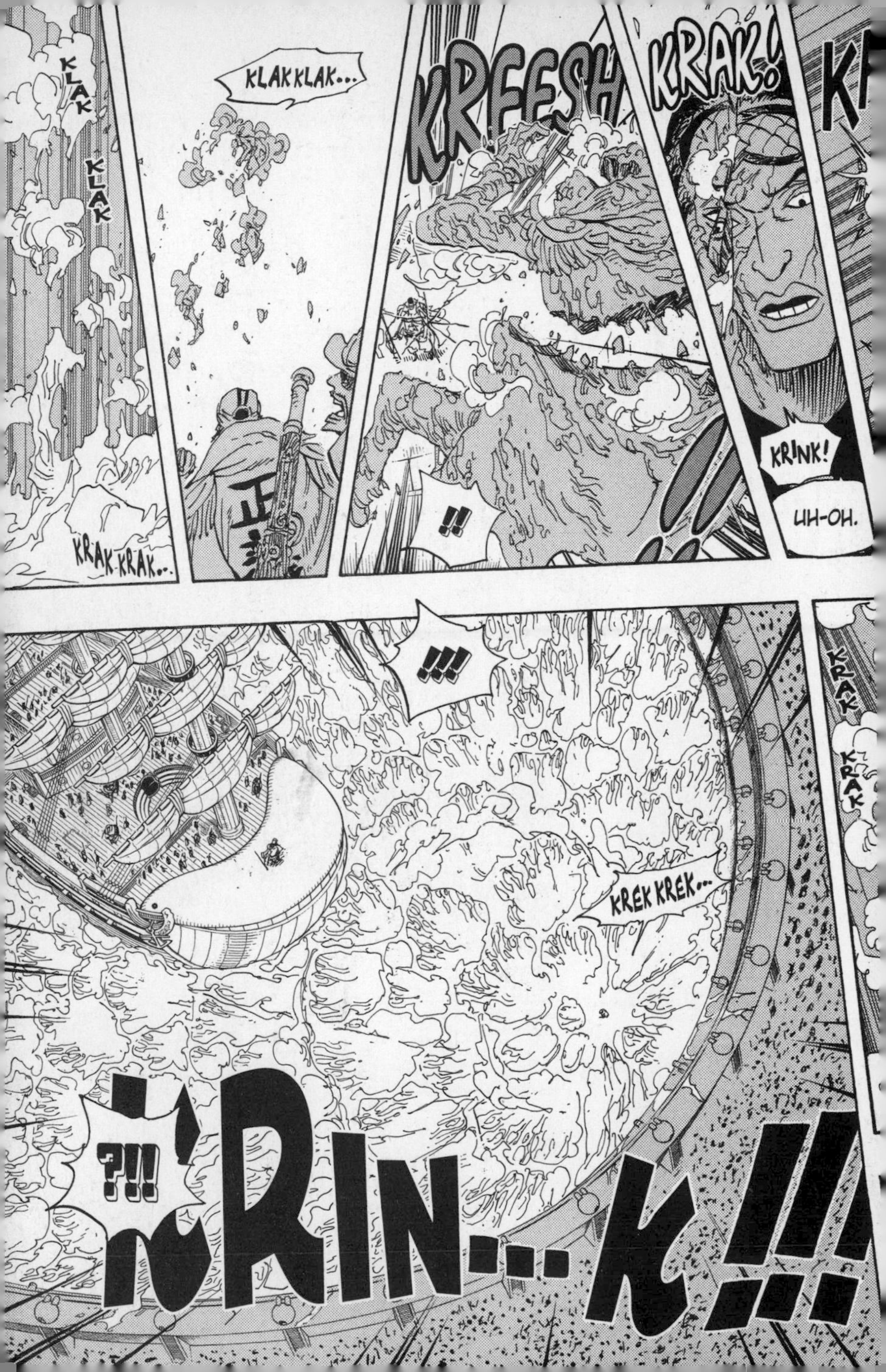
KRAK!
KRINK!
UH-OH.
KREESH
!!
KLAKKLAK...
KLAK
KLAK
KRAK KRAK...
KRAK
KRAK
!!!
KREK KREK...
?!!
KRIN...K!!!

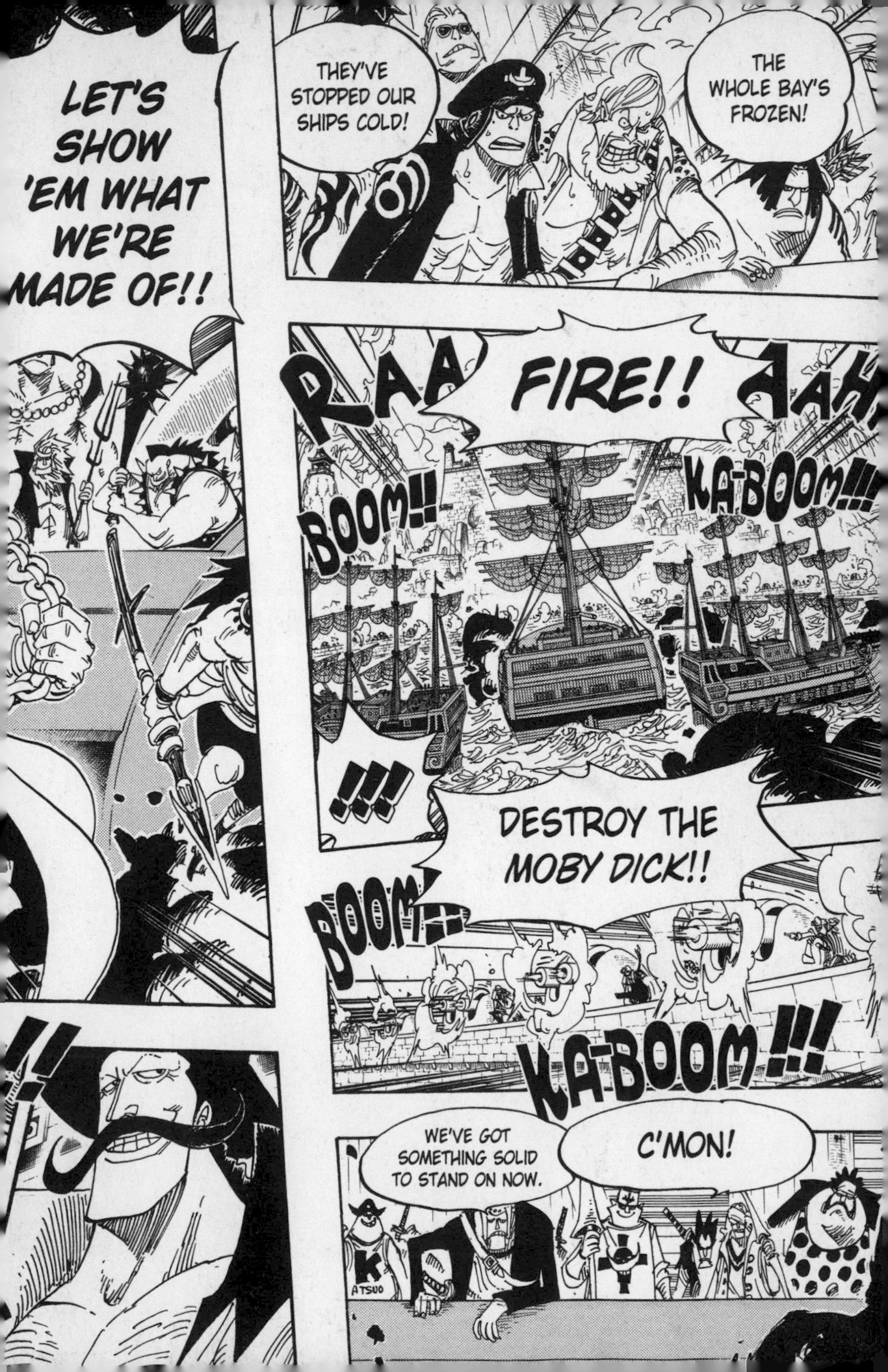
THE WHOLE BAY'S FROZEN!
THEY'VE STOPPED OUR SHIPS COLD!
LET'S SHOW 'EM WHAT WE'RE MADE OF!!
RAA
AAH
FIRE!!
KA-BOOM!!!
BOOM!!
!!!
DESTROY THE MOBY DICK!!
BOOM!!
KA-BOOM!!!
C'MON!
WE'VE GOT SOMETHING SOLID TO STAND ON NOW.
!!

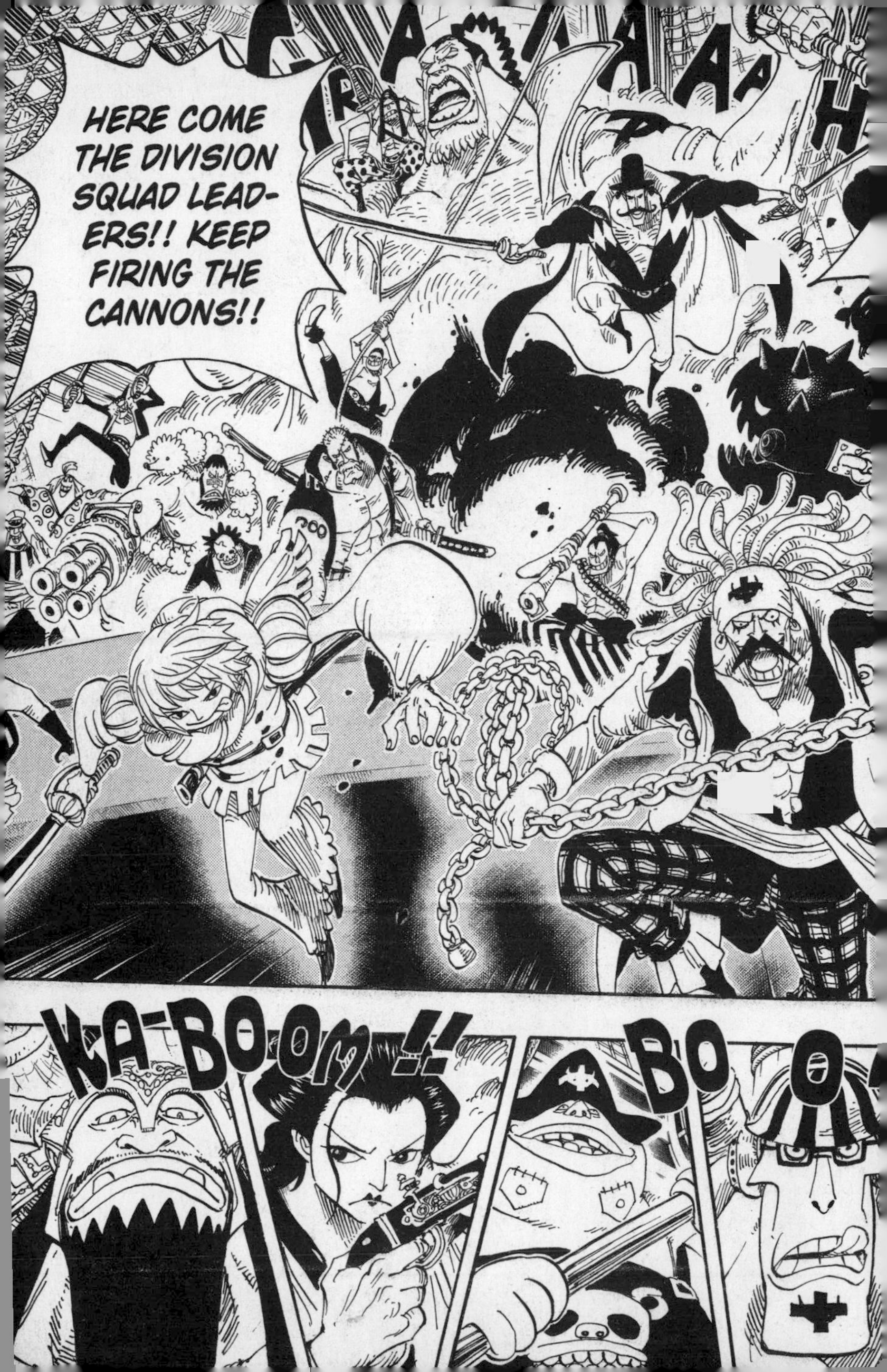
HERE COME THE DIVISION SQUAD LEADERS!! KEEP FIRING THE CANNONS!!
BO-O
KA-BOOM!!

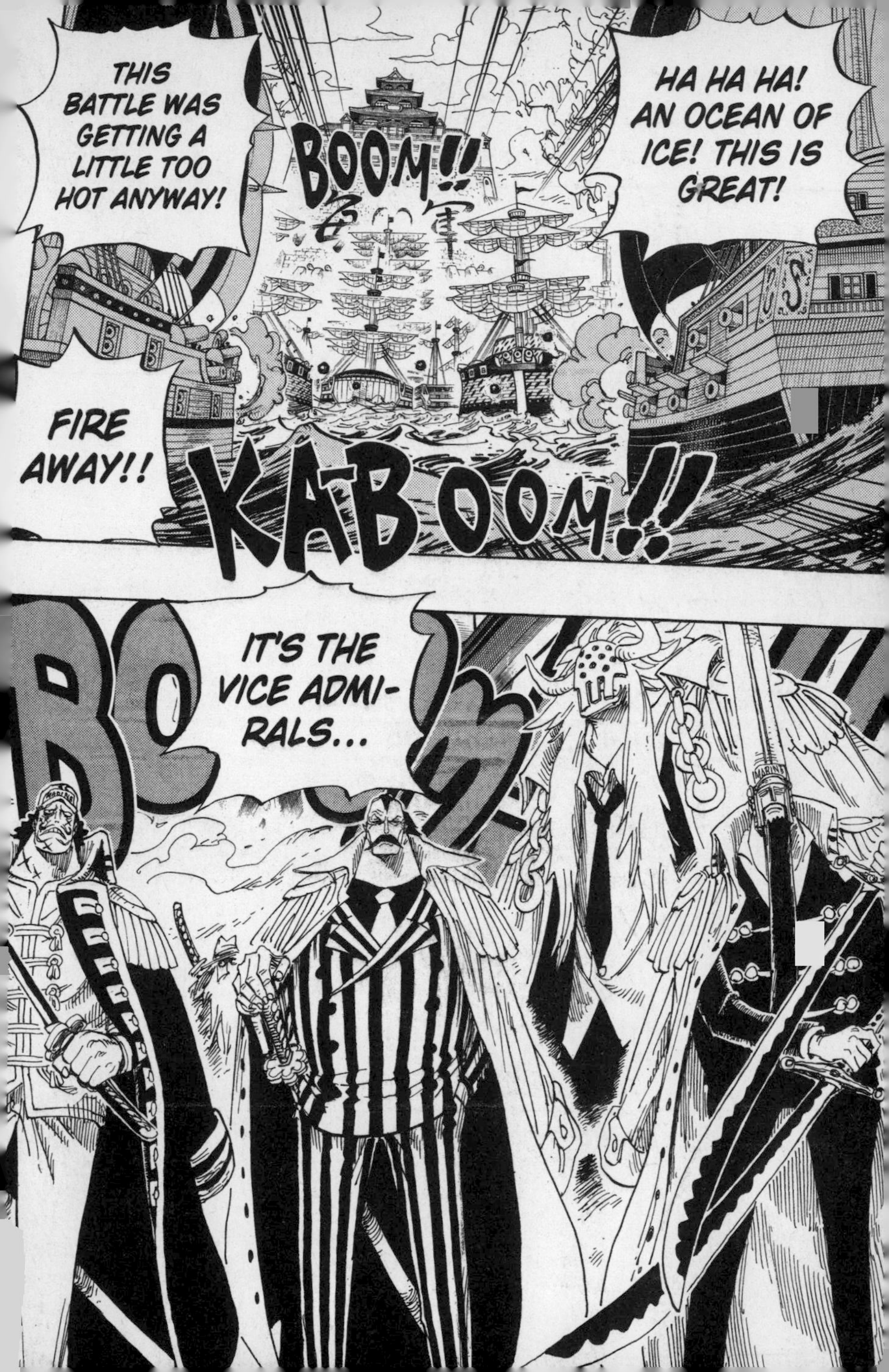
HA HA HA! AN OCEAN OF ICE! THIS IS GREAT!
BOOM!!
THIS BATTLE WAS GETTING A LITTLE TOO HOT ANYWAY!
FIRE AWAY!!
KABOOM!!
IT'S THE VICE ADMIRALS...

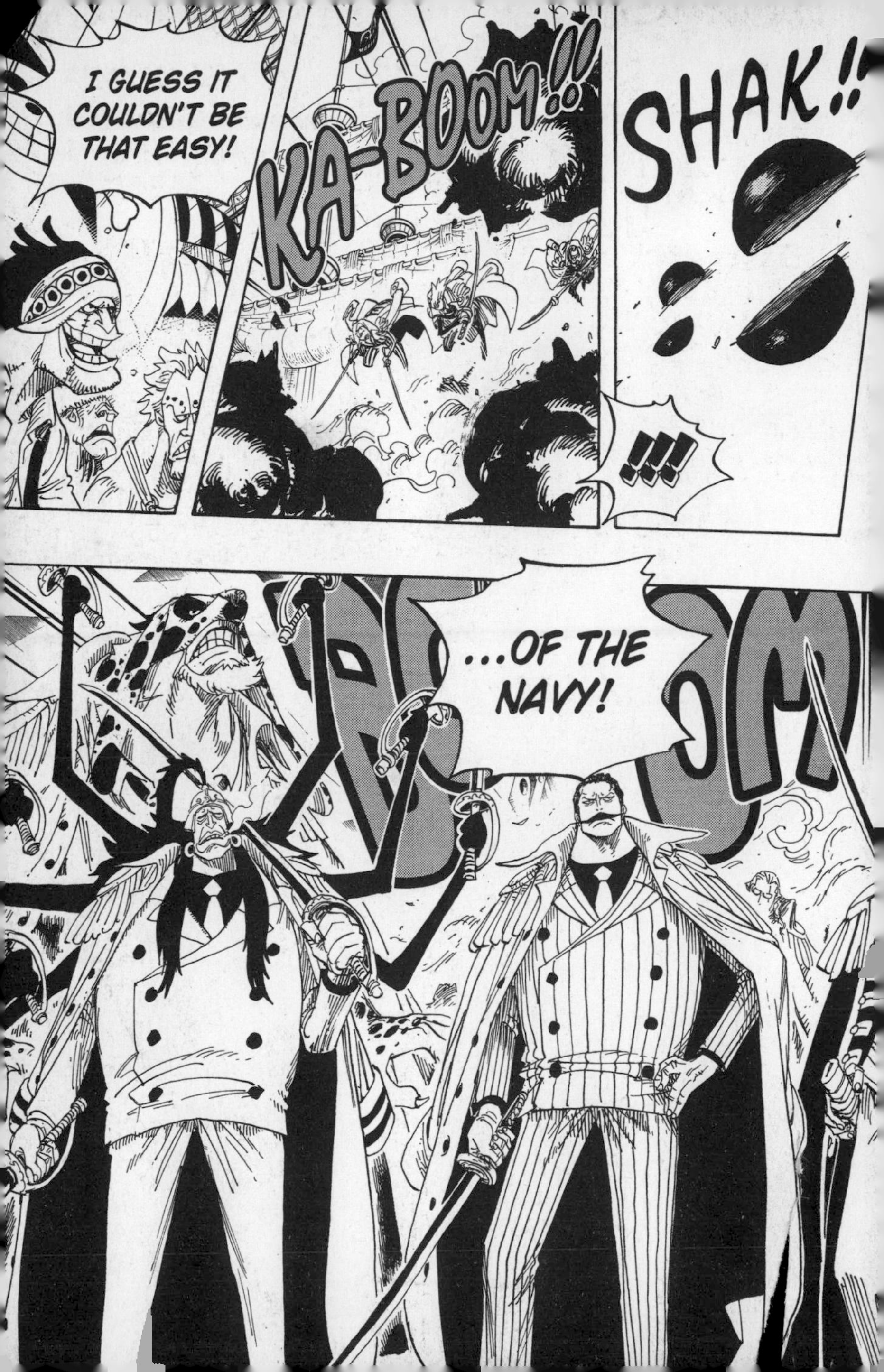
SHAK!!
!!!
KA-BOOM!!
I GUESS IT COULDN'T BE THAT EASY!
...OF THE NAVY!

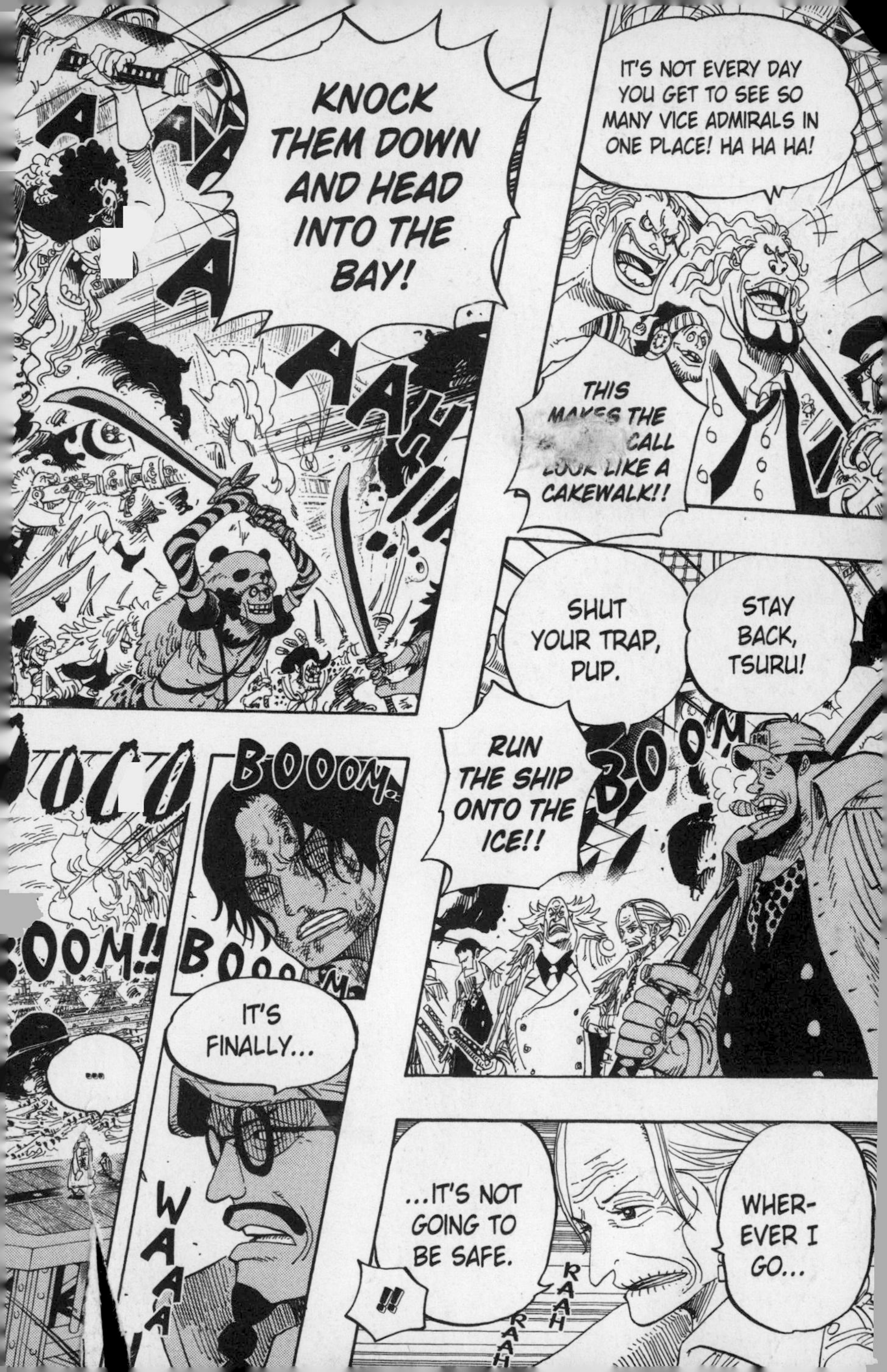
IT'S NOT EVERY DAY YOU GET TO SEE SO MANY VICE ADMIRALS IN ONE PLACE! HA HA HA!
THIS MAKES THE CALL LOOK LIKE A CAKEWALK!!
KNOCK THEM DOWN AND HEAD INTO THE BAY!
AAAAAAAH!!!
STAY BACK, TSURU!
SHUT YOUR TRAP, PUP.
RUN THE SHIP ONTO THE ICE!!
BOOOM
BOOOM
BOOOM
BOOM!!
IT'S FINALLY...
WAAAA
...
WHER-EVER I GO...
...IT'S NOT GOING TO BE SAFE.
!!
RAAAH
RAAAH

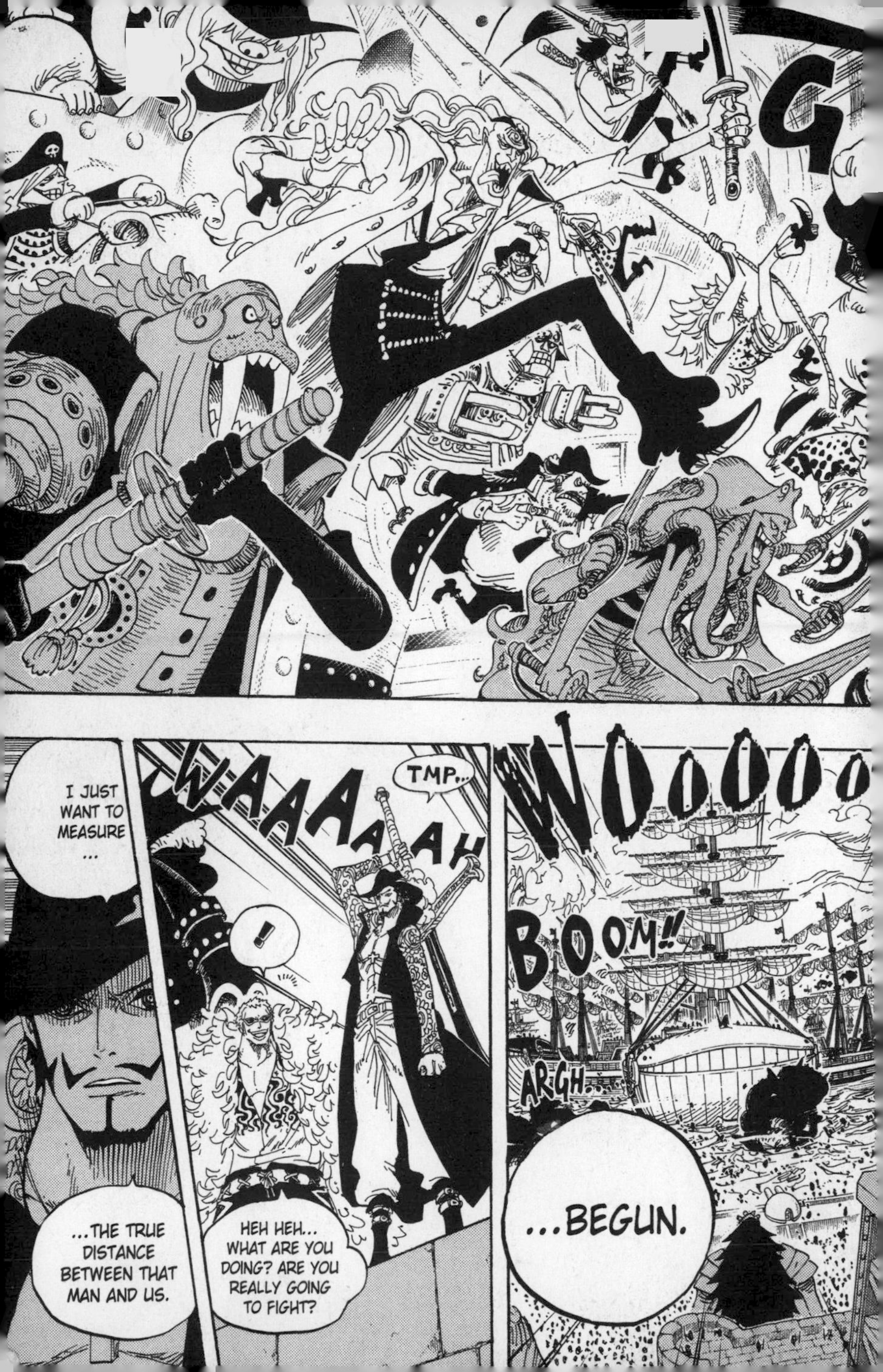
WOOOOO
BOOM!!
ARGH
...BEGUN.
WAAAAAAH
TMP...
!
HEH HEH... WHAT ARE YOU DOING? ARE YOU REALLY GOING TO FIGHT?
I JUST WANT TO MEASURE ...
...THE TRUE DISTANCE BETWEEN THAT MAN AND US.

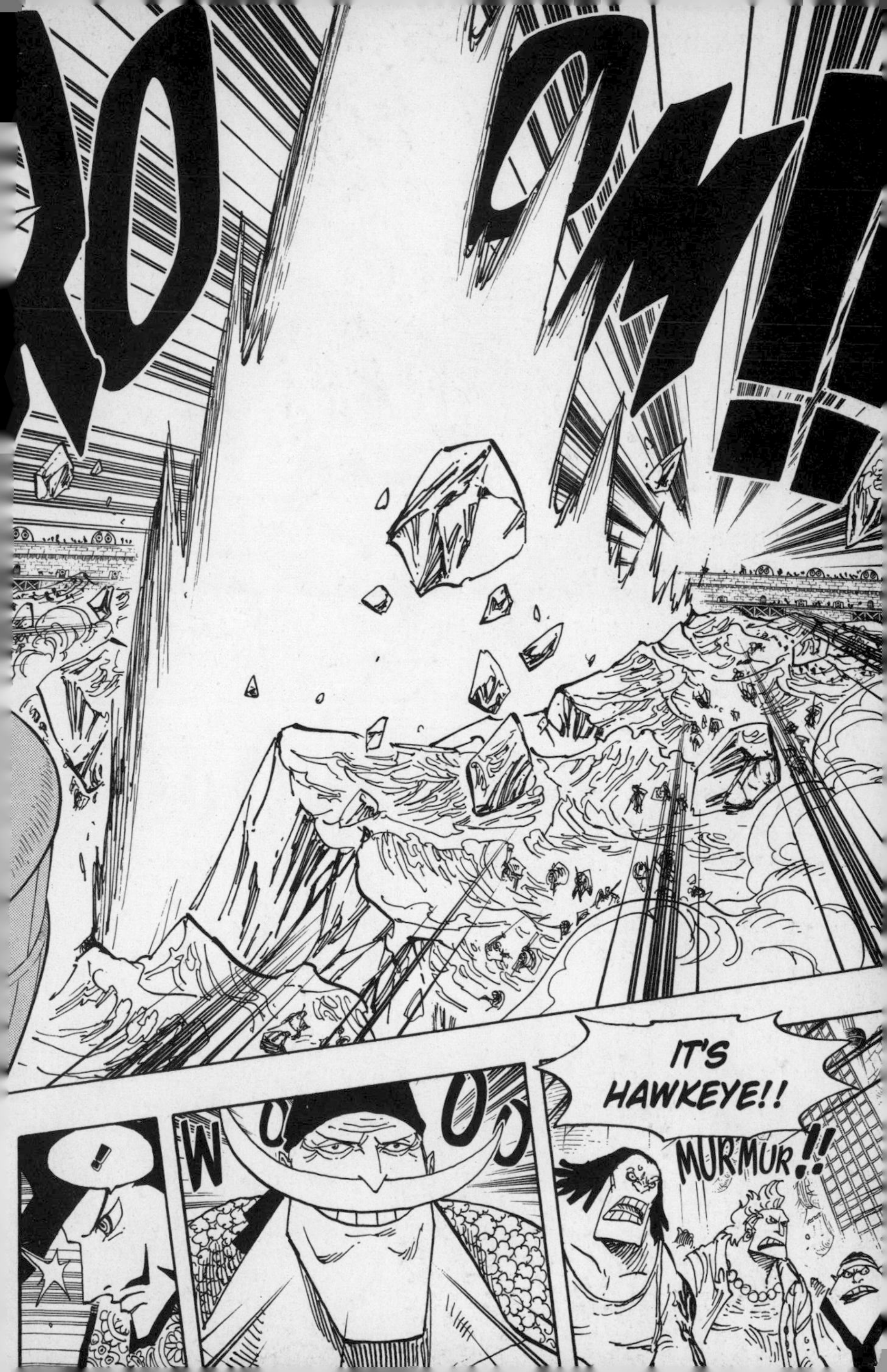
OOM!!
IT'S HAWKEYE!!
MURMUR!!
WOOO
!

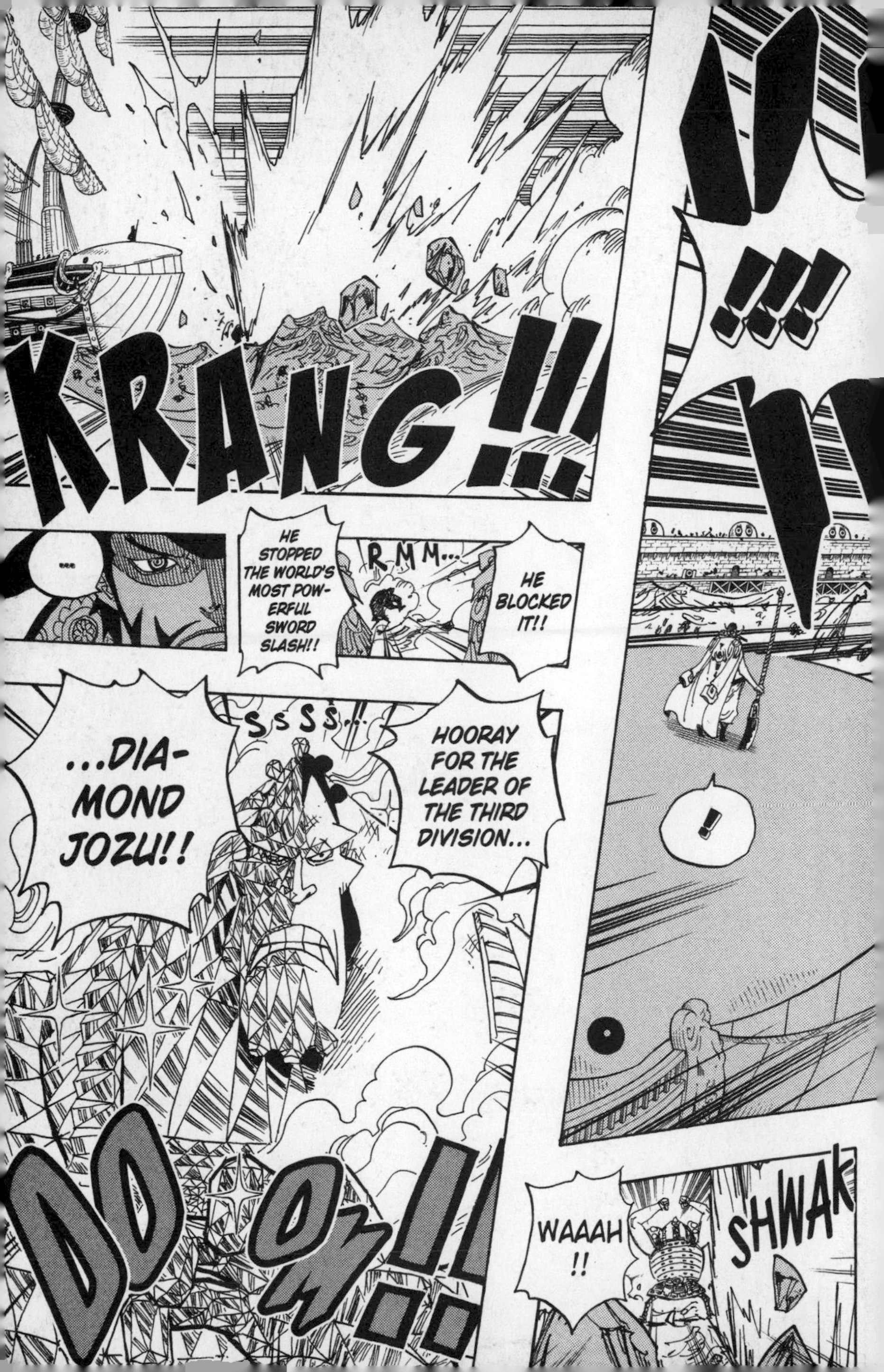
!!!
!
KRANG!!
HE BLOCKED IT!!
HE STOPPED THE WORLD'S MOST POWERFUL SWORD SLASH!!
RMM...
...
HOORAY FOR THE LEADER OF THE THIRD DIVISION...
...DIAMOND JOZU!!
SSSS...
DOOM!!
WAAAH!!
SHWAK

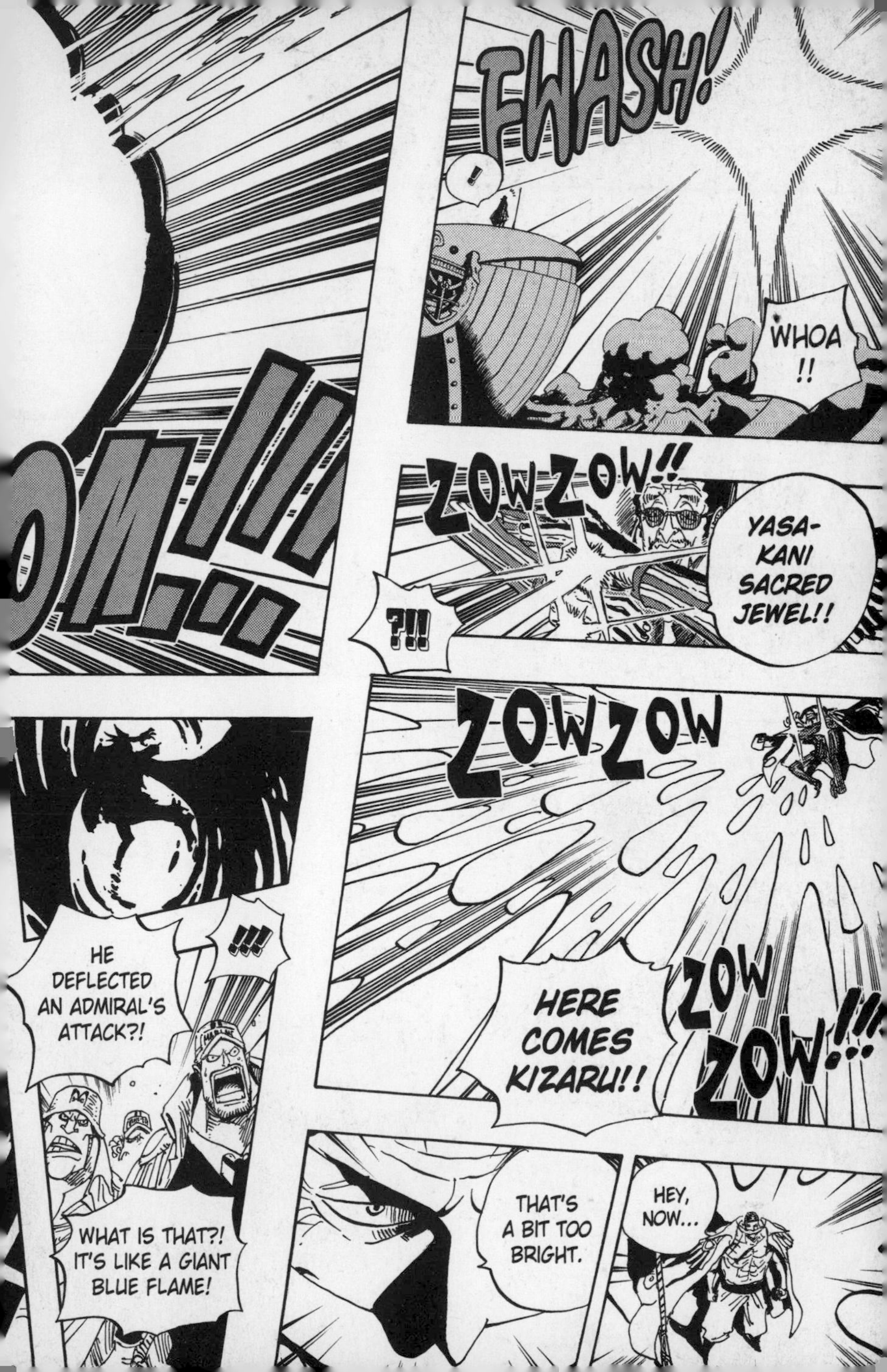
FWASH!
!
WHOA!!
ZOWZOW!!
YASA-KANI SACRED JEWEL!!
?!!
ZOWZOW
HERE COMES KIZARU!!
ZOW ZOW!!!
!!!
HE DEFLECTED AN ADMIRAL'S ATTACK?!
WHAT IS THAT?! IT'S LIKE A GIANT BLUE FLAME!
HEY, NOW...
THAT'S A BIT TOO BRIGHT.

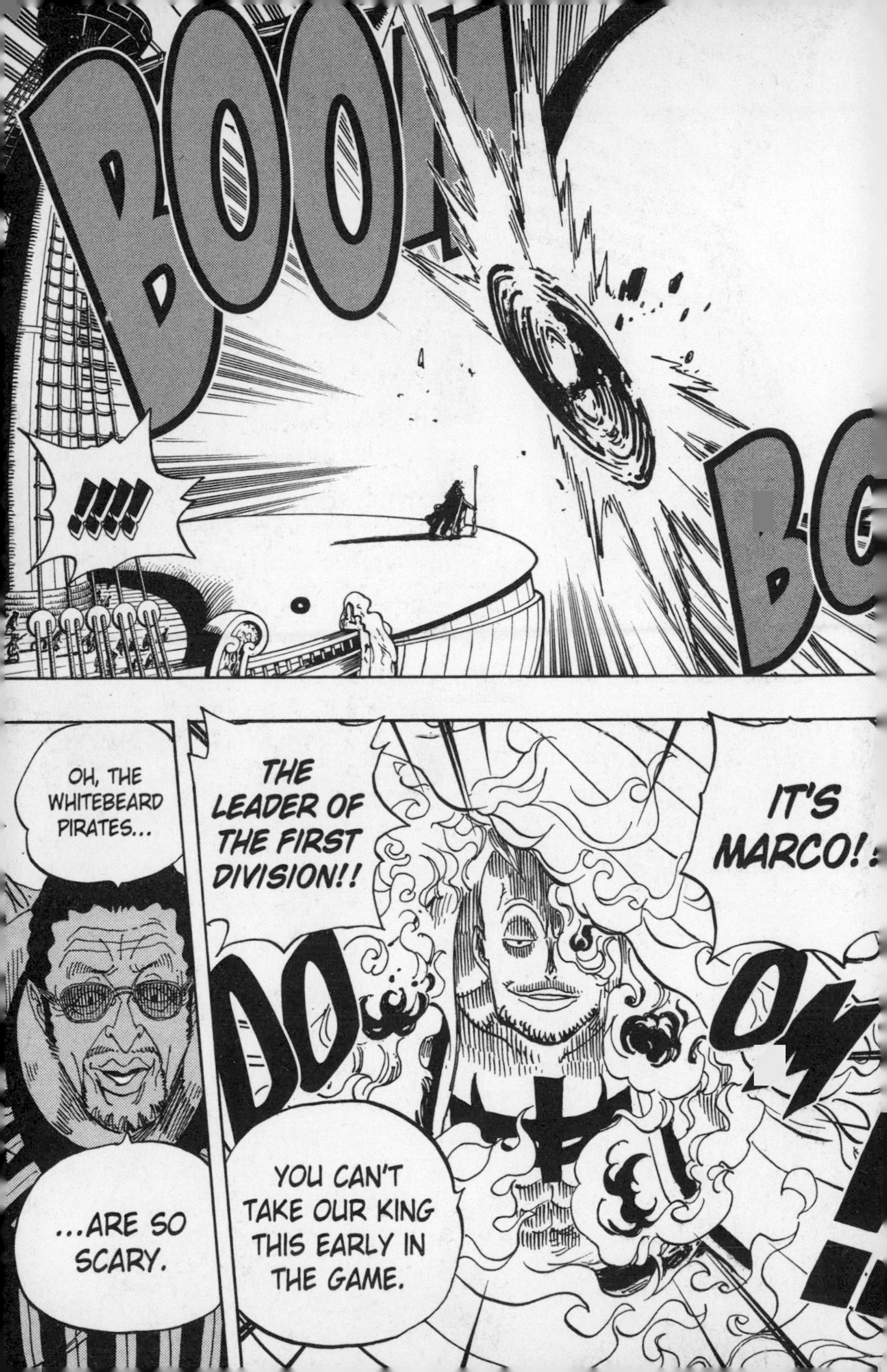
!!!!
IT'S MARCO!!
THE LEADER OF THE FIRST DIVISION!!
YOU CAN'T TAKE OUR KING THIS EARLY IN THE GAME.
OH, THE WHITEBEARD PIRATES...
...ARE SO SCARY.

SBS Question Corner

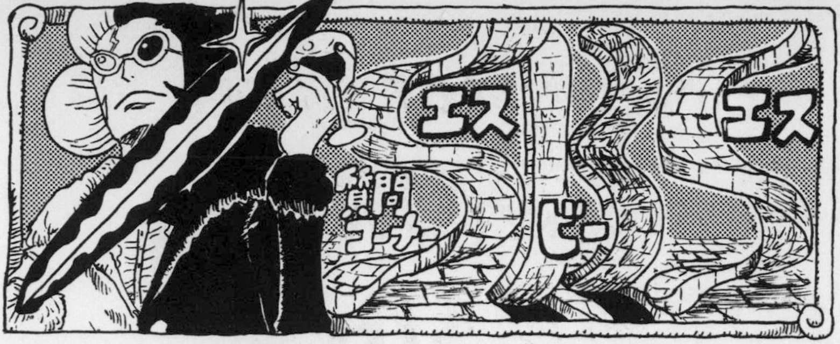
エス
ビー
エス
質問コーナー
(Ponio, Hokkaido)

Oda (A): Okay. Let's start the SBS! Let's go! Yeah!

Reader (Q): Mr. Oda. Good morning/day/evening. My friend Shota, (you can call him Mr. S if you want), really really likes Kana (you can call her Ms. K if you want). But Kana is dating someone else. What should I do?

--D. Hosokawa (Age 14)

A: Oh, okay. You're on your own! Yeah!

Q: Hey, Odacchi! I got a question for you! Can the former Baroque Works Mr. 1 cut anything with his "weiner"?! I really really can't stop thinking about it and it keeps me up at night!

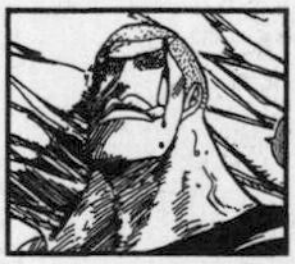

--28 in 8th Grade

A: Okay! Then don't sleep! Yeah!

Q: Eiichiro… Look at you! All grown up!

--Nice Man Poser

A: Whatever. I don't care about this page anymore. I'll make the next SBS page as fun as I can though! Oh, and thank you to all my fans who watched the latest One Piece movie, Strong World. Thanks to all of you, it's a hit. It would be great if you could give me your continued support!

Chapter 554:
ADMIRAL AKAINU

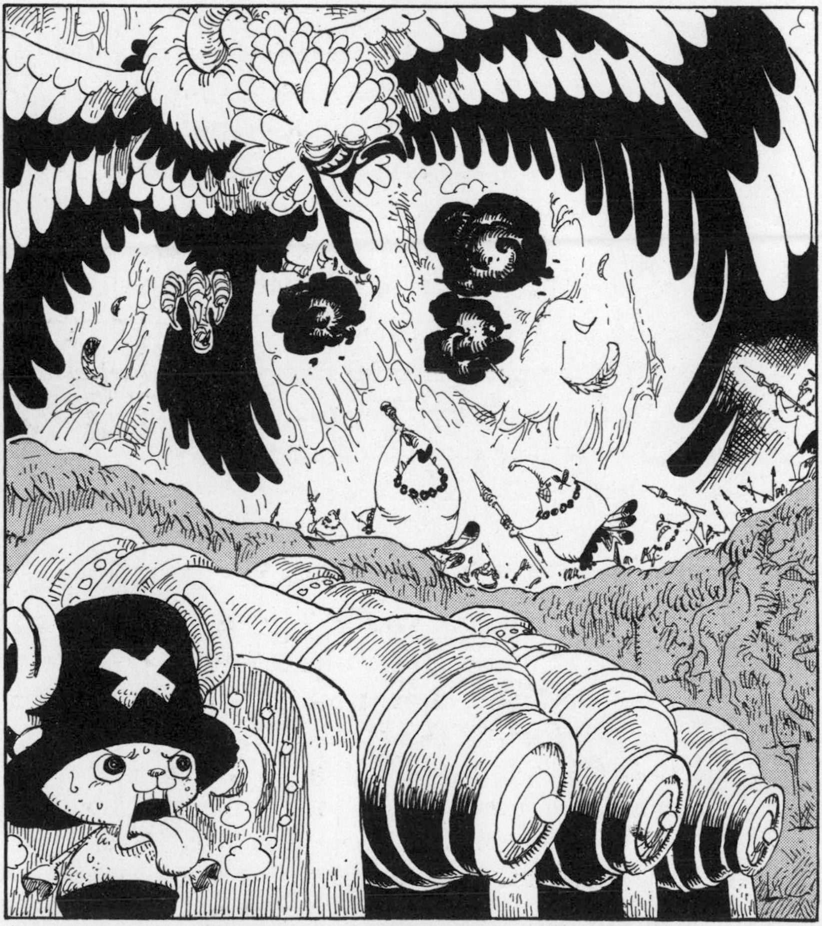

CHOPPER'S "I'M NOT FOOD, YOU JERKS!!"
FINAL VOLUME: "MAN VS. BIRD"

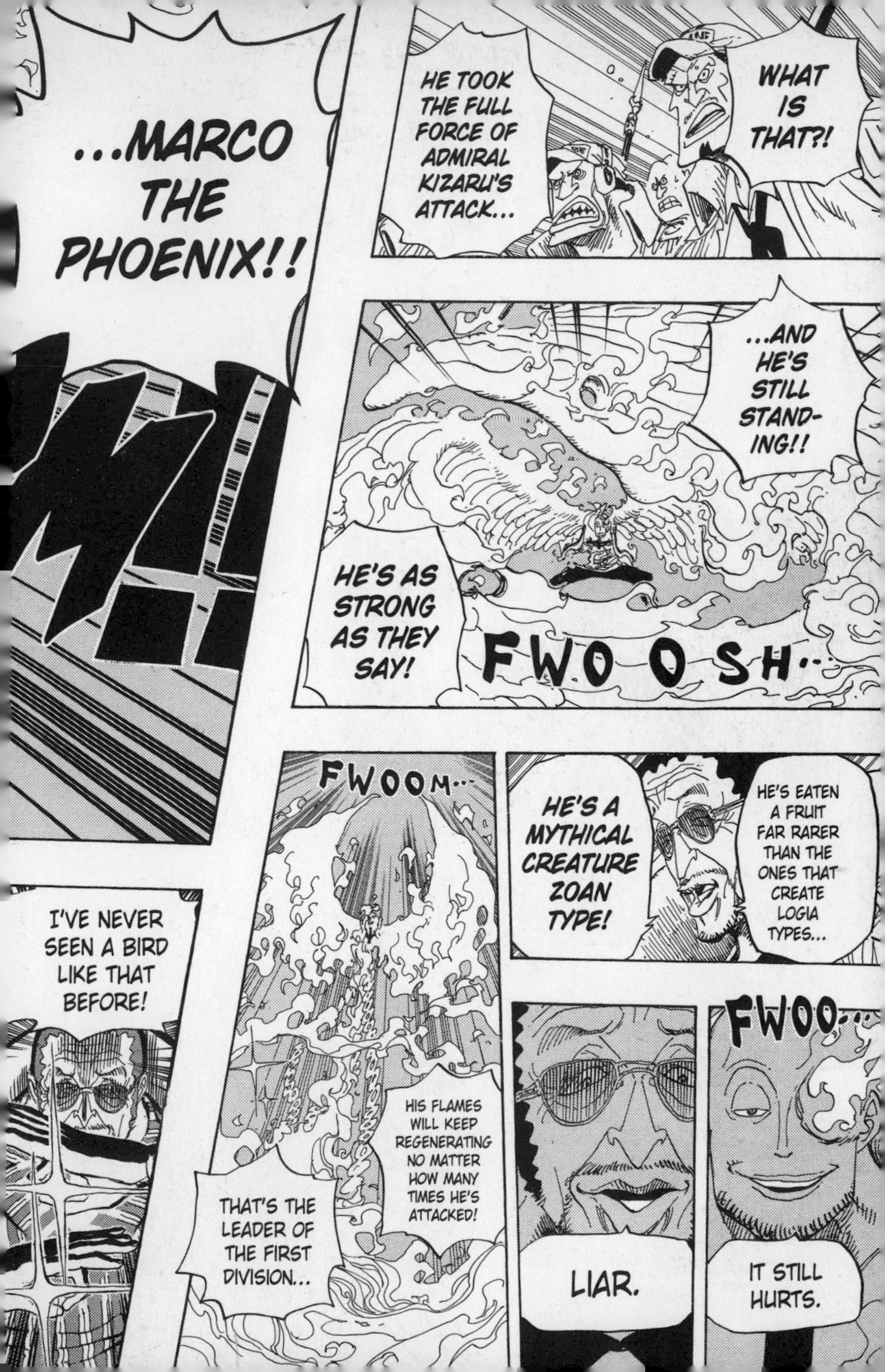
WHAT IS THAT?!
HE TOOK THE FULL FORCE OF ADMIRAL KIZARU'S ATTACK...
...AND HE'S STILL STANDING!!
HE'S AS STRONG AS THEY SAY!
FWOOSH...
...MARCO THE PHOENIX!!
HE'S EATEN A FRUIT FAR RARER THAN THE ONES THAT CREATE LOGIA TYPES...
HE'S A MYTHICAL CREATURE ZOAN TYPE!
FWOO...
IT STILL HURTS.
LIAR.
FWOOM...
HIS FLAMES WILL KEEP REGENERATING NO MATTER HOW MANY TIMES HE'S ATTACKED!
THAT'S THE LEADER OF THE FIRST DIVISION...
I'VE NEVER SEEN A BIRD LIKE THAT BEFORE!

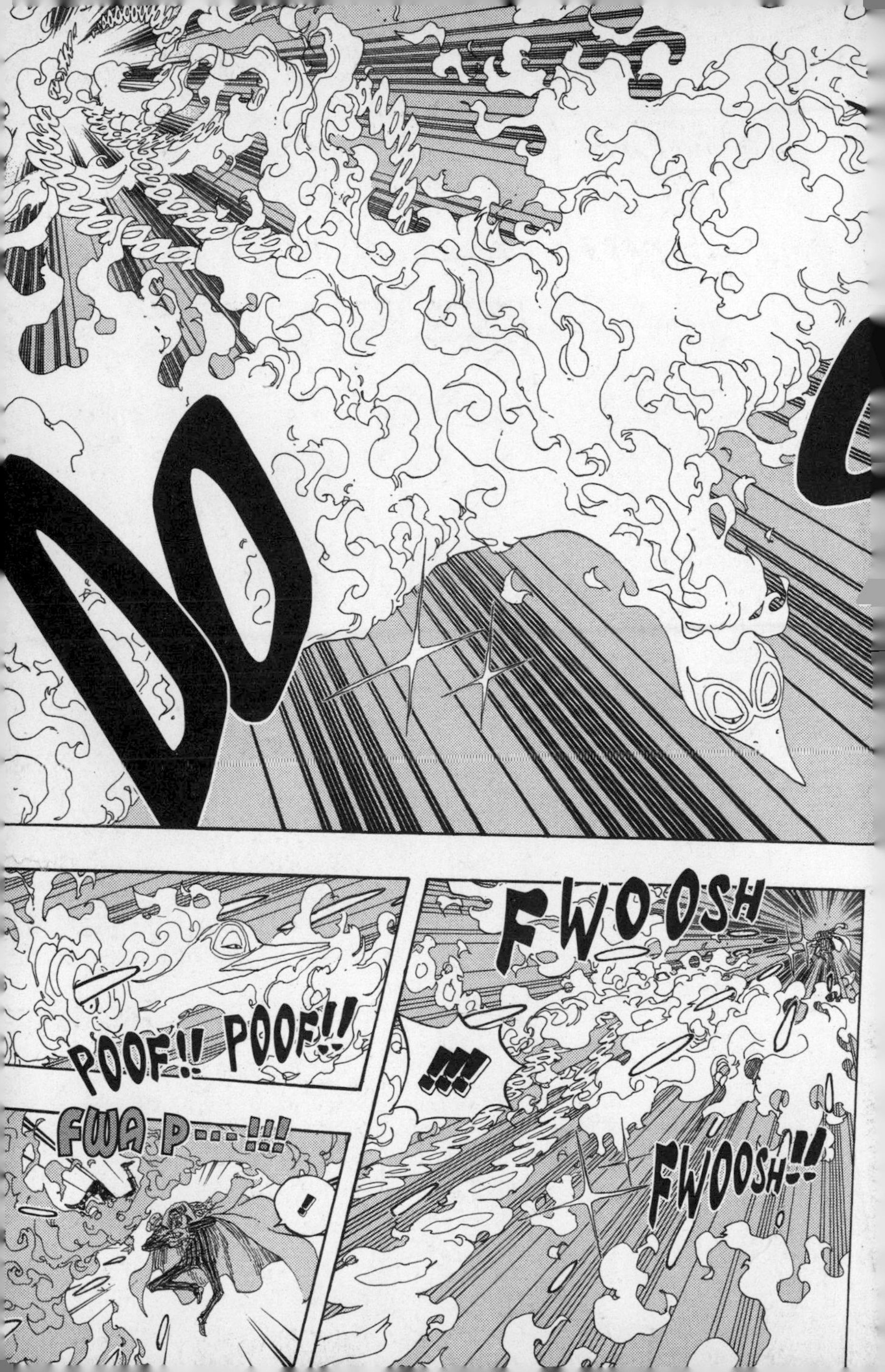
FWOOSH
!!!
FWOOSH!!
POOF!! POOF!!
FWAP...!!!
!

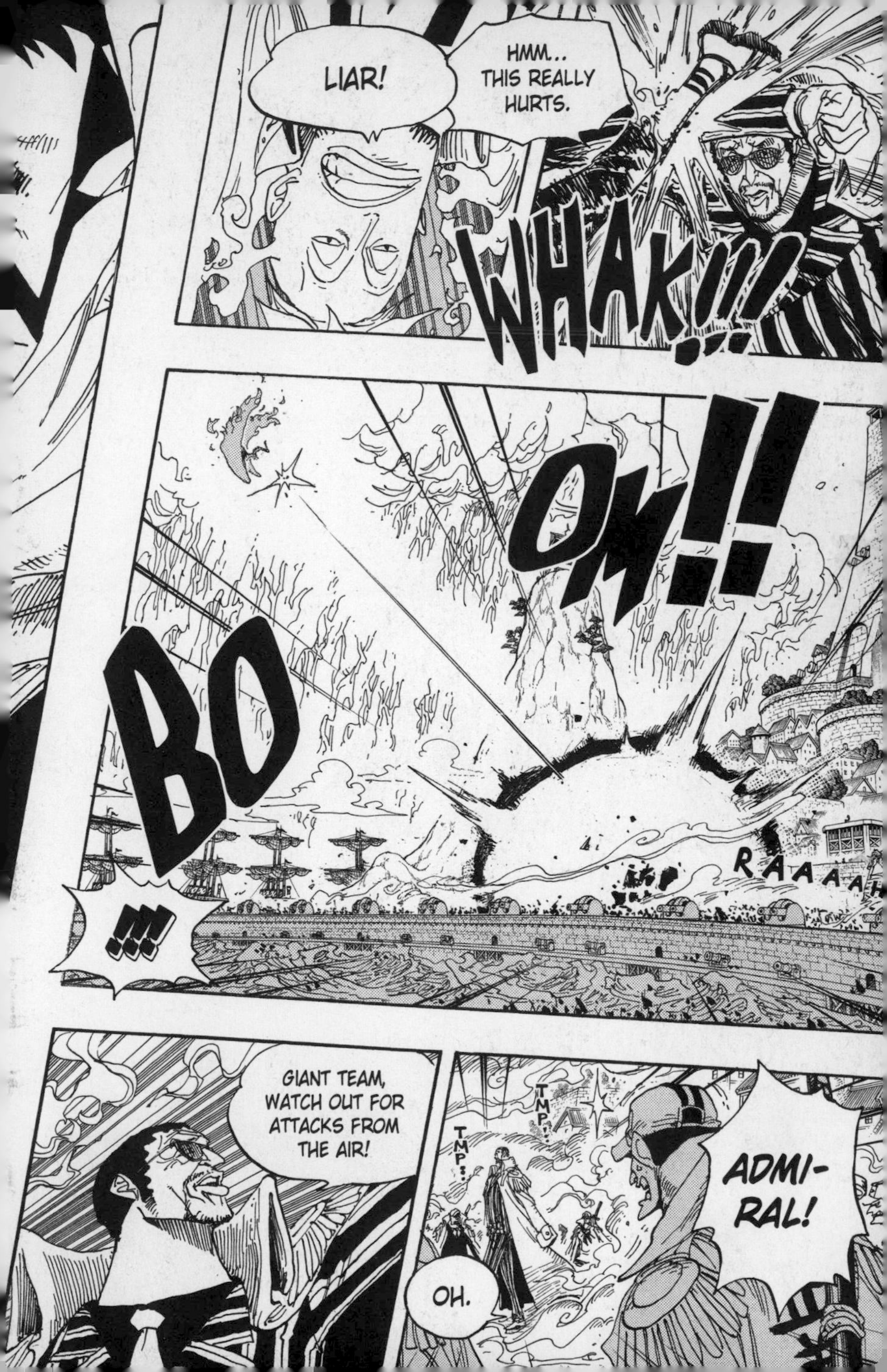
HMM.. THIS REALLY HURTS.
WHAK!!!
LIAR!
BOOM!!
RAAAAH
!!!
ADMI-RAL!
TMP...
TMP...
OH.
GIANT TEAM, WATCH OUT FOR ATTACKS FROM THE AIR!

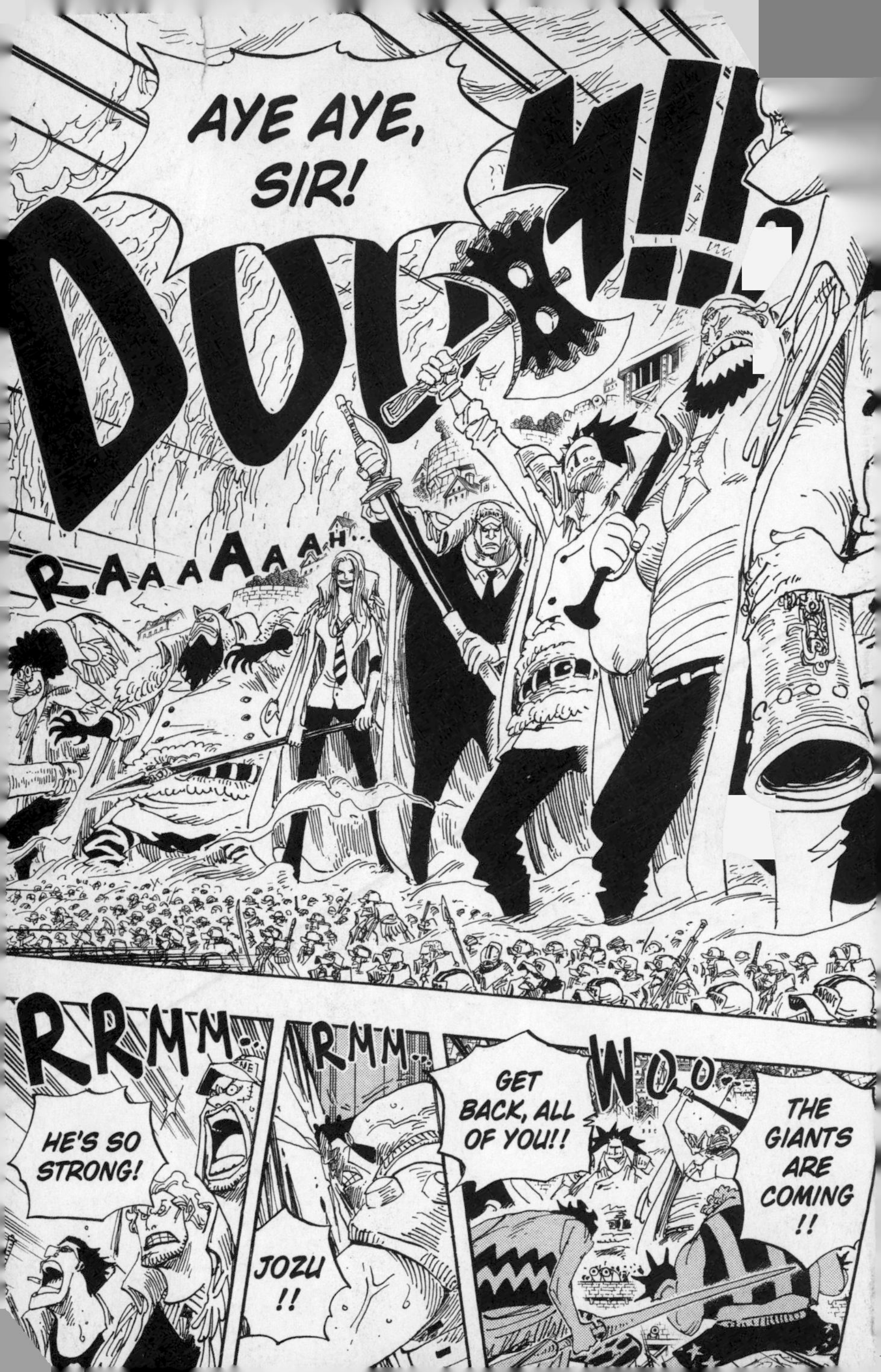
AYE AYE, SIR!
DOOM!!
RAAAAAAAH...
WOO..
THE GIANTS ARE COMING!!
GET BACK, ALL OF YOU!!
RMM..
JOZU!!
RRMM..
HE'S SO STRONG!

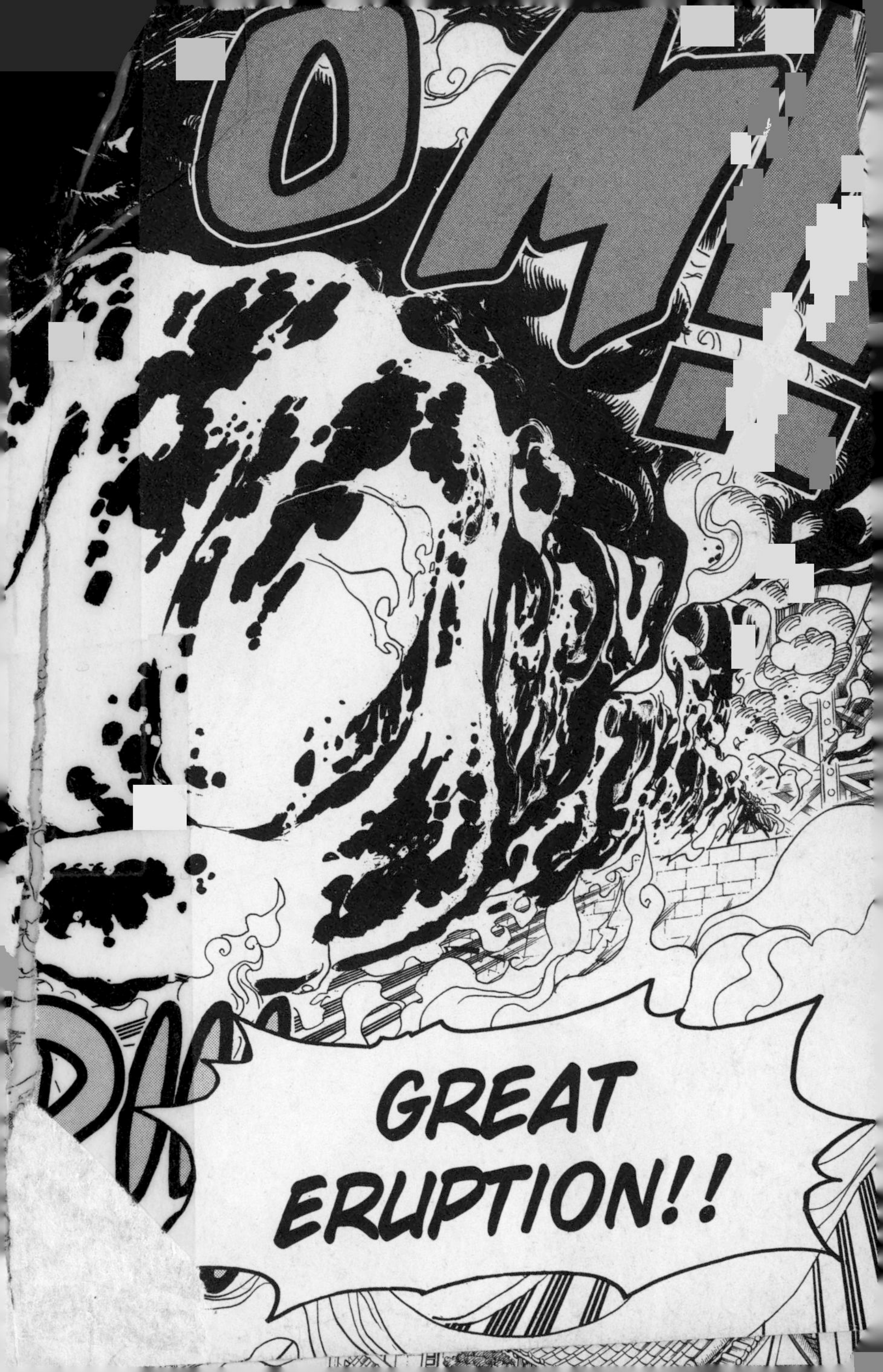
GREAT
ERUPTION!!

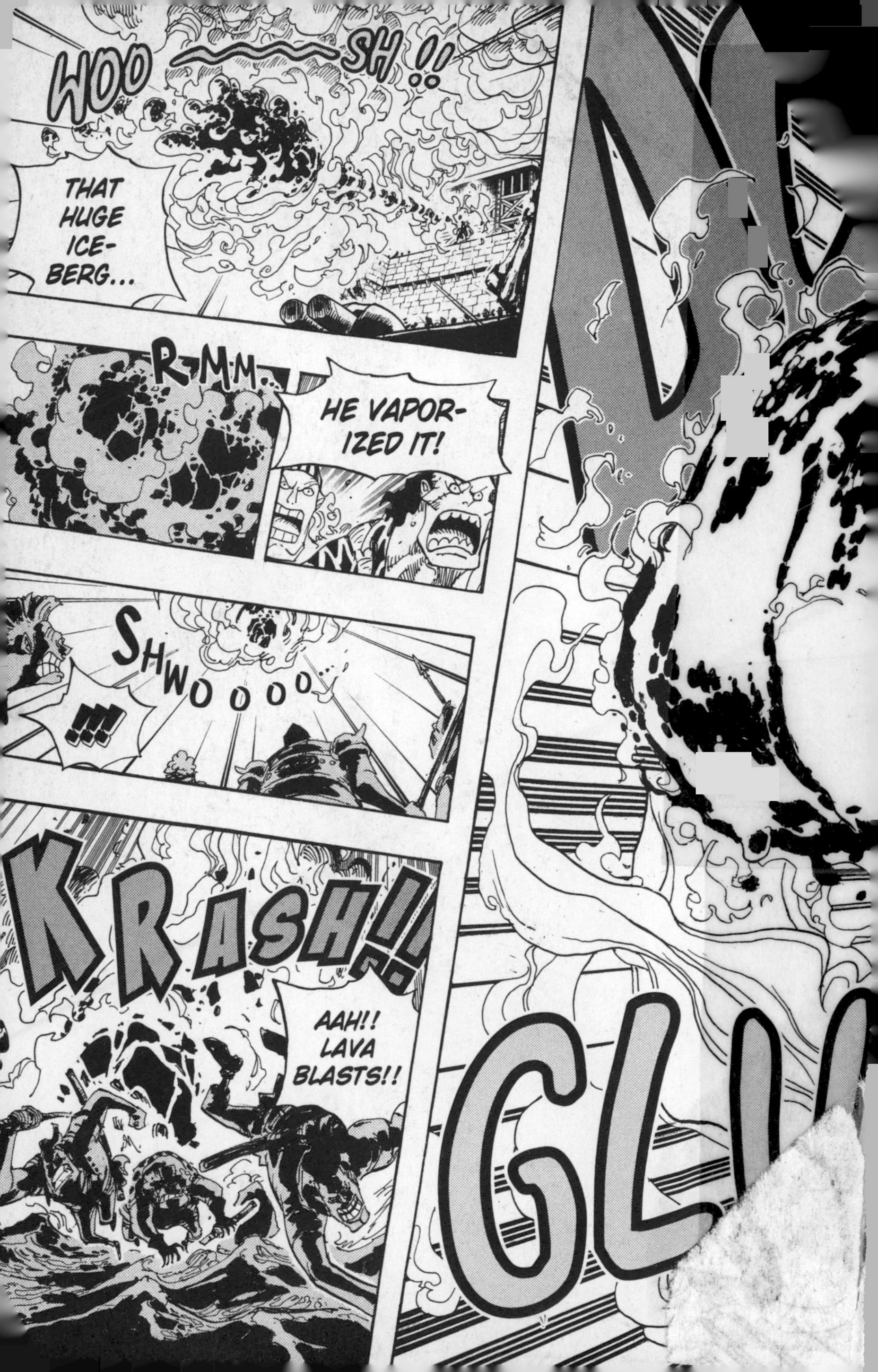
GLU
WOO————SH!!
THAT HUGE ICE-BERG...
HE VAPOR-IZED IT!
RMM
SHWOOOOO...
!!!
KRASH!!
AAH!! LAVA BLASTS!!

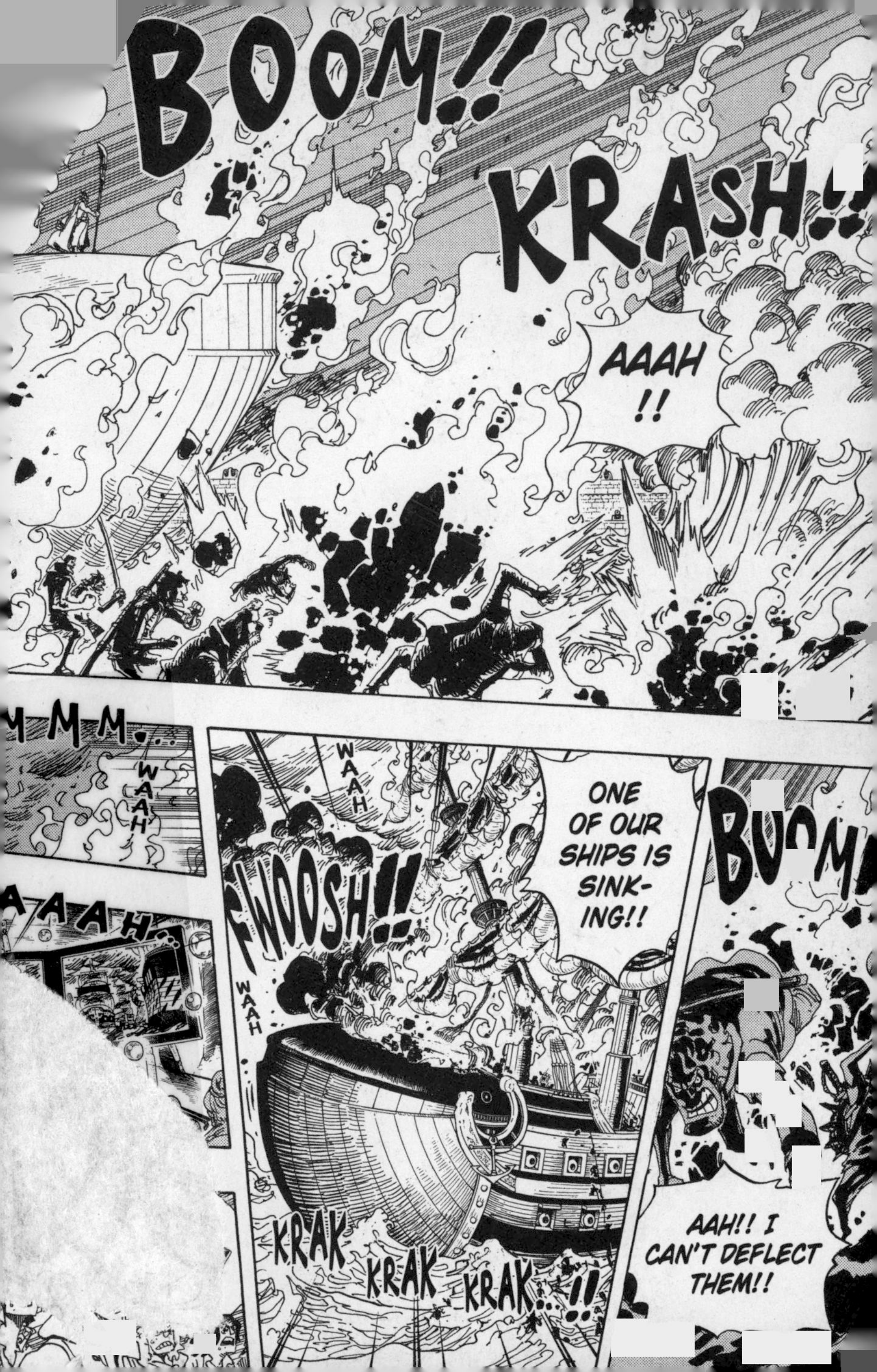
BOOM!!
KRASH!!
AAAH!!
AAH!! I CAN'T DEFLECT THEM!!
WAAH
ONE OF OUR SHIPS IS SINKING!!
FWOOSH!!
WAAH
KRAK
KRAK
KRAK...!!
MMM...
WAAH
AAAH...

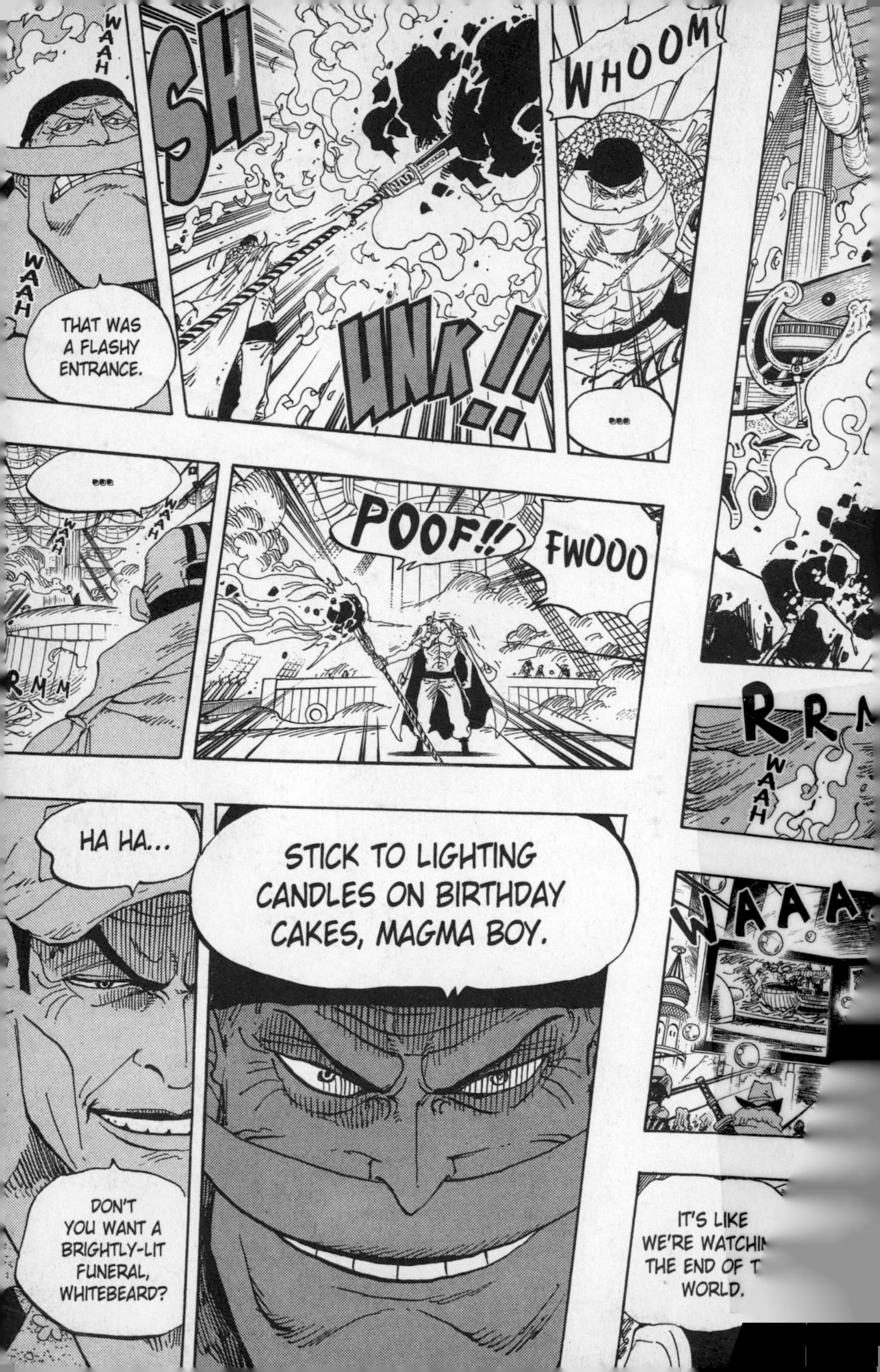
WHOOM
...
SH
UNK!!
WAAH
WAAH
THAT WAS A FLASHY ENTRANCE.
RR
WAAH
POOF!!
FWOOO
...
WAAH
WAAH
RMN
WAAA
IT'S LIKE WE'RE WATCHIN THE END OF T WORLD.
STICK TO LIGHTING CANDLES ON BIRTHDAY CAKES, MAGMA BOY.
HA HA...
DON'T YOU WANT A BRIGHTLY-LIT FUNERAL, WHITEBEARD?

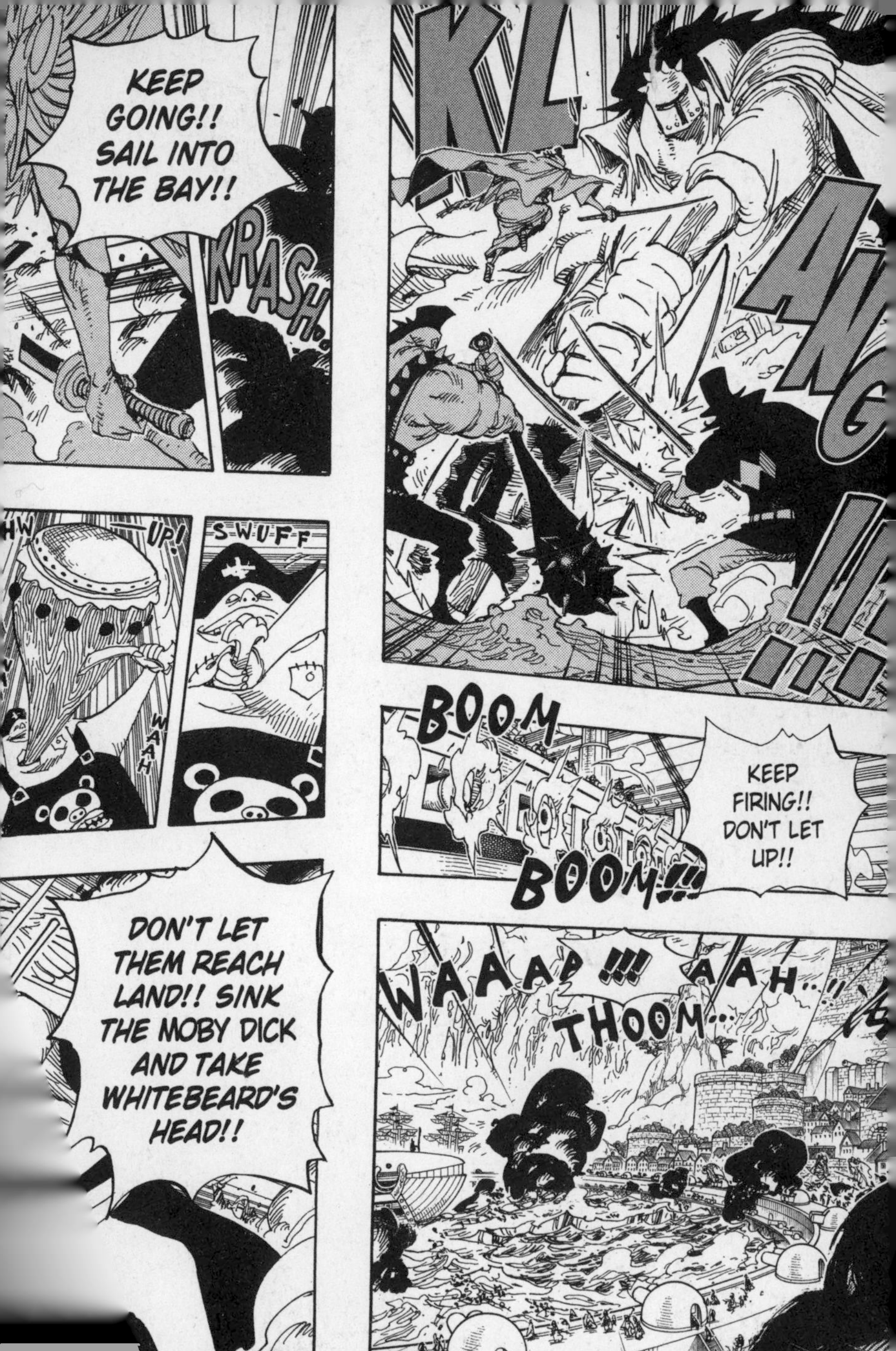
KL
ANG!!
KEEP GOING!! SAIL INTO THE BAY!!
KRASH
S-W-U-F-F
WAAH
HWUP!
BOOM
BOOM!!!
KEEP FIRING!! DON'T LET UP!!
WAAAH!!!
AAH...!!
THOOM...
DON'T LET THEM REACH LAND!! SINK THE MOBY DICK AND TAKE WHITEBEARD'S HEAD!!

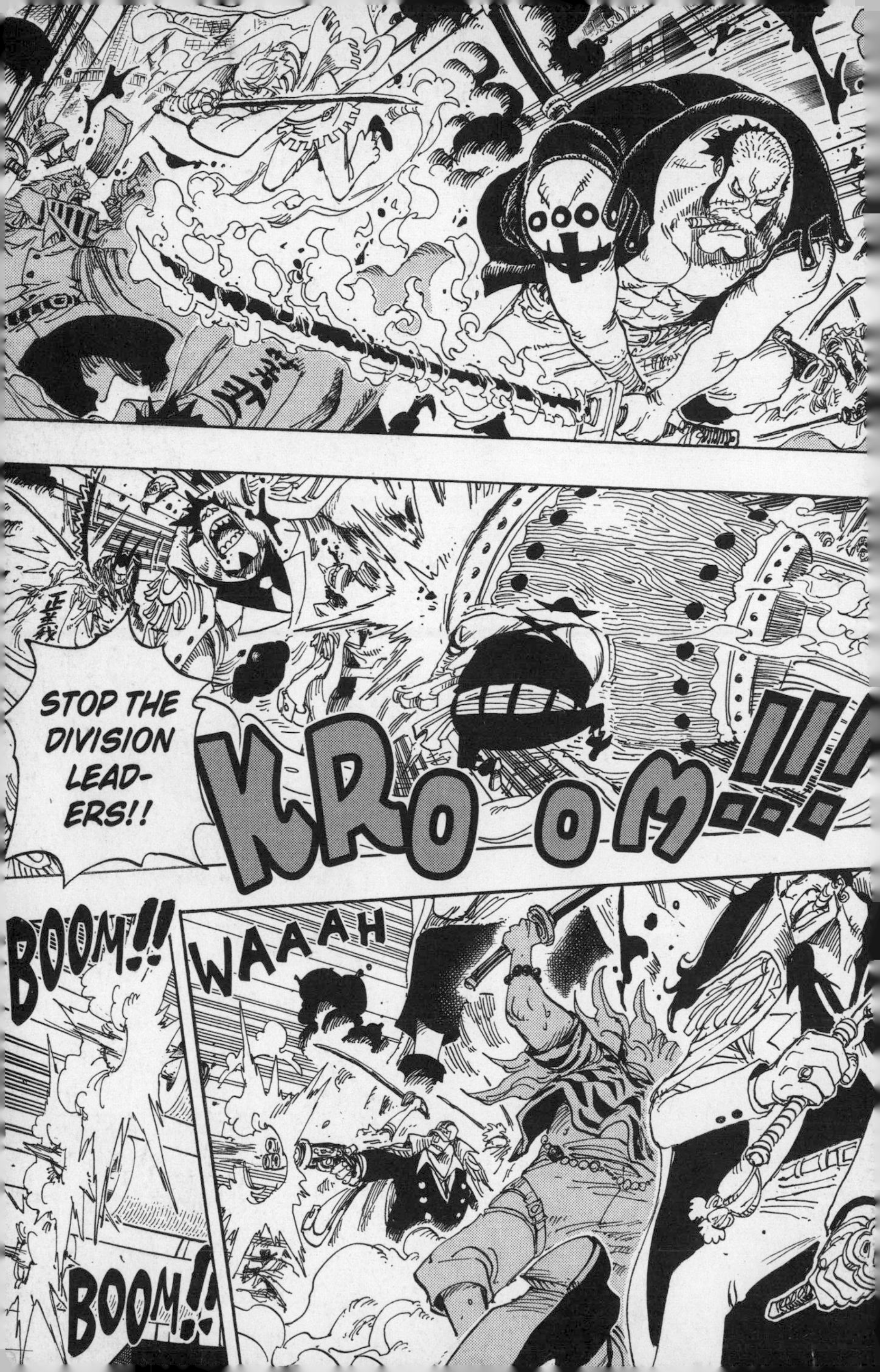
KROOM!!!
STOP THE DIVISION LEADERS!!
WAAAH
BOOM!!
BOOM!!

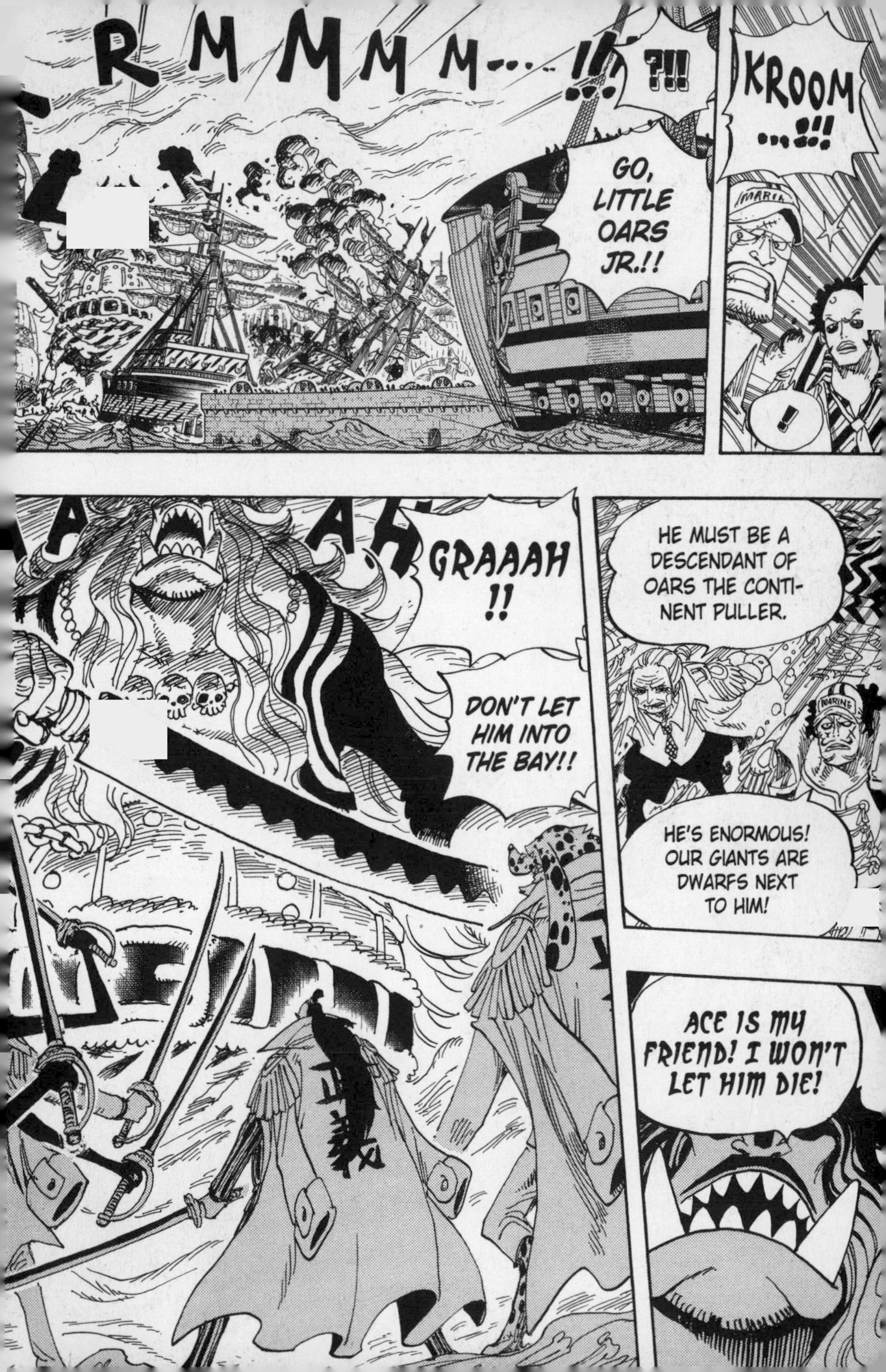
KROOM
...!!
?!!
RMMMM...!!
GO, LITTLE OARS JR.!!
HE MUST BE A DESCENDANT OF OARS THE CONTINENT PULLER.
HE'S ENORMOUS! OUR GIANTS ARE DWARFS NEXT TO HIM!
ACE IS MY FRIEND! I WON'T LET HIM DIE!
GRAAAH!!
DON'T LET HIM INTO THE BAY!!

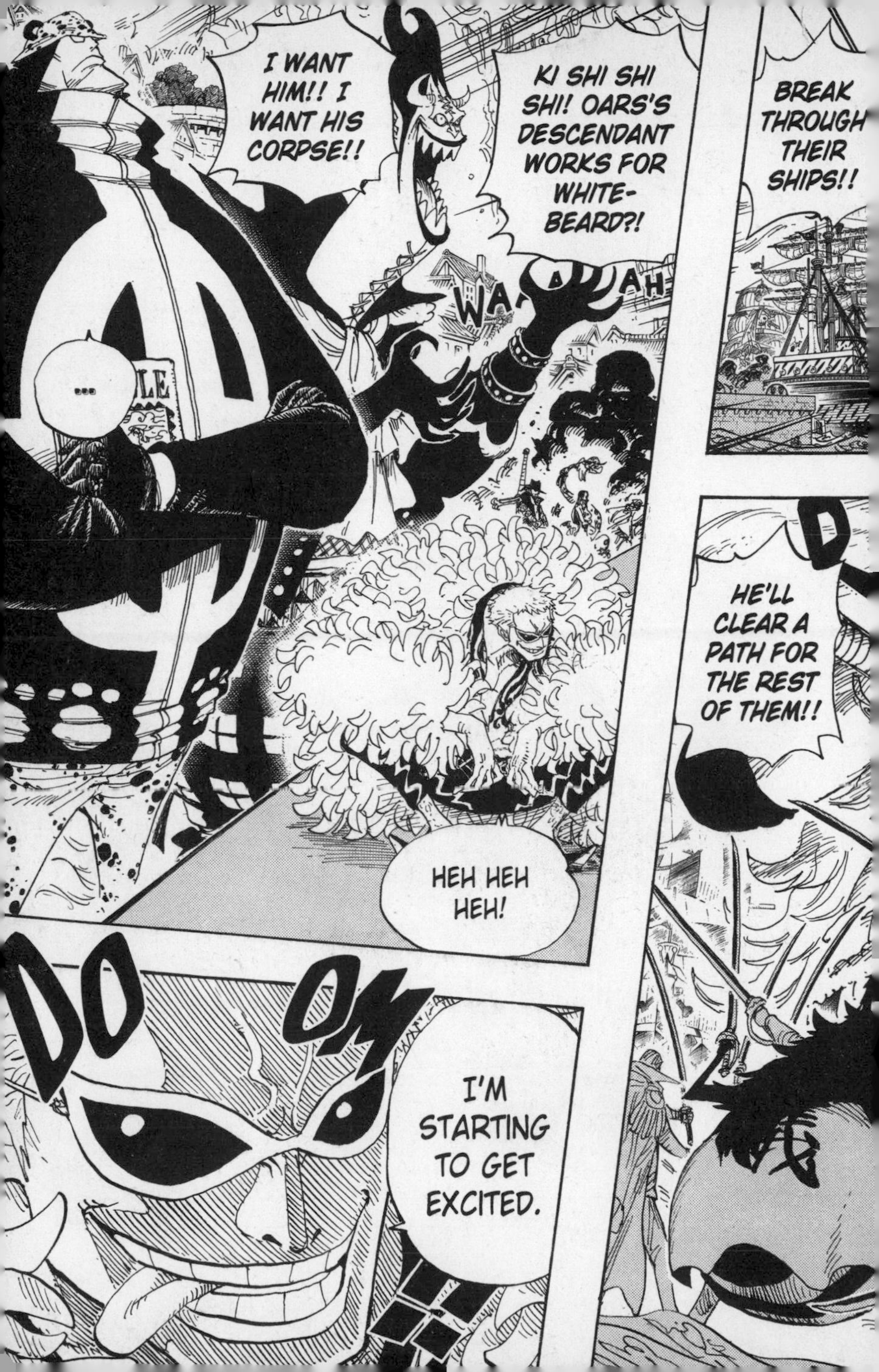
BREAK THROUGH THEIR SHIPS!!
KI SHI SHI SHI! OARS'S DESCENDANT WORKS FOR WHITE-BEARD?!
I WANT HIM!! I WANT HIS CORPSE!!
WA AH
HEH HEH HEH!
HE'LL CLEAR A PATH FOR THE REST OF THEM!!
DO ON
I'M STARTING TO GET EXCITED.

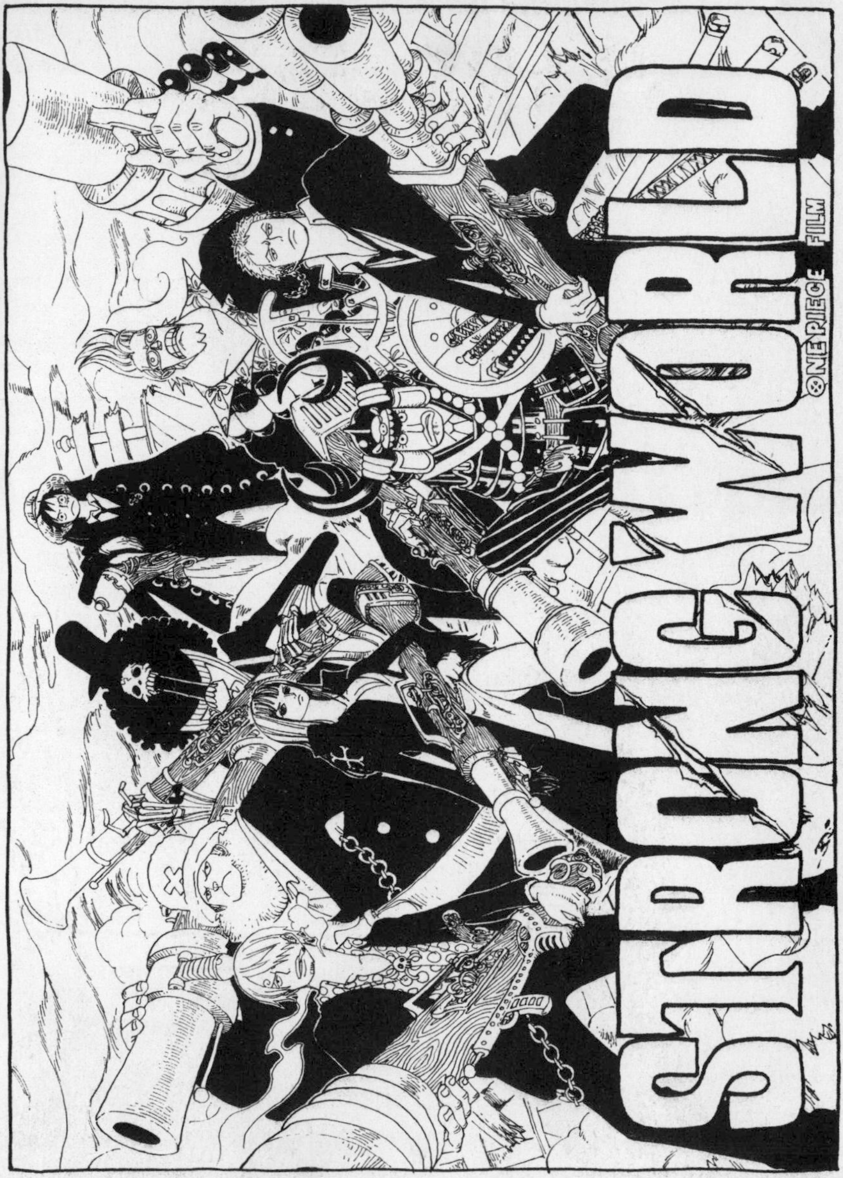
ONE PIECE FILM
STRONG WORLD

Chapter 555: OARS AND THE HAT

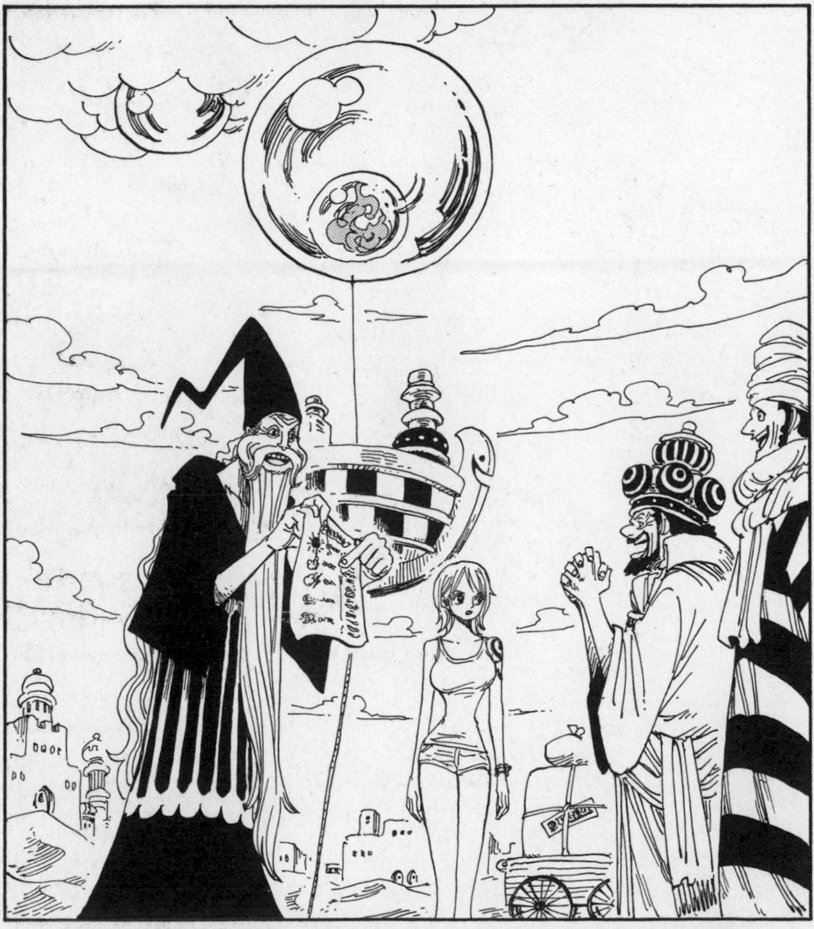

LIMITED COVER SERIES, NO. 16: NAMI'S WEATHER REPORT VOL. 1: "THE BUSINESS OF THE LEGENDARY SKY ISLAND WEATHERIA"

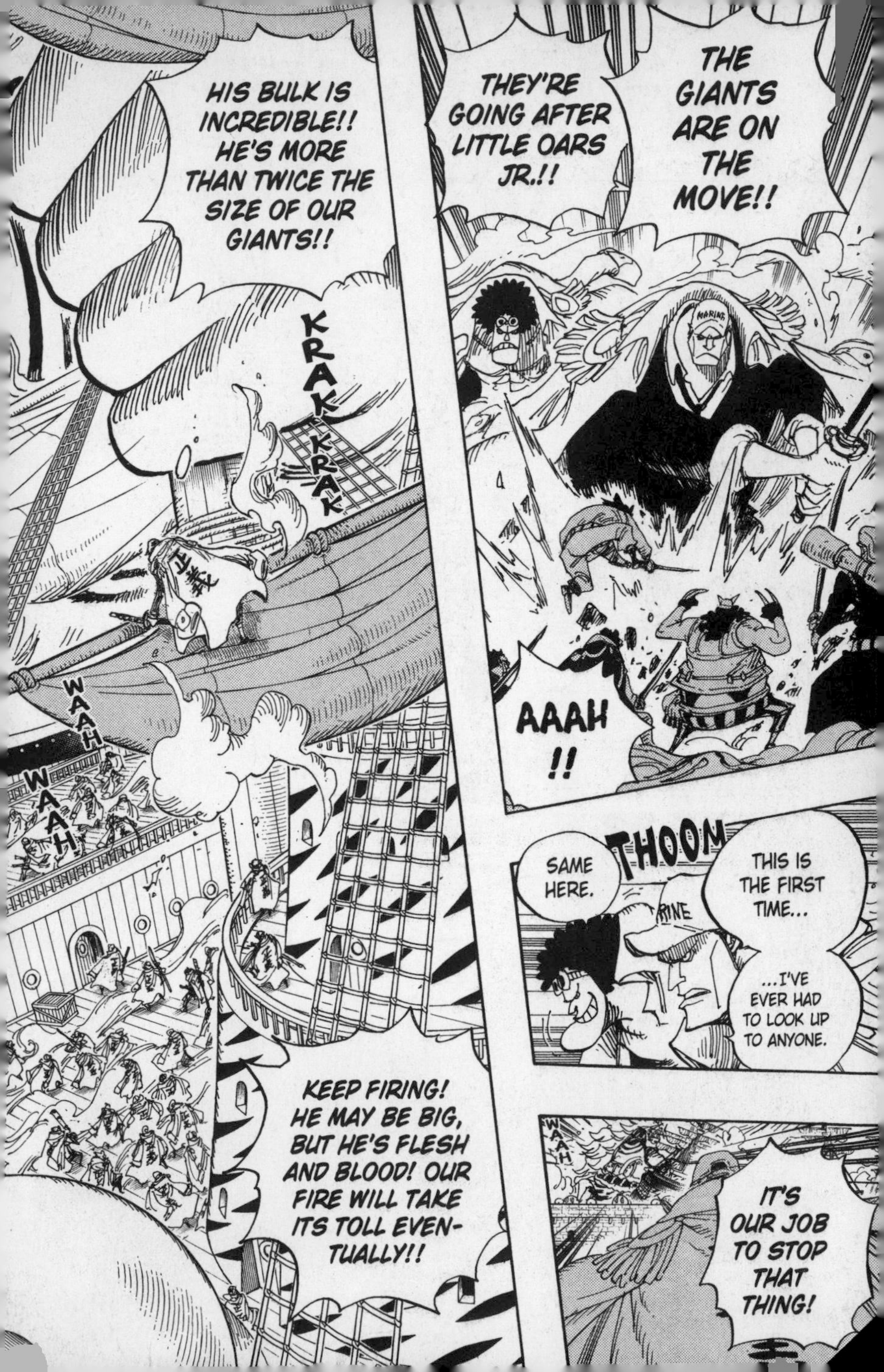
THE GIANTS ARE ON THE MOVE!!
THEY'RE GOING AFTER LITTLE OARS JR.!!
AAAH !!
THIS IS THE FIRST TIME...
...I'VE EVER HAD TO LOOK UP TO ANYONE.
THOOM
SAME HERE.
WAAH
IT'S OUR JOB TO STOP THAT THING!
HIS BULK IS INCREDIBLE!! HE'S MORE THAN TWICE THE SIZE OF OUR GIANTS!!
KRAK KRAK KRAK
WAAH
WAAH
KEEP FIRING! HE MAY BE BIG, BUT HE'S FLESH AND BLOOD! OUR FIRE WILL TAKE ITS TOLL EVEN-TUALLY!!

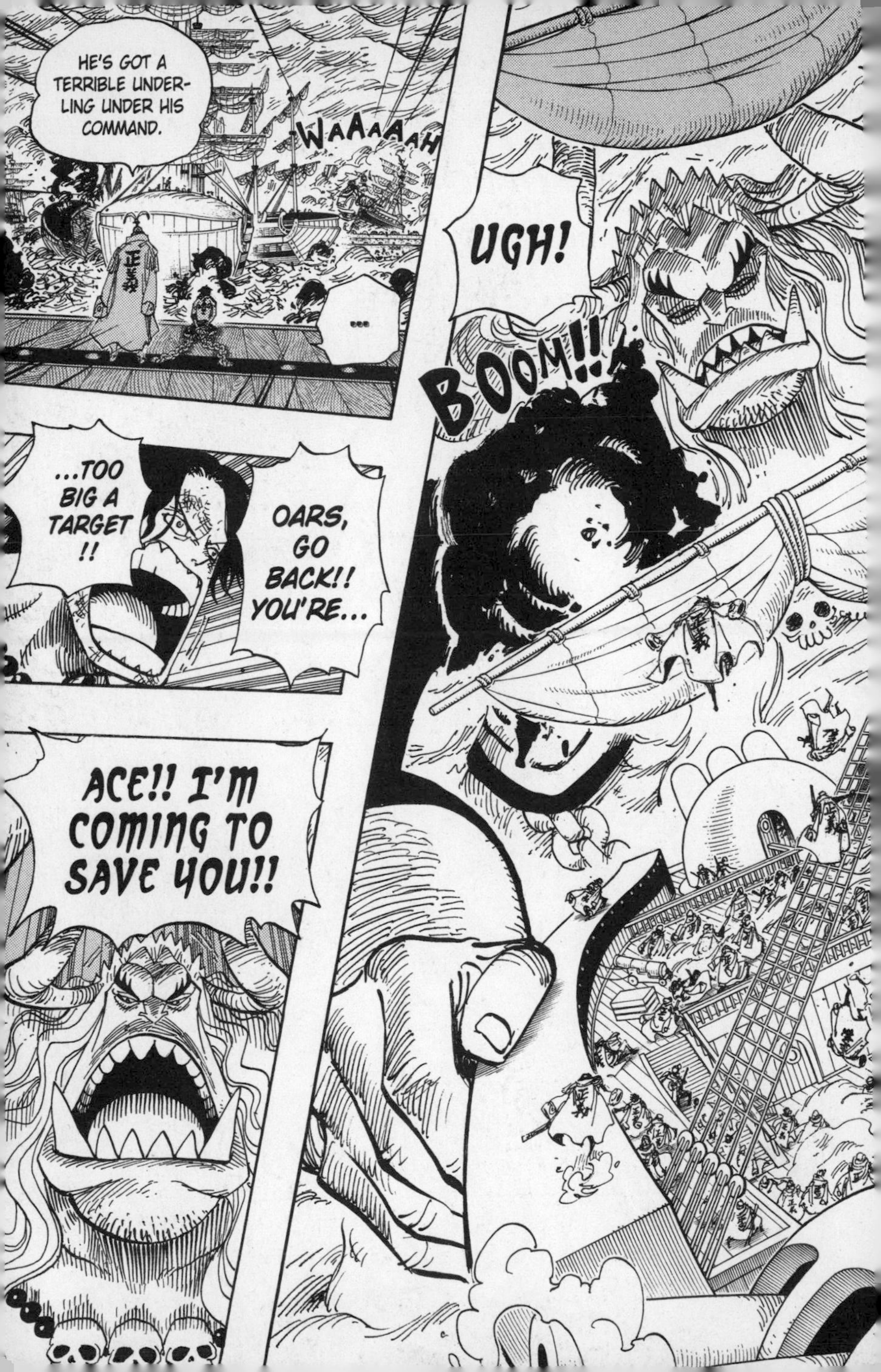
UGH!
BOOM!!
HE'S GOT A TERRIBLE UNDERLING UNDER HIS COMMAND.
WAAAAAH
...
OARS, GO BACK!! YOU'RE...
...TOO BIG A TARGET!!
ACE!! I'M COMING TO SAVE YOU!!

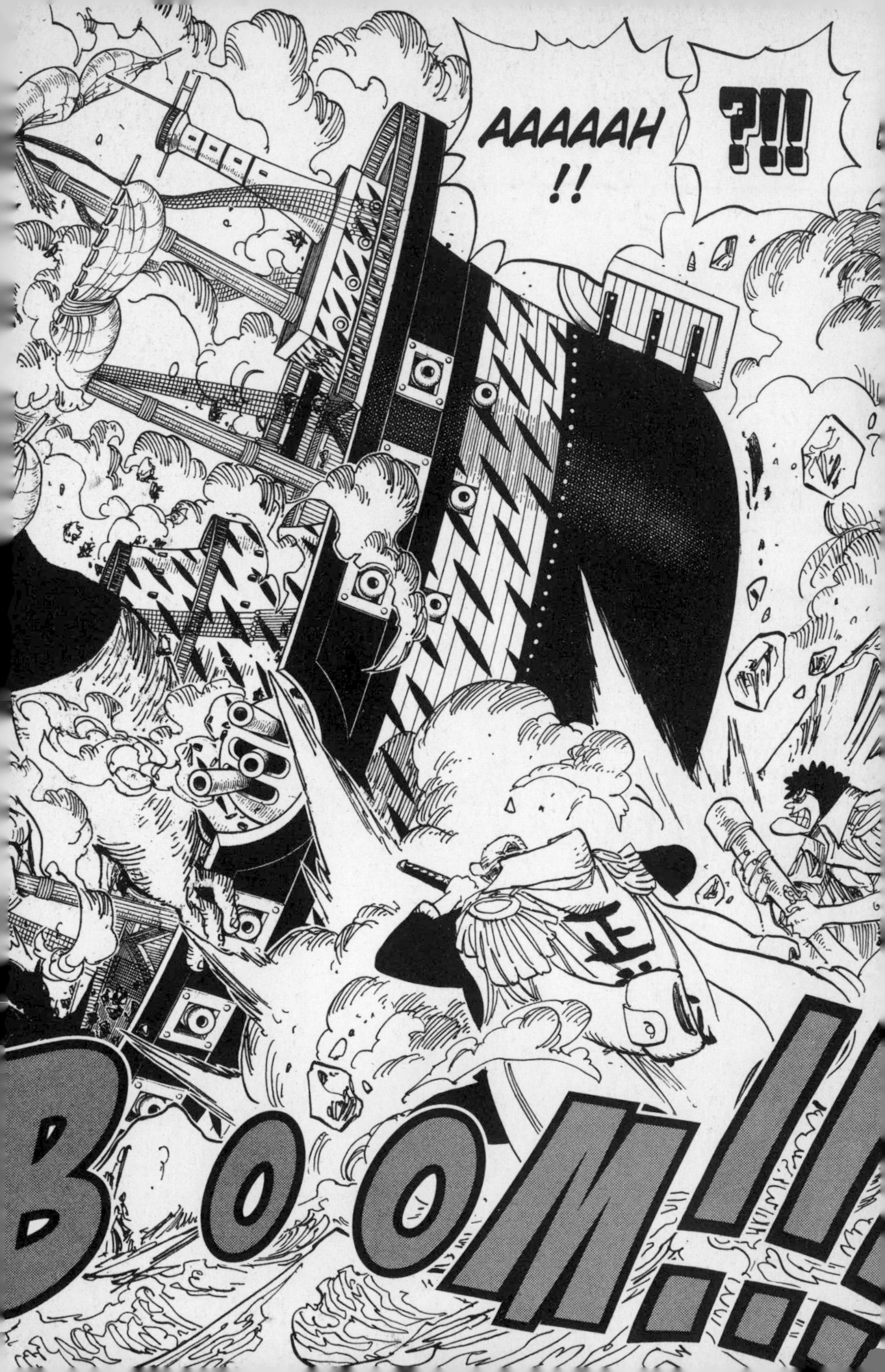
?!!
AAAAAH !!
BOOM...!!

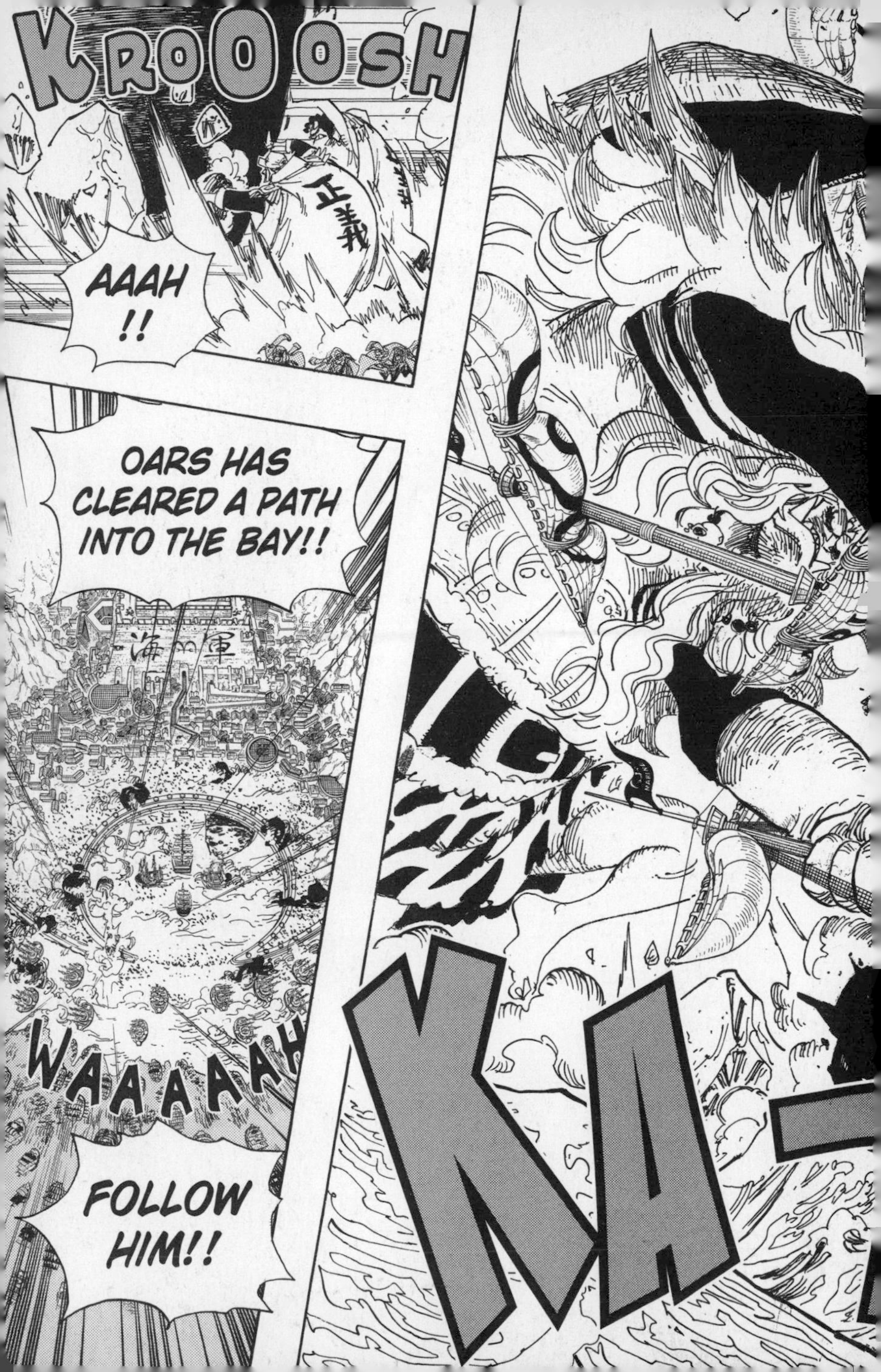
KA-
KROOOOSH
正義
AAAH!!
OARS HAS CLEARED A PATH INTO THE BAY!!
海軍
WAAAAAH
FOLLOW HIM!!

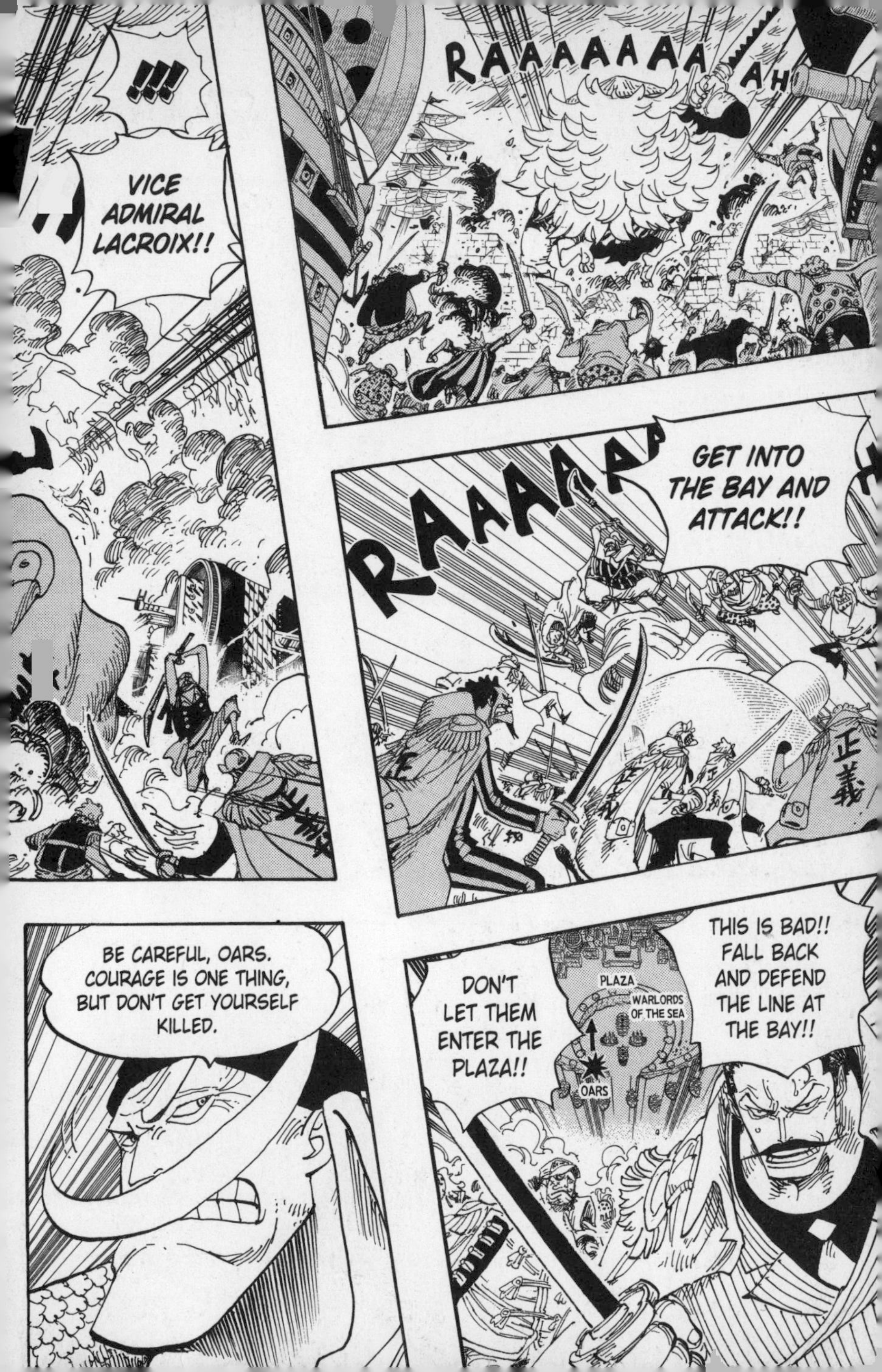
RAAAAAAAAH
GET INTO THE BAY AND ATTACK!!
RAAAAAA
!!!!
VICE ADMIRAL LACROIX!!
THIS IS BAD!! FALL BACK AND DEFEND THE LINE AT THE BAY!!
PLAZA
WARLORDS OF THE SEA
OARS
DON'T LET THEM ENTER THE PLAZA!!
BE CAREFUL, OARS. COURAGE IS ONE THING, BUT DON'T GET YOURSELF KILLED.
正義

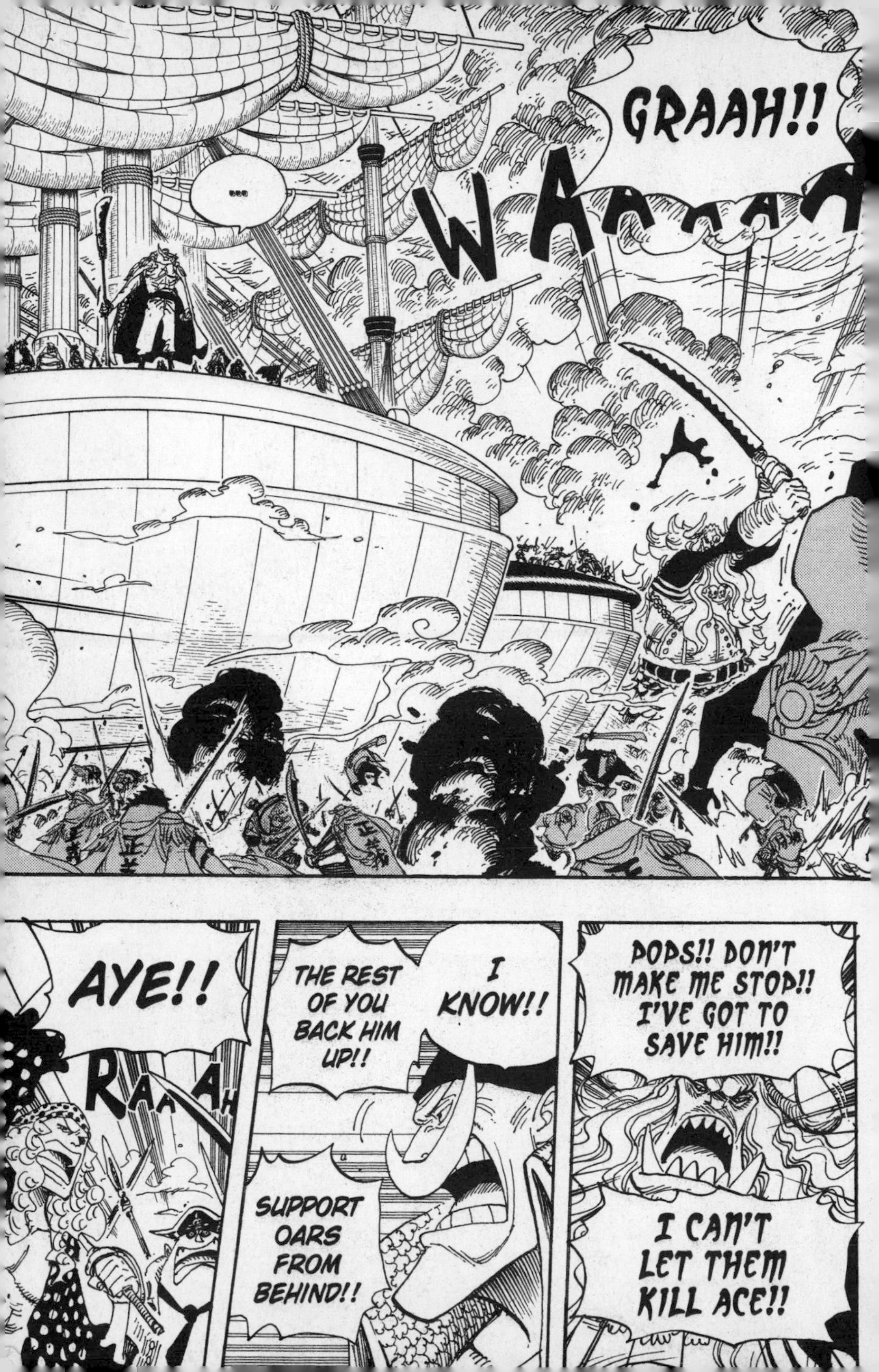
GRAAH!!
WAAAAA
...
POPS!! DON'T MAKE ME STOP!! I'VE GOT TO SAVE HIM!!
I CAN'T LET THEM KILL ACE!!
I KNOW!!
THE REST OF YOU BACK HIM UP!!
SUPPORT OARS FROM BEHIND!!
AYE!!
RAAAH

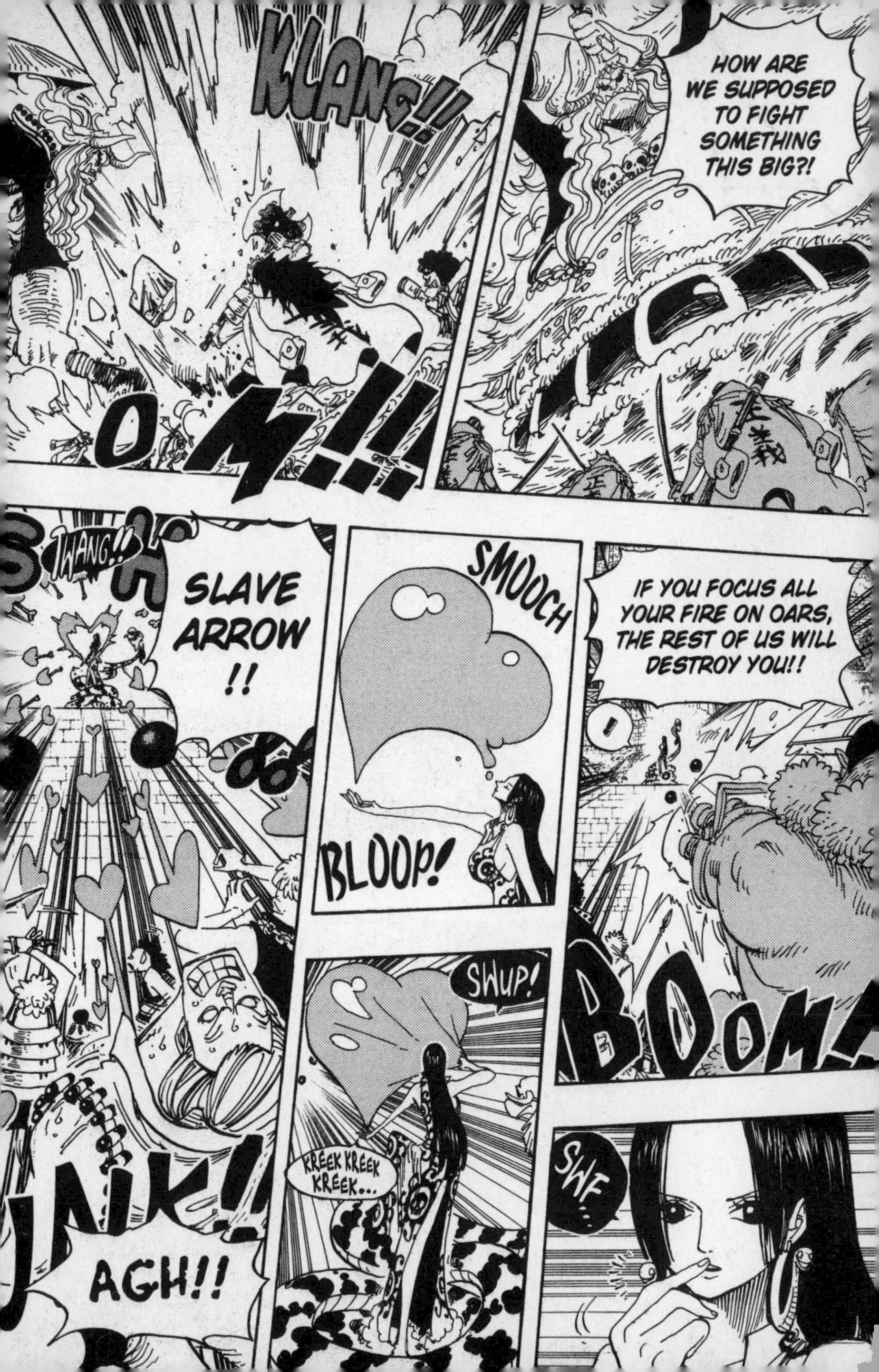
HOW ARE WE SUPPOSED TO FIGHT SOMETHING THIS BIG?!
KLANG!!
IF YOU FOCUS ALL YOUR FIRE ON OARS, THE REST OF US WILL DESTROY YOU!!
BOOM
SWF
SMOOCH
BLOOP!
SWUP!
KREEK KREEK KREEK...
TWANG!!
SLAVE ARROW!!
AGH!!

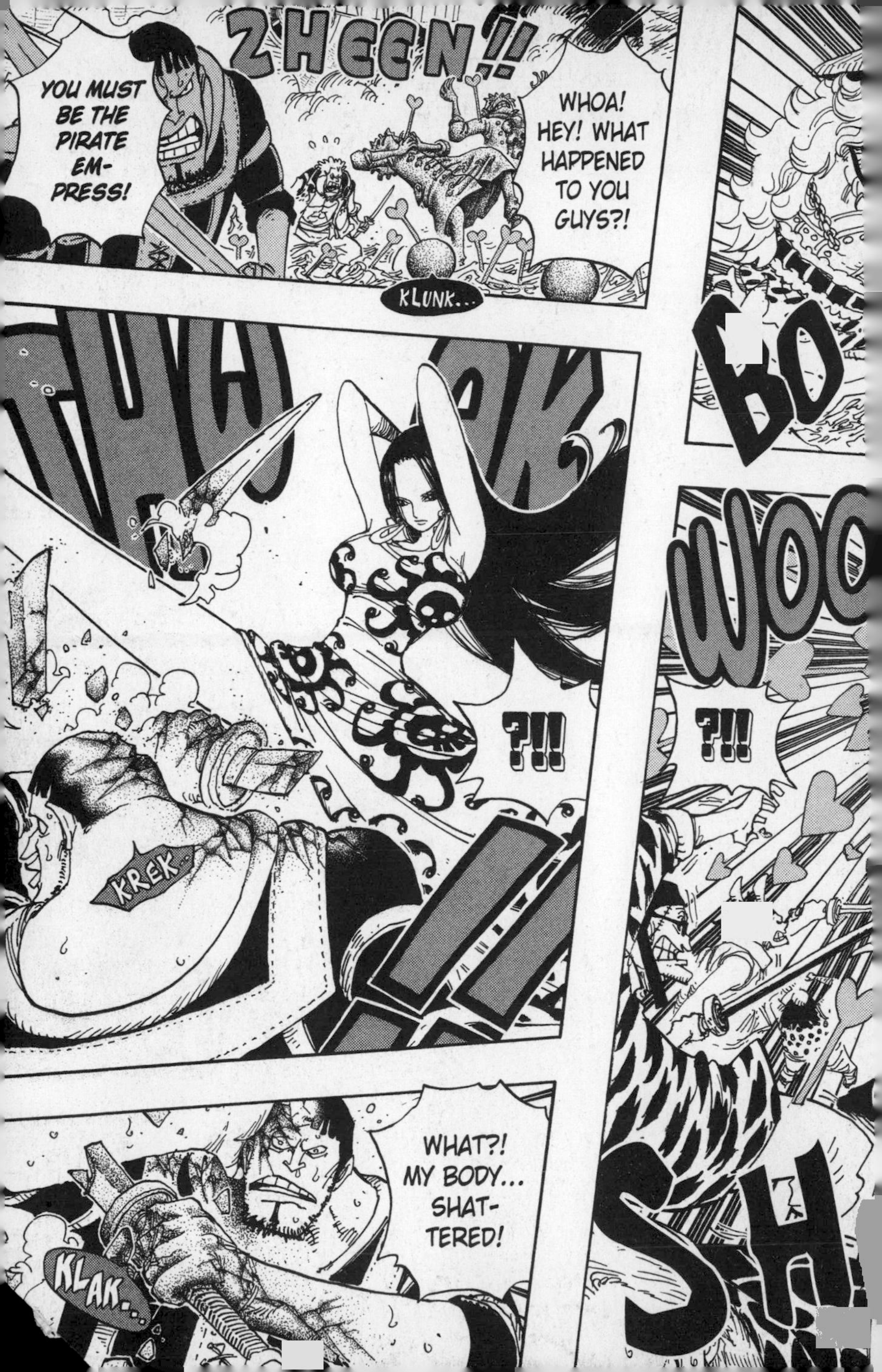
BO
WOO
?!!
SH
ZHEEN!!
WHOA! HEY! WHAT HAPPENED TO YOU GUYS?!
YOU MUST BE THE PIRATE EMPRESS!
KLUNK...
THWOK
?!!
KREK
WHAT?! MY BODY... SHATTERED!
KLAK...

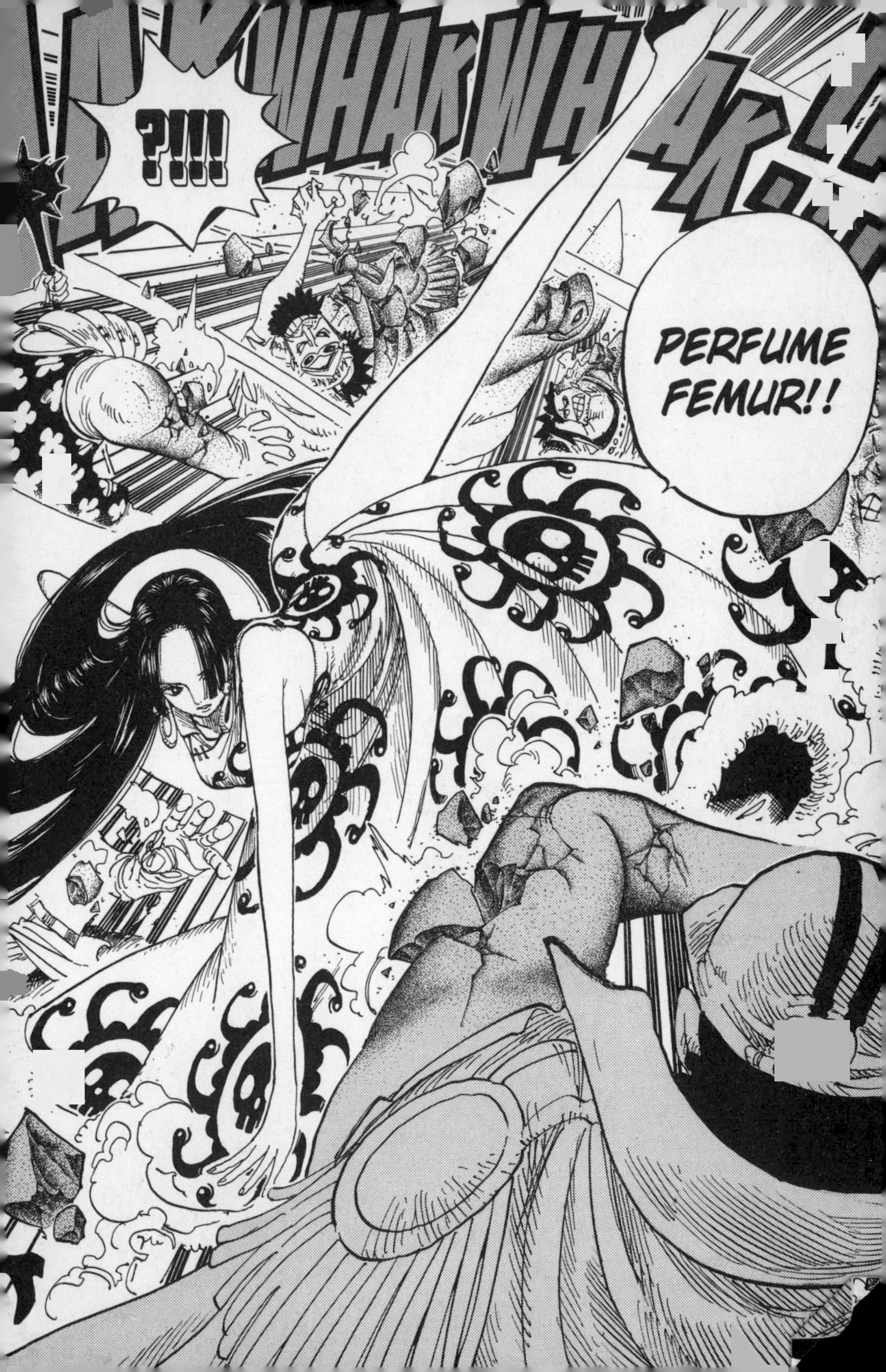
PERFUME FEMUR!!
?!!!

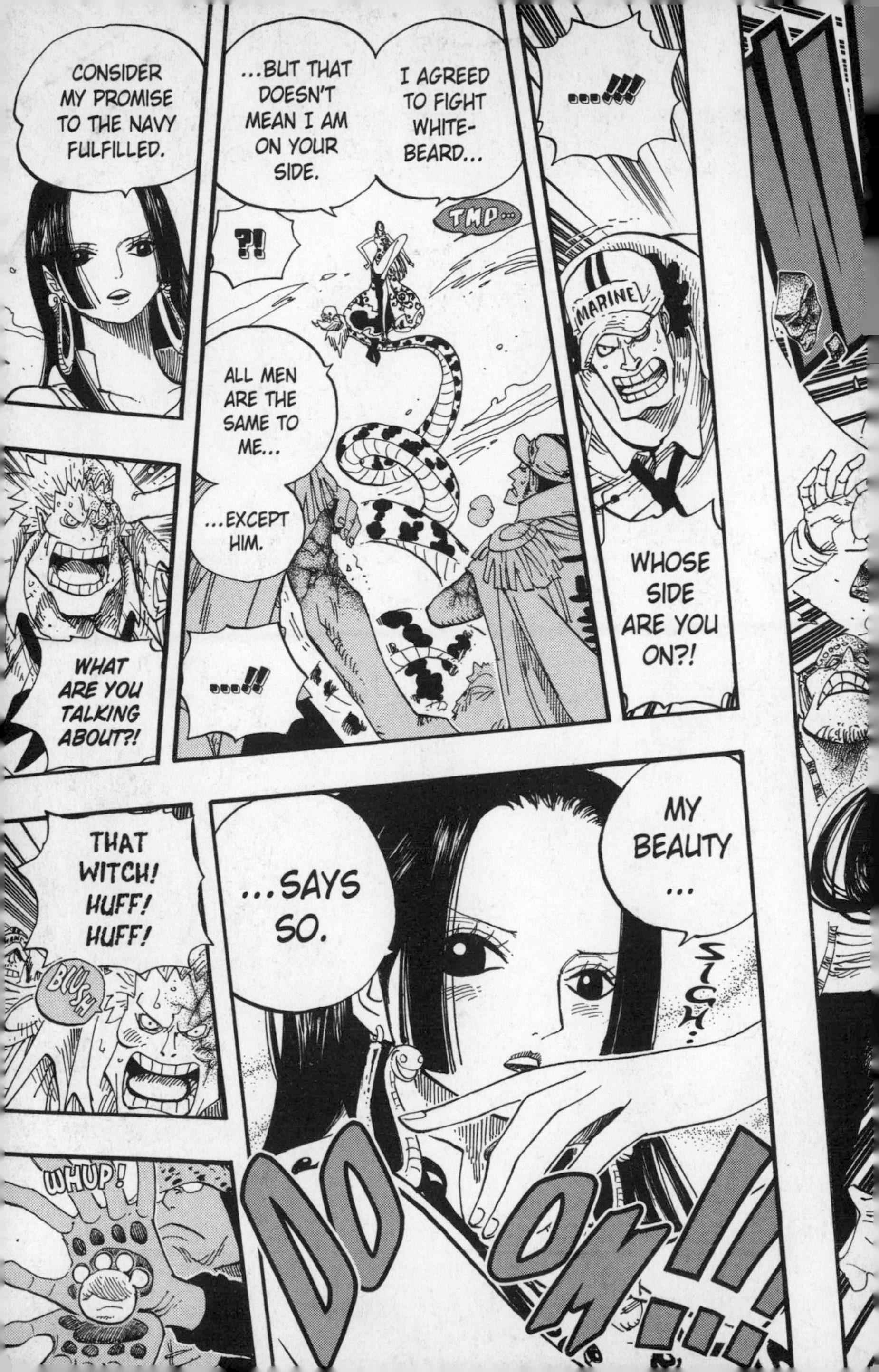
...!!!
WHOSE SIDE ARE YOU ON?!
I AGREED TO FIGHT WHITE-BEARD...
...BUT THAT DOESN'T MEAN I AM ON YOUR SIDE.
TMP...
?!
ALL MEN ARE THE SAME TO ME...
...EXCEPT HIM.
...!!
CONSIDER MY PROMISE TO THE NAVY FULFILLED.
WHAT ARE YOU TALKING ABOUT?!
MY BEAUTY ...
...SAYS SO.
SIGH...
DOOM!!...
THAT WITCH! HUFF! HUFF!
BLUSH
WHUP!

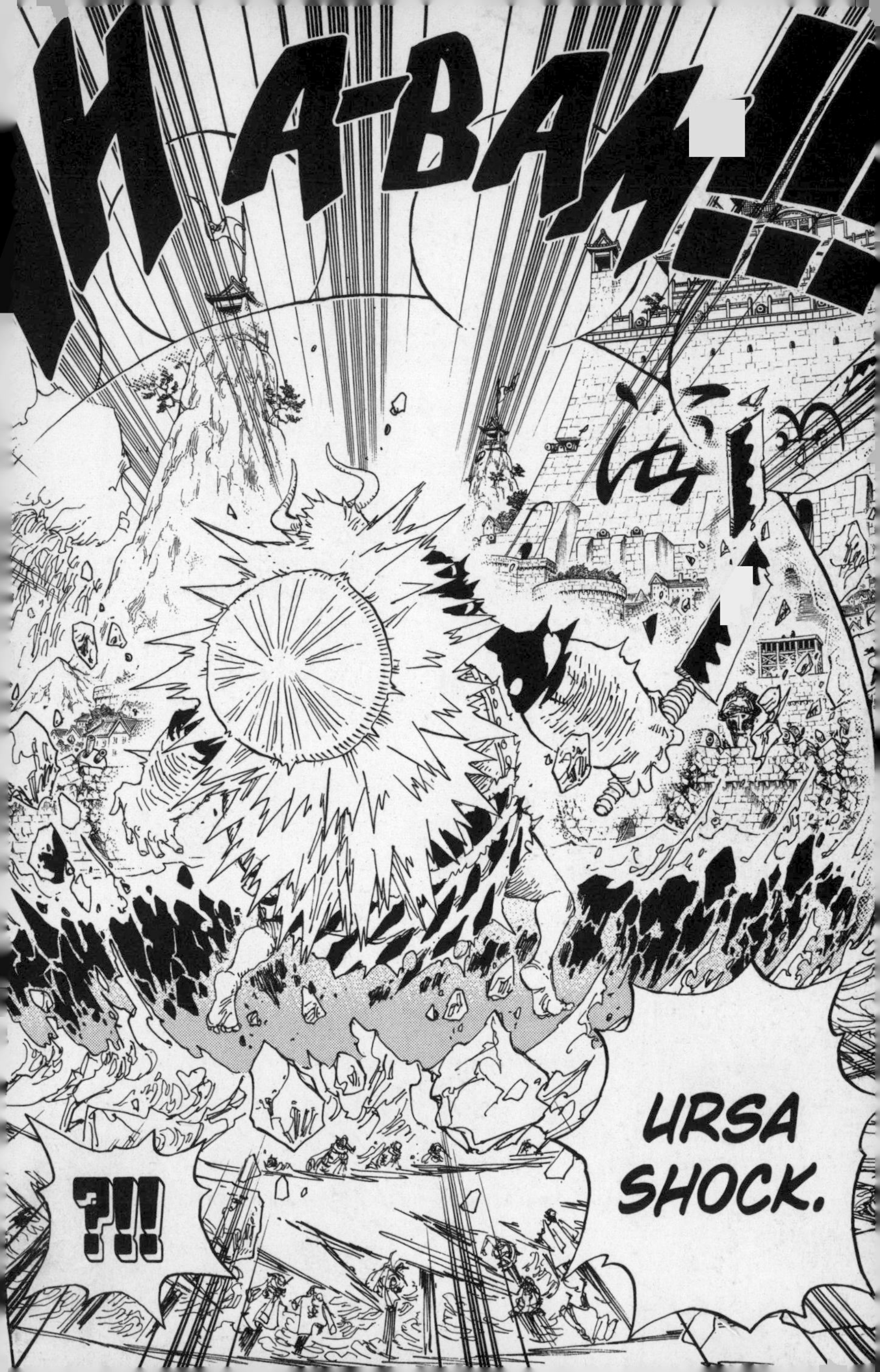
KA-BAM!!!
URSA SHOCK.
?!!

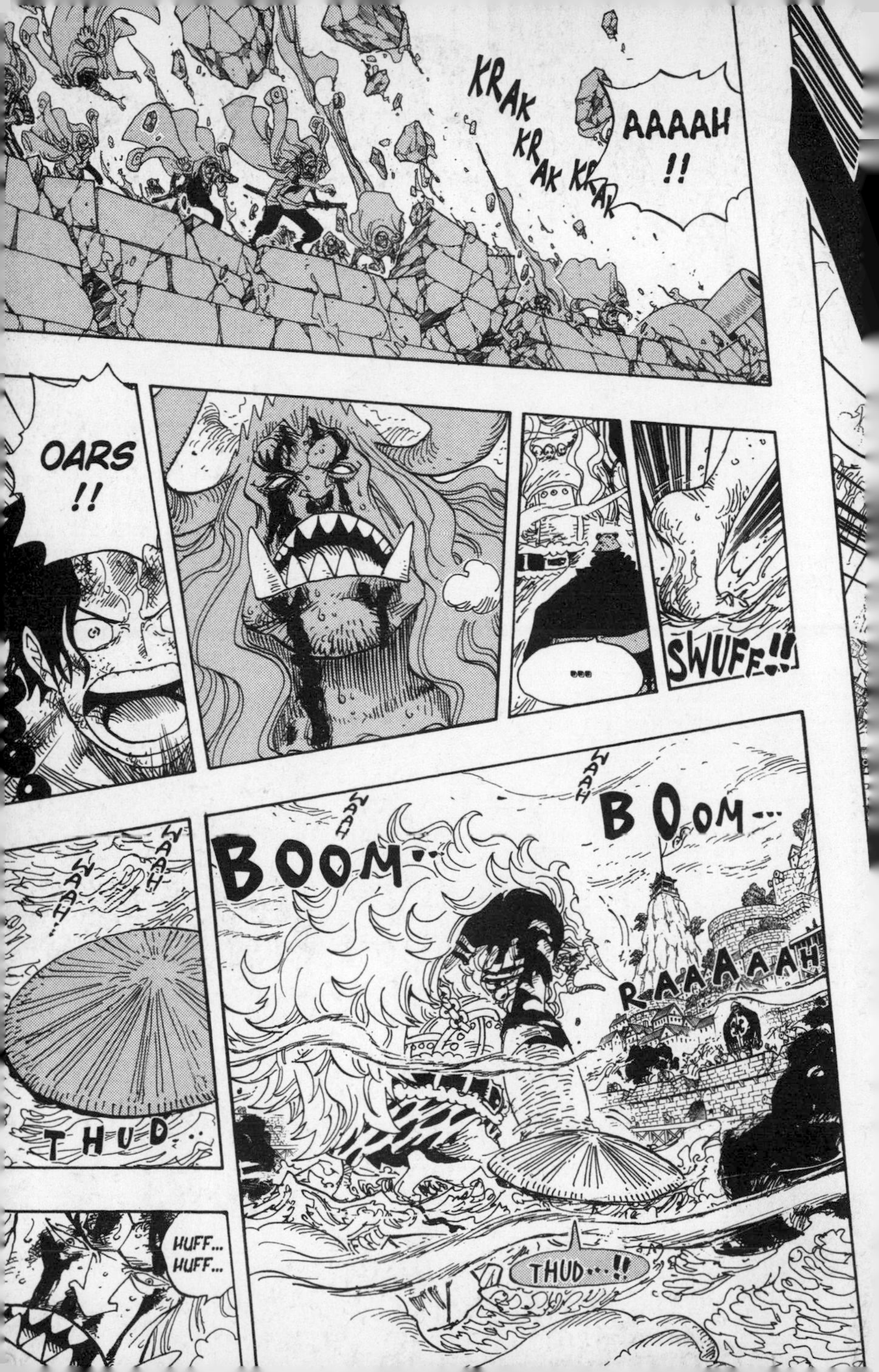

KRAK KRAK KRAK KRAK
AAAAH !!
SWUFF!!
...
OARS !!
WAAH
BOOM...
WAAH
BOOM...
RAAAAAH
THUD...!!
WAAAH!
WAAAH!
THUD
HUFF... HUFF...

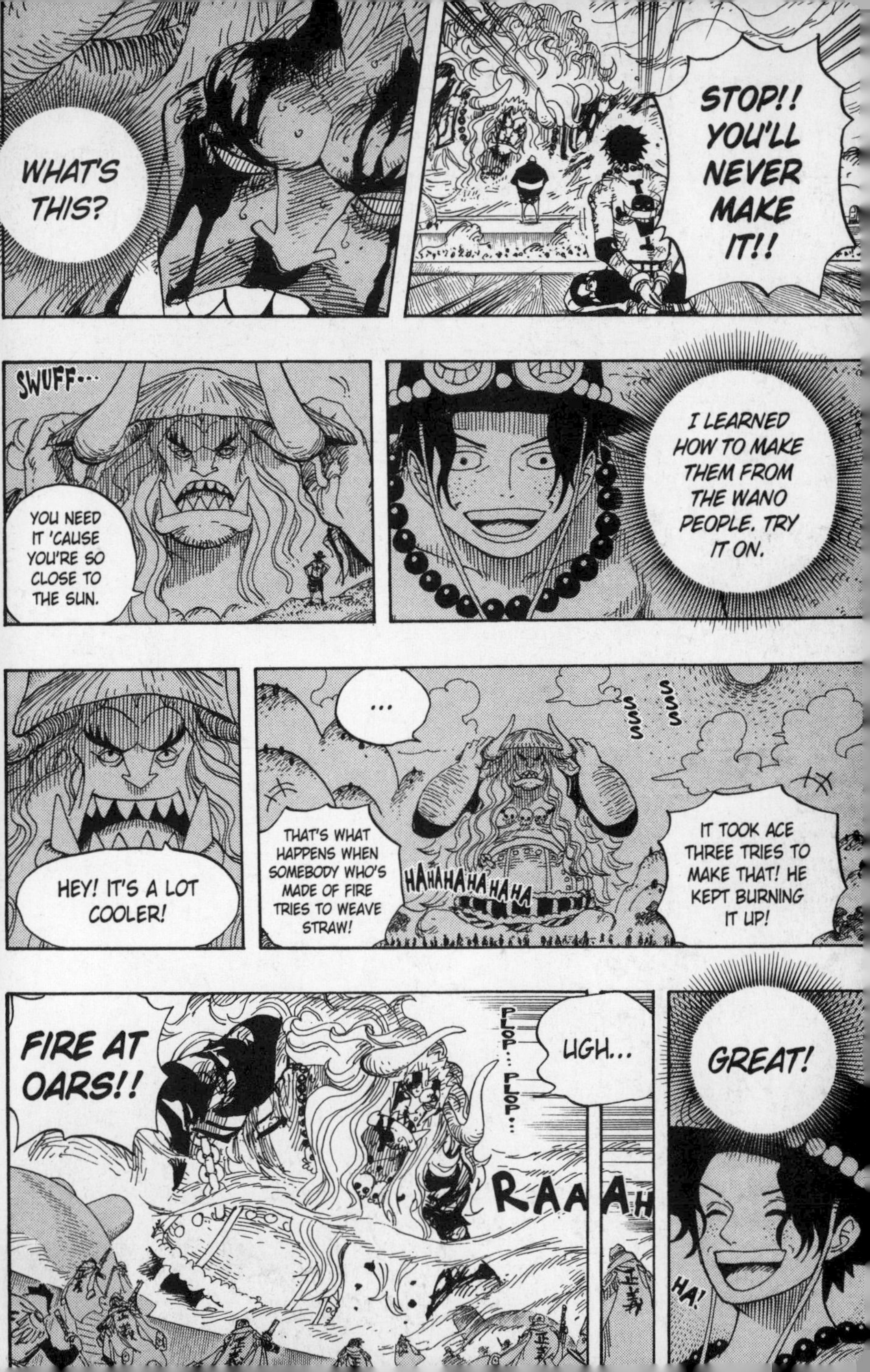
STOP!! YOU'LL NEVER MAKE IT!!
WHAT'S THIS?
I LEARNED HOW TO MAKE THEM FROM THE WANO PEOPLE. TRY IT ON.
SWUFF...
YOU NEED IT 'CAUSE YOU'RE SO CLOSE TO THE SUN.
...
SSSS
SSSS
IT TOOK ACE THREE TRIES TO MAKE THAT! HE KEPT BURNING IT UP!
HAHAHAHAHAHAHA
THAT'S WHAT HAPPENS WHEN SOMEBODY WHO'S MADE OF FIRE TRIES TO WEAVE STRAW!
HEY! IT'S A LOT COOLER!
GREAT!
HA!
UGH...
PLOP... PLOP...
RAAAH
FIRE AT OARS!!

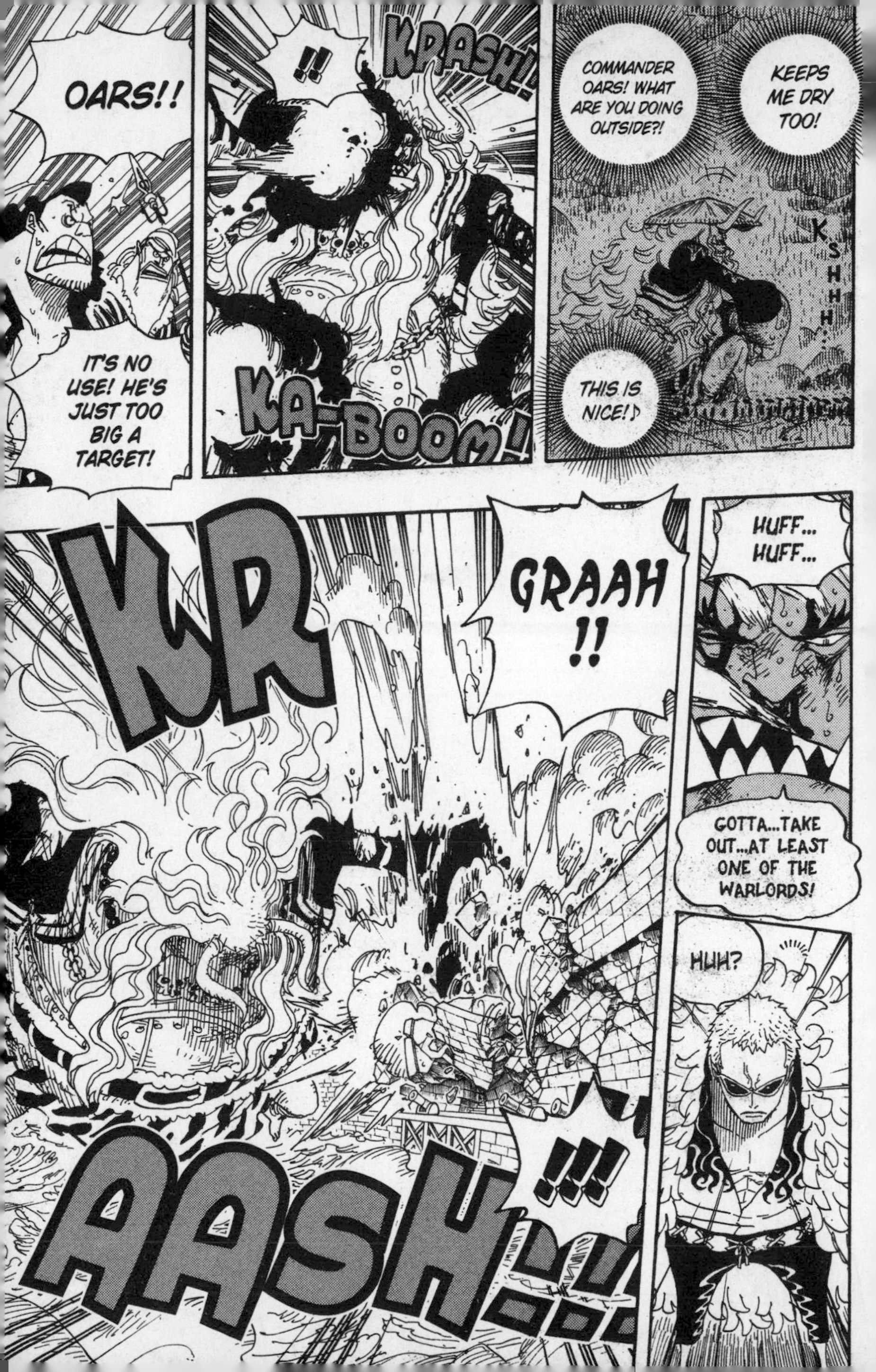
KEEPS ME DRY TOO!
COMMANDER OARS! WHAT ARE YOU DOING OUTSIDE?!
KSHHH...
THIS IS NICE!♪
KRASH!!
!!
KA-BOOM!
OARS!!
IT'S NO USE! HE'S JUST TOO BIG A TARGET!
HUFF... HUFF...
GOTTA...TAKE OUT...AT LEAST ONE OF THE WARLORDS!
HUH?
GRAAH!!
KR
AASH!!!

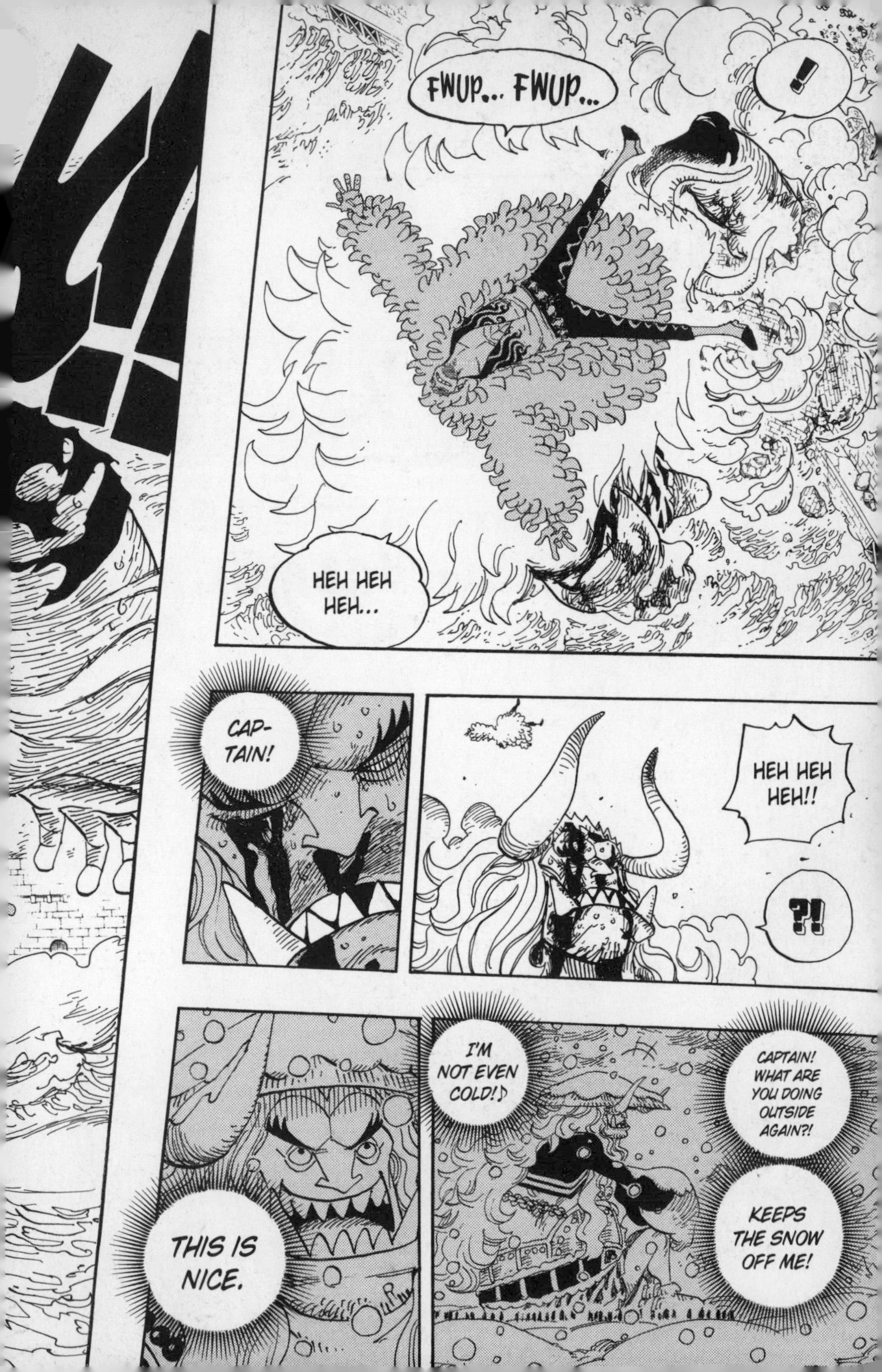
!
FWUP... FWUP...
HEH HEH HEH...
HEH HEH HEH!!
?!
CAP-TAIN!
CAPTAIN! WHAT ARE YOU DOING OUTSIDE AGAIN?!
KEEPS THE SNOW OFF ME!
I'M NOT EVEN COLD!♪
THIS IS NICE.

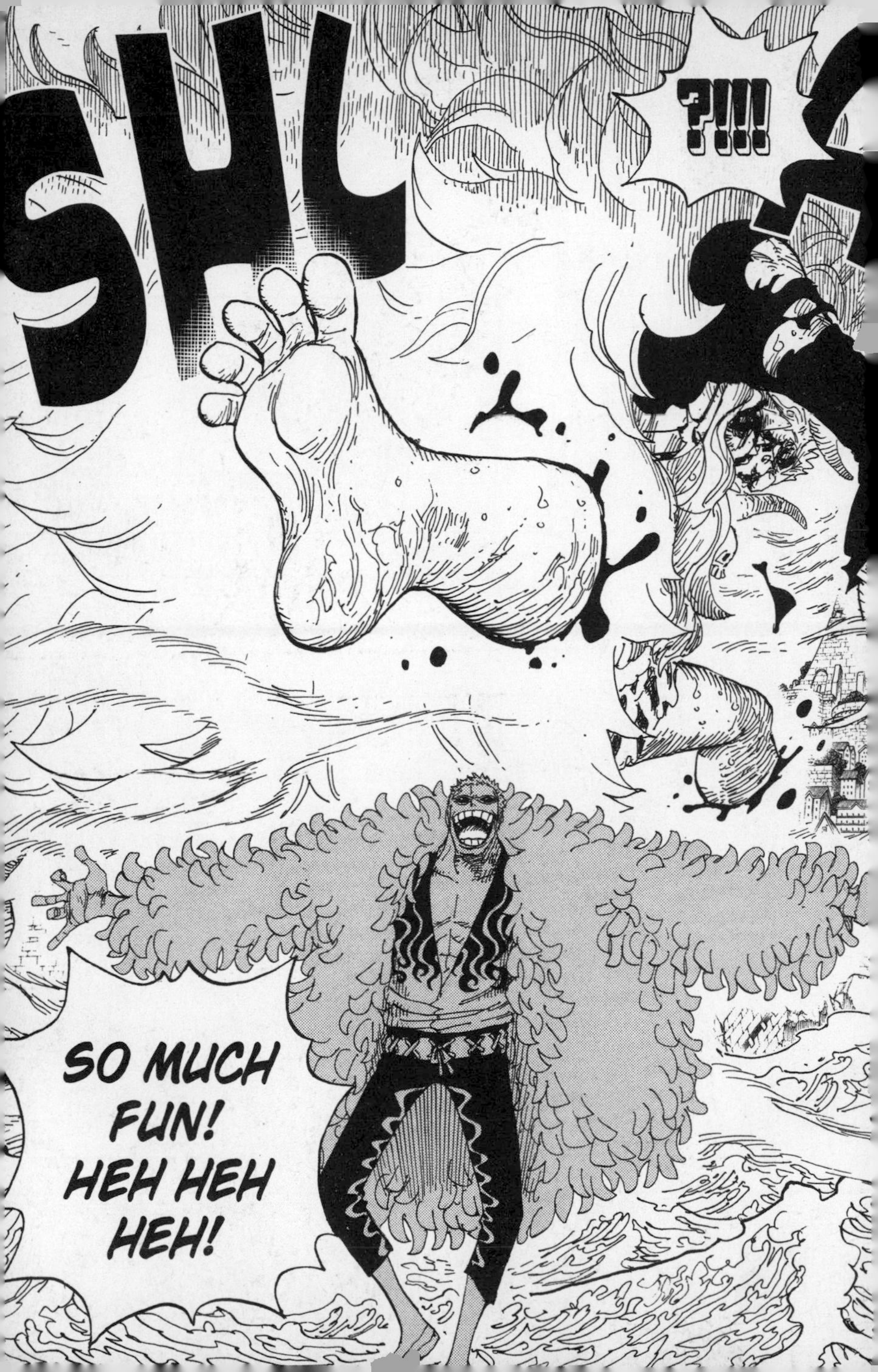
?!!!
SHL
SO MUCH FUN! HEH HEH HEH!

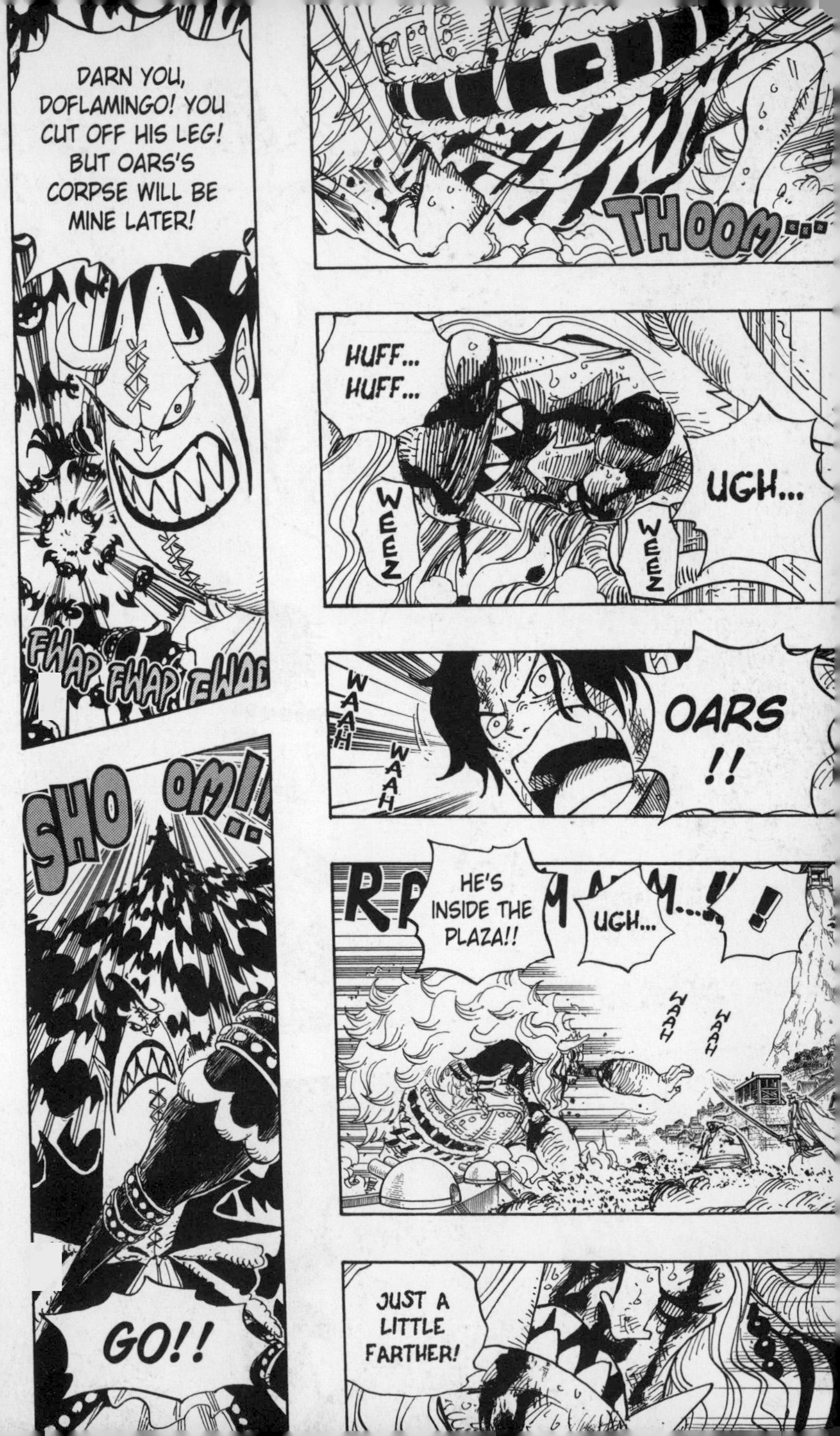
THOOM...
UGH...
WEEZ
HUFF... HUFF...
WEEZ
OARS!!
WAAH
WAAH
UGH...
HE'S INSIDE THE PLAZA!!
WAAH
WAAH
JUST A LITTLE FARTHER!
DARN YOU, DOFLAMINGO! YOU CUT OFF HIS LEG! BUT OARS'S CORPSE WILL BE MINE LATER!
FWAP FWAP
SHOOM!!
GO!!

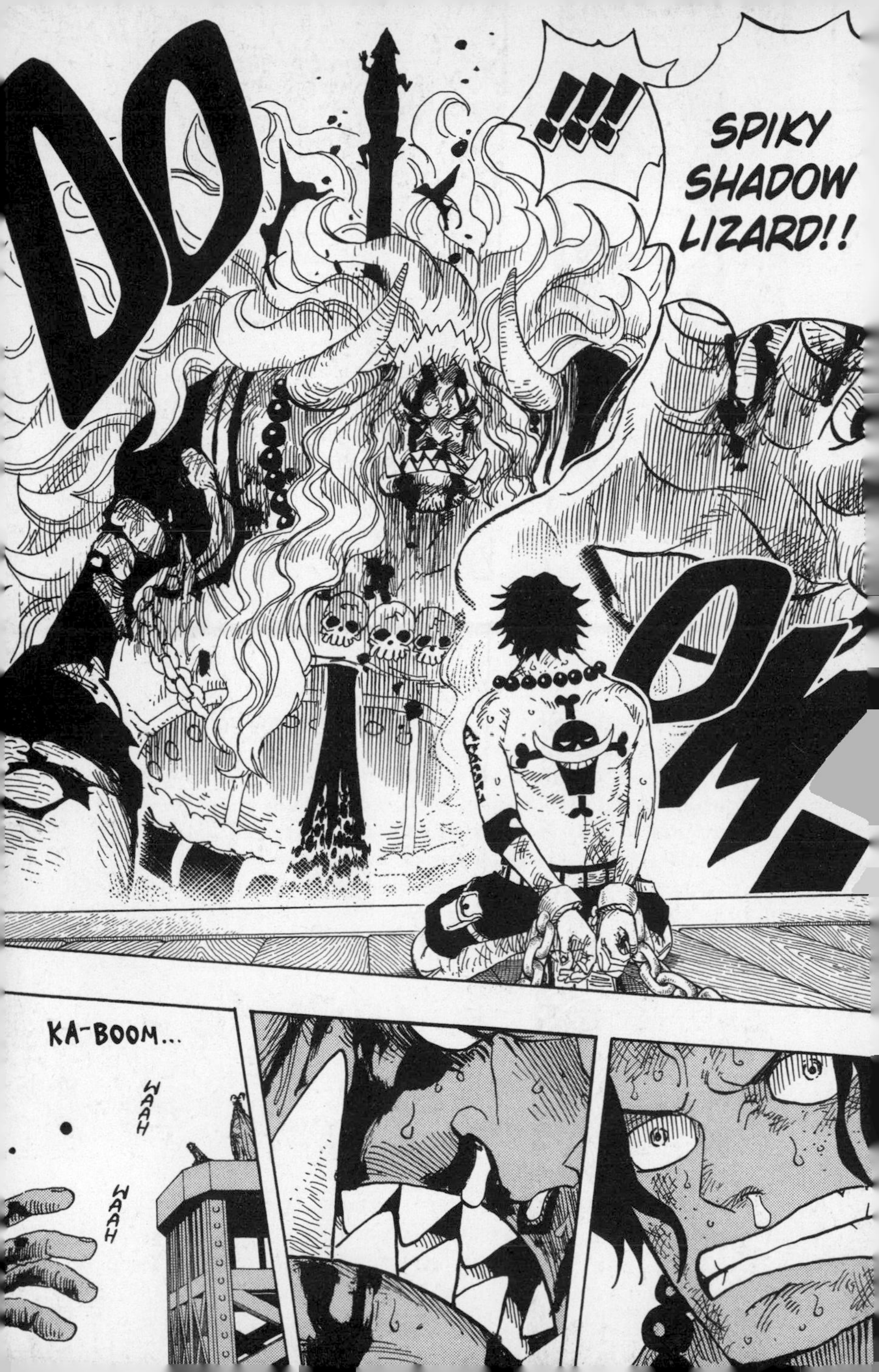
!!!
SPIKY SHADOW LIZARD!!
DOOM
KA-BOOM...
WAAH
WAAH

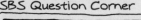

(Make Me Law's Girl, Hiroshima)

Q: I see Luffy eat a lot but he never gets fat. Now I'm jealous.
--Chikusa 10422

A: Hold on. He eats a lot but he also runs around a ton. It'd be weird if he got fat.

Q: I have a question. Whenever the Straw Hat Pirates defeat enemies, they only use the word "defeat." As it describes, I'm guessing that none of the enemies are dead. So is the reason why you don't use words like "kill" or "crush," because you're insisting that you "don't put an end to their lives?" Or is there some other reason for it?
--Tochisaki

I WANNA KICK CROCO-DILE'S BUTT!!!

A: Near the beginning of my serialization, my Grandma in Kumamoto said, "Don't say stuff like 'kill this' or 'kill that' too much." It's natural for Luffy and his crew to not say it, but I think it's inevitable that the enemies do. But every time a friend or acquaintance died, I matured and understood how bad those words really are. Well, I still use those words as part of jokes or when they're said by REALLY bad guys. But I do think that they're bad words. So don't try it at home, okay?

I GOT BEAT UP QUITE BADLY, BUT I'LL SEE WHETHER OR NOT THERE'S STILL HOPE FOR ME...

Q: Is Urouge's weapon a pencil? Or is that a chocolate bat?
--Puffball No. 1

A: It's a pencil, I guess. So because Urouge couldn't find a pencil sharpener, did he go out to sea to get one? (Is that a 2B pencil?)

Q: I represent the northern Kanto region and came for an official request. Please make Whitebeard's birthday April 6 since it can be pronounced to sound like Shiro (White).
--Wealthy Class in Gunma

A: Okay.

Chapter 556:
JUSTICE WILL PREVAIL!

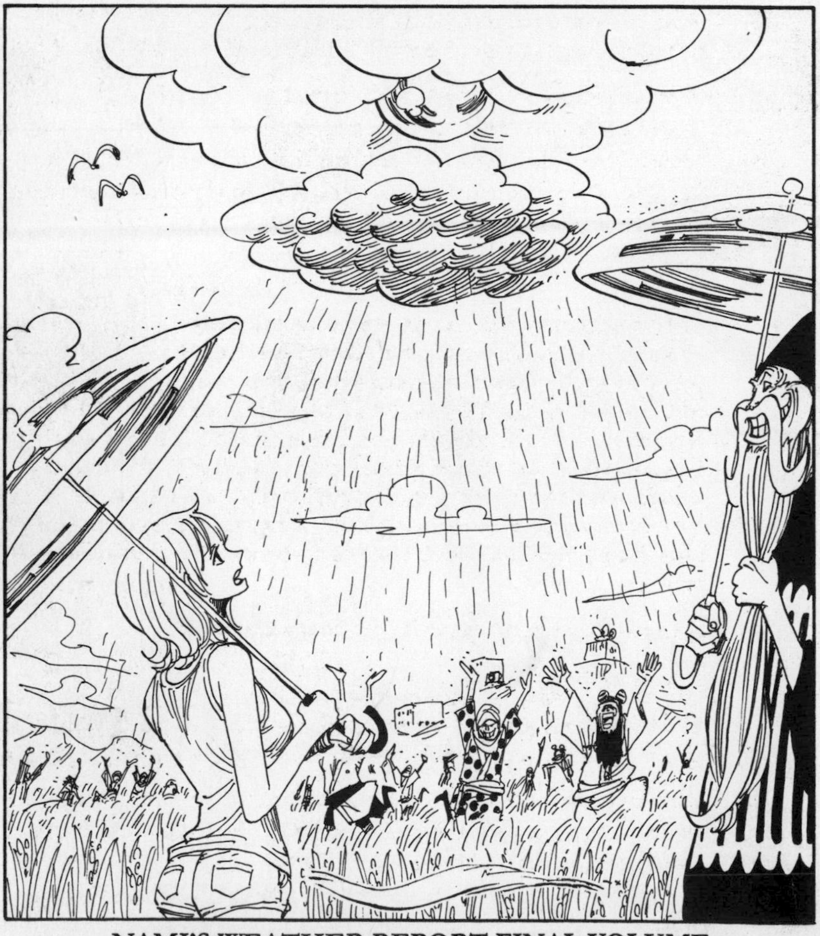

NAMI'S WEATHER REPORT FINAL VOLUME:
"THE WEATHER SCIENCE OF WEATHERIA"

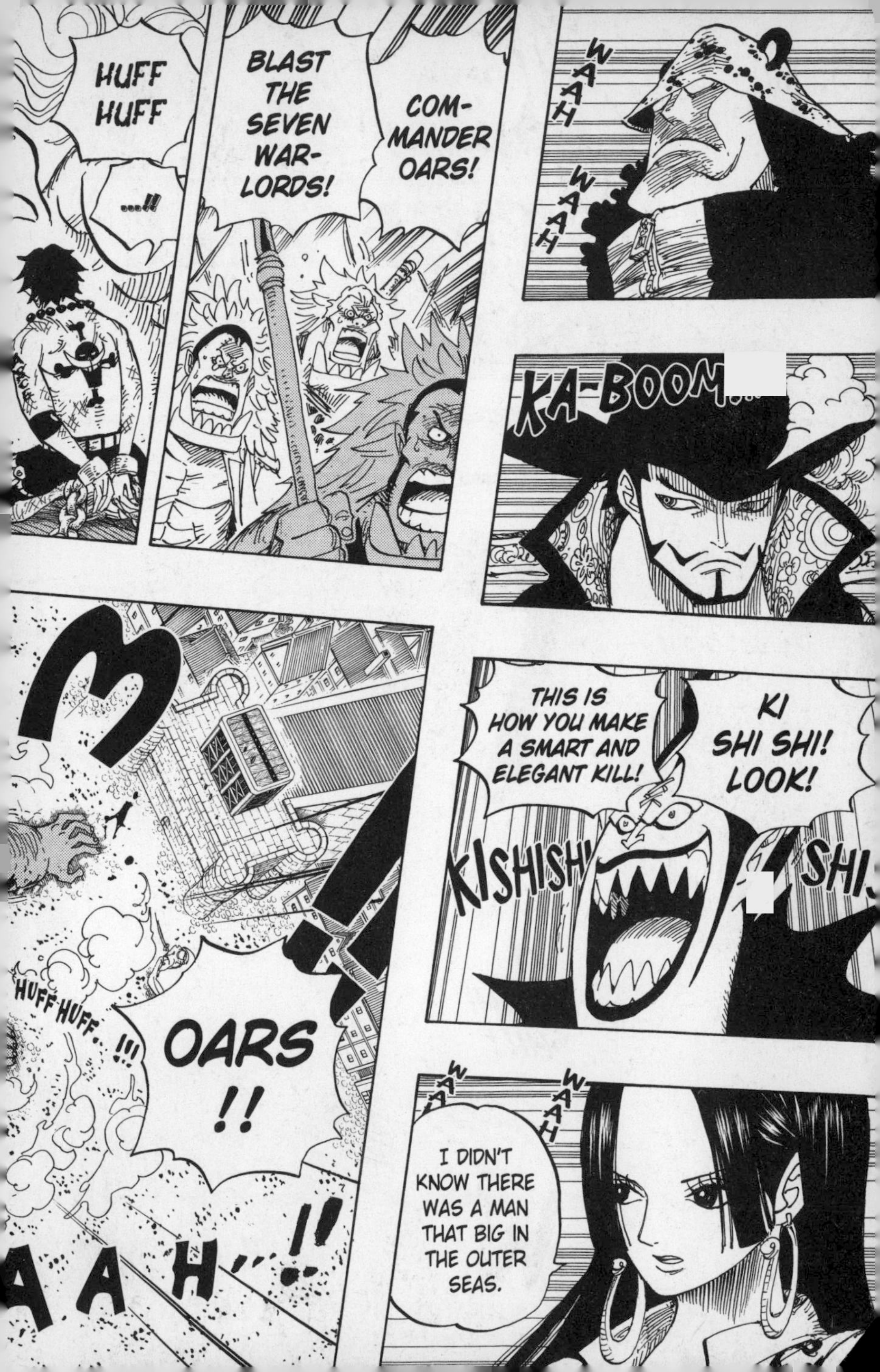
WAAH
WAAH
COM-MANDER OARS!
BLAST THE SEVEN WAR-LORDS!
HUFF HUFF
...!!
KA-BOOM
KI SHI SHI! LOOK!
THIS IS HOW YOU MAKE A SMART AND ELEGANT KILL!
KISHISHI
SHI
M
HUFF HUFF...!!!
OARS !!
AAH...!!
WAAH
WAAH
I DIDN'T KNOW THERE WAS A MAN THAT BIG IN THE OUTER SEAS.

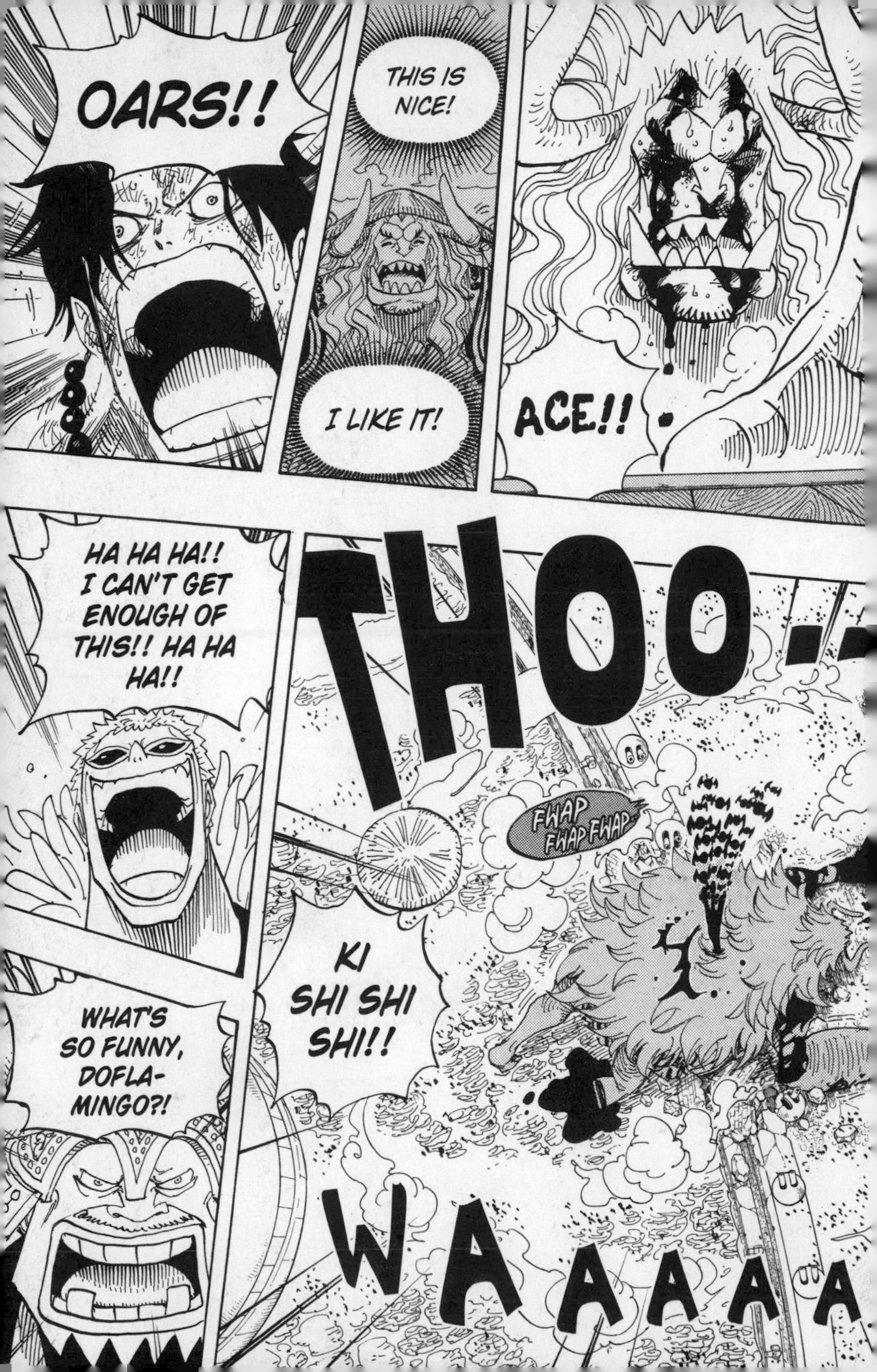
ACE!!
THIS IS NICE!
I LIKE IT!
OARS!!
THOO--
FWAP FWAP FWAP
KI SHI SHI SHI!!
WAAAAA
HA HA HA!! I CAN'T GET ENOUGH OF THIS!! HA HA HA!!
WHAT'S SO FUNNY, DOFLA-MINGO?!

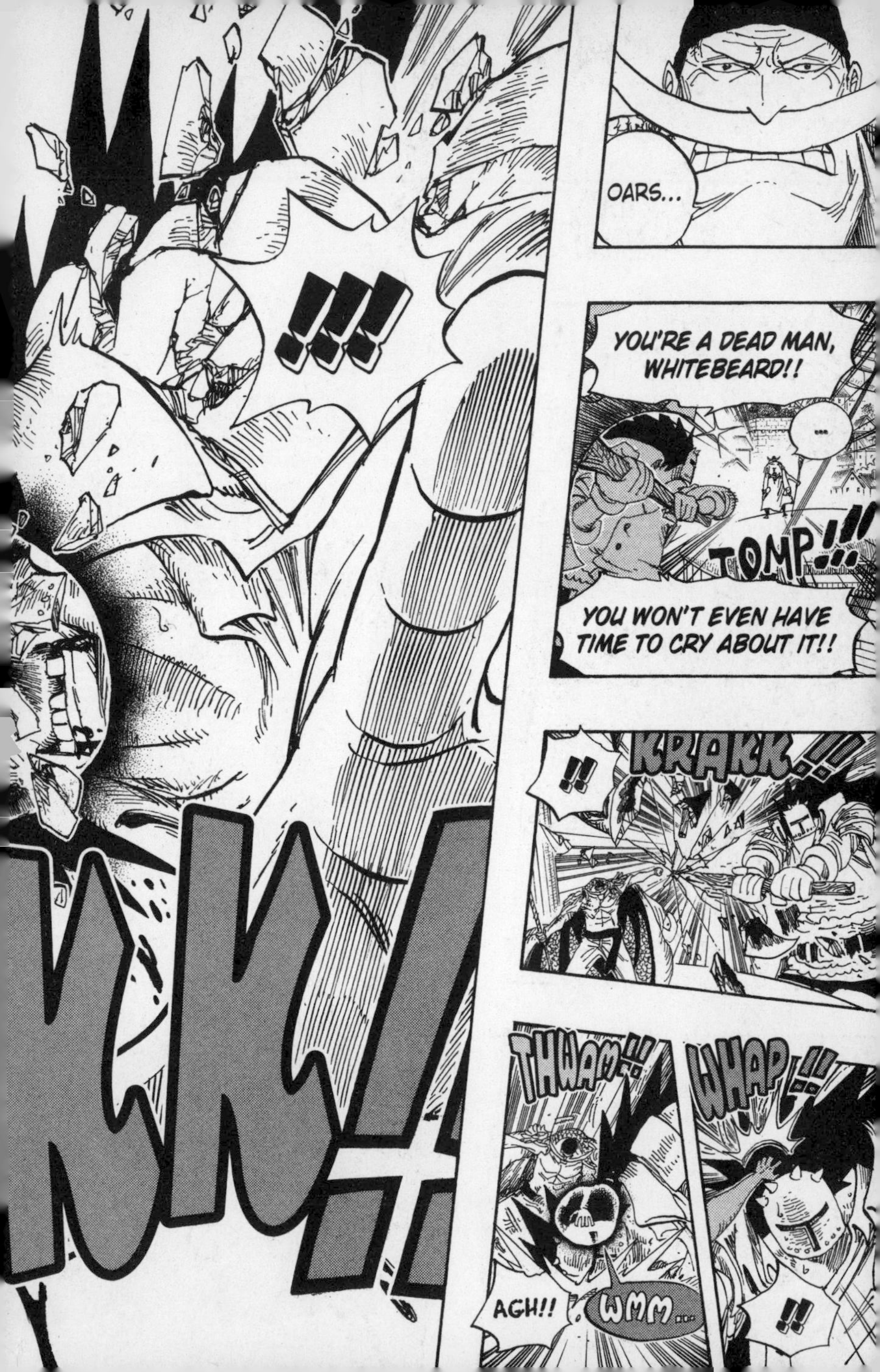
OARS...
YOU'RE A DEAD MAN, WHITEBEARD!!
...
TOMP!!!
YOU WON'T EVEN HAVE TIME TO CRY ABOUT IT!!
!!
KRAKK!!!
WHAP!!!
!!
THWAM!!!
AGH!!
WMM...
!!!

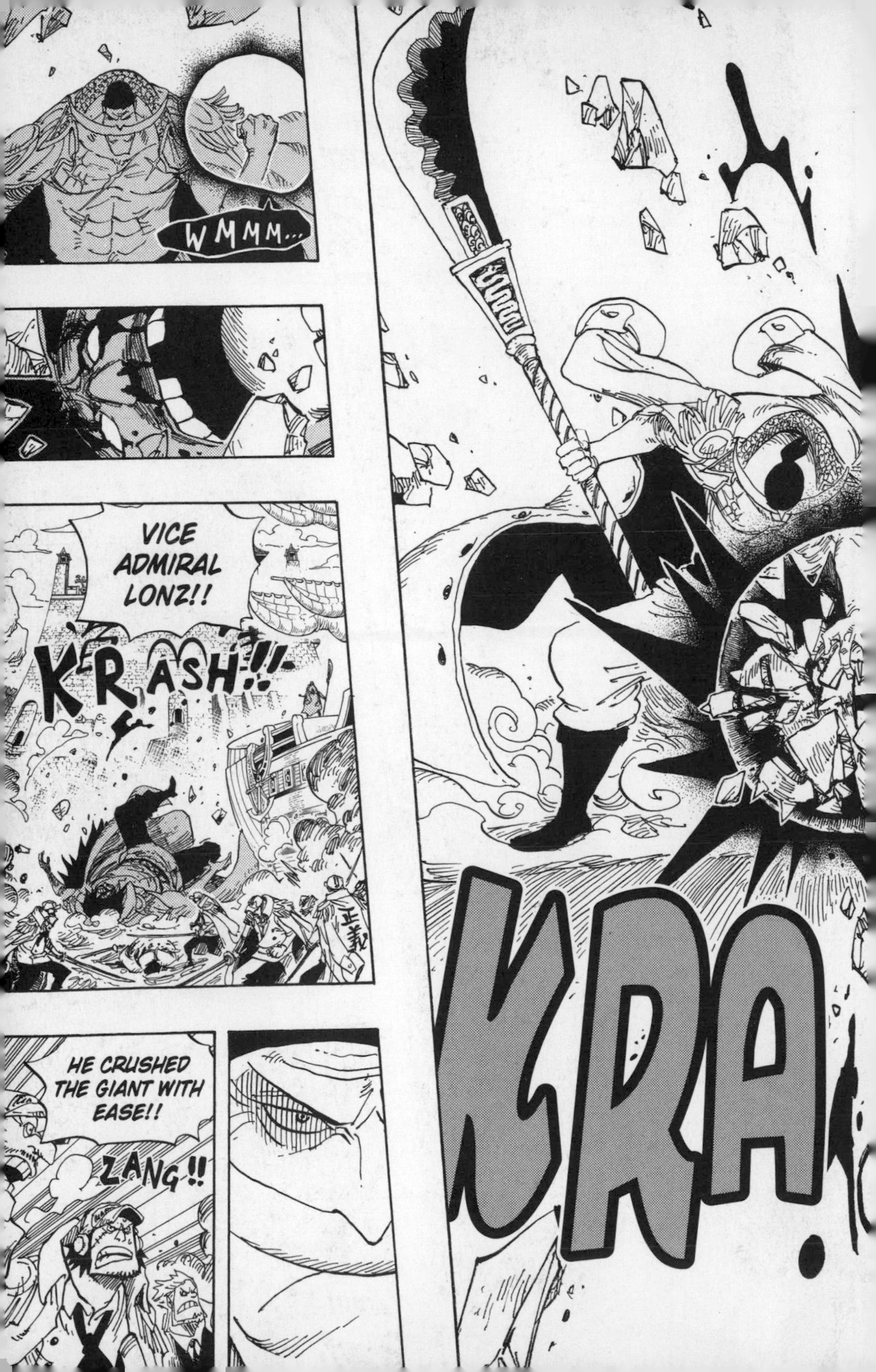
KRA!
WMMM...
VICE ADMIRAL LONZ!!
KRASH!!
HE CRUSHED THE GIANT WITH EASE!!
ZANG!!

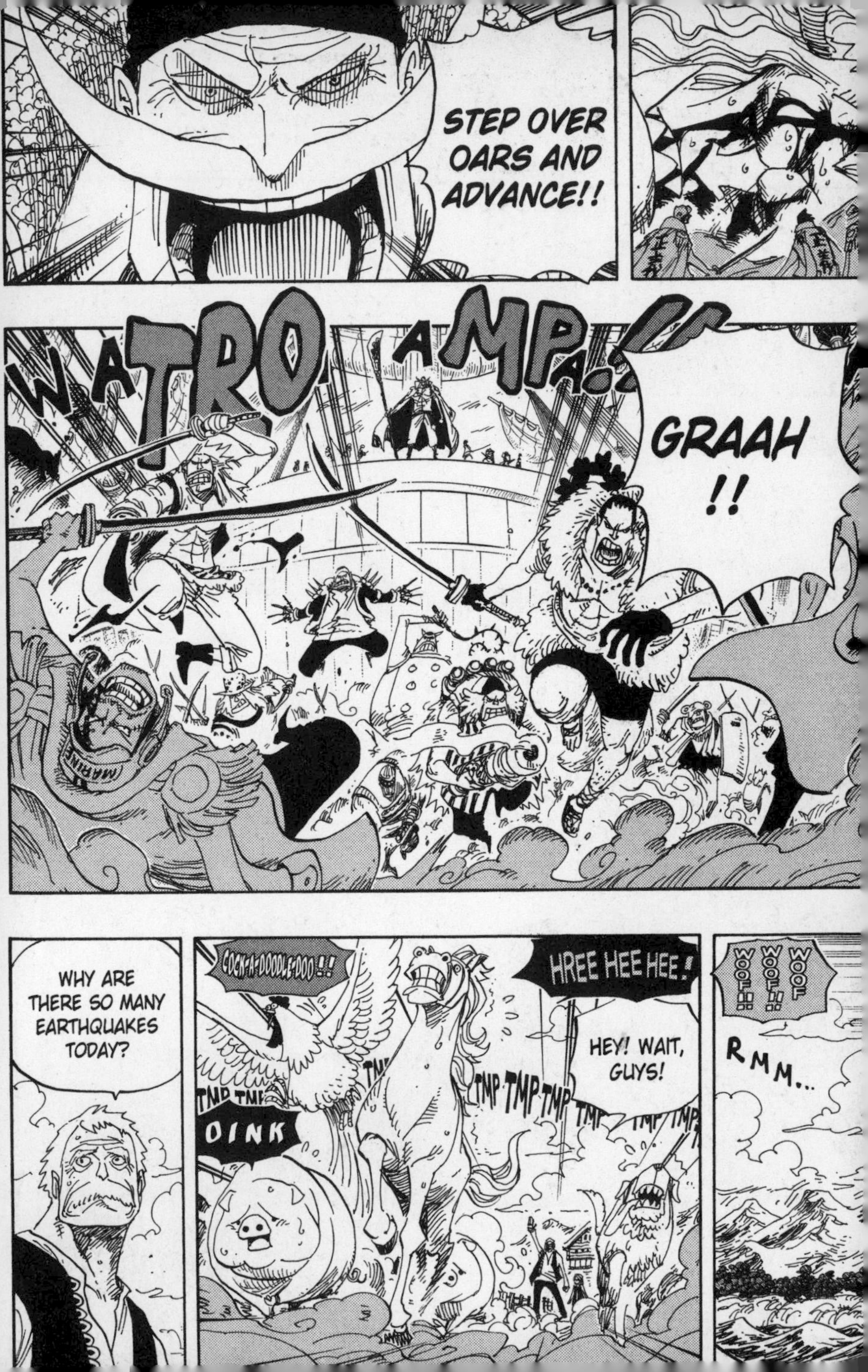
STEP OVER OARS AND ADVANCE!!
WATRO AMPA!!
GRAAH!!
WOOF!! WOOF!! WOOF
RMMM...
HREE HEE HEE!
HEY! WAIT, GUYS!
COCK-A-DOODLE-DOO!!
TMP TMP TMP TMP TMP
TMP TMP
OINK
WHY ARE THERE SO MANY EARTHQUAKES TODAY?

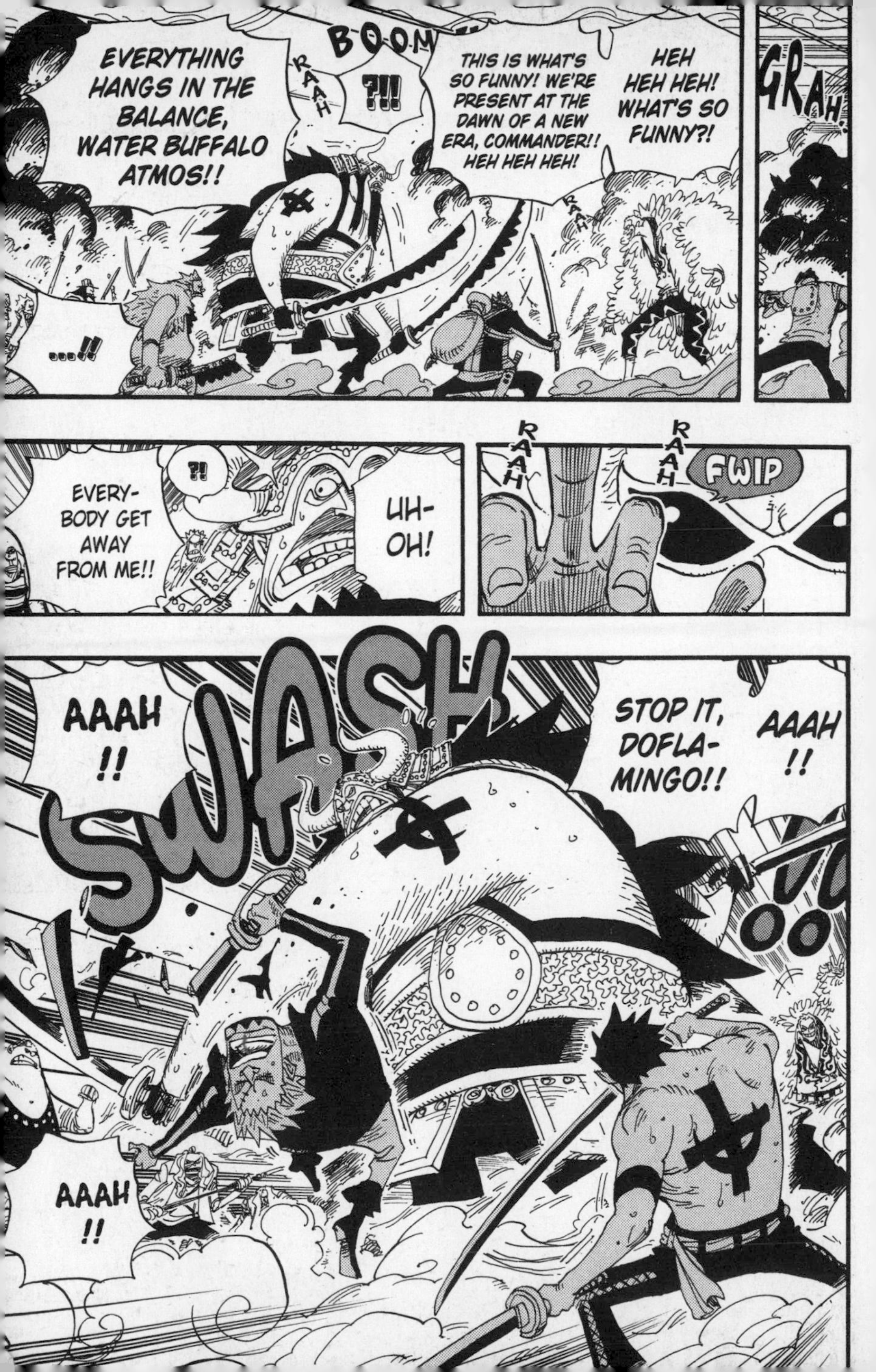
GRAH
HEH HEH HEH! WHAT'S SO FUNNY?!
RAAH
THIS IS WHAT'S SO FUNNY! WE'RE PRESENT AT THE DAWN OF A NEW ERA, COMMANDER!! HEH HEH HEH!
BOOM
?!!
RAAH
EVERYTHING HANGS IN THE BALANCE, WATER BUFFALO ATMOS!!
...!!
RAAH
FWIP
RAAH
UH-OH!
?!
EVERYBODY GET AWAY FROM ME!!
AAAH !!
STOP IT, DOFLAMINGO!!
SWASH
AAAH !!
AAAH !!

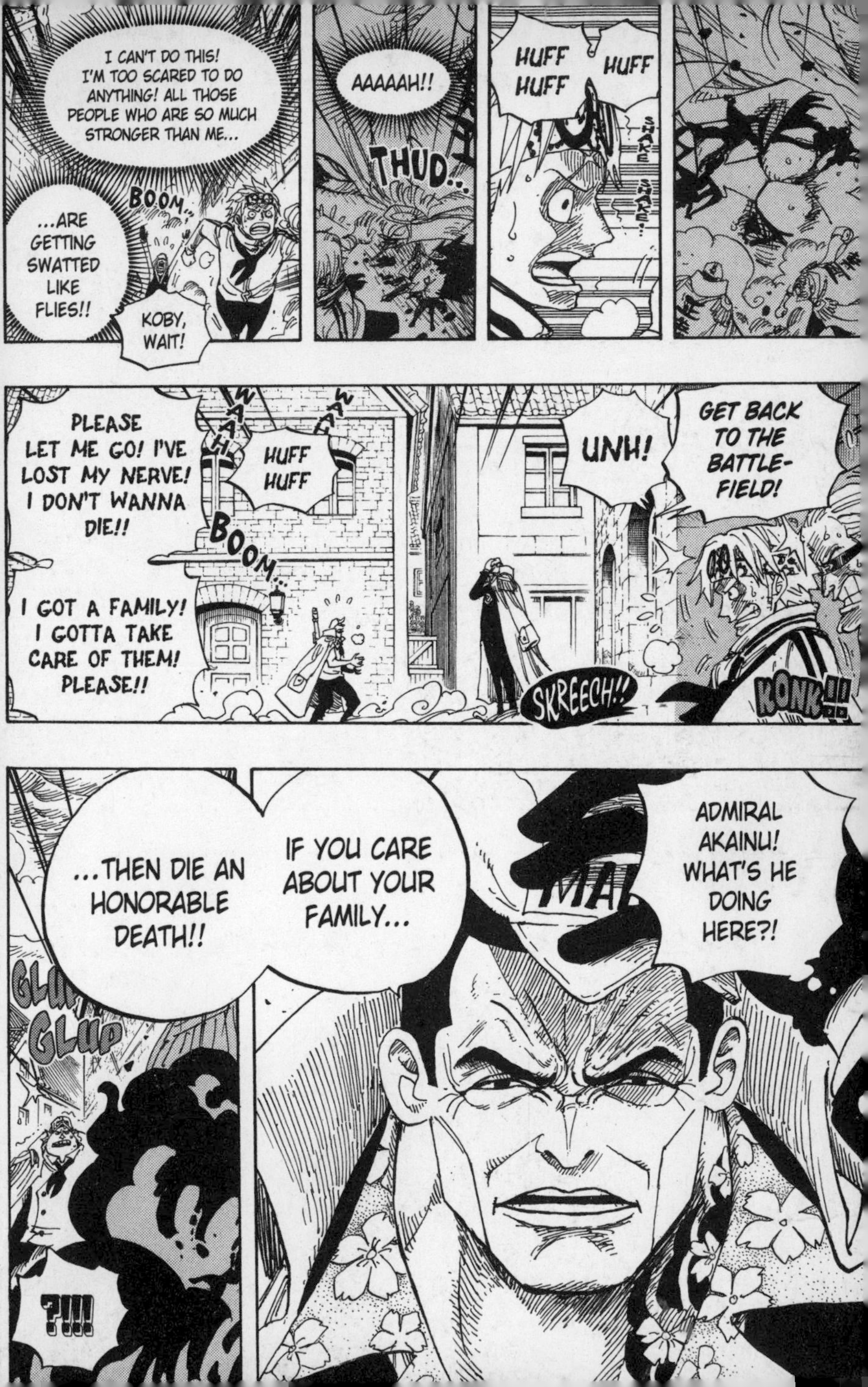
HUFF HUFF
HUFF
SHAKE SHAKE
AAAAAH!!
THUD...
I CAN'T DO THIS! I'M TOO SCARED TO DO ANYTHING! ALL THOSE PEOPLE WHO ARE SO MUCH STRONGER THAN ME...
BOOM...
...ARE GETTING SWATTED LIKE FLIES!!
KOBY, WAIT!
GET BACK TO THE BATTLE-FIELD!
UNH!
KONK!!
SKREECH!!
HUFF HUFF
WAAH WAAH
PLEASE LET ME GO! I'VE LOST MY NERVE! I DON'T WANNA DIE!!
BOOM...
I GOT A FAMILY! I GOTTA TAKE CARE OF THEM! PLEASE!!
ADMIRAL AKAINU! WHAT'S HE DOING HERE?!
IF YOU CARE ABOUT YOUR FAMILY...
...THEN DIE AN HONORABLE DEATH!!
GLUP GLUP
?!!!

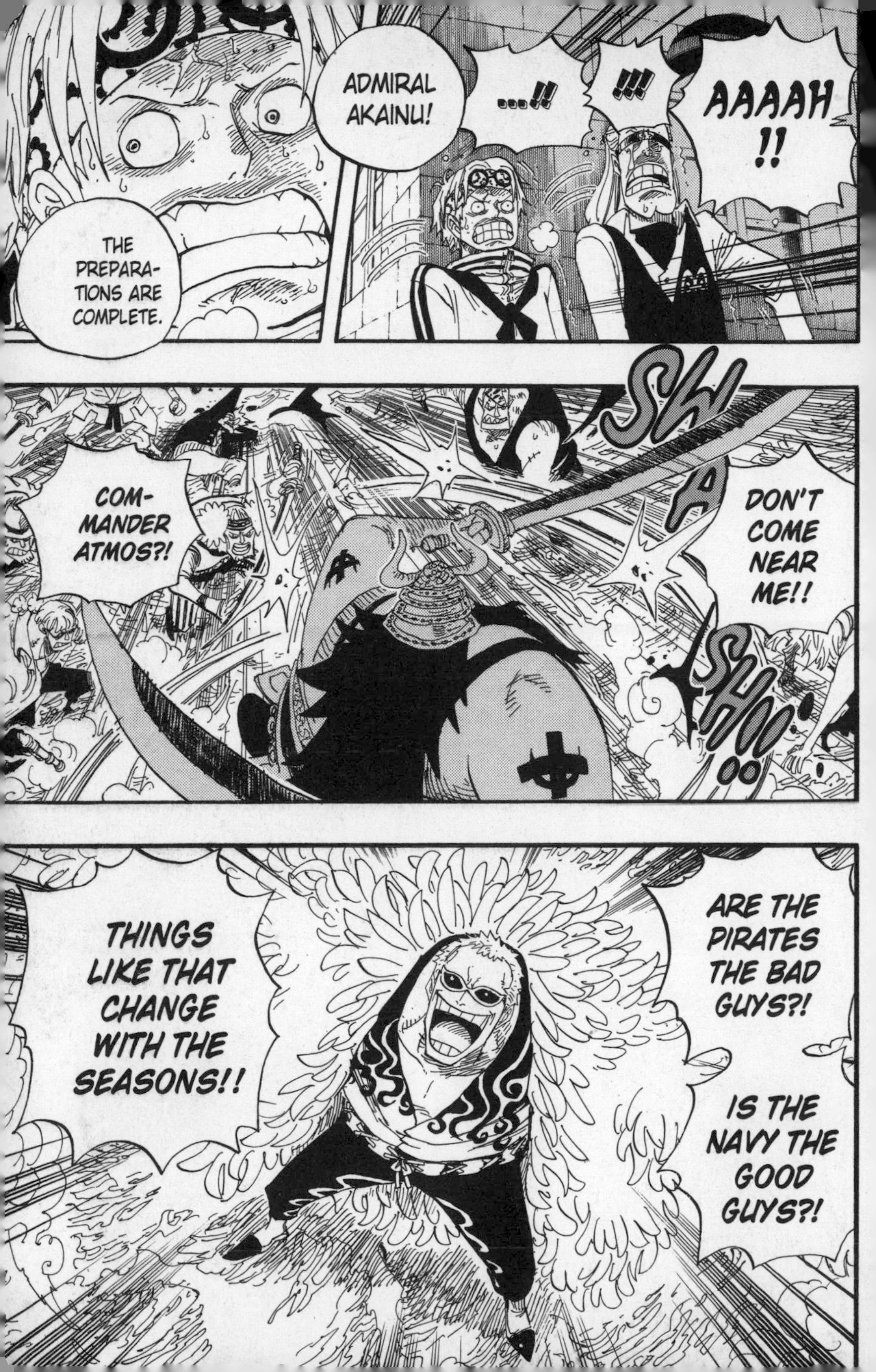
AAAAH !!
!!!
...!!
ADMIRAL AKAINU!
THE PREPARATIONS ARE COMPLETE.
SWA
DON'T COME NEAR ME!!
SHH!!
COMMANDER ATMOS?!
ARE THE PIRATES THE BAD GUYS?!
IS THE NAVY THE GOOD GUYS?!
THINGS LIKE THAT CHANGE WITH THE SEASONS!!

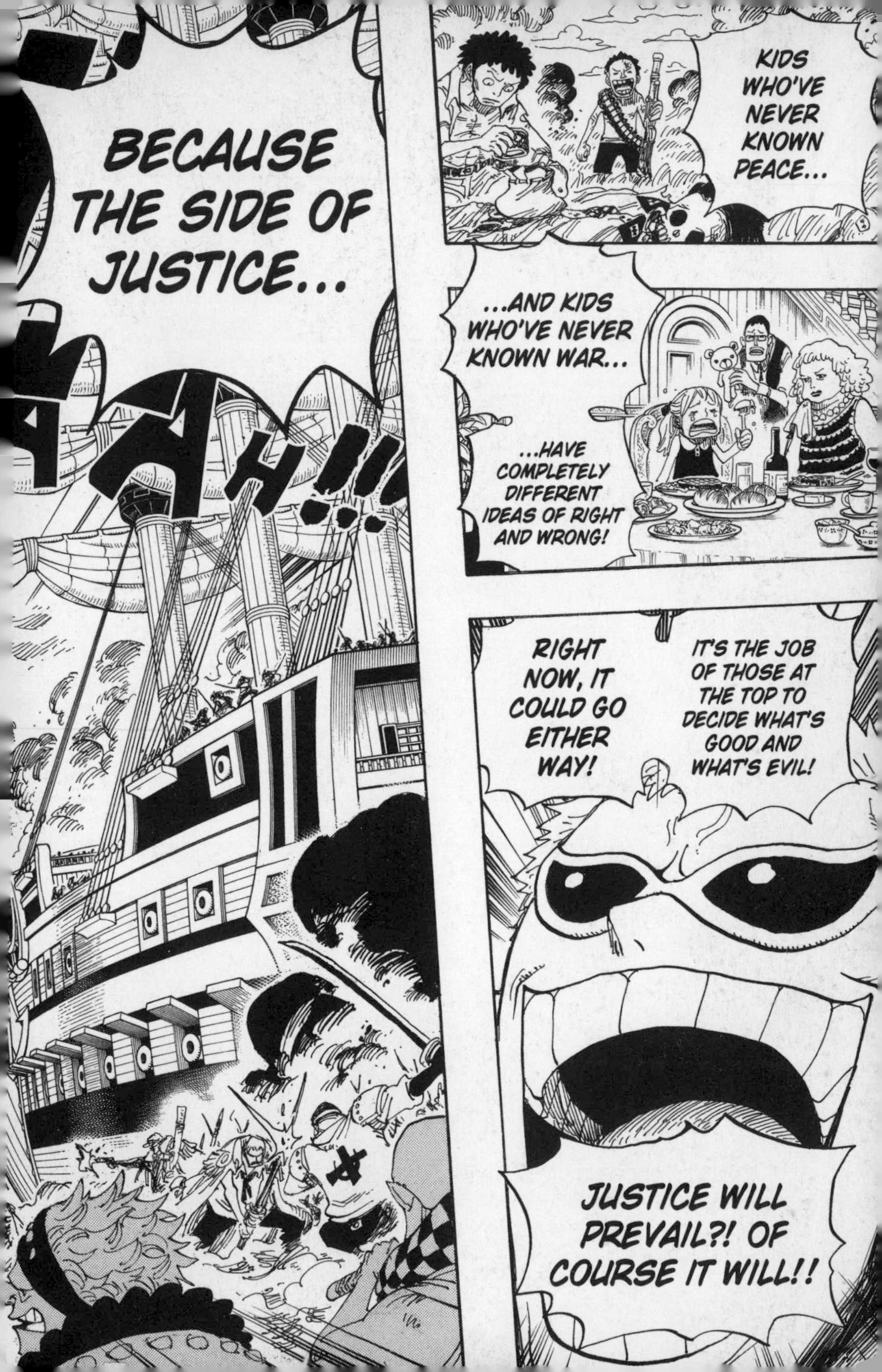
KIDS WHO'VE NEVER KNOWN PEACE...
...AND KIDS WHO'VE NEVER KNOWN WAR...
...HAVE COMPLETELY DIFFERENT IDEAS OF RIGHT AND WRONG!
IT'S THE JOB OF THOSE AT THE TOP TO DECIDE WHAT'S GOOD AND WHAT'S EVIL!
RIGHT NOW, IT COULD GO EITHER WAY!
JUSTICE WILL PREVAIL?! OF COURSE IT WILL!!
BECAUSE THE SIDE OF JUSTICE...
AH!!!

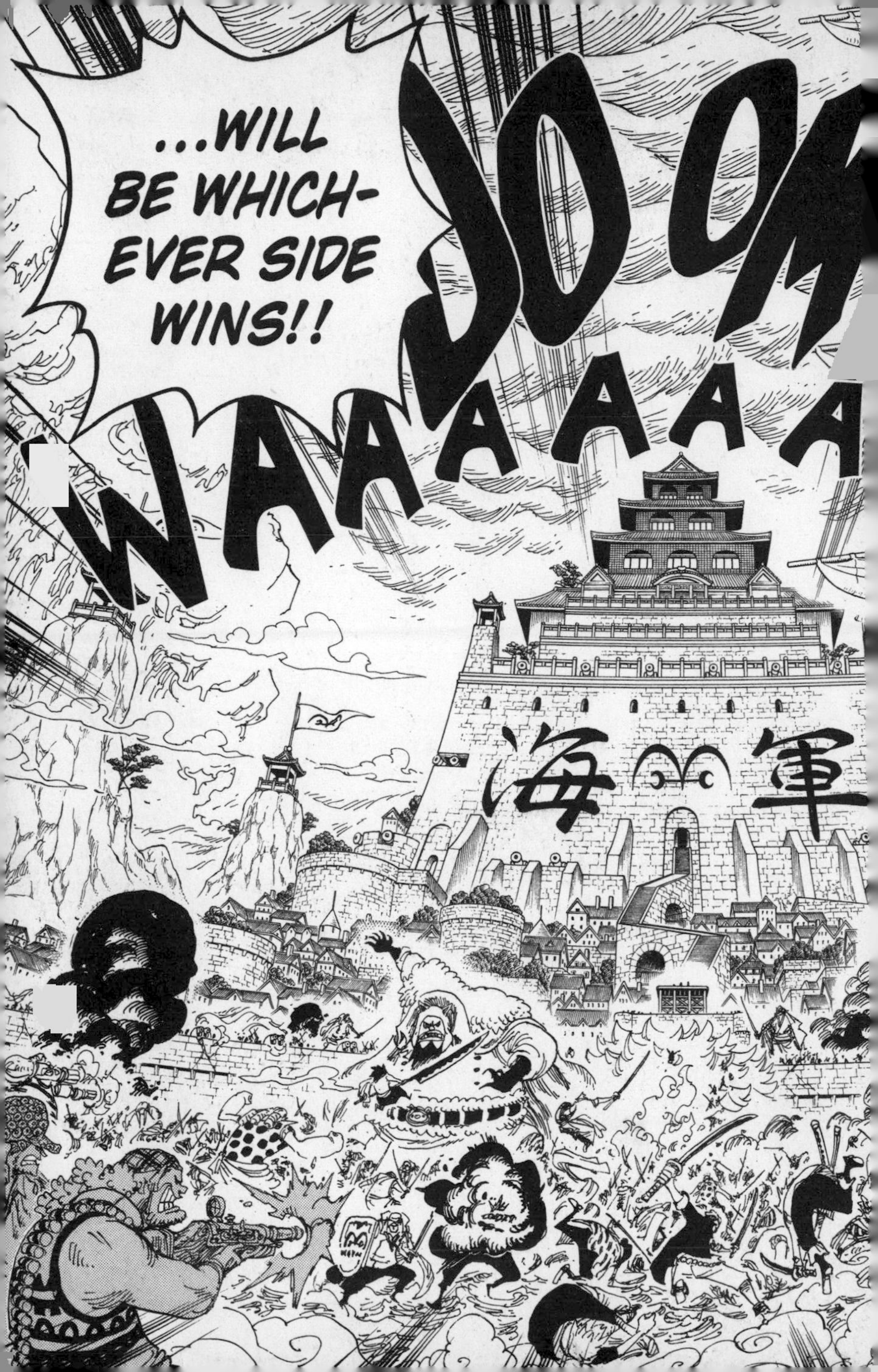
...WILL BE WHICH-EVER SIDE WINS!!
DOOM
WAAAAAAA
海軍

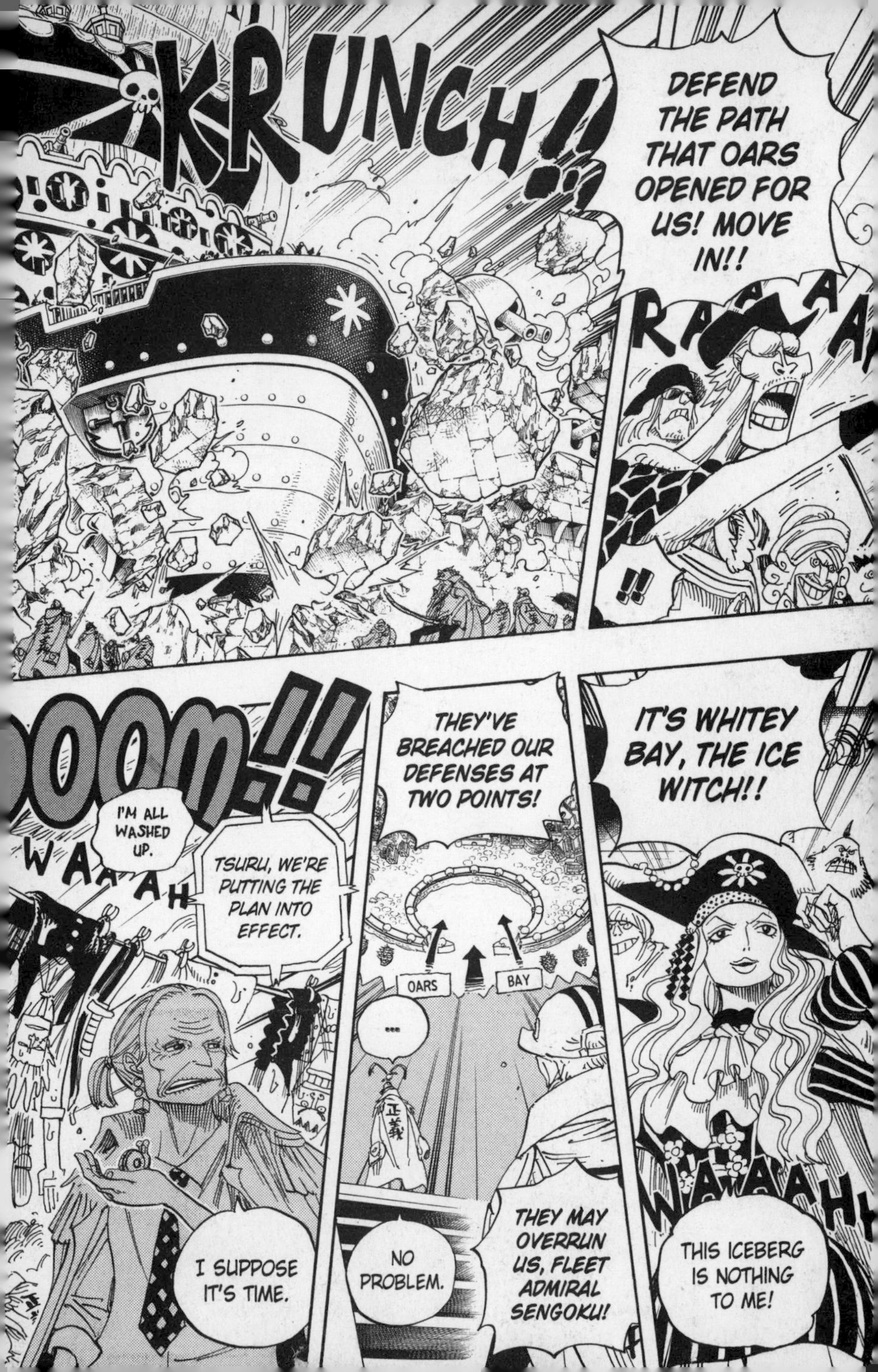
DEFEND THE PATH THAT OARS OPENED FOR US! MOVE IN!!
RAAAA
!!
KRUNCH!!
IT'S WHITEY BAY, THE ICE WITCH!!
WAAAAH
THIS ICEBERG IS NOTHING TO ME!
THEY'VE BREACHED OUR DEFENSES AT TWO POINTS!
BAY
OARS
...
THEY MAY OVERRUN US, FLEET ADMIRAL SENGOKU!
NO PROBLEM.
OOOM!!
WAAAAH
TSURU, WE'RE PUTTING THE PLAN INTO EFFECT.
I'M ALL WASHED UP.
I SUPPOSE IT'S TIME.

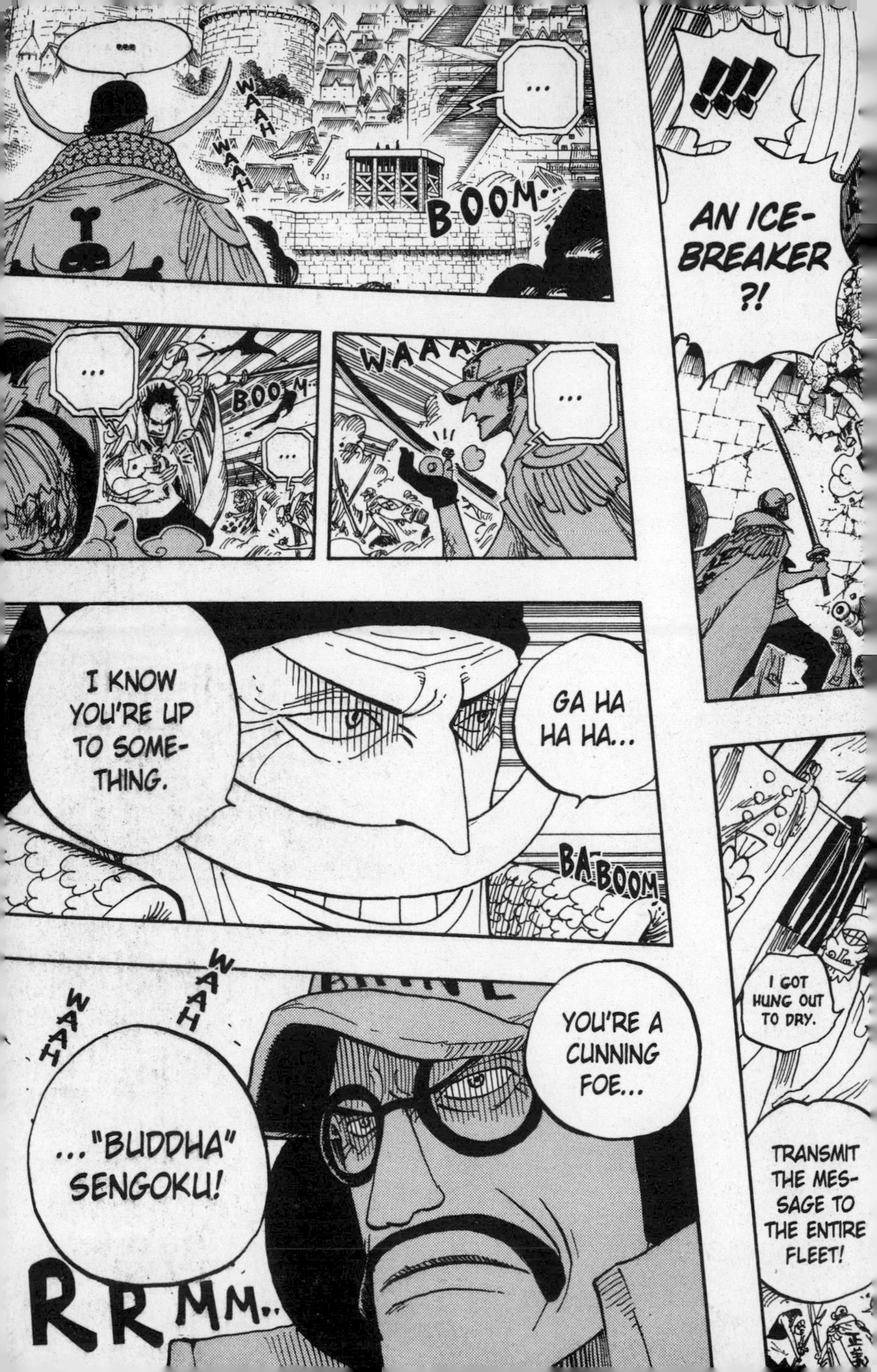
!!!
AN ICE-BREAKER ?!
...
WAAH WAAH
BOOM...
...
...
WAAAA
BOOM
...
...
GA HA HA HA...
I KNOW YOU'RE UP TO SOME-THING.
BA-BOOM
I GOT HUNG OUT TO DRY.
TRANSMIT THE MES-SAGE TO THE ENTIRE FLEET!
YOU'RE A CUNNING FOE...
WAAH
WAAH
..."BUDDHA" SENGOKU!
RRMM..

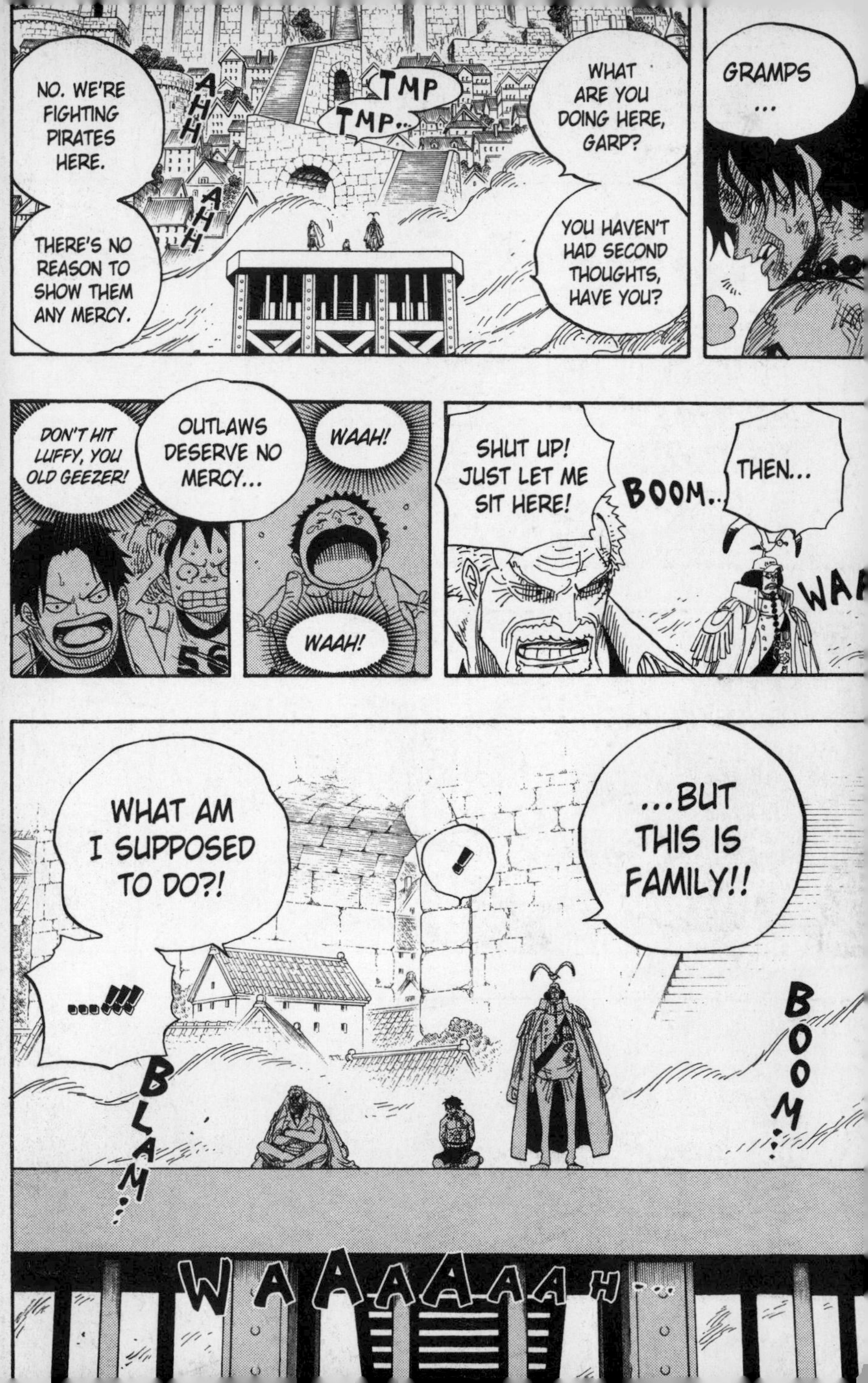
GRAMPS ...
WHAT ARE YOU DOING HERE, GARP?
YOU HAVEN'T HAD SECOND THOUGHTS, HAVE YOU?
TMP
TMP...
AHHH
AHHH
NO. WE'RE FIGHTING PIRATES HERE.
THERE'S NO REASON TO SHOW THEM ANY MERCY.
THEN...
WA
BOOM..
SHUT UP! JUST LET ME SIT HERE!
WAAH!
WAAH!
OUTLAWS DESERVE NO MERCY...
DON'T HIT LUFFY, YOU OLD GEEZER!
56
...BUT THIS IS FAMILY!!
!
WHAT AM I SUPPOSED TO DO?!
BOOM..
...!!!
BLAM..
WAAAAAAH...

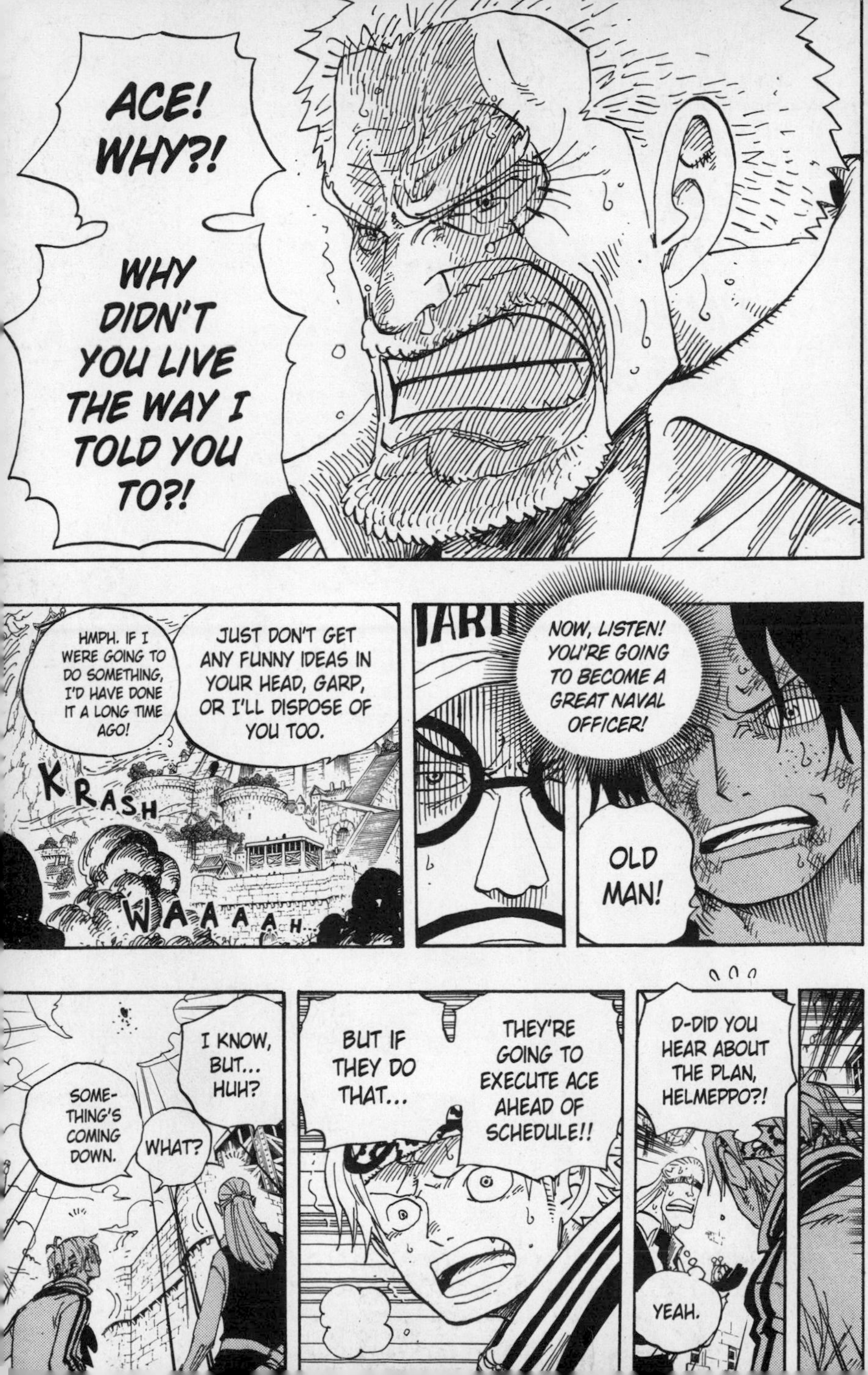
ACE! WHY?!
WHY DIDN'T YOU LIVE THE WAY I TOLD YOU TO?!
NOW, LISTEN! YOU'RE GOING TO BECOME A GREAT NAVAL OFFICER!
OLD MAN!
JUST DON'T GET ANY FUNNY IDEAS IN YOUR HEAD, GARP, OR I'LL DISPOSE OF YOU TOO.
HMPH. IF I WERE GOING TO DO SOMETHING, I'D HAVE DONE IT A LONG TIME AGO!
KRASH
WAAAAH...
D-DID YOU HEAR ABOUT THE PLAN, HELMEPPO?!
YEAH.
THEY'RE GOING TO EXECUTE ACE AHEAD OF SCHEDULE!!
BUT IF THEY DO THAT...
I KNOW, BUT... HUH?
WHAT?
SOME-THING'S COMING DOWN.

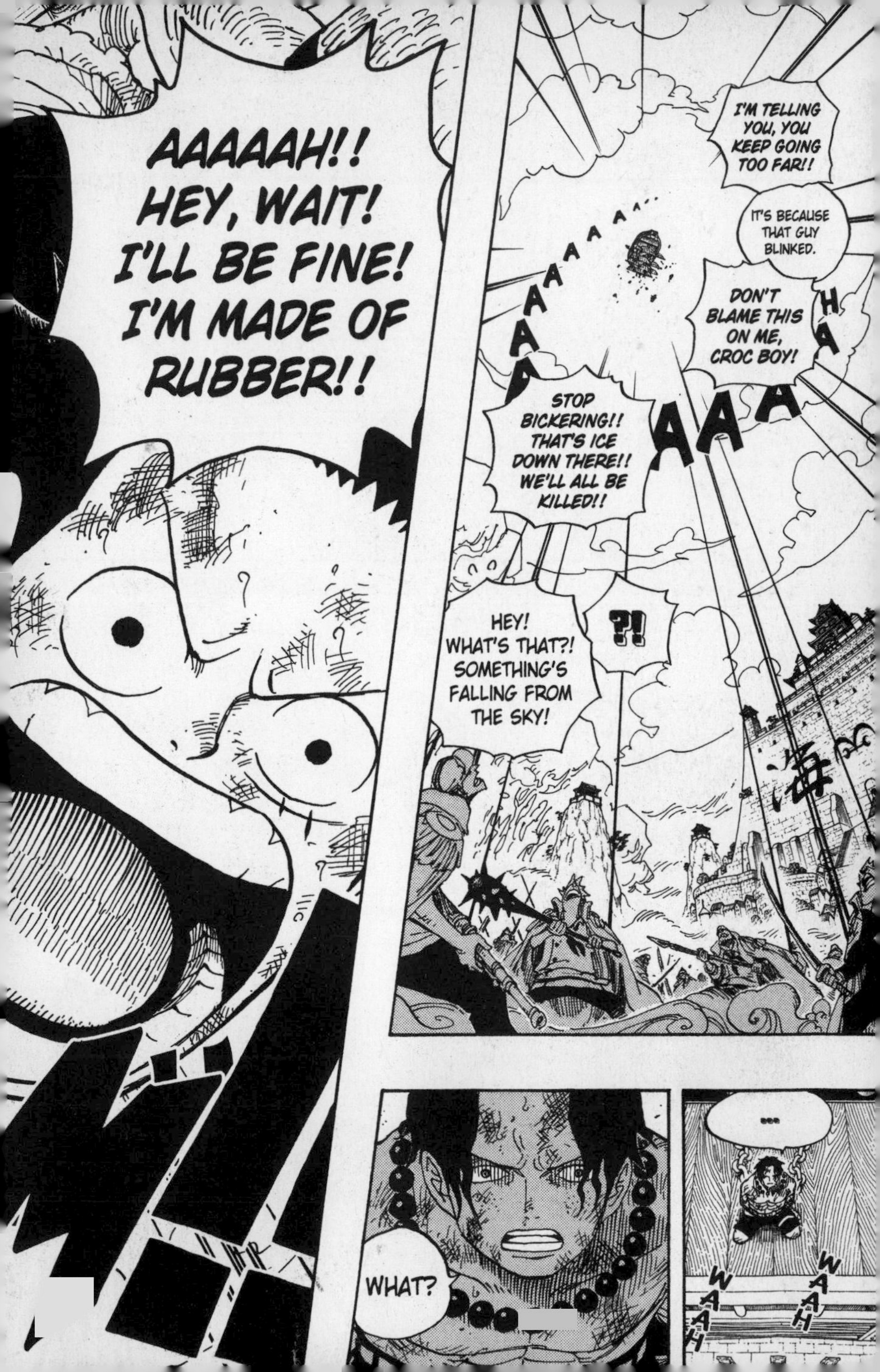
I'M TELLING YOU, YOU KEEP GOING TOO FAR!!
IT'S BECAUSE THAT GUY BLINKED.
DON'T BLAME THIS ON ME, CROC BOY!
AAAAAAAAA...
AAAHA
STOP BICKERING!! THAT'S ICE DOWN THERE!! WE'LL ALL BE KILLED!!
?!
HEY! WHAT'S THAT?! SOMETHING'S FALLING FROM THE SKY!
...
WAAH
WAAH
WHAT?
AAAAAH!! HEY, WAIT! I'LL BE FINE! I'M MADE OF RUBBER!!

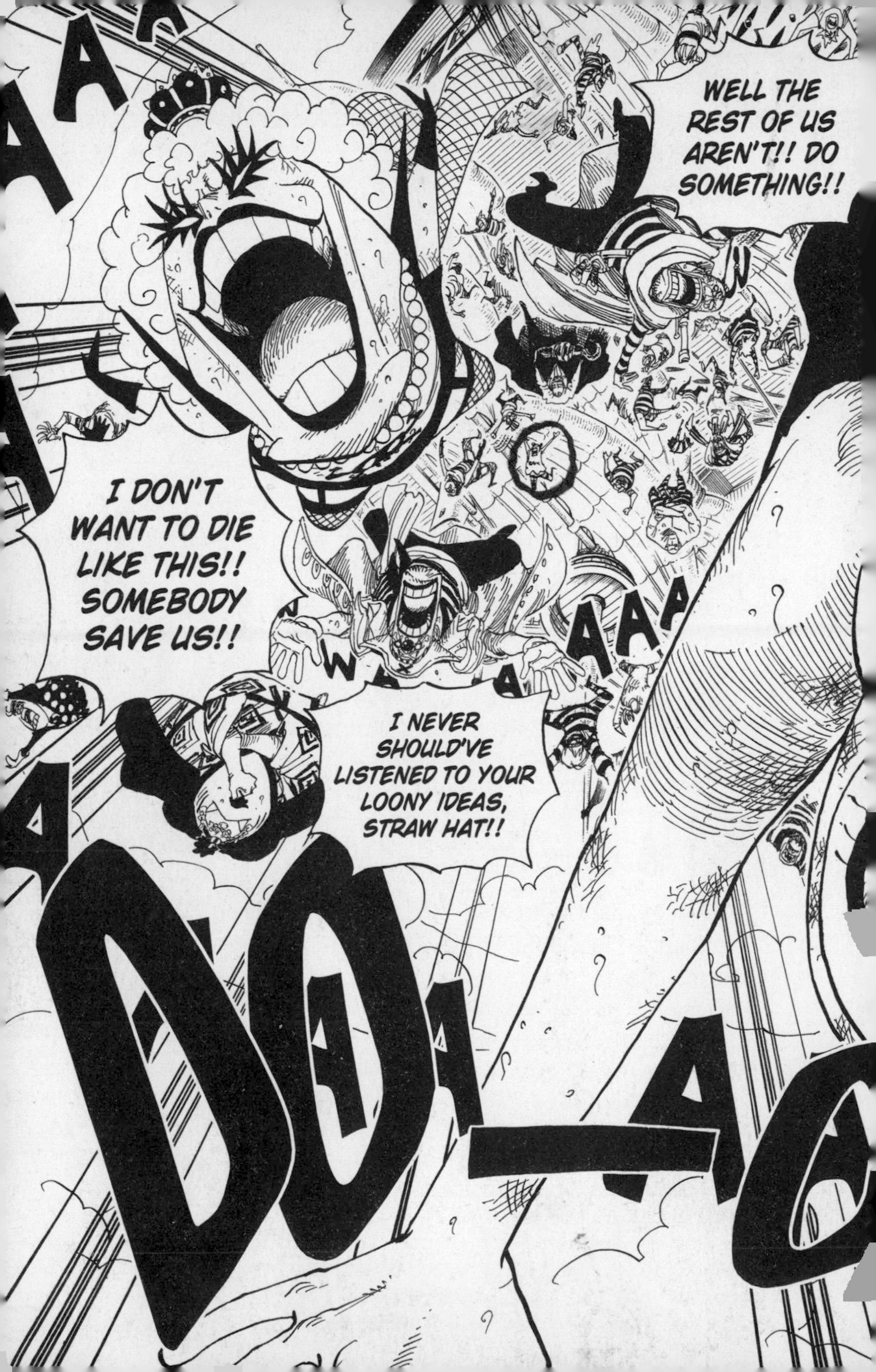
WELL THE REST OF US AREN'T!! DO SOMETHING!!
I DON'T WANT TO DIE LIKE THIS!! SOMEBODY SAVE US!!
I NEVER SHOULD'VE LISTENED TO YOUR LOONY IDEAS, STRAW HAT!!

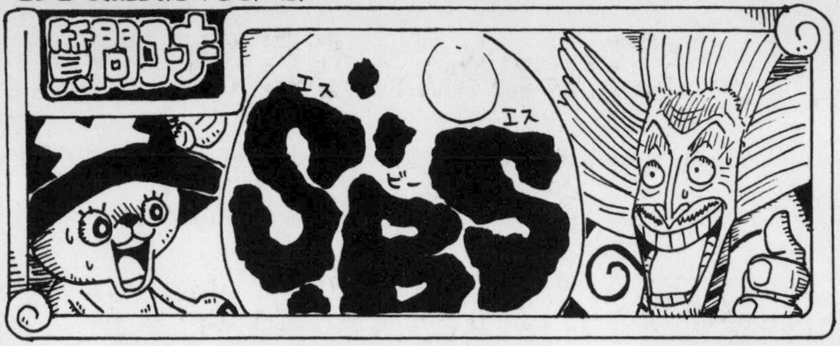
質問コーナー
SBS

(Skull Yukichi, Iwate)

Q: Odacchi! Hi! I have a serious question. Tell me about your daily schedule!

--I'm Glad I'm Japanese

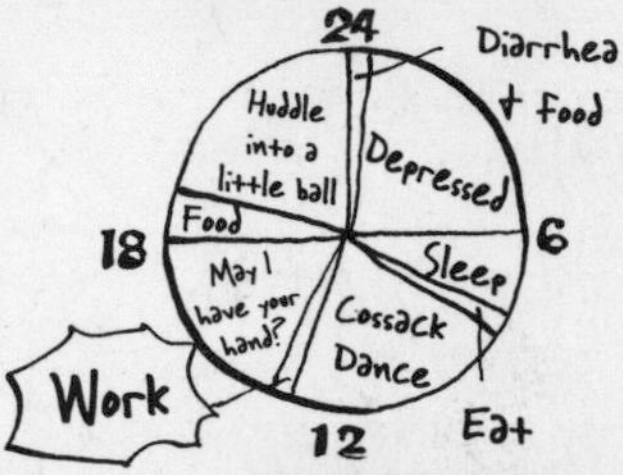
24
Diarrhea + Food
Huddle into a little ball
Depressed
6
Sleep
Cossack Dance
Eat
12
Work
May I have your hand?
Food
18

A: A serious question! All right. My schedule looks like this. ➡ Use it for reference if you want to become a comic author!

Q: I remember laughing my head off in volume 55, chapter 537, when I saw Hannyabal's underwear. It had a strawberry pattern, didn't it? Does he like cute underwear like that? Aside from strawberries, what other underwear does he have?

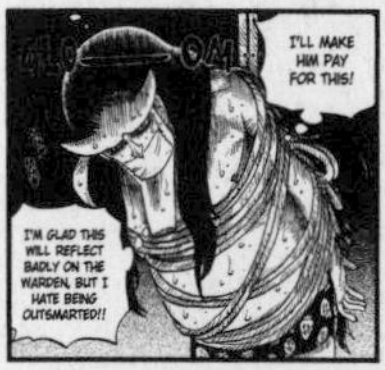
I'LL MAKE HIM PAY FOR THIS!
I'M GLAD THIS WILL REFLECT BADLY ON THE WARDEN, BUT I HATE BEING OUTSMARTED!!

A: I'm glad you noticed Hannyabal's horrible taste in clothes. But I do hear that Hannyabal's collection is quite something.

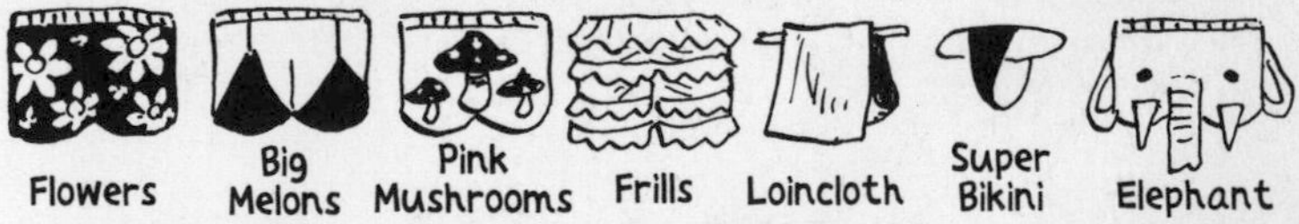
Flowers
Big Melons
Pink Mushrooms
Frills
Loincloth
Super Bikini
Elephant

Q: What's up! I'm a girl! Oh! I love fish cakes. By the way, there's something I want to ask you, Odacchi! Are Inazuma's glasses (or sunglasses) 3-D glasses? They have different colors so it made me do a double take. If they weren't 3-D glasses, wouldn't everything look jumbled up because of the different colors? Please tell me! =3

--Masaking

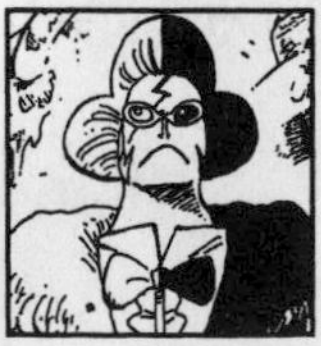

A: I see! I guess that would be it. Well, he would be able to see all the 3-D movies he wants. But everything he sees will start jumping out at him because of those glasses. Like when he'd see kids on the curb, he'd yell out "Look before you walk!" to them. Or when he meets Wanze, he'll go, "Your eyes are popping out way too much!" Wait, I guess his eyes have always been like that. Yup... Oh, yeah. I think those are 3-D glasses.

Chapter 557:

LUFFY AND WHITEBEARD

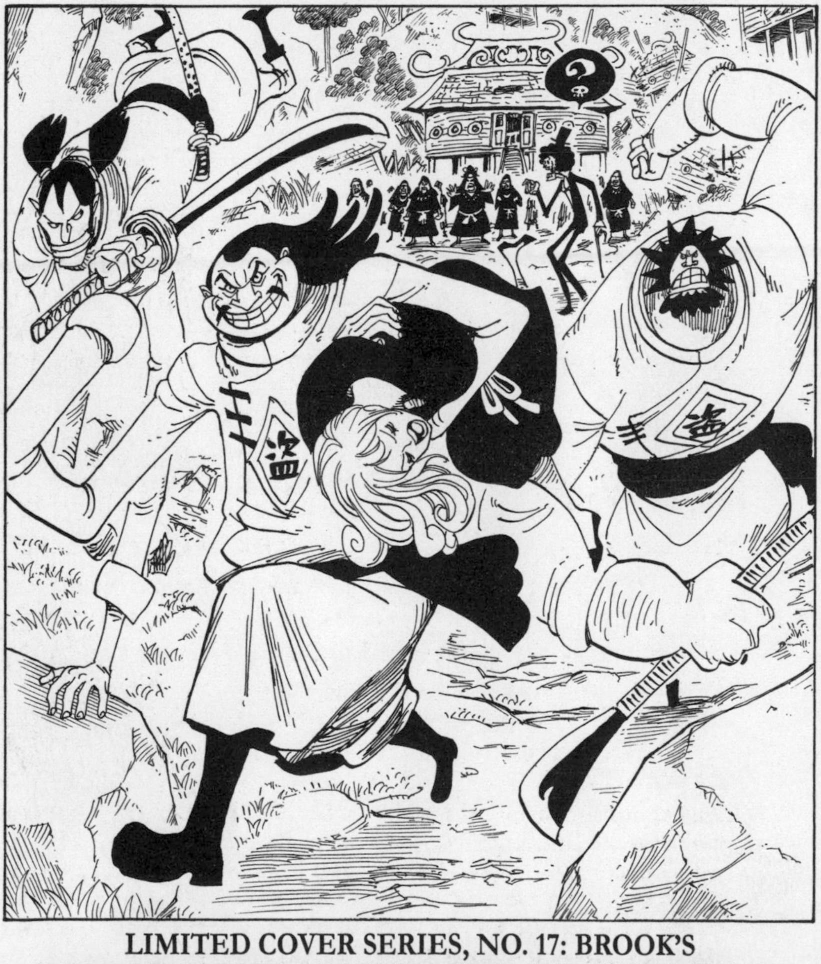

LIMITED COVER SERIES, NO. 17: BROOK'S "REPAYMENT FOR A NIGHT'S STAY AND UNDERWEAR" VOL. 1: "PEOPLE WHO DO NOT FIGHT"

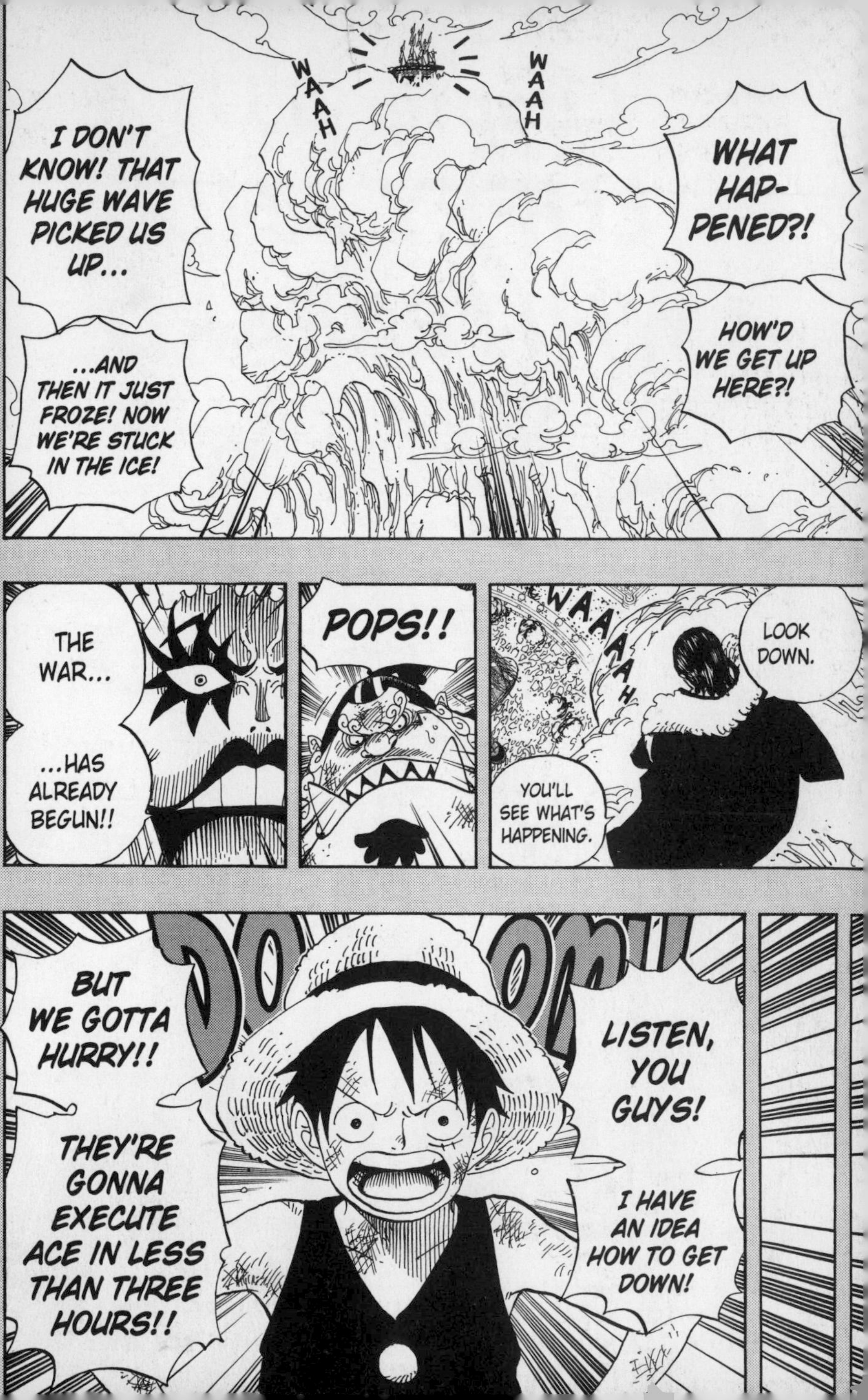
WAAH
WAAH
WHAT HAP-PENED?!
HOW'D WE GET UP HERE?!
I DON'T KNOW! THAT HUGE WAVE PICKED US UP...
...AND THEN IT JUST FROZE! NOW WE'RE STUCK IN THE ICE!
WAAAAAH
LOOK DOWN.
YOU'LL SEE WHAT'S HAPPENING.
POPS!!
THE WAR...
...HAS ALREADY BEGUN!!
LISTEN, YOU GUYS!
I HAVE AN IDEA HOW TO GET DOWN!
BUT WE GOTTA HURRY!!
THEY'RE GONNA EXECUTE ACE IN LESS THAN THREE HOURS!!

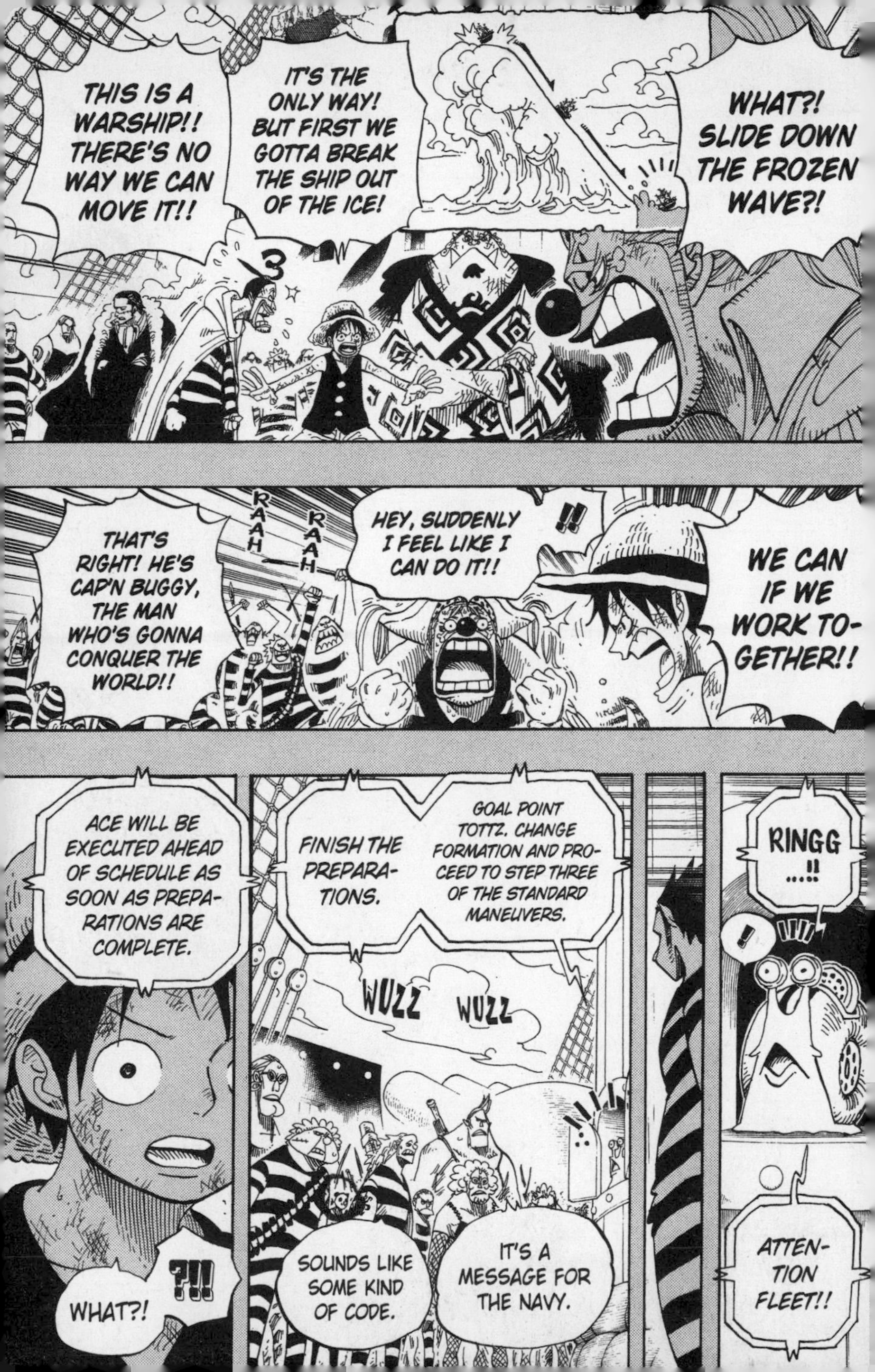
WHAT?! SLIDE DOWN THE FROZEN WAVE?!
IT'S THE ONLY WAY! BUT FIRST WE GOTTA BREAK THE SHIP OUT OF THE ICE!
THIS IS A WARSHIP!! THERE'S NO WAY WE CAN MOVE IT!!
WE CAN IF WE WORK TO-GETHER!!
!!
HEY, SUDDENLY I FEEL LIKE I CAN DO IT!!
RAAH RAAH
THAT'S RIGHT! HE'S CAP'N BUGGY, THE MAN WHO'S GONNA CONQUER THE WORLD!!
RINGG ...!!
!
ATTEN-TION FLEET!!
GOAL POINT TOTTZ. CHANGE FORMATION AND PRO-CEED TO STEP THREE OF THE STANDARD MANEUVERS.
FINISH THE PREPARA-TIONS.
WUZZ WUZZ
IT'S A MESSAGE FOR THE NAVY.
SOUNDS LIKE SOME KIND OF CODE.
ACE WILL BE EXECUTED AHEAD OF SCHEDULE AS SOON AS PREPA-RATIONS ARE COMPLETE.
?!!
WHAT?!

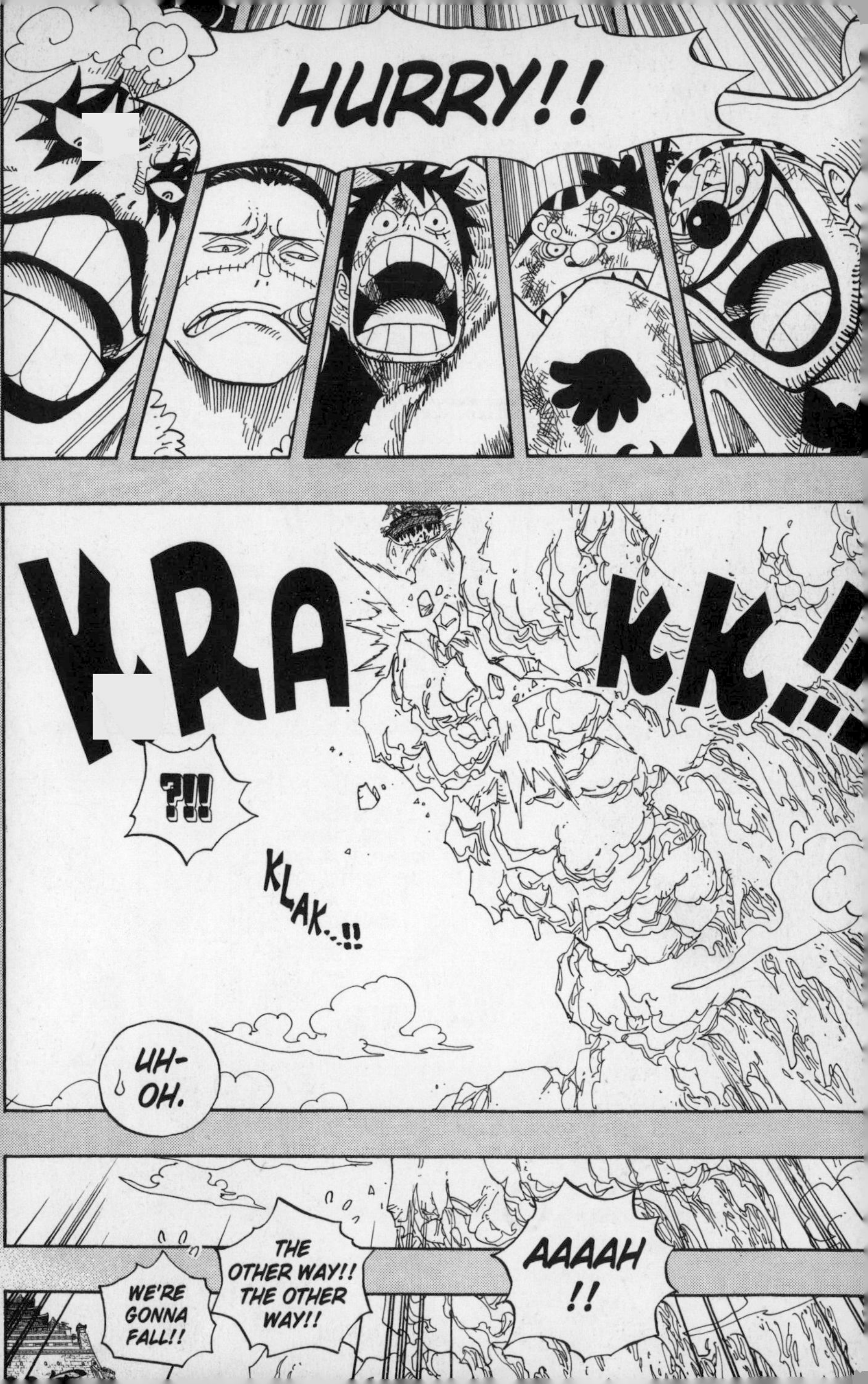
HURRY!!
KRAKK!!
?!!
KLAK..!!
UH-OH.
AAAAH!!
THE OTHER WAY!! THE OTHER WAY!!
WE'RE GONNA FALL!!

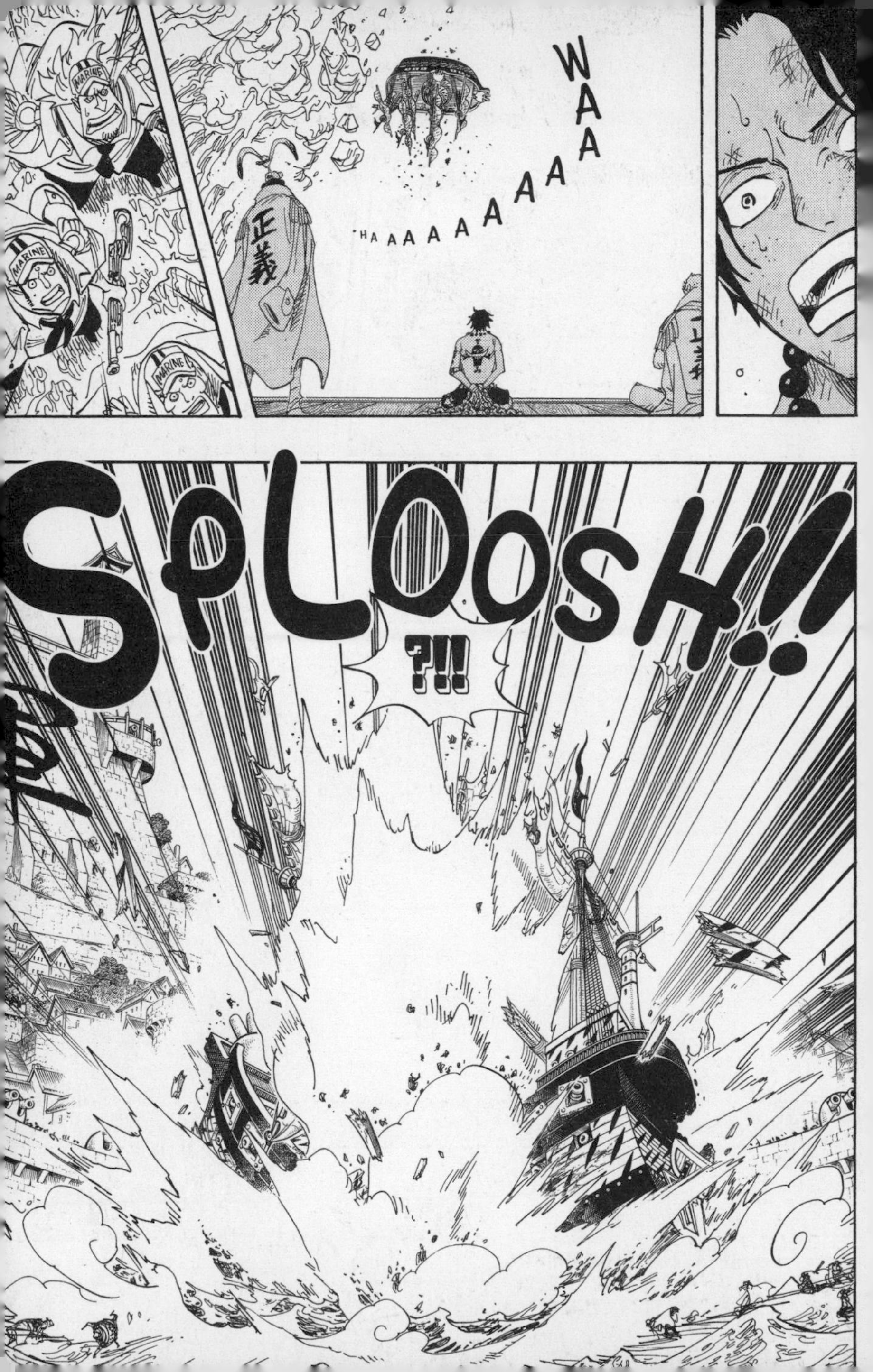
WAAAAAAAAA
THAAAAAAA
正義
SPLOOSH!!
?!!

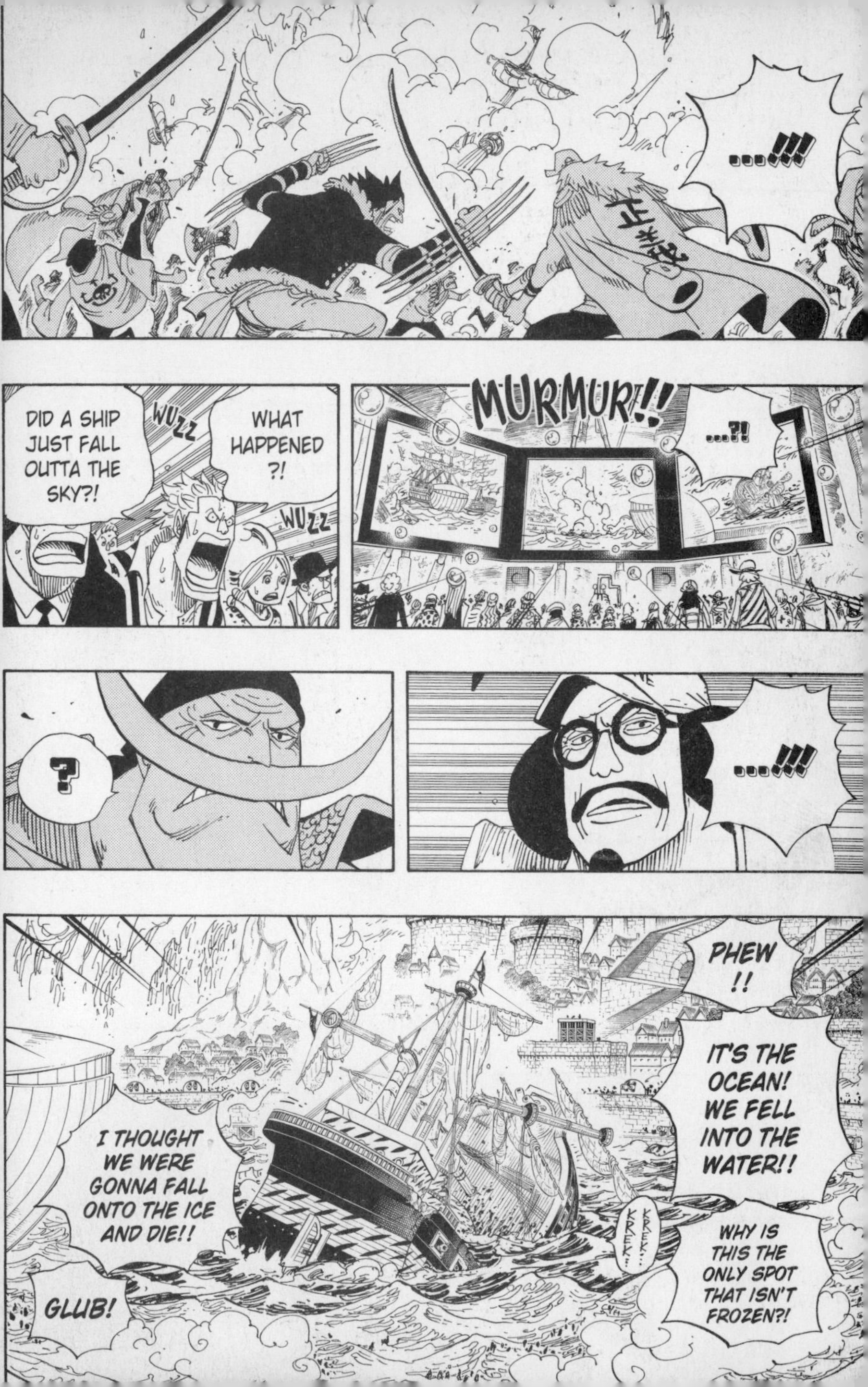
...!!!
MURMUR!!
...?!
WUZZ
WHAT HAPPENED ?!
WUZZ
DID A SHIP JUST FALL OUTTA THE SKY?!
...!!!
?
PHEW !!
IT'S THE OCEAN! WE FELL INTO THE WATER!!
WHY IS THIS THE ONLY SPOT THAT ISN'T FROZEN?!
KREK... KREK...
I THOUGHT WE WERE GONNA FALL ONTO THE ICE AND DIE!!
GLUB!

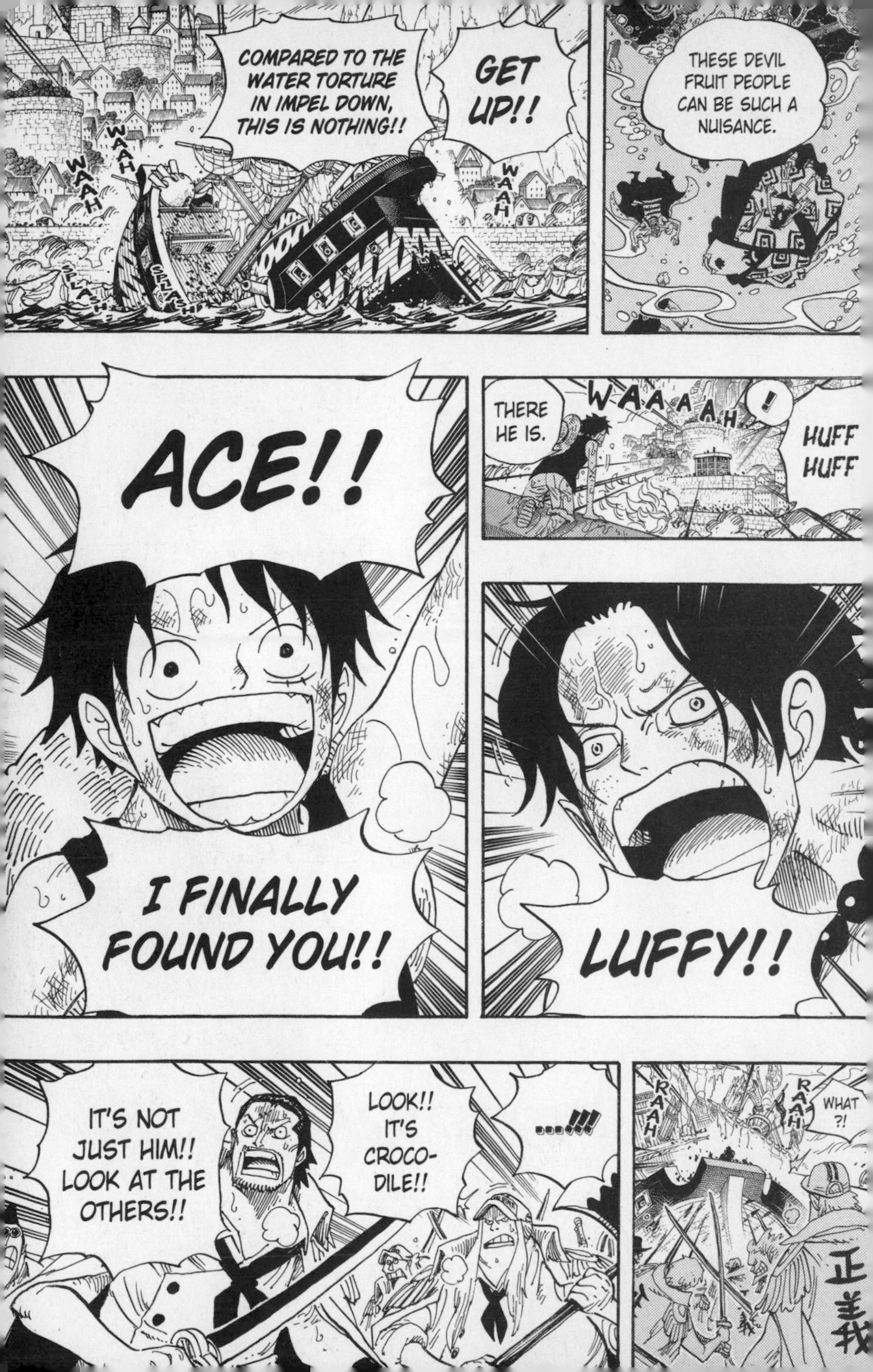
THESE DEVIL FRUIT PEOPLE CAN BE SUCH A NUISANCE.
GET UP!!
COMPARED TO THE WATER TORTURE IN IMPEL DOWN, THIS IS NOTHING!!
WAAH
WAAH WAAH
SPLASH SPLASH
HUFF HUFF
WAAAAH!
THERE HE IS.
LUFFY!!
ACE!!
I FINALLY FOUND YOU!!
WHAT?!
RAAH
RAAH
正義
...!!!
LOOK!! IT'S CROCO-DILE!!
IT'S NOT JUST HIM!! LOOK AT THE OTHERS!!

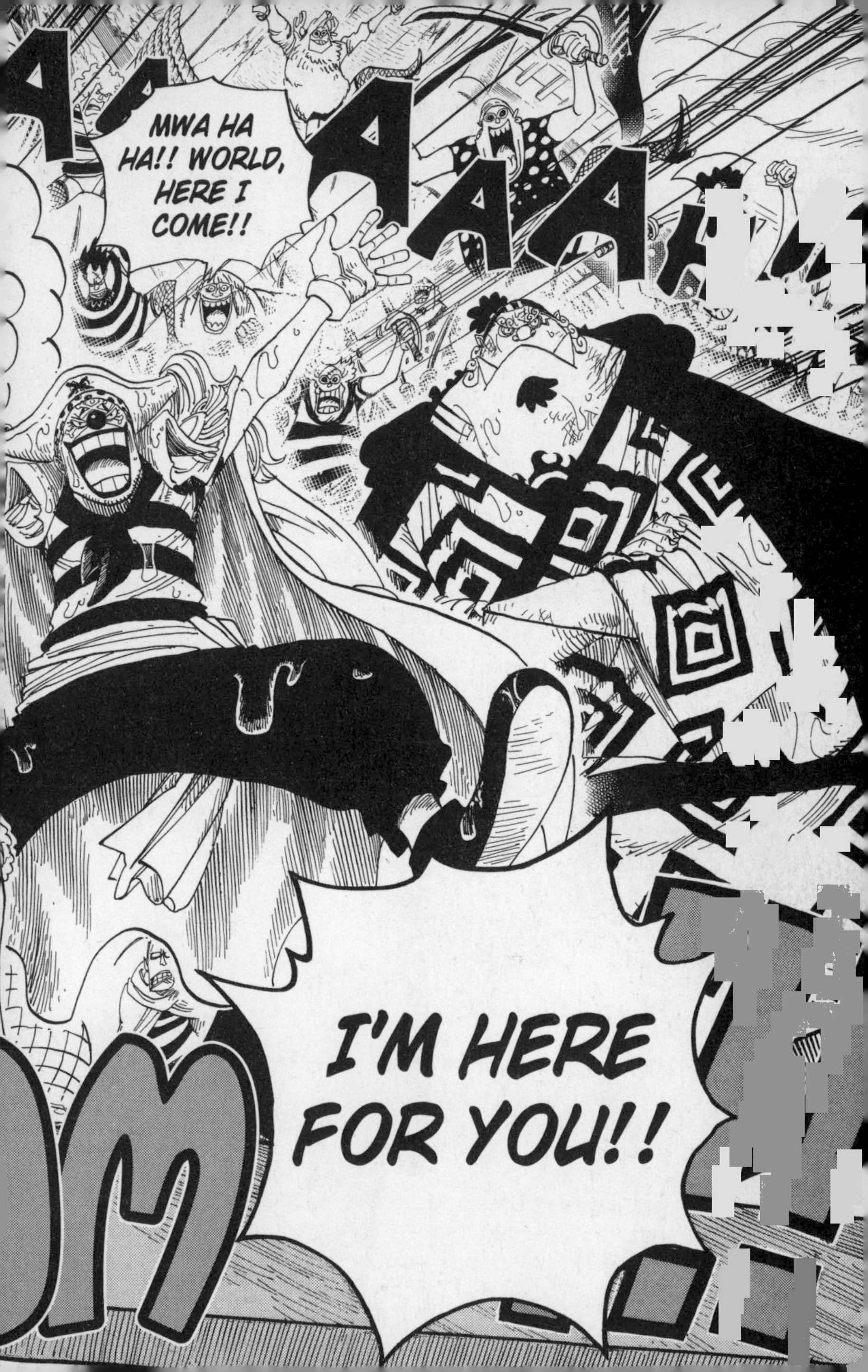
MWA HA HA!! WORLD, HERE I COME!!
I'M HERE FOR YOU!!

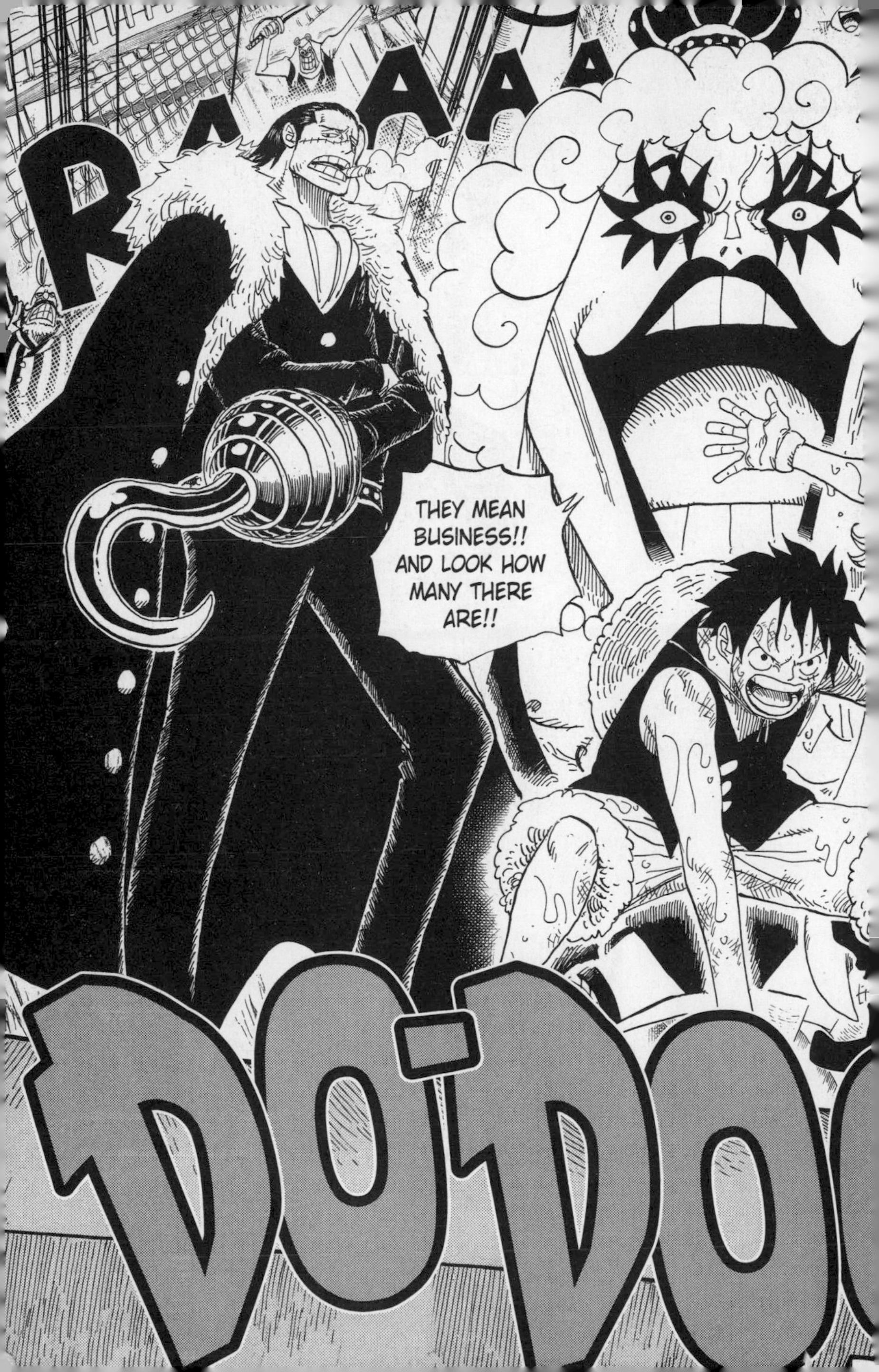
RAAAA
THEY MEAN BUSINESS!! AND LOOK HOW MANY THERE ARE!!
DO-DO

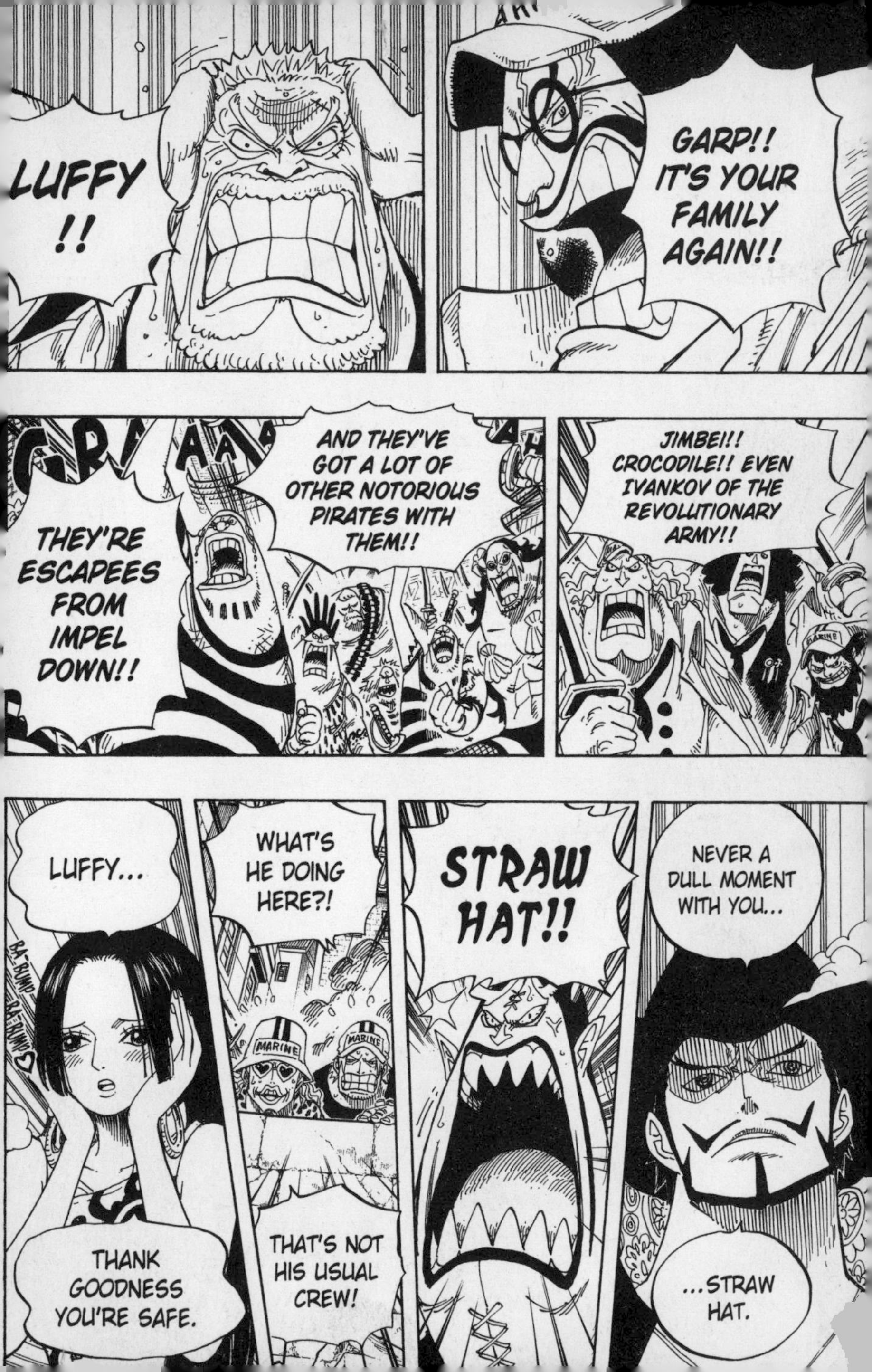
GARP!! IT'S YOUR FAMILY AGAIN!!
LUFFY !!
JIMBEI!!! CROCODILE!! EVEN IVANKOV OF THE REVOLUTIONARY ARMY!!
AND THEY'VE GOT A LOT OF OTHER NOTORIOUS PIRATES WITH THEM!!
THEY'RE ESCAPEES FROM IMPEL DOWN!!
NEVER A DULL MOMENT WITH YOU...
...STRAW HAT.
STRAW HAT!!
WHAT'S HE DOING HERE?!
THAT'S NOT HIS USUAL CREW!
LUFFY...
BA-BUMP
BA-BUMP
THANK GOODNESS YOU'RE SAFE.

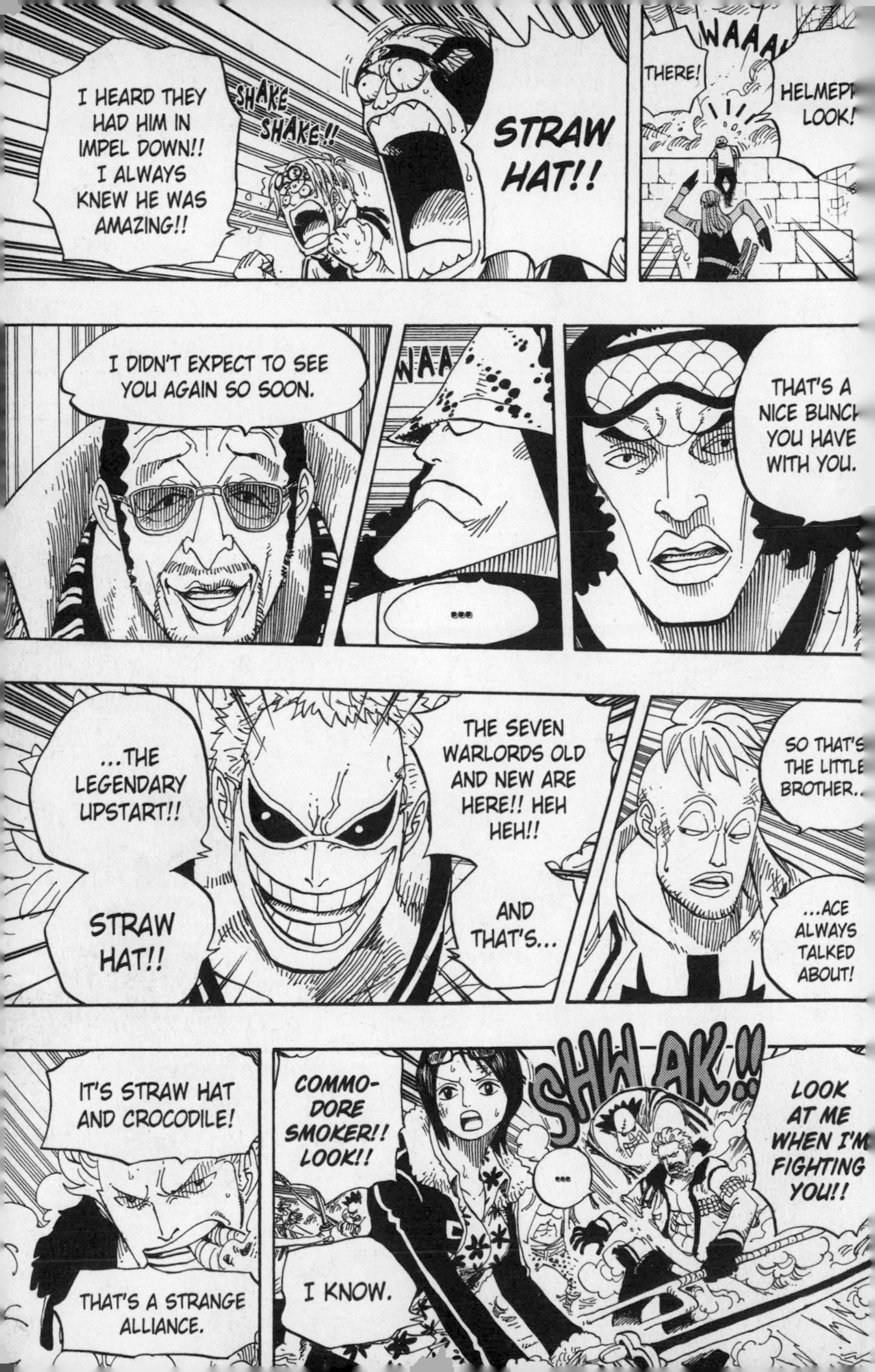
WAAA
THERE!
HELMEPP LOOK!
STRAW HAT!!
SHAKE SHAKE!!
I HEARD THEY HAD HIM IN IMPEL DOWN!! I ALWAYS KNEW HE WAS AMAZING!!
THAT'S A NICE BUNCH YOU HAVE WITH YOU.
WAA
...
I DIDN'T EXPECT TO SEE YOU AGAIN SO SOON.
SO THAT'S THE LITTLE BROTHER...
...ACE ALWAYS TALKED ABOUT!
THE SEVEN WARLORDS OLD AND NEW ARE HERE!! HEH HEH!!
...THE LEGENDARY UPSTART!!
AND THAT'S...
STRAW HAT!!
SHWAK!!
LOOK AT ME WHEN I'M FIGHTING YOU!!
...
COMMODORE SMOKER!! LOOK!!
I KNOW.
IT'S STRAW HAT AND CROCODILE!
THAT'S A STRANGE ALLIANCE.

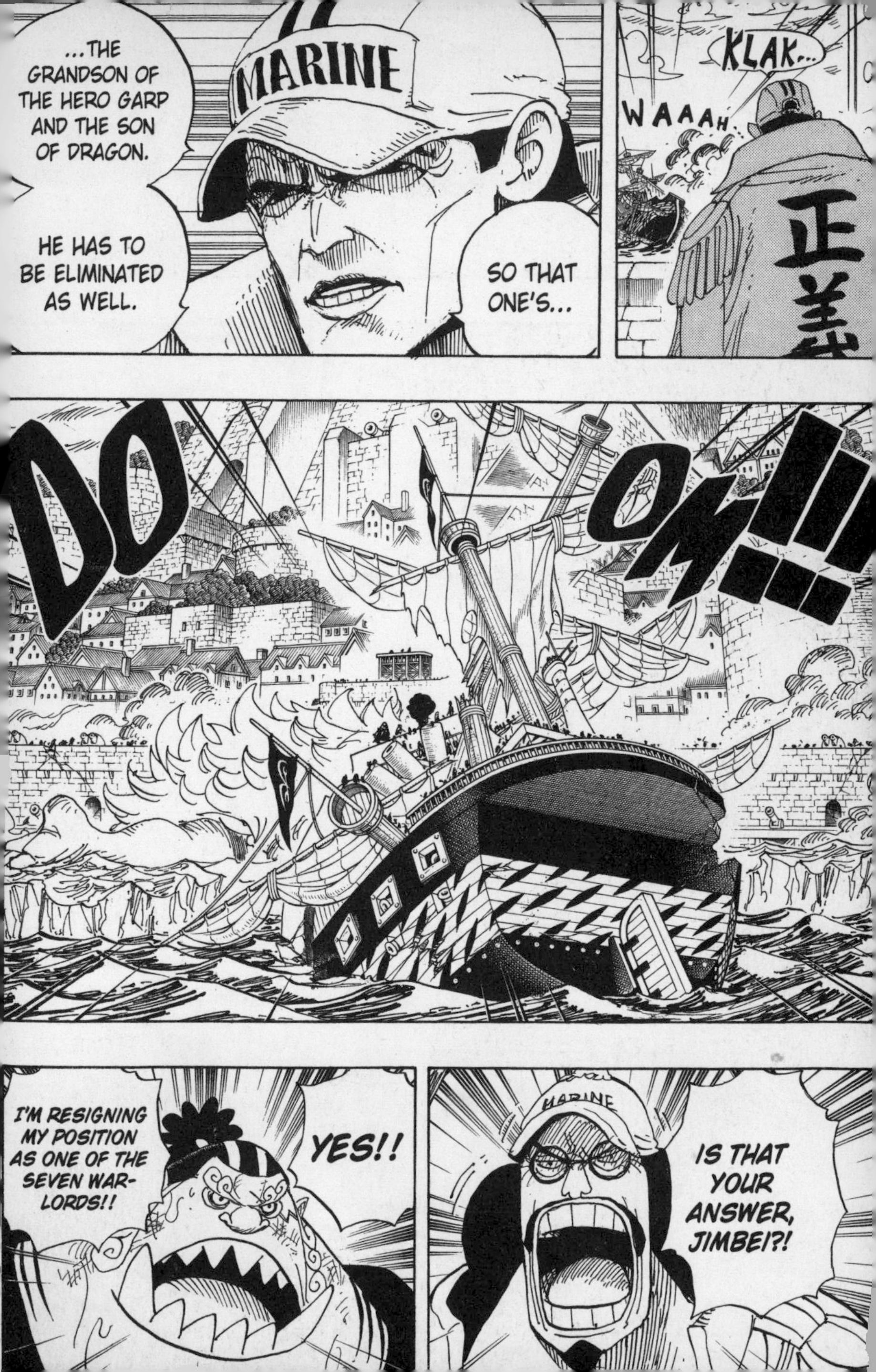
KLAK...
WAAAH
正義
SO THAT ONE'S...
...THE GRANDSON OF THE HERO GARP AND THE SON OF DRAGON.
HE HAS TO BE ELIMINATED AS WELL.
DOON!!!
IS THAT YOUR ANSWER, JIMBEI?!
YES!!
I'M RESIGNING MY POSITION AS ONE OF THE SEVEN WAR-LORDS!!

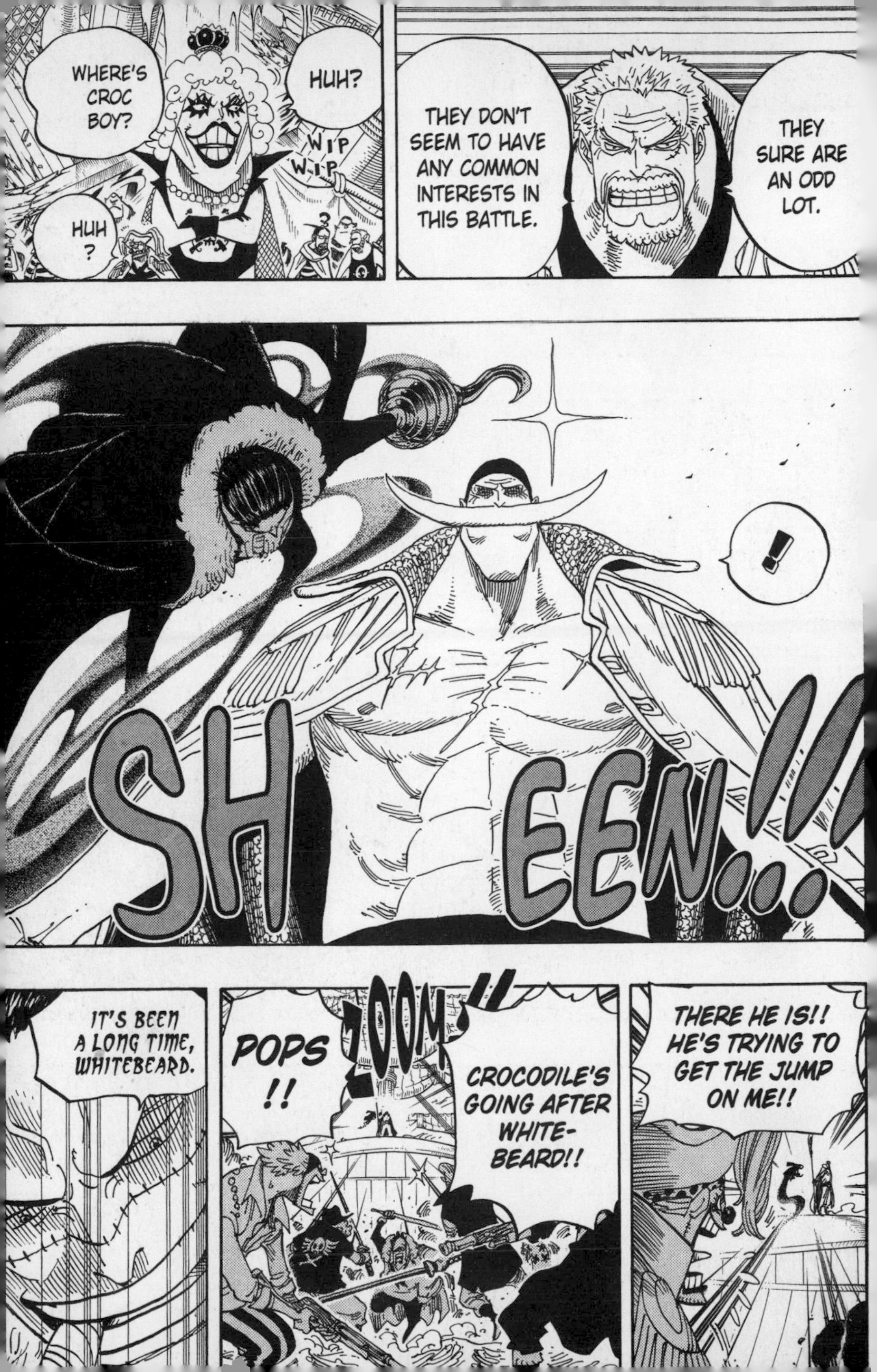
THEY SURE ARE AN ODD LOT.
THEY DON'T SEEM TO HAVE ANY COMMON INTERESTS IN THIS BATTLE.
HUH?
WHERE'S CROC BOY?
WIP WIP
HUH ?
!
SH EEN...!!!
THERE HE IS!! HE'S TRYING TO GET THE JUMP ON ME!!
ZOOM!!
CROCODILE'S GOING AFTER WHITE-BEARD!!
POPS !!
IT'S BEEN A LONG TIME, WHITEBEARD.

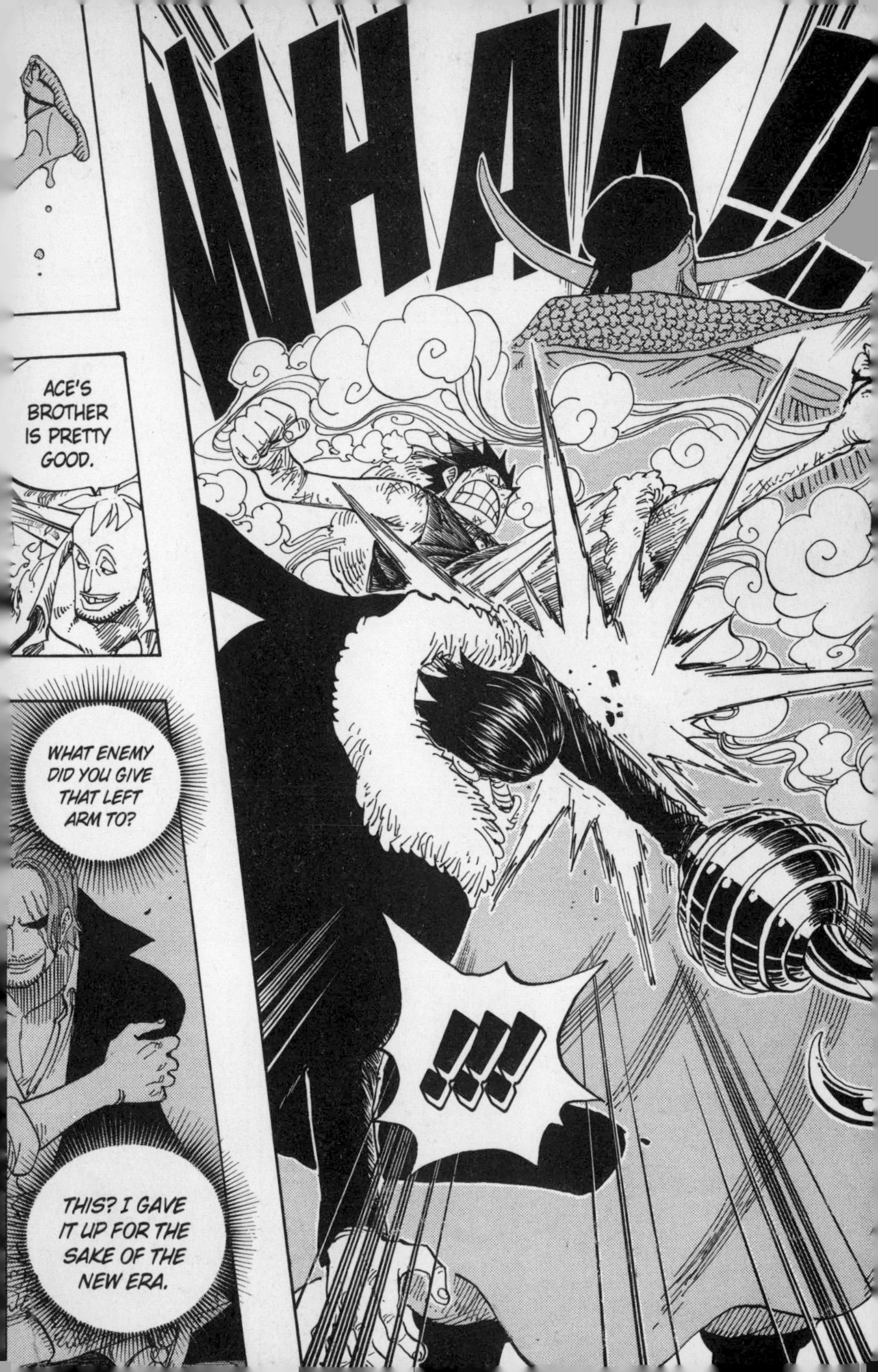
WHAK!
!!!
ACE'S BROTHER IS PRETTY GOOD.
WHAT ENEMY DID YOU GIVE THAT LEFT ARM TO?
THIS? I GAVE IT UP FOR THE SAKE OF THE NEW ERA.

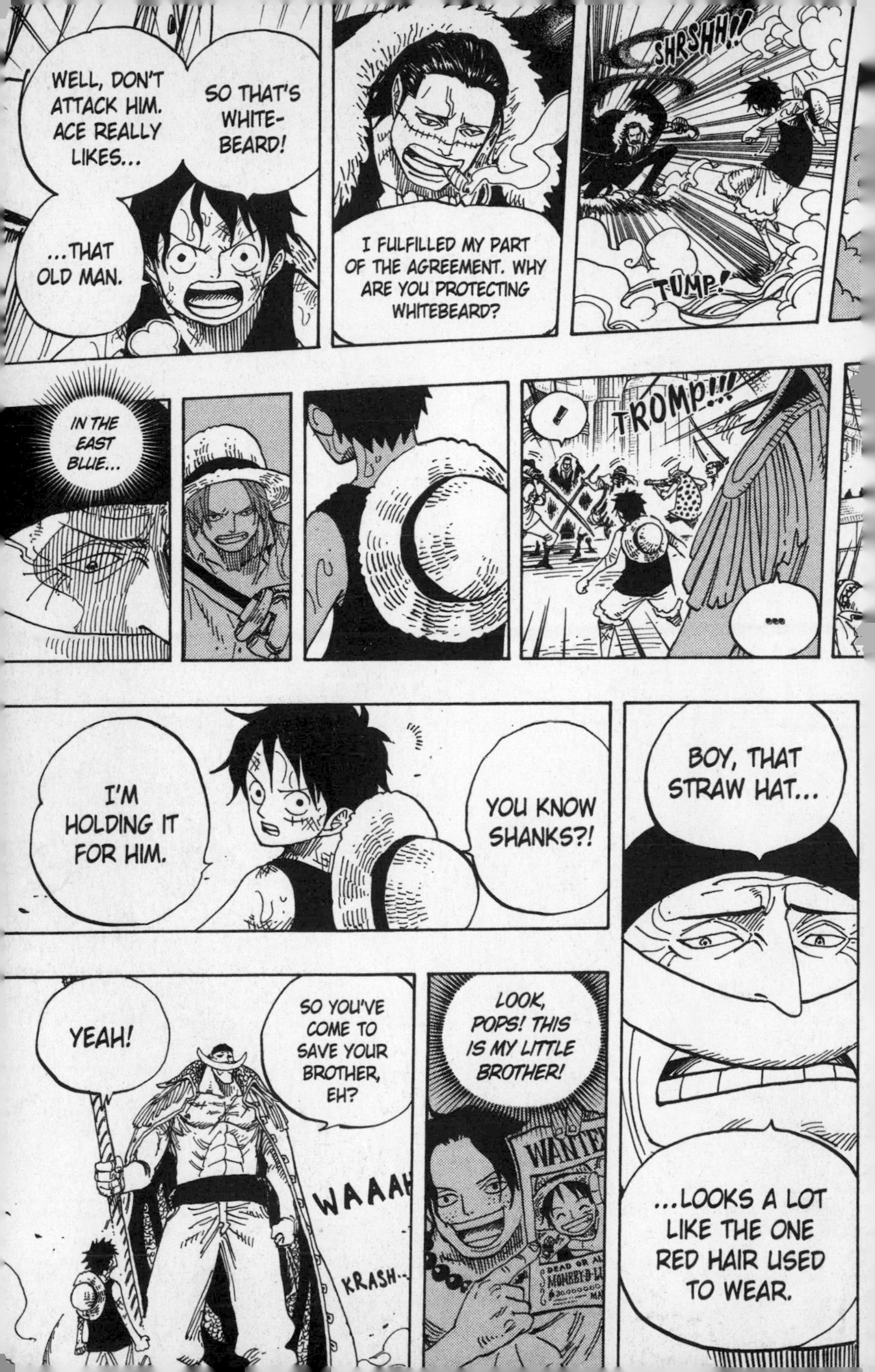
SHRSHH!!
TUMP!
I FULFILLED MY PART OF THE AGREEMENT. WHY ARE YOU PROTECTING WHITEBEARD?
SO THAT'S WHITE-BEARD!
WELL, DON'T ATTACK HIM. ACE REALLY LIKES...
...THAT OLD MAN.
...
!
TROMP!!!
IN THE EAST BLUE...
BOY, THAT STRAW HAT...
...LOOKS A LOT LIKE THE ONE RED HAIR USED TO WEAR.
YOU KNOW SHANKS?!
I'M HOLDING IT FOR HIM.
LOOK, POPS! THIS IS MY LITTLE BROTHER!
WANTED
DEAD OR ALIVE
SO YOU'VE COME TO SAVE YOUR BROTHER, EH?
YEAH!
WAAAH
KRASH...

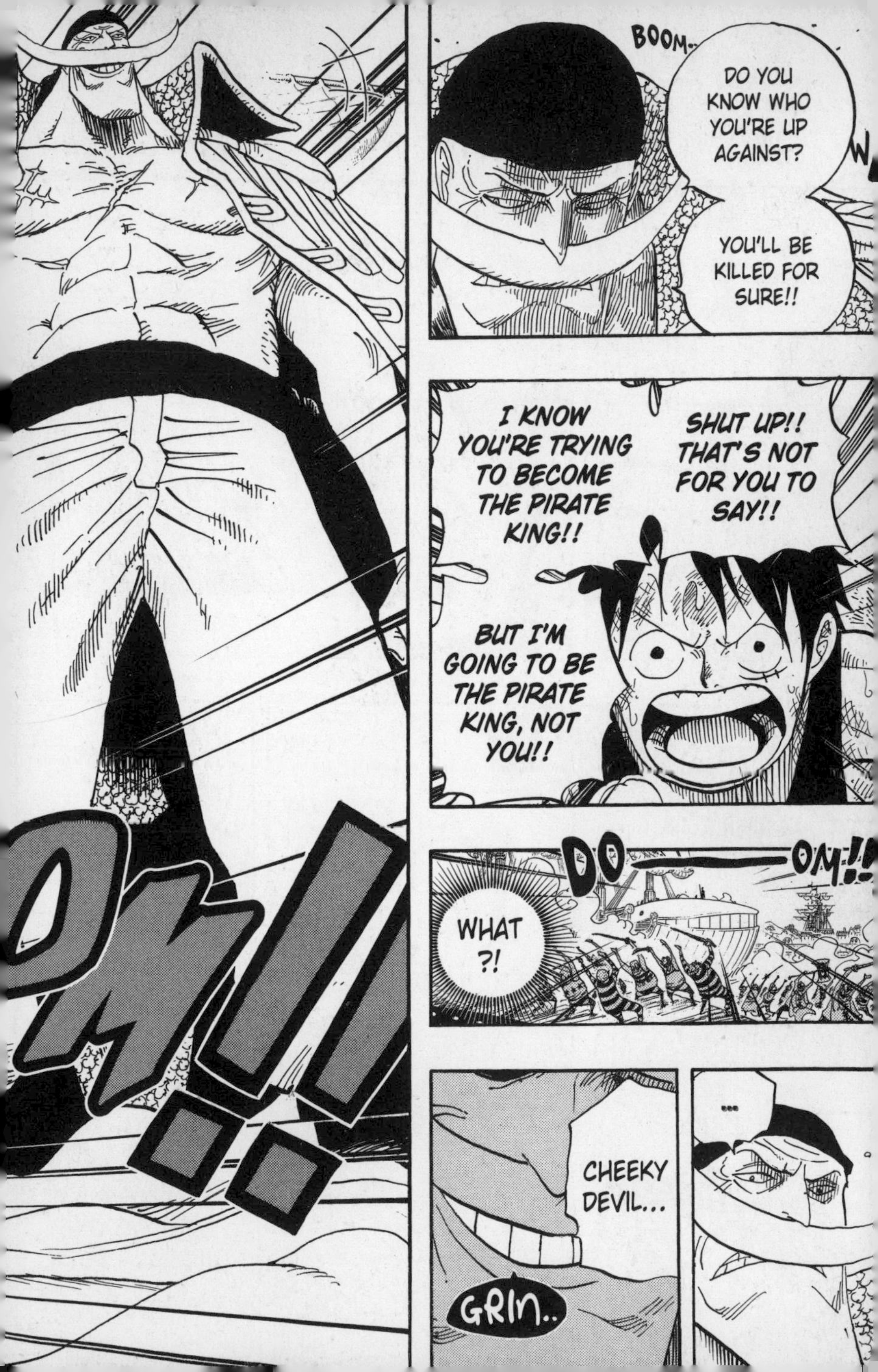
BOOM..
DO YOU KNOW WHO YOU'RE UP AGAINST?
YOU'LL BE KILLED FOR SURE!!
SHUT UP!! THAT'S NOT FOR YOU TO SAY!!
I KNOW YOU'RE TRYING TO BECOME THE PIRATE KING!!
BUT I'M GOING TO BE THE PIRATE KING, NOT YOU!!
DO———OM!!
WHAT ?!
...
CHEEKY DEVIL...
GRIN..

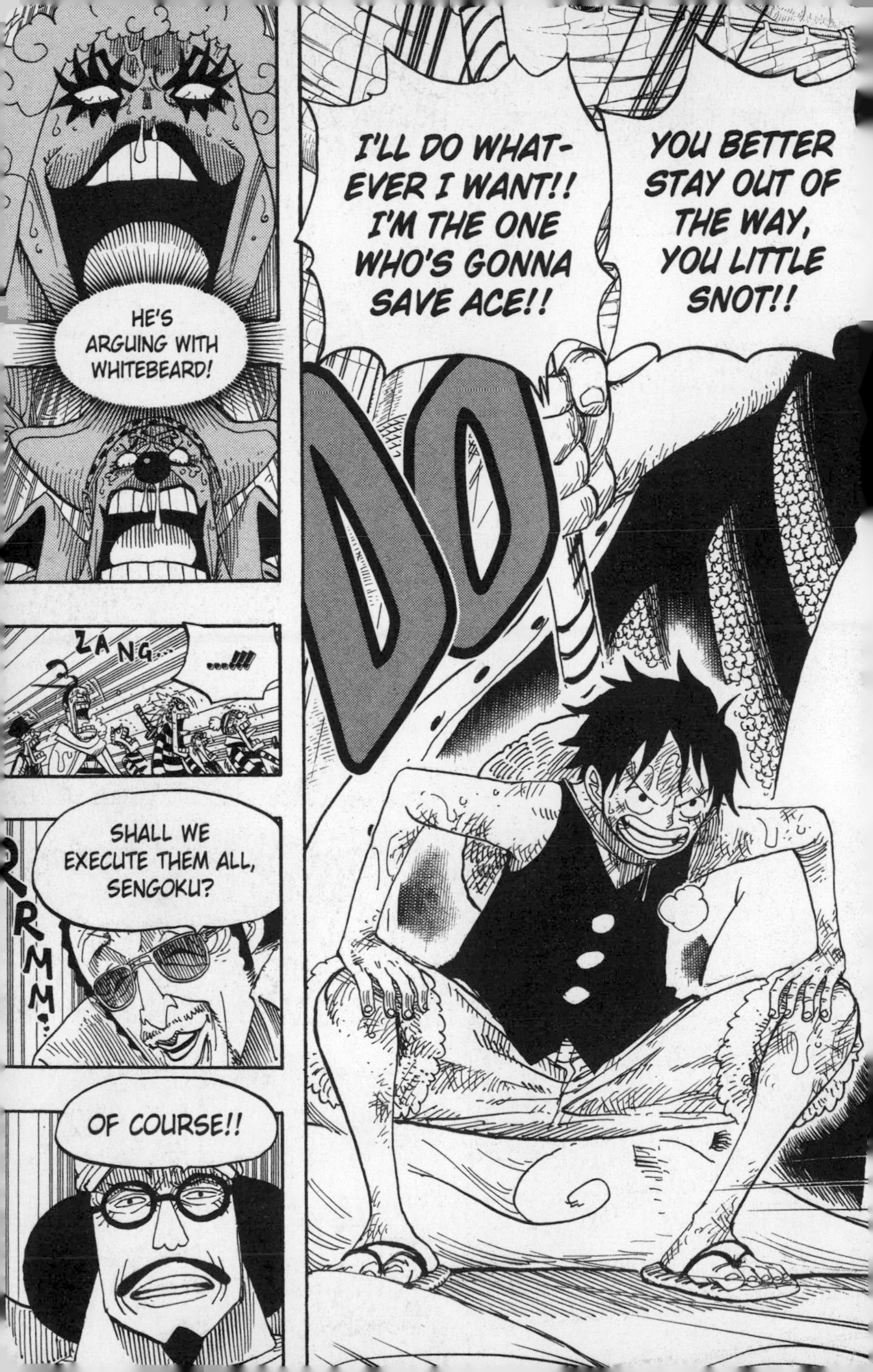
YOU BETTER STAY OUT OF THE WAY, YOU LITTLE SNOT!!
I'LL DO WHATEVER I WANT!! I'M THE ONE WHO'S GONNA SAVE ACE!!
DO
HE'S ARGUING WITH WHITEBEARD!
...!!!
ZANG...
SHALL WE EXECUTE THEM ALL, SENGOKU?
RRMM
OF COURSE!!

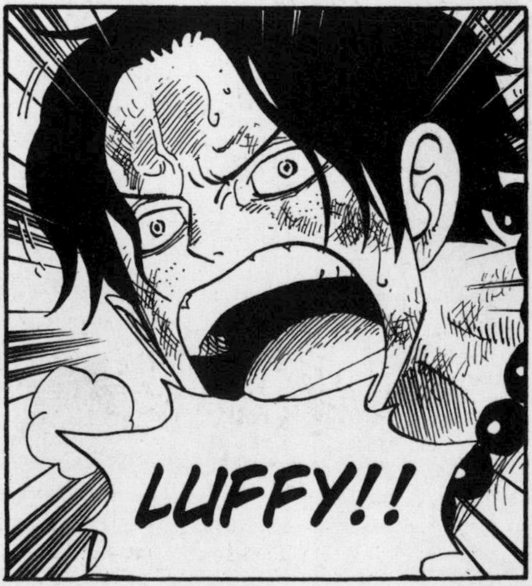
LUFFY!!

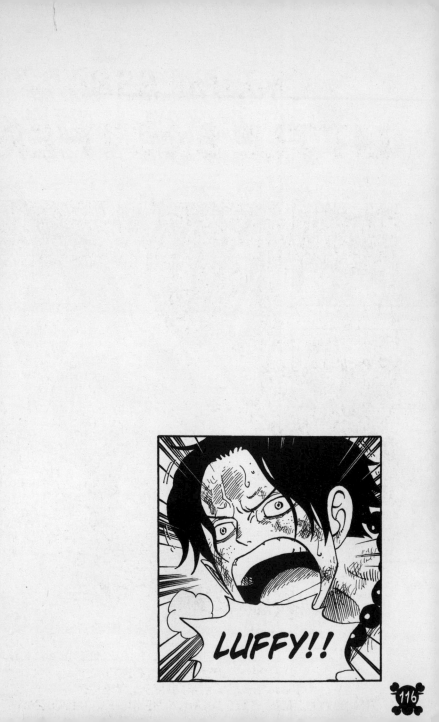

Chapter 558:
LITTLE BROTHER

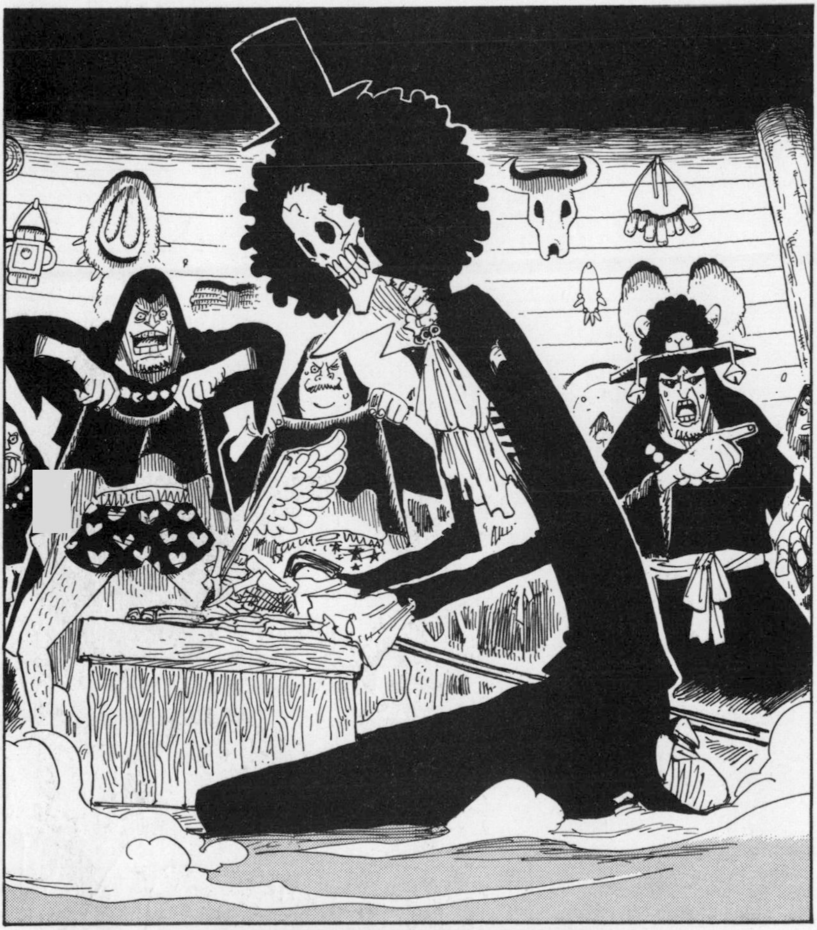

BROOK'S "REPAYMENT FOR A NIGHT'S STAY AND UNDERWEAR"
FINAL VOLUME: "THE DEMON BEGINS COMPOSING"

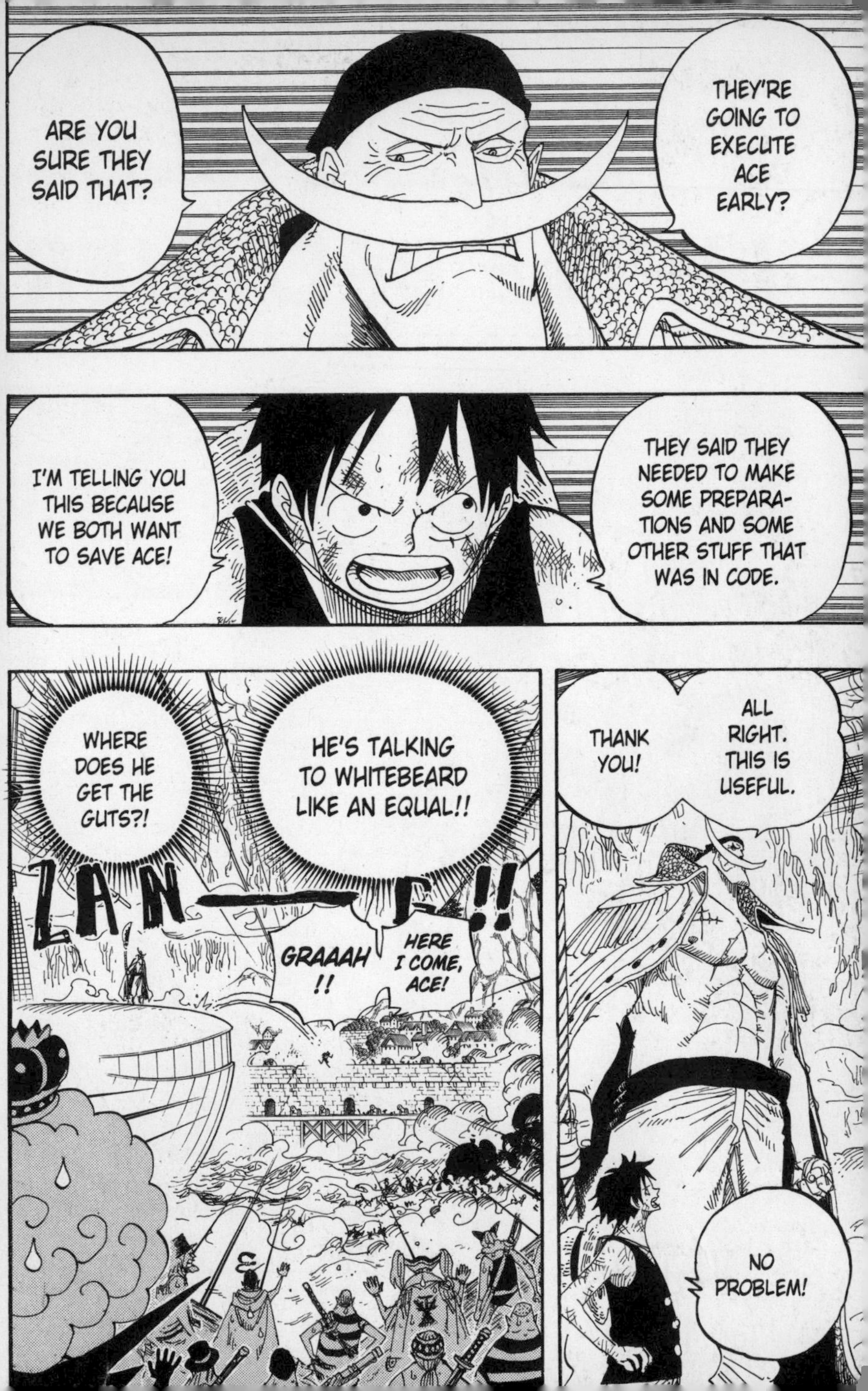
THEY'RE GOING TO EXECUTE ACE EARLY?
ARE YOU SURE THEY SAID THAT?
THEY SAID THEY NEEDED TO MAKE SOME PREPARATIONS AND SOME OTHER STUFF THAT WAS IN CODE.
I'M TELLING YOU THIS BECAUSE WE BOTH WANT TO SAVE ACE!
ALL RIGHT. THIS IS USEFUL.
THANK YOU!
NO PROBLEM!
HE'S TALKING TO WHITEBEARD LIKE AN EQUAL!!
WHERE DOES HE GET THE GUTS?!
ZAN——G!!
HERE I COME, ACE!
GRAAAH!!

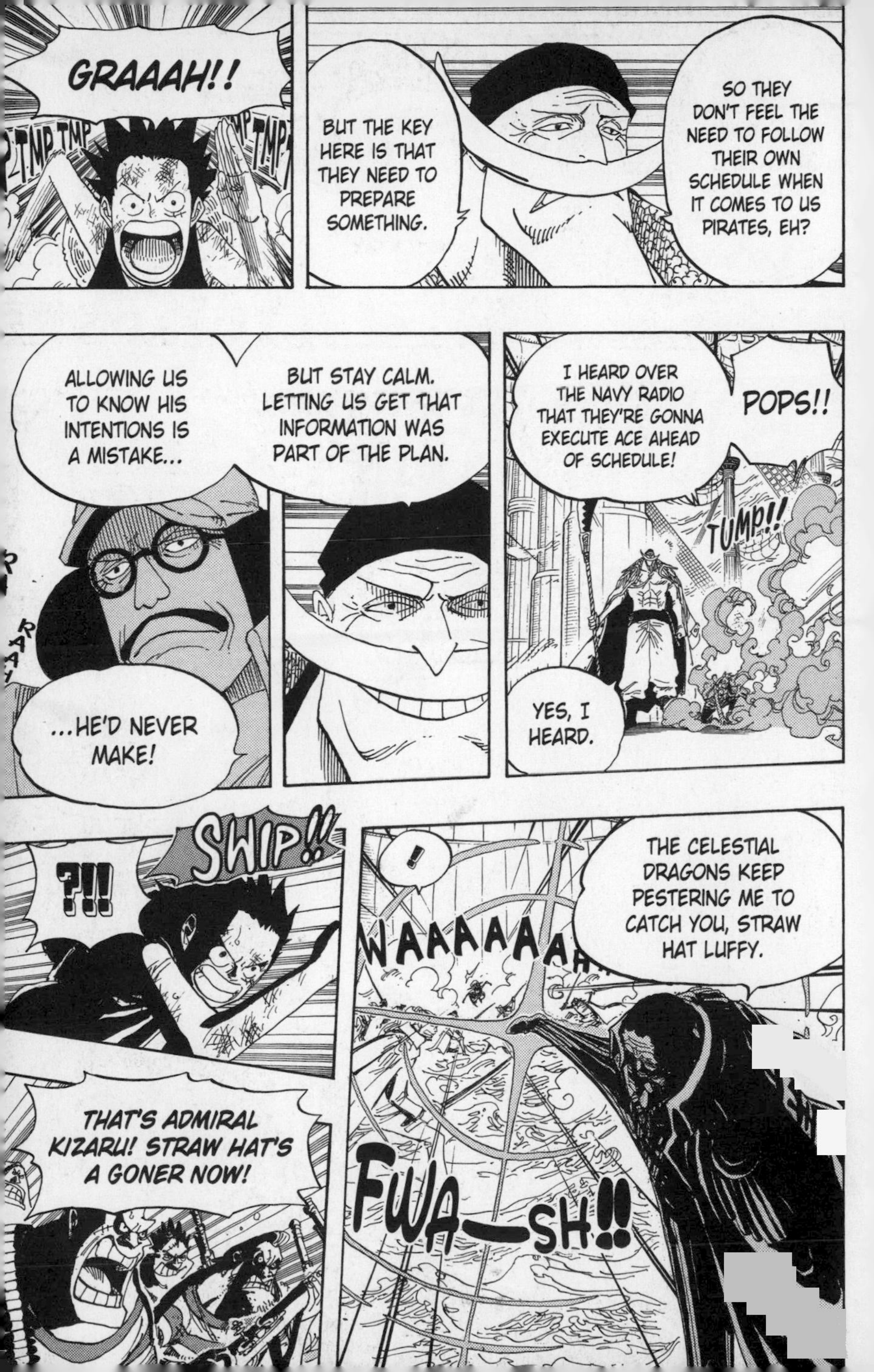
SO THEY DON'T FEEL THE NEED TO FOLLOW THEIR OWN SCHEDULE WHEN IT COMES TO US PIRATES, EH?
BUT THE KEY HERE IS THAT THEY NEED TO PREPARE SOMETHING.
GRAAAH!!
TMP TMP
TMP TMP
POPS!!
I HEARD OVER THE NAVY RADIO THAT THEY'RE GONNA EXECUTE ACE AHEAD OF SCHEDULE!
TUMP!!
YES, I HEARD.
BUT STAY CALM. LETTING US GET THAT INFORMATION WAS PART OF THE PLAN.
ALLOWING US TO KNOW HIS INTENTIONS IS A MISTAKE...
...HE'D NEVER MAKE!
!
THE CELESTIAL DRAGONS KEEP PESTERING ME TO CATCH YOU, STRAW HAT LUFFY.
WAAAAAAAH..
FWA—SH!!
SHIP!!
?!!
THAT'S ADMIRAL KIZARU! STRAW HAT'S A GONER NOW!

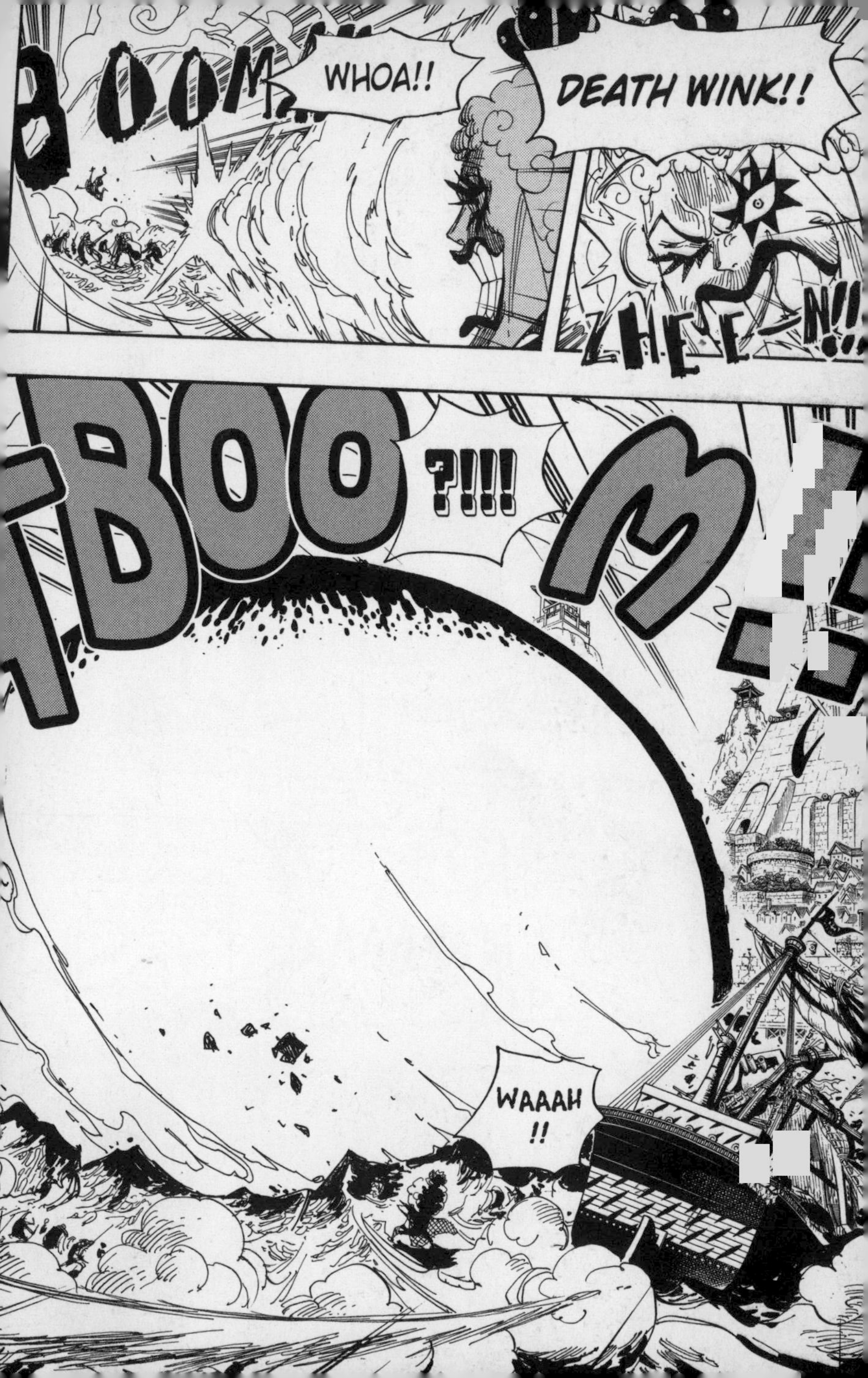
DEATH WINK!!
ZHEE-N!!
WHOA!!
BOOM
BOOM
?!!!
WAAAH !!

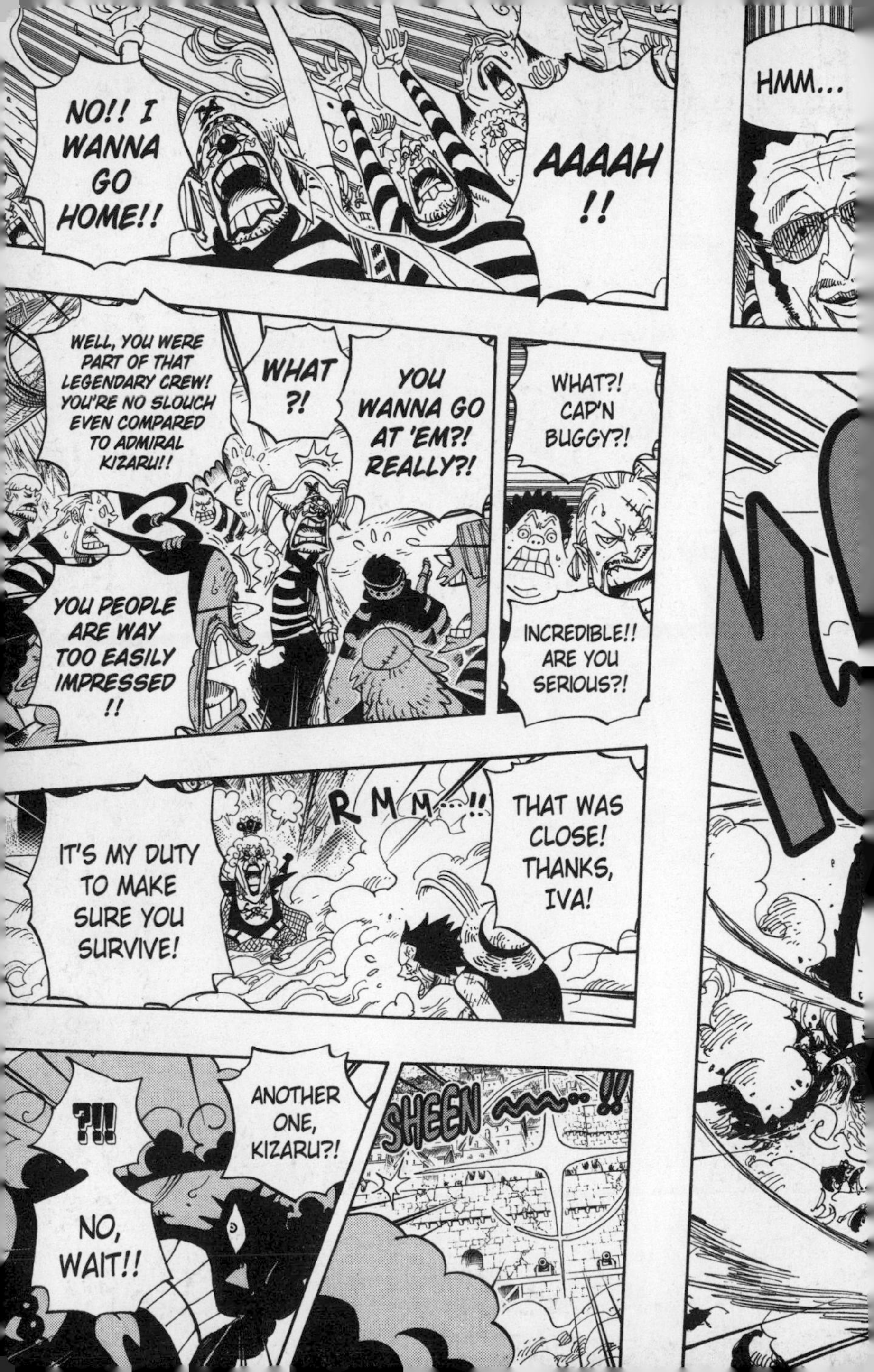
HMM...
AAAAH!!
NO!! I WANNA GO HOME!!
WHAT?! CAP'N BUGGY?!
INCREDIBLE!! ARE YOU SERIOUS?!
YOU WANNA GO AT 'EM?! REALLY?!
WHAT?!
WELL, YOU WERE PART OF THAT LEGENDARY CREW! YOU'RE NO SLOUCH EVEN COMPARED TO ADMIRAL KIZARU!!
YOU PEOPLE ARE WAY TOO EASILY IMPRESSED!!
THAT WAS CLOSE! THANKS, IVA!
RMM...!!
IT'S MY DUTY TO MAKE SURE YOU SURVIVE!
SHEEN ~~..!!
ANOTHER ONE, KIZARU?!
?!!
NO, WAIT!!

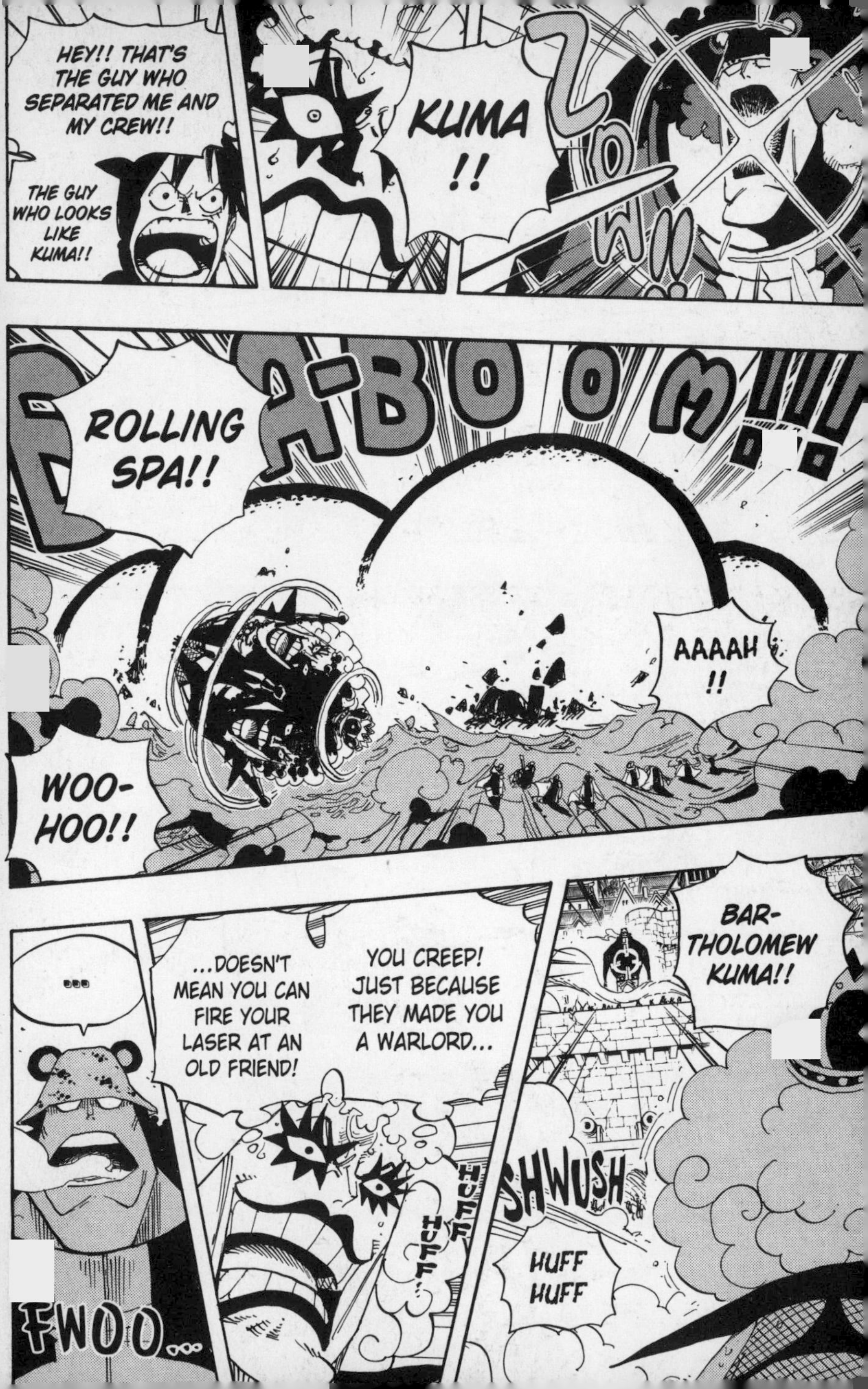
ZOW!!
KUMA!!
HEY!! THAT'S THE GUY WHO SEPARATED ME AND MY CREW!!
THE GUY WHO LOOKS LIKE KUMA!!
BOOM!!!!
AAAAH!!
ROLLING SPA!!
WOO-HOO!!
BAR-THOLOMEW KUMA!!
SHWUSH
HUFF HUFF
YOU CREEP! JUST BECAUSE THEY MADE YOU A WARLORD...
...DOESN'T MEAN YOU CAN FIRE YOUR LASER AT AN OLD FRIEND!
HUFF
HUFF HUFF
...
FWOO...

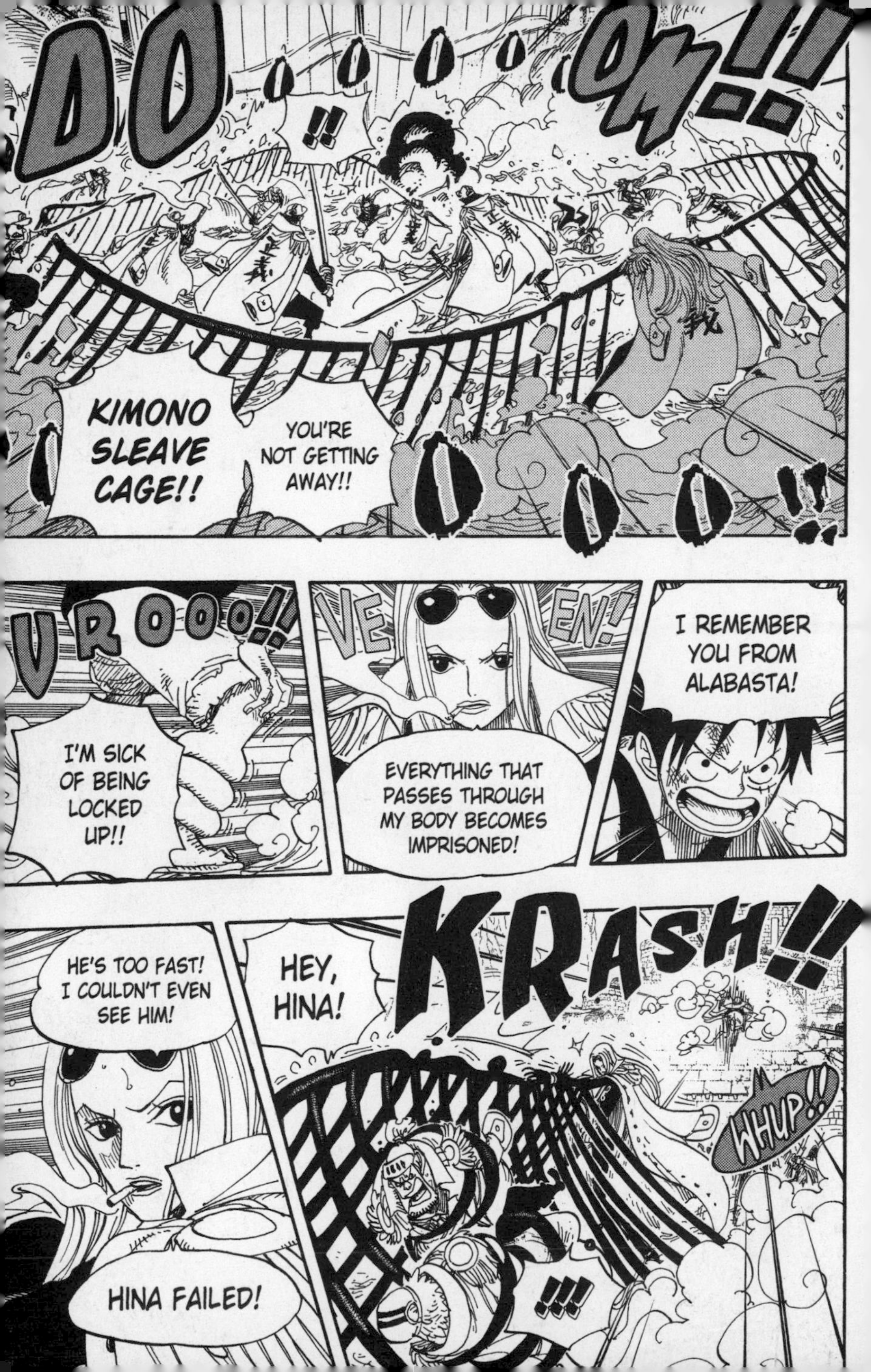
DOOOOOOOM!!
YOU'RE NOT GETTING AWAY!!
KIMONO SLEAVE CAGE!!
OOO!!
I REMEMBER YOU FROM ALABASTA!
VEEN!
EVERYTHING THAT PASSES THROUGH MY BODY BECOMES IMPRISONED!
VROOOO!!
I'M SICK OF BEING LOCKED UP!!
KRASH!!
HEY, HINA!
WHUP!!
!!!
HE'S TOO FAST! I COULDN'T EVEN SEE HIM!
HINA FAILED!

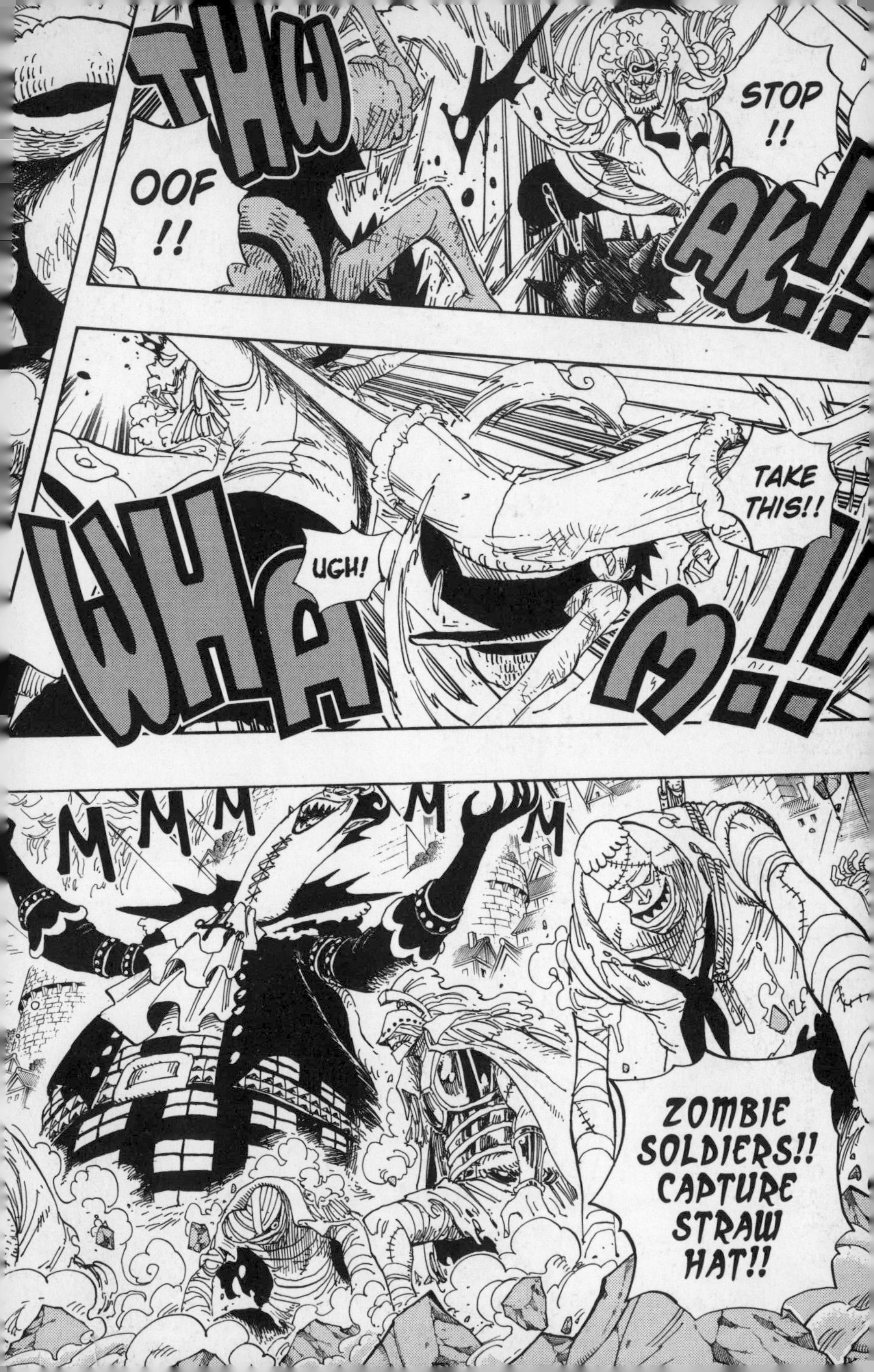
STOP!!
THW
AK..!!
OOF!!
TAKE THIS!!
UGH!
WHA
M..!!
M M M M M
ZOMBIE SOLDIERS!! CAPTURE STRAW HAT!!

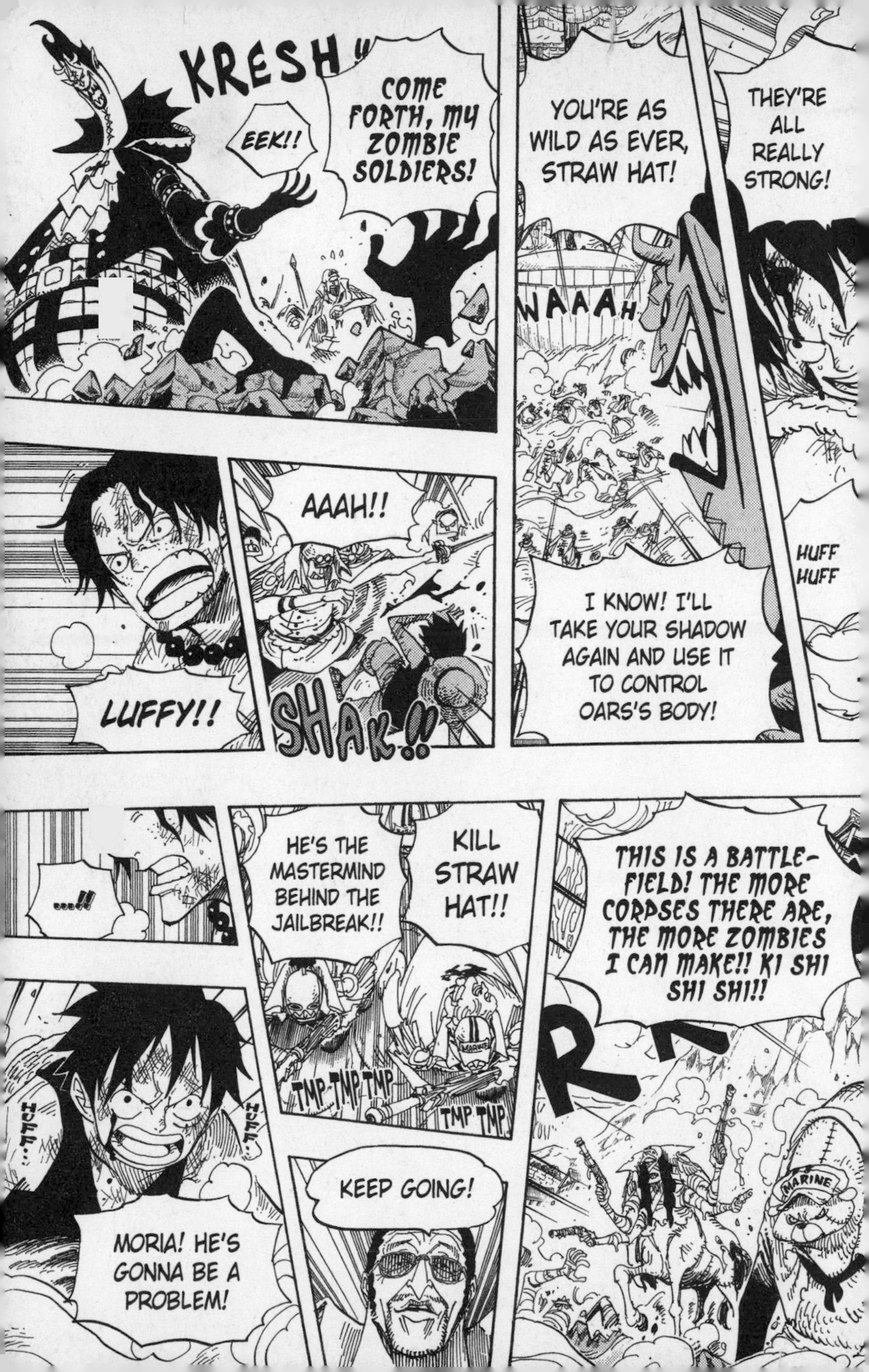

THEY'RE ALL REALLY STRONG!
HUFF HUFF
YOU'RE AS WILD AS EVER, STRAW HAT!
WAAAH
I KNOW! I'LL TAKE YOUR SHADOW AGAIN AND USE IT TO CONTROL OARS'S BODY!
COME FORTH, MY ZOMBIE SOLDIERS!
KRESH!!
EEK!!
AAAH!!
SHAK!!
LUFFY!!
THIS IS A BATTLEFIELD! THE MORE CORPSES THERE ARE, THE MORE ZOMBIES I CAN MAKE!! KI SHI SHI SHI!!
KILL STRAW HAT!!
HE'S THE MASTERMIND BEHIND THE JAILBREAK!!
TMP TMP TMP
TMP TMP
KEEP GOING!
...!!
HUFF...
HUFF...
MORIA! HE'S GONNA BE A PROBLEM!

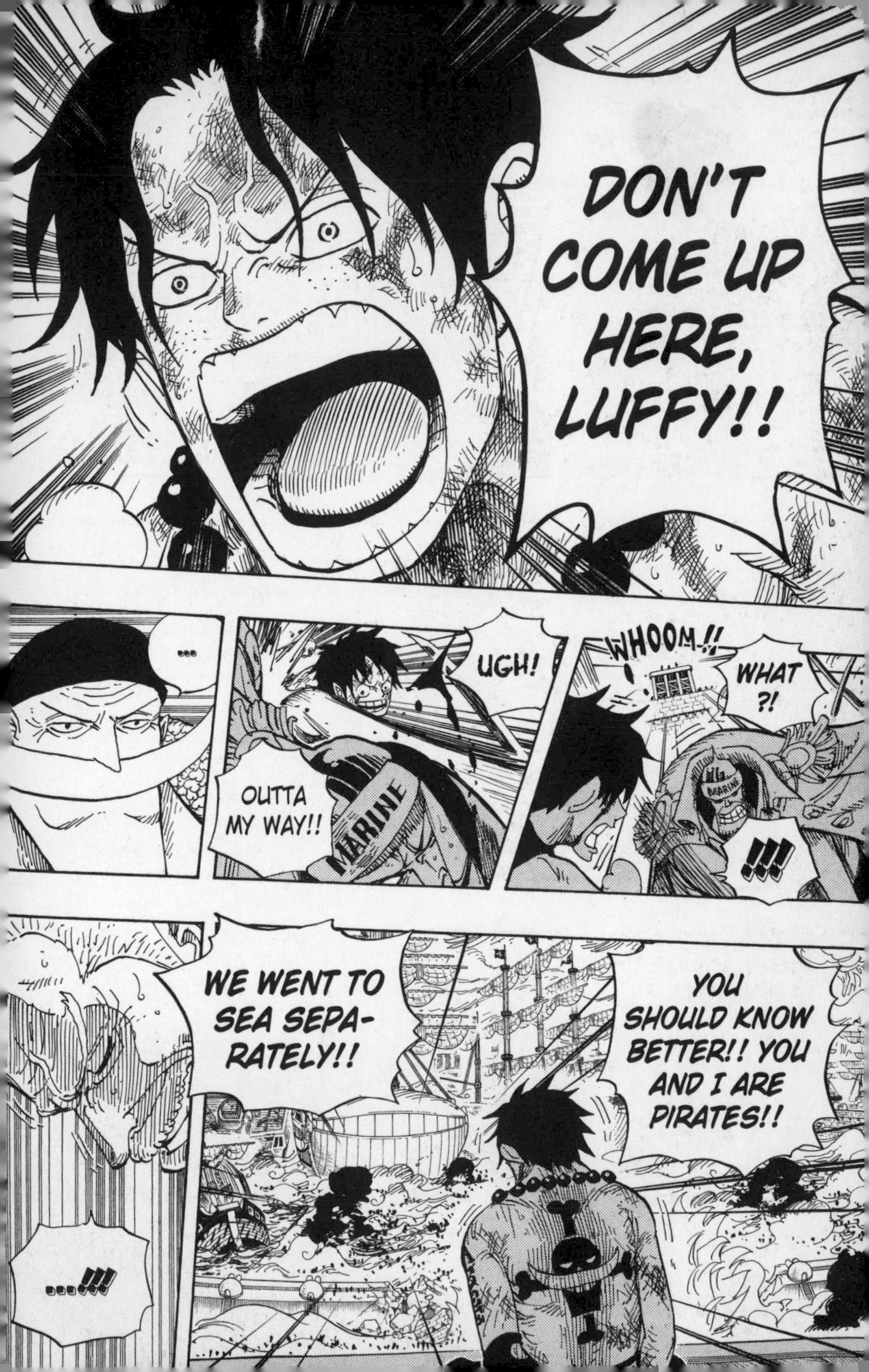
DON'T COME UP HERE, LUFFY!!
WHOOM!!
WHAT ?!
!!!
UGH!
OUTTA MY WAY!!
...
YOU SHOULD KNOW BETTER!! YOU AND I ARE PIRATES!!
WE WENT TO SEA SEPA- RATELY!!
...!!!

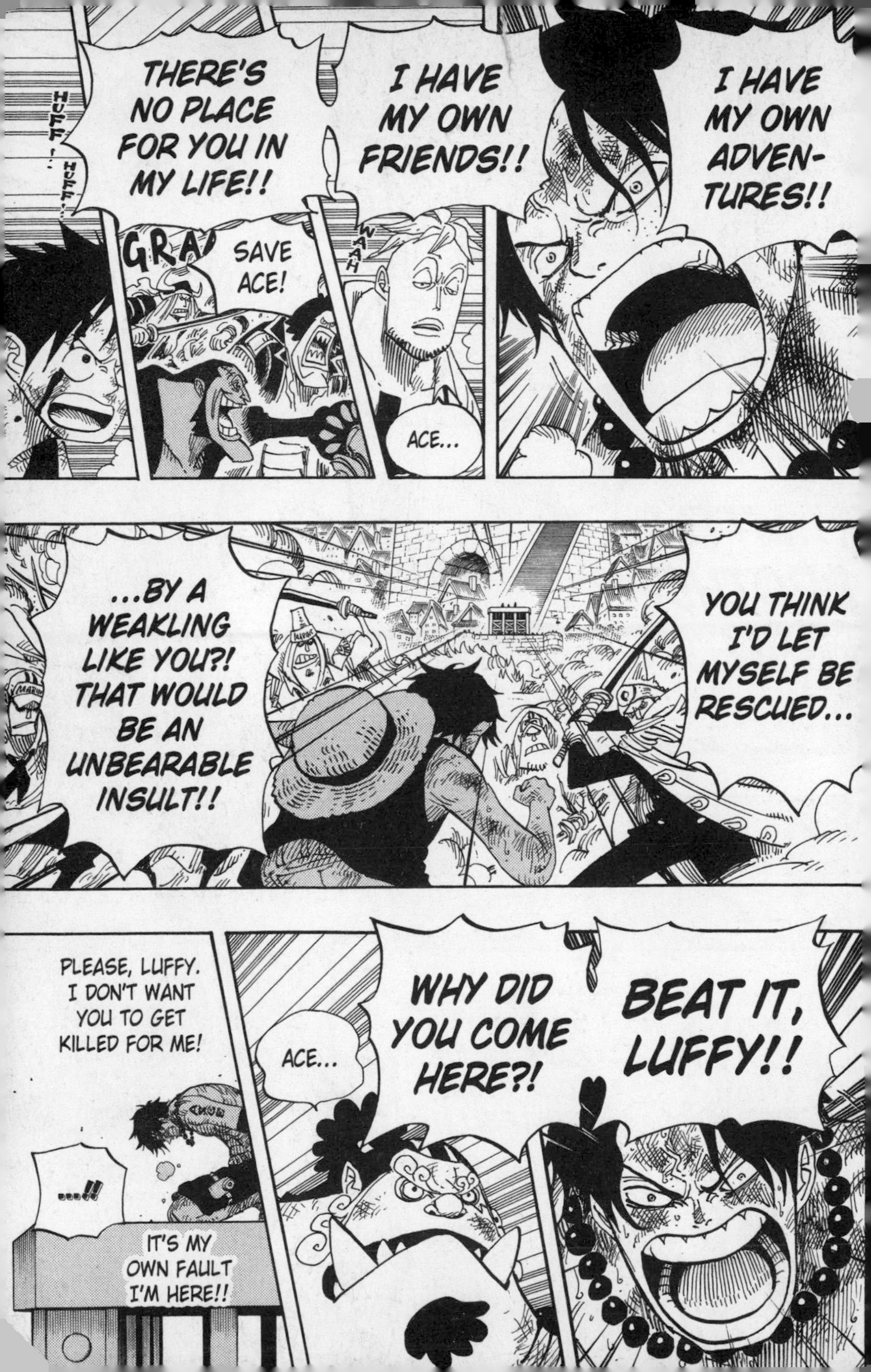
I HAVE MY OWN ADVENTURES!!
I HAVE MY OWN FRIENDS!!
WAAH
ACE...
SAVE ACE!
GRA
THERE'S NO PLACE FOR YOU IN MY LIFE!!
HUFF!!
HUFF!!
YOU THINK I'D LET MYSELF BE RESCUED...
...BY A WEAKLING LIKE YOU?! THAT WOULD BE AN UNBEARABLE INSULT!!
BEAT IT, LUFFY!!
WHY DID YOU COME HERE?!
ACE...
PLEASE, LUFFY. I DON'T WANT YOU TO GET KILLED FOR ME!
...!!
IT'S MY OWN FAULT I'M HERE!!

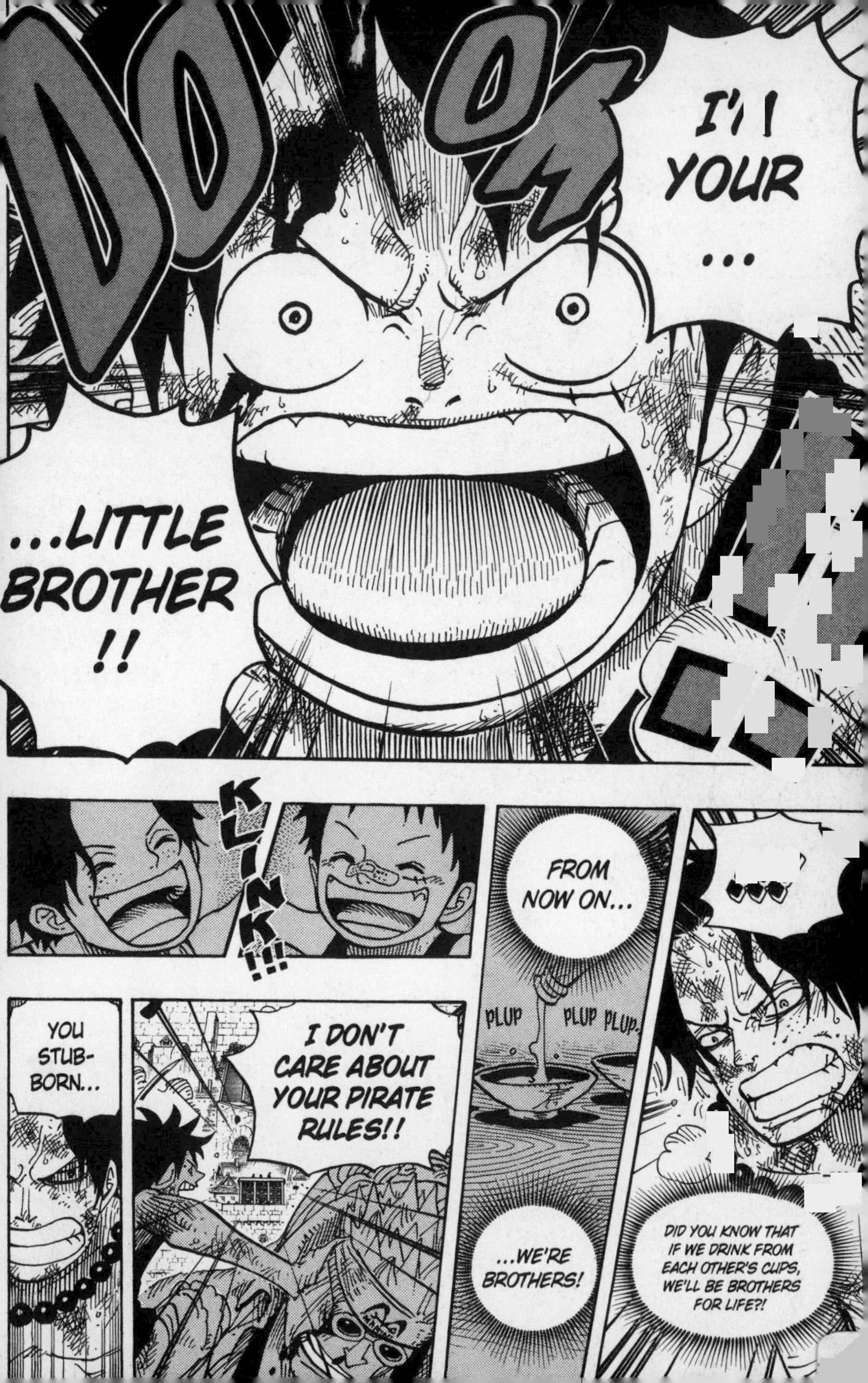
DOOM
I'M YOUR ...
...LITTLE BROTHER!!
DID YOU KNOW THAT IF WE DRINK FROM EACH OTHER'S CUPS, WE'LL BE BROTHERS FOR LIFE?!
FROM NOW ON...
PLUP PLUP PLUP
...WE'RE BROTHERS!
KLINK!!!
I DON'T CARE ABOUT YOUR PIRATE RULES!!
YOU STUB-BORN...

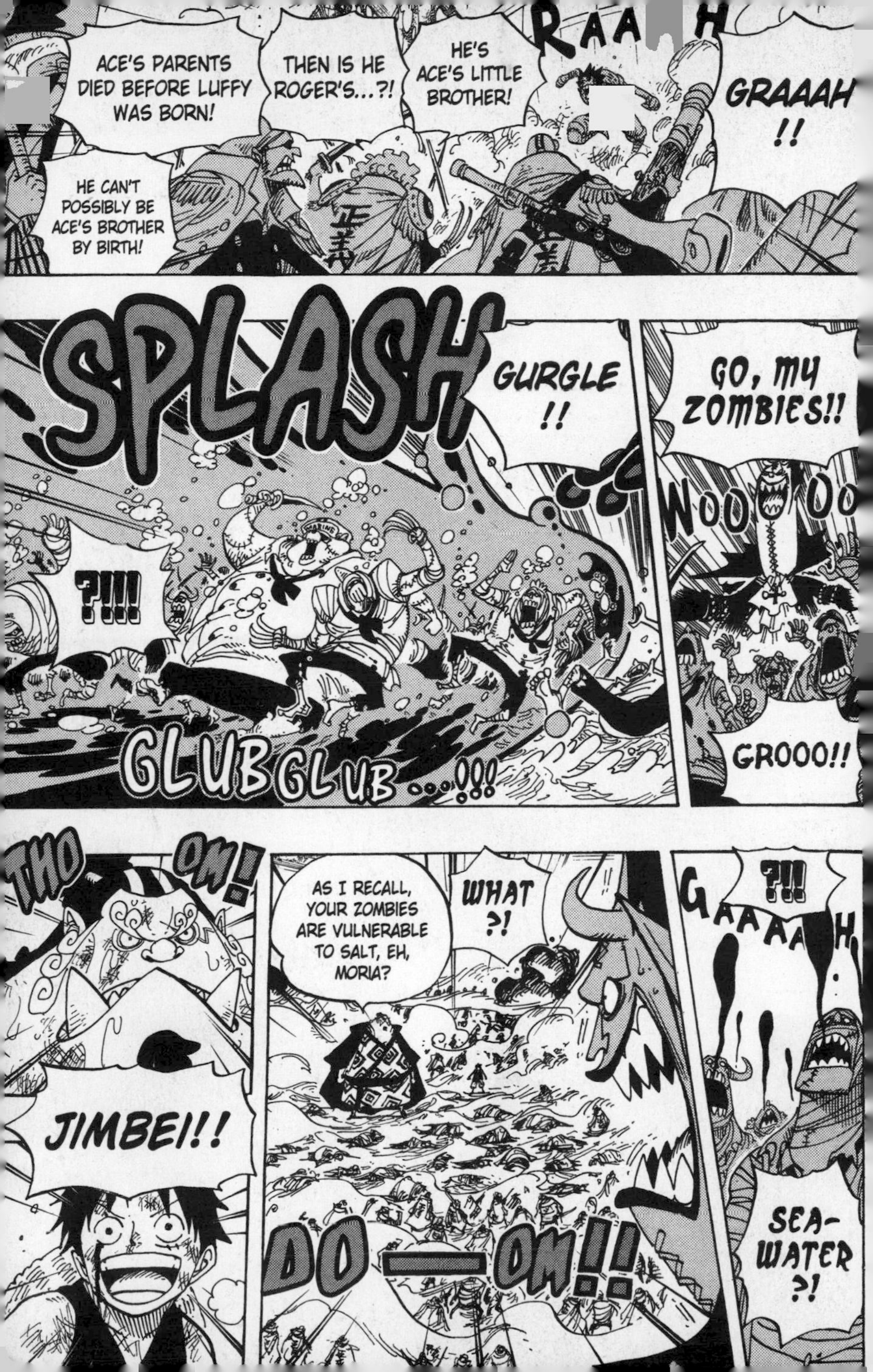
GRAAAH !!
RAA H
HE'S ACE'S LITTLE BROTHER!
THEN IS HE ROGER'S...?!
ACE'S PARENTS DIED BEFORE LUFFY WAS BORN!
HE CAN'T POSSIBLY BE ACE'S BROTHER BY BIRTH!
GO, MY ZOMBIES!!
WOOOO
GROOO!!
GURGLE !!
SPLASH
?!!!
GLUB GLUB...!!!
?!!
GAAAAH
SEA-WATER ?!
WHAT ?!
AS I RECALL, YOUR ZOMBIES ARE VULNERABLE TO SALT, EH, MORIA?
DO—OM!!
THOOM!
JIMBEI!!

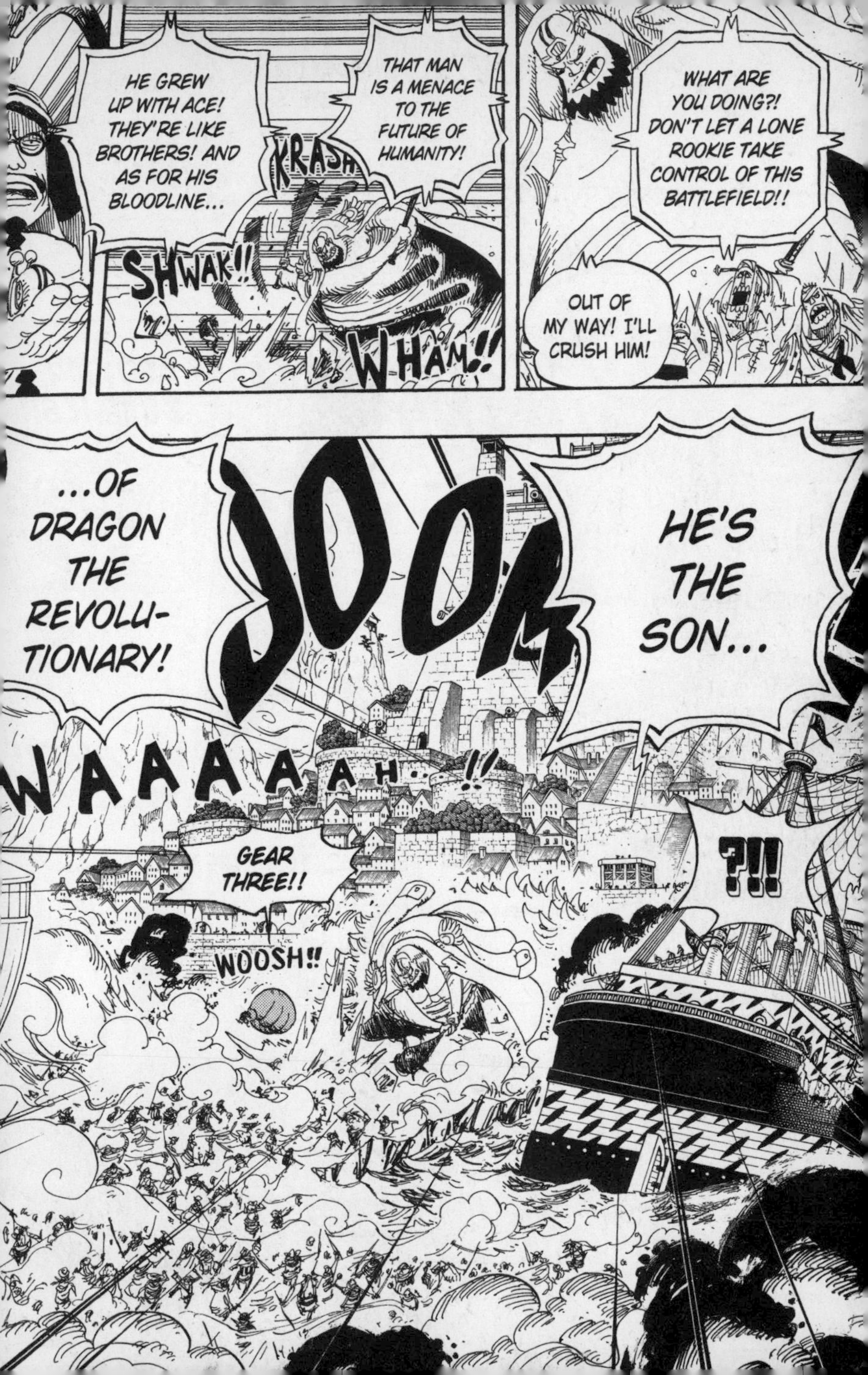
WHAT ARE YOU DOING?! DON'T LET A LONE ROOKIE TAKE CONTROL OF THIS BATTLEFIELD!!
OUT OF MY WAY! I'LL CRUSH HIM!
THAT MAN IS A MENACE TO THE FUTURE OF HUMANITY!
KRASH
SHWAK!!
WHAM!!
HE GREW UP WITH ACE! THEY'RE LIKE BROTHERS! AND AS FOR HIS BLOODLINE...
HE'S THE SON...
...OF DRAGON THE REVOLUTIONARY!
DOOM
?!!
WAAAAAH!!
GEAR THREE!!
WOOSH!!

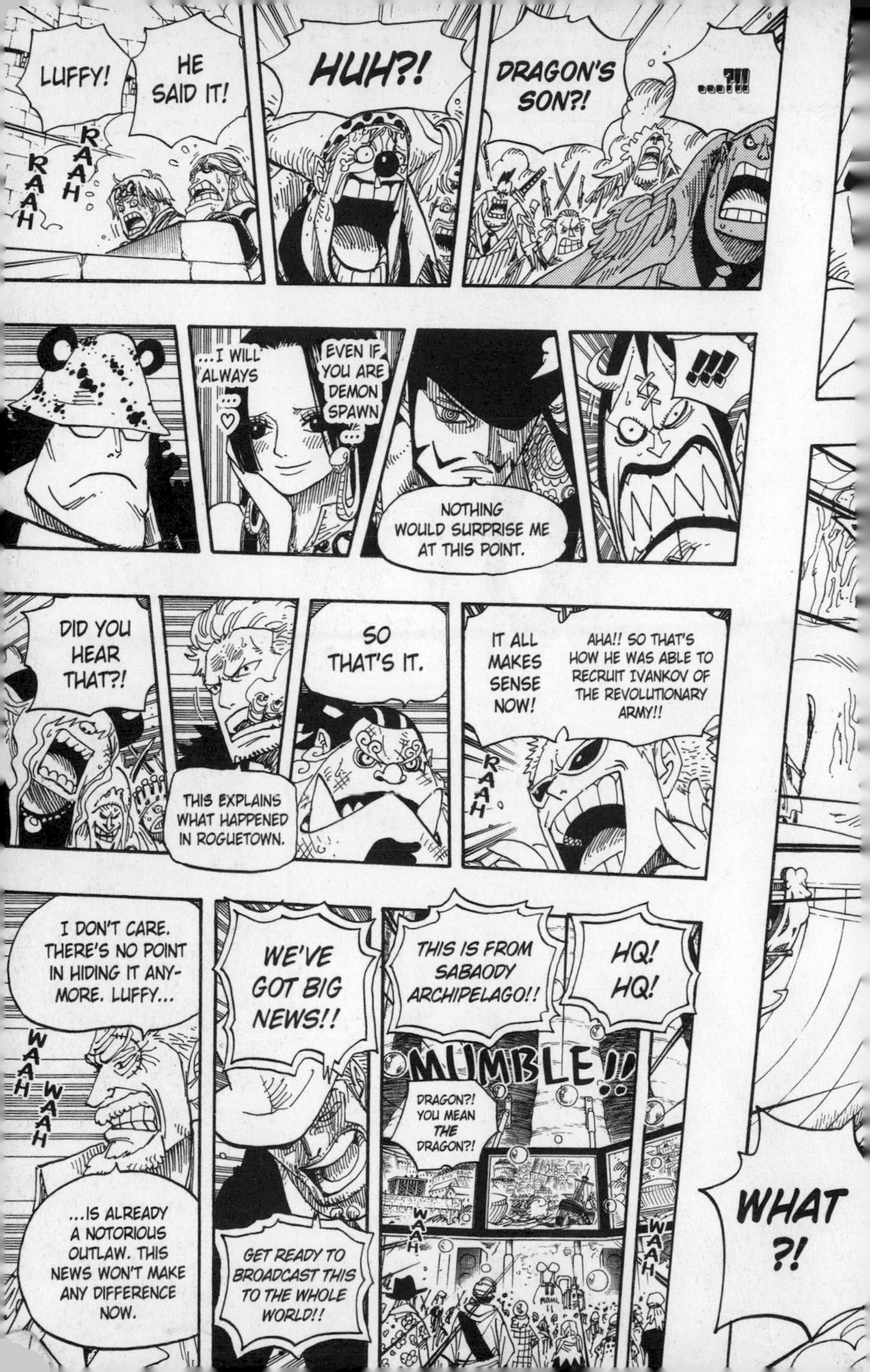
...?!!
DRAGON'S SON?!
HUH?!
HE SAID IT!
LUFFY!
RAAH
RAAH
!!!
NOTHING WOULD SURPRISE ME AT THIS POINT.
EVEN IF YOU ARE DEMON SPAWN
...
...I WILL ALWAYS
...
♥
AHA!! SO THAT'S HOW HE WAS ABLE TO RECRUIT IVANKOV OF THE REVOLUTIONARY ARMY!!
IT ALL MAKES SENSE NOW!
RAAH
SO THAT'S IT.
THIS EXPLAINS WHAT HAPPENED IN ROGUETOWN.
DID YOU HEAR THAT?!
HQ! HQ!
THIS IS FROM SABAODY ARCHIPELAGO!!
MUMBLE!!
DRAGON?! YOU MEAN THE DRAGON?!
WAAH
WAAH
WE'VE GOT BIG NEWS!!
GET READY TO BROADCAST THIS TO THE WHOLE WORLD!!
I DON'T CARE. THERE'S NO POINT IN HIDING IT ANY-MORE. LUFFY...
WAAH
WAAH
...IS ALREADY A NOTORIOUS OUTLAW. THIS NEWS WON'T MAKE ANY DIFFERENCE NOW.
WHAT ?!

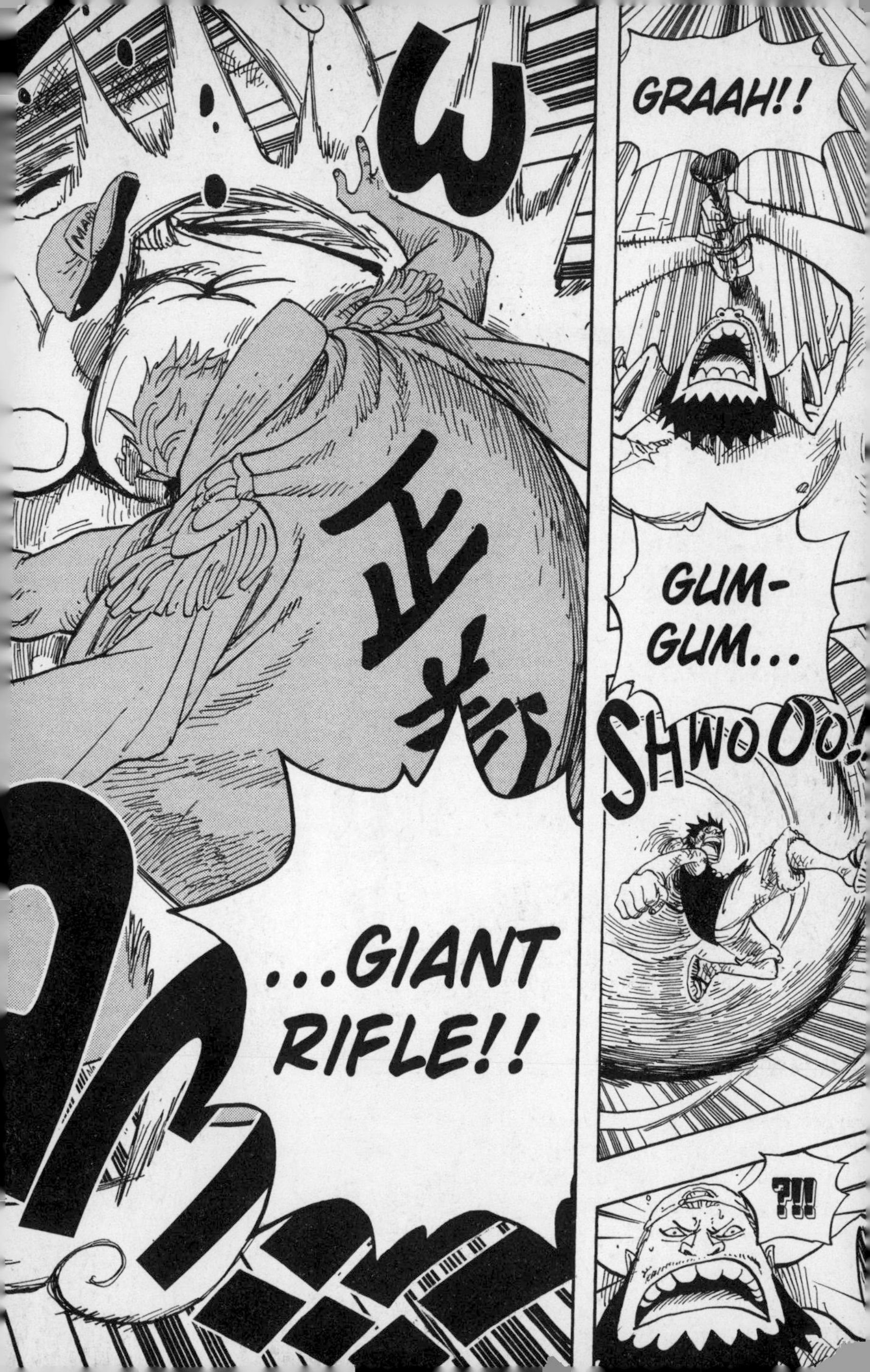
GRAAH!!
GUM-GUM...
SHWOOO!
?!!
...GIANT RIFLE!!

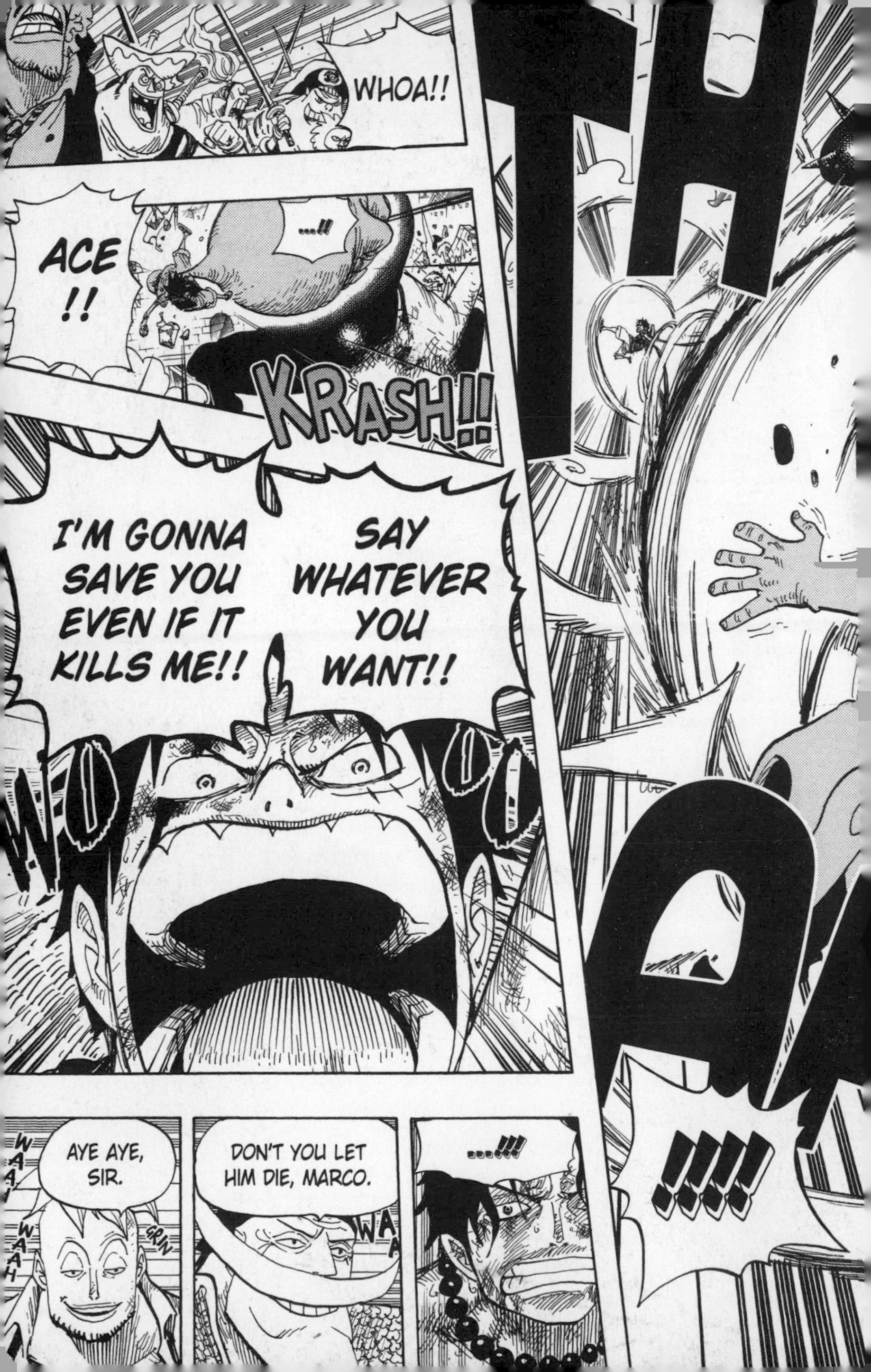
!!!!
WHOA!!
ACE !!
...!!
KRASH!!
I'M GONNA SAVE YOU EVEN IF IT KILLS ME!!
SAY WHATEVER YOU WANT!!
...!!!
DON'T YOU LET HIM DIE, MARCO.
AYE AYE, SIR.
GRIN
WAAH

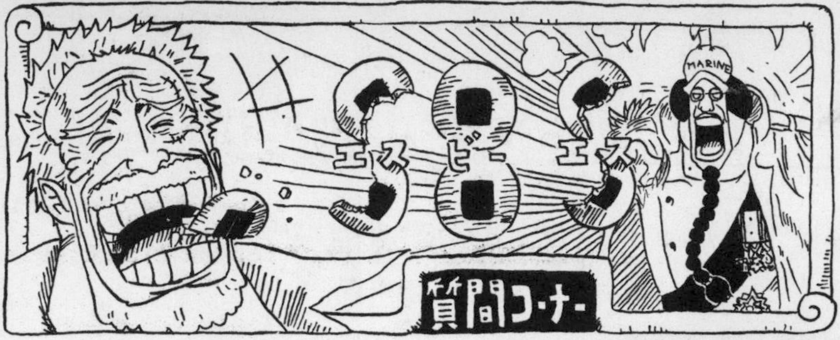
エスビーエス
質問コーナー

(Naoto Kozuka, Aichi)

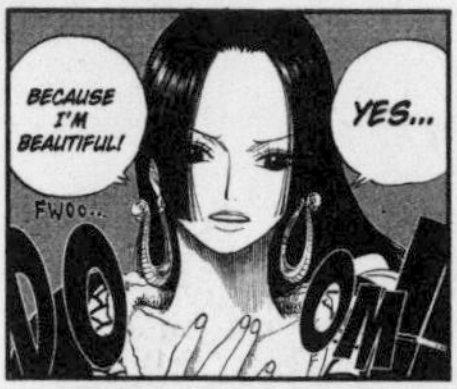
YES...
BECAUSE I'M BEAUTIFUL!
FWOO...
DOOM!

Q: Will Hancock fall in love when she meets me?

--Native Hokkaidoan

A: You're Hannyabal, aren't you! I just know it!

Q: Hello, Mr. Oda! I have a question. Are the three marine "admirals" based on…?

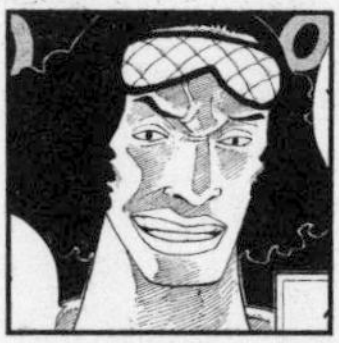

Aokiji
↓
Yusaku Matsuda

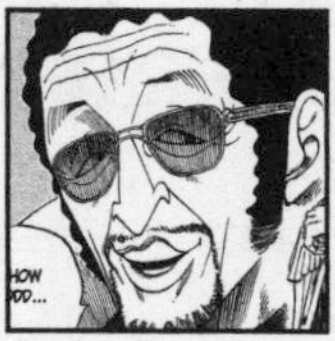

Kizaru
↓
Kunie Tanaka

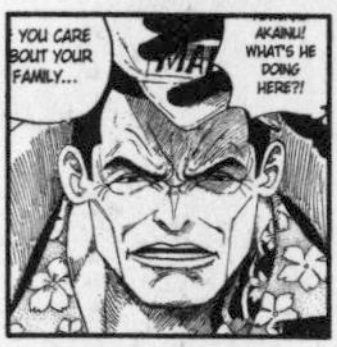
AKAINU! WHAT'S HE DOING HERE?!
YOU CARE BOUT YOUR FAMILY...

Akainu
↓
Bunta Sugawara

Am I right? I'm sorry if I'm not. If possible, can you tell us the reason for picking them too?!

--Mossball

A: Yup. You got all of them. The readers that are still in school right now probably don't know who they are. They are all great Japanese actors. As for why I chose those three, it's because I like them. For Bunta Sugawara, I wanted to use his face from the movie *Battles Without Honor or Humanity*, but his distinctive crew cut hairstyle is hidden under his hat. In short, you can pretty much ignore this because it's just a personal preference of mine. To all the people who didn't know, just think of them as awesome-looking old men. (By the way, he also voiced a role in *Spirited Away*.)

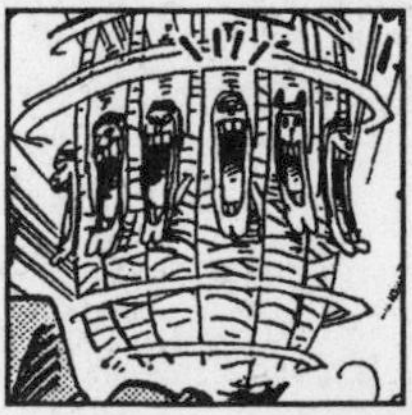

Q: On page 183 of volume 55, Bon turned into Panda Man when he was spinning around. Has Bon touched the face of Panda Man before?

--Man Who Ate the Skinny-Skinny Fruit

A: Hey, you're right! It's there! That does make it true that he touched Panda Man's face. But I have no idea when he did it. Bon has so many surprises.

Chapter 559:
DESTINY

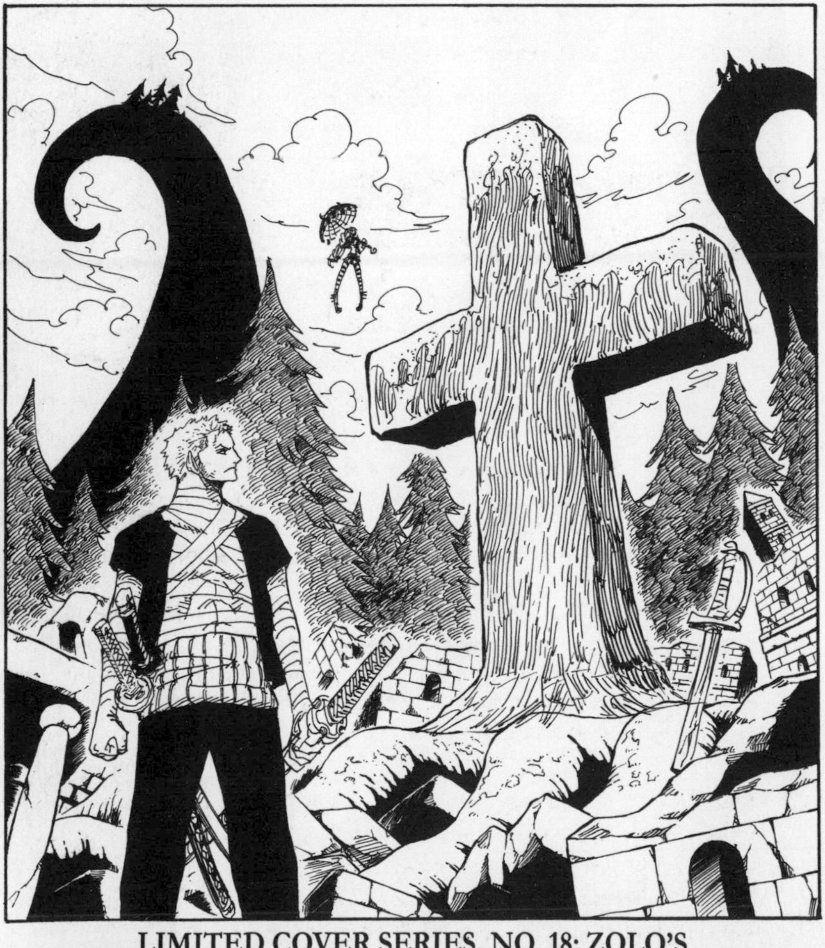

LIMITED COVER SERIES, NO. 18: ZOLO'S
"WHERE ARE THEY? WHAT A PAIN" VOL. 1: "THE GIANT
TOMBSTONE ON THE OUTSKIRTS OF THE RUINS"

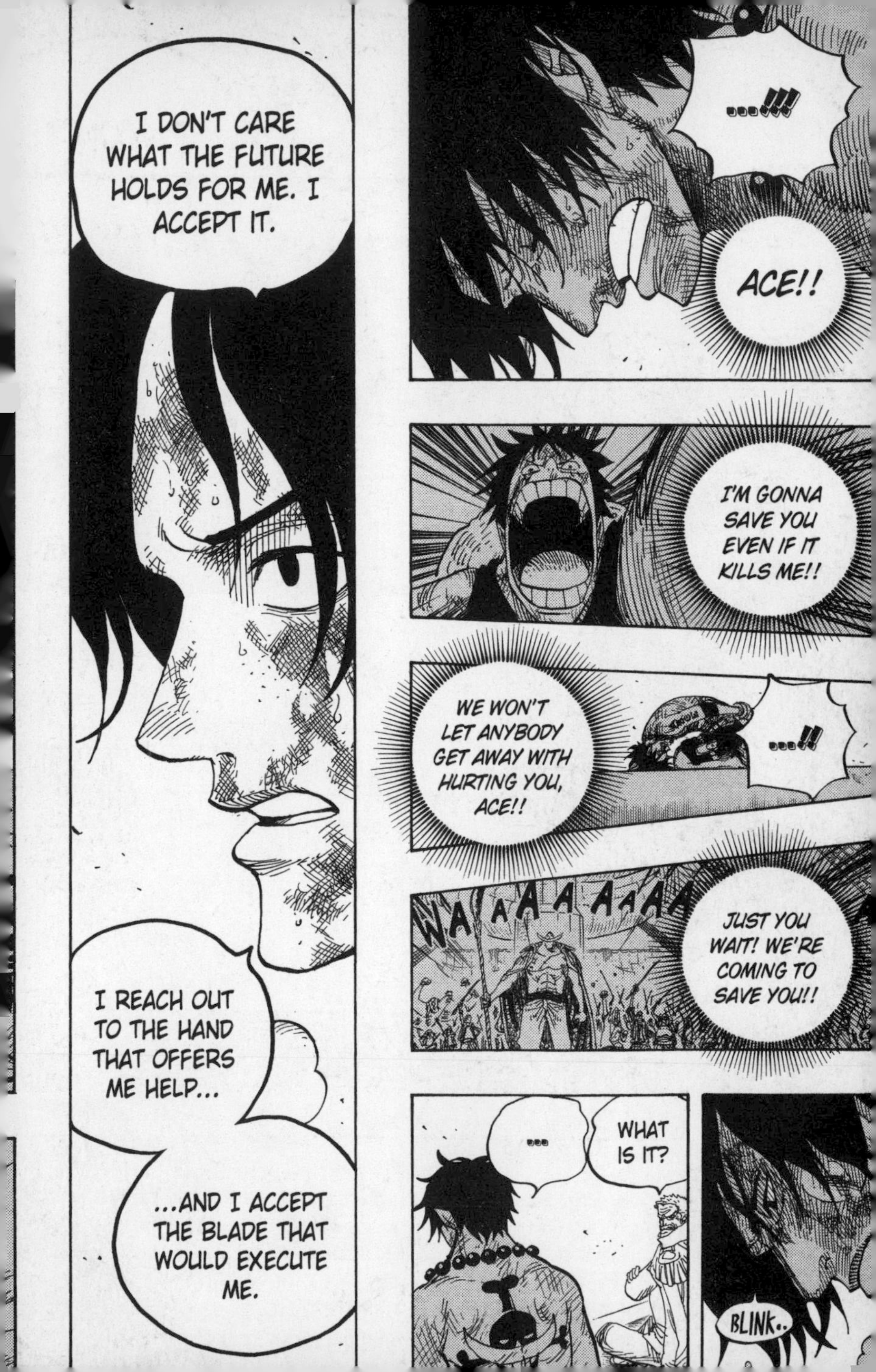
...!!!
ACE!!
I'M GONNA SAVE YOU EVEN IF IT KILLS ME!!
...!!
WE WON'T LET ANYBODY GET AWAY WITH HURTING YOU, ACE!!
JUST YOU WAIT! WE'RE COMING TO SAVE YOU!!
WAAAAAAAAA
BLINK..
WHAT IS IT?
...
I DON'T CARE WHAT THE FUTURE HOLDS FOR ME. I ACCEPT IT.
I REACH OUT TO THE HAND THAT OFFERS ME HELP...
...AND I ACCEPT THE BLADE THAT WOULD EXECUTE ME.

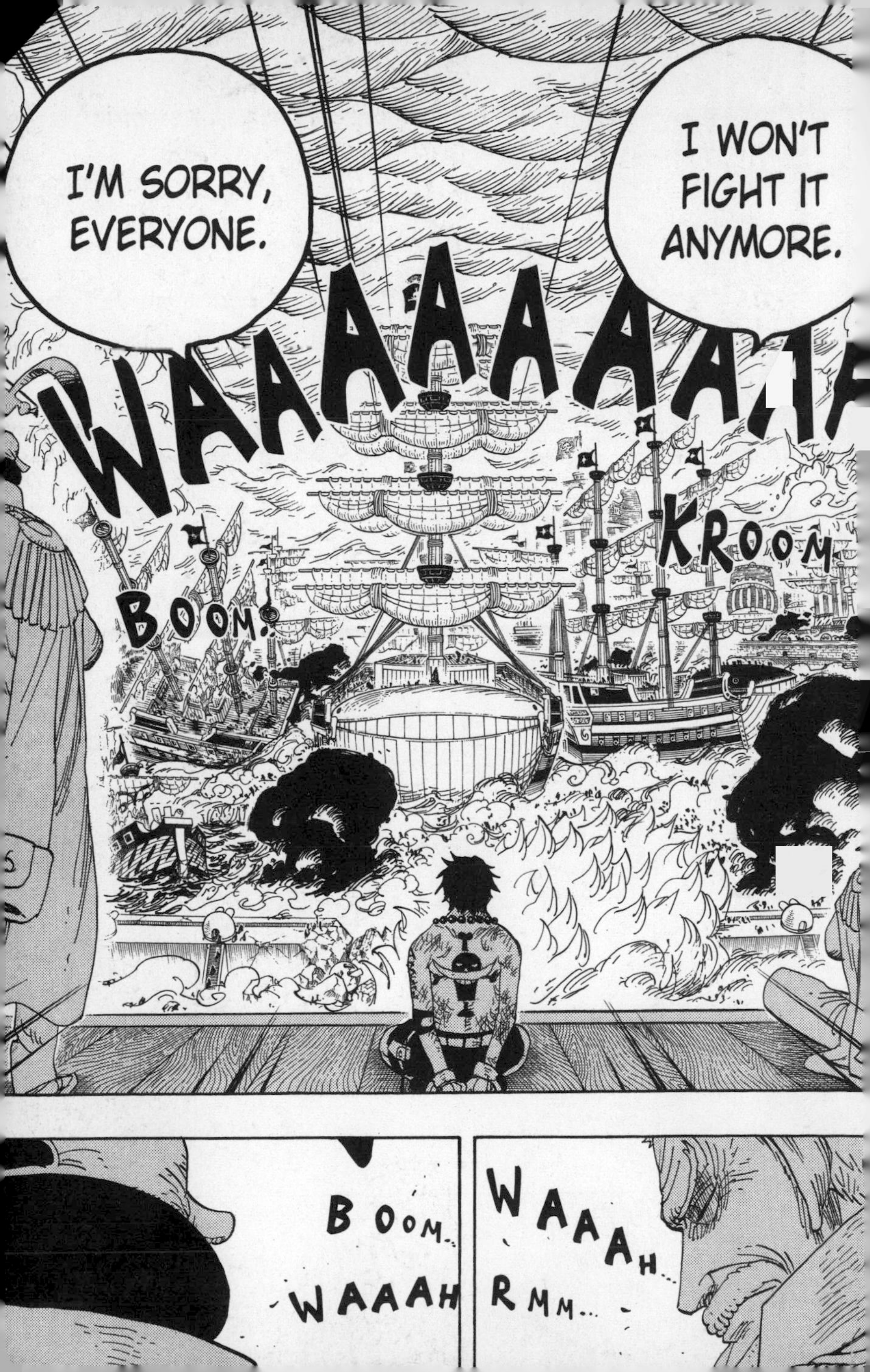
I WON'T FIGHT IT ANYMORE.
I'M SORRY, EVERYONE.
WAAAAAAA
KROOM
BOOM
WAAAH...
RMM...
BOOM...
WAAAH

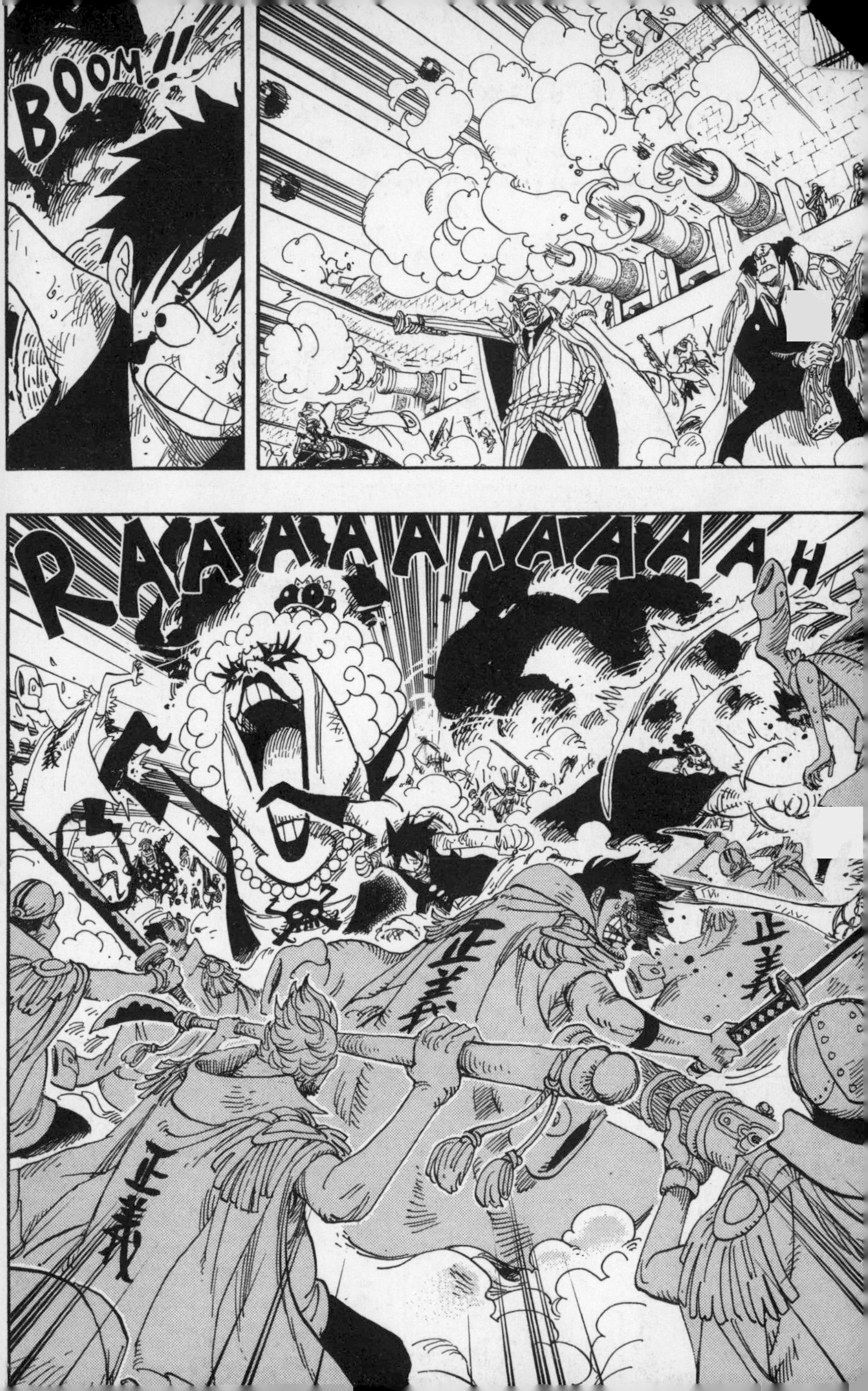
BOOM!!
RAAAAAAAAAAH
正義

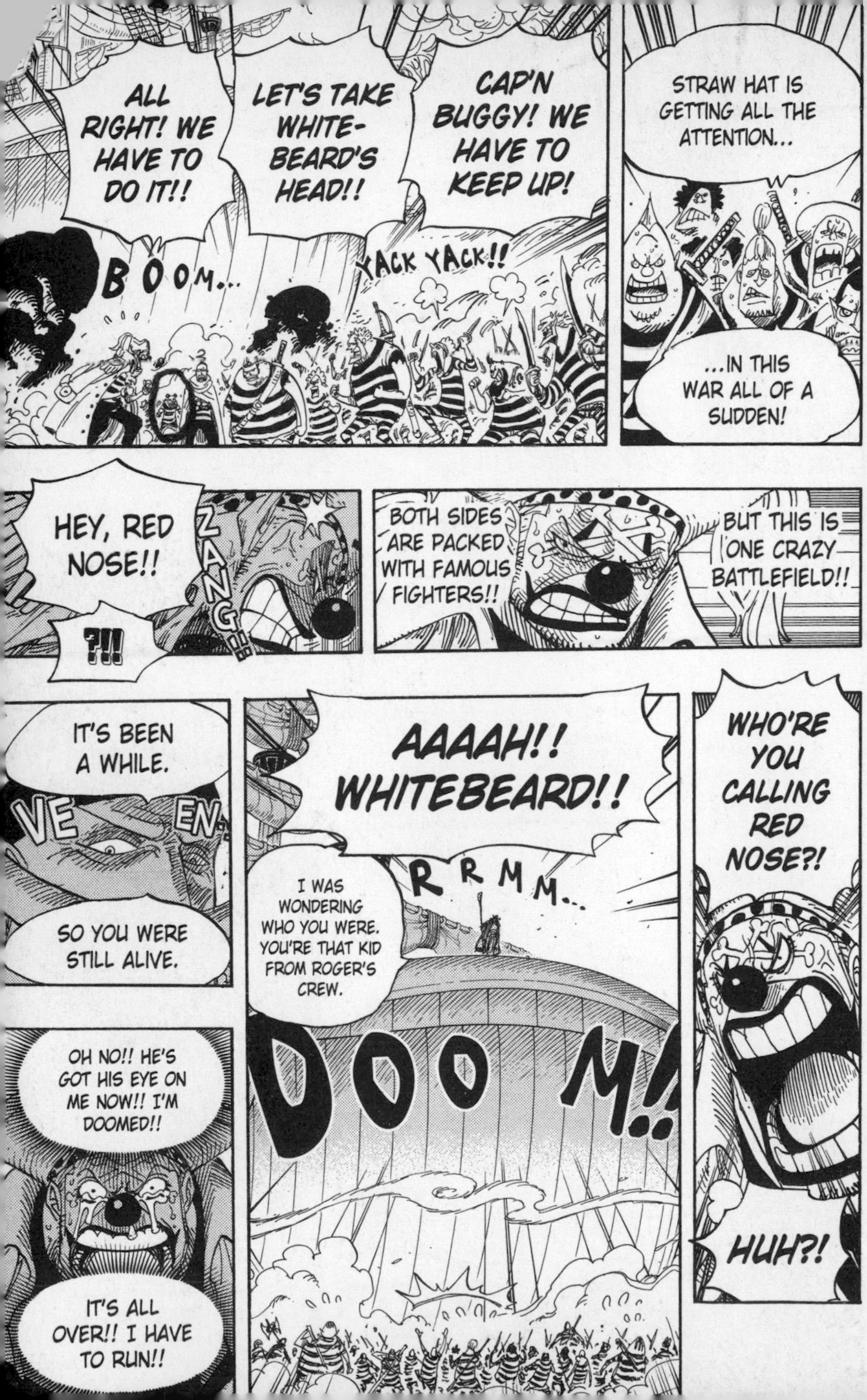
STRAW HAT IS GETTING ALL THE ATTENTION...
...IN THIS WAR ALL OF A SUDDEN!
CAP'N BUGGY! WE HAVE TO KEEP UP!
LET'S TAKE WHITE-BEARD'S HEAD!!
ALL RIGHT! WE HAVE TO DO IT!!
YACK YACK!!
BOOM...
BUT THIS IS ONE CRAZY BATTLEFIELD!!
BOTH SIDES ARE PACKED WITH FAMOUS FIGHTERS!!
ZANG!!
HEY, RED NOSE!!
?!!
WHO'RE YOU CALLING RED NOSE?!
HUH?!
AAAAH!! WHITEBEARD!!
RRMM...
I WAS WONDERING WHO YOU WERE. YOU'RE THAT KID FROM ROGER'S CREW.
DOOM!!
IT'S BEEN A WHILE.
SO YOU WERE STILL ALIVE.
OH NO!! HE'S GOT HIS EYE ON ME NOW!! I'M DOOMED!!
IT'S ALL OVER!! I HAVE TO RUN!!

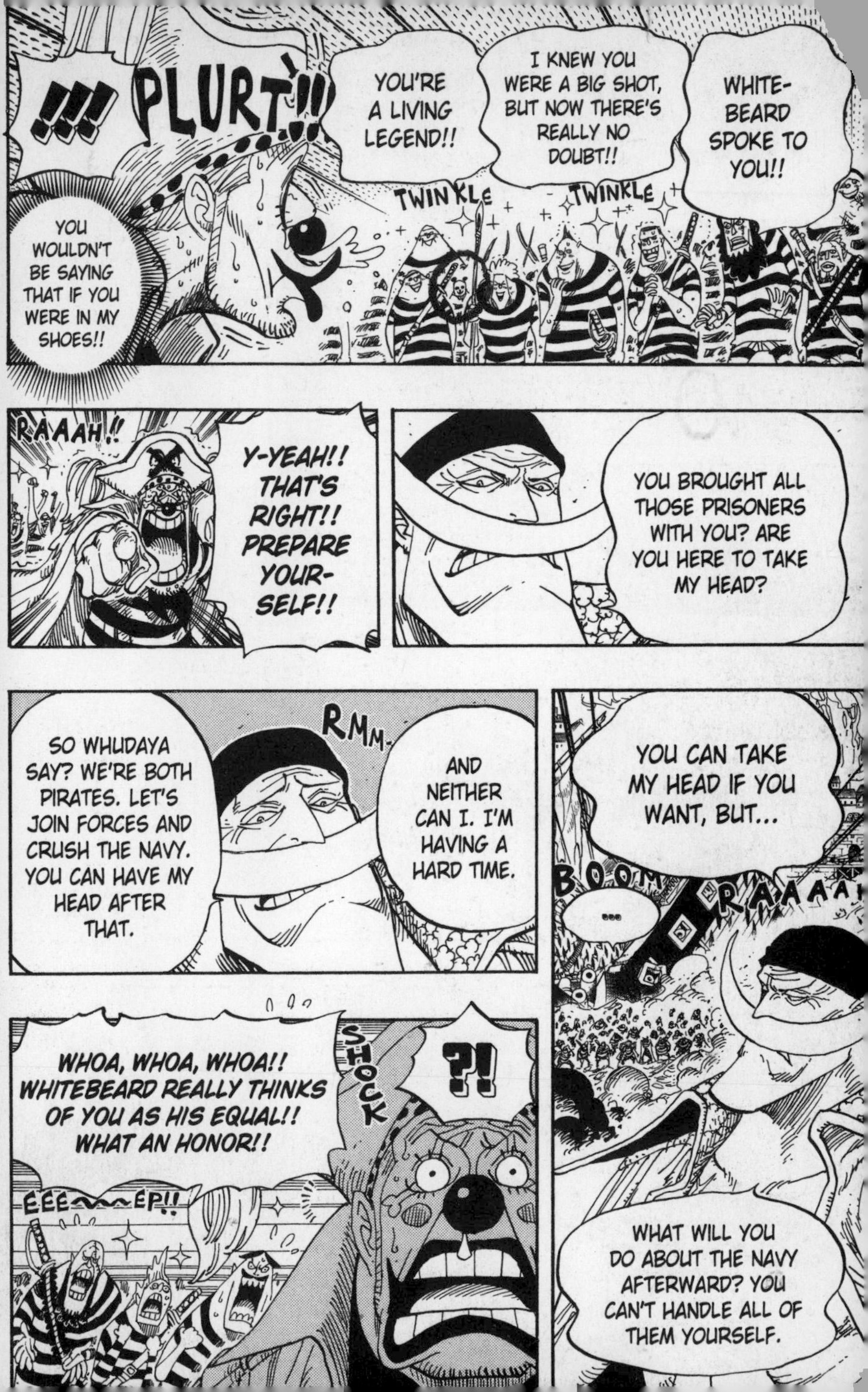
WHITE-BEARD SPOKE TO YOU!!
I KNEW YOU WERE A BIG SHOT, BUT NOW THERE'S REALLY NO DOUBT!!
YOU'RE A LIVING LEGEND!!
TWINKLE
TWINKLE
PLURT!!
!!!
YOU WOULDN'T BE SAYING THAT IF YOU WERE IN MY SHOES!!
YOU BROUGHT ALL THOSE PRISONERS WITH YOU? ARE YOU HERE TO TAKE MY HEAD?
Y-YEAH!! THAT'S RIGHT!! PREPARE YOURSELF!!
RAAAH!!
YOU CAN TAKE MY HEAD IF YOU WANT, BUT...
BOOM
RAAAA!
...
WHAT WILL YOU DO ABOUT THE NAVY AFTERWARD? YOU CAN'T HANDLE ALL OF THEM YOURSELF.
RMM-
AND NEITHER CAN I. I'M HAVING A HARD TIME.
SO WHUDAYA SAY? WE'RE BOTH PIRATES. LET'S JOIN FORCES AND CRUSH THE NAVY. YOU CAN HAVE MY HEAD AFTER THAT.
?!
SHOCK
WHOA, WHOA, WHOA!! WHITEBEARD REALLY THINKS OF YOU AS HIS EQUAL!! WHAT AN HONOR!!
EEE~~EP!!

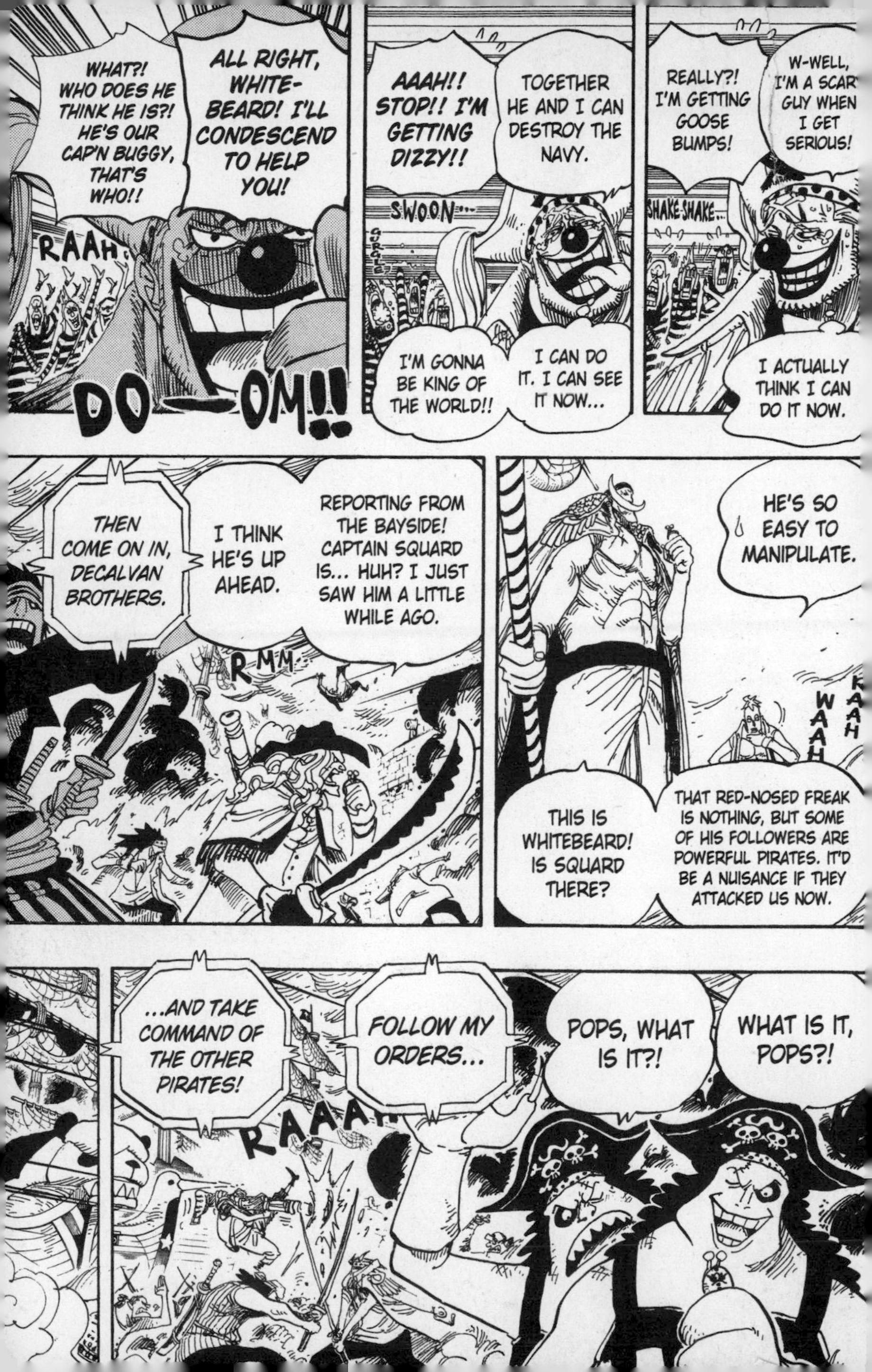
W-WELL, I'M A SCAR GUY WHEN I GET SERIOUS!
REALLY?! I'M GETTING GOOSE BUMPS!
SHAKE SHAKE...
I ACTUALLY THINK I CAN DO IT NOW.
TOGETHER HE AND I CAN DESTROY THE NAVY.
AAAH!! STOP!! I'M GETTING DIZZY!!
SWOON...
GURGLE
I CAN DO IT. I CAN SEE IT NOW...
I'M GONNA BE KING OF THE WORLD!!
ALL RIGHT, WHITE-BEARD! I'LL CONDESCEND TO HELP YOU!
WHAT?! WHO DOES HE THINK HE IS?! HE'S OUR CAP'N BUGGY, THAT'S WHO!!
RAAH
DO—OM!!
HE'S SO EASY TO MANIPULATE.
WAAAH
KAAAH
THAT RED-NOSED FREAK IS NOTHING, BUT SOME OF HIS FOLLOWERS ARE POWERFUL PIRATES. IT'D BE A NUISANCE IF THEY ATTACKED US NOW.
THIS IS WHITEBEARD! IS SQUARD THERE?
REPORTING FROM THE BAYSIDE! CAPTAIN SQUARD IS... HUH? I JUST SAW HIM A LITTLE WHILE AGO.
I THINK HE'S UP AHEAD.
THEN COME ON IN, DECALVAN BROTHERS.
RMM
WHAT IS IT, POPS?!
POPS, WHAT IS IT?!
FOLLOW MY ORDERS...
...AND TAKE COMMAND OF THE OTHER PIRATES!
RAAA

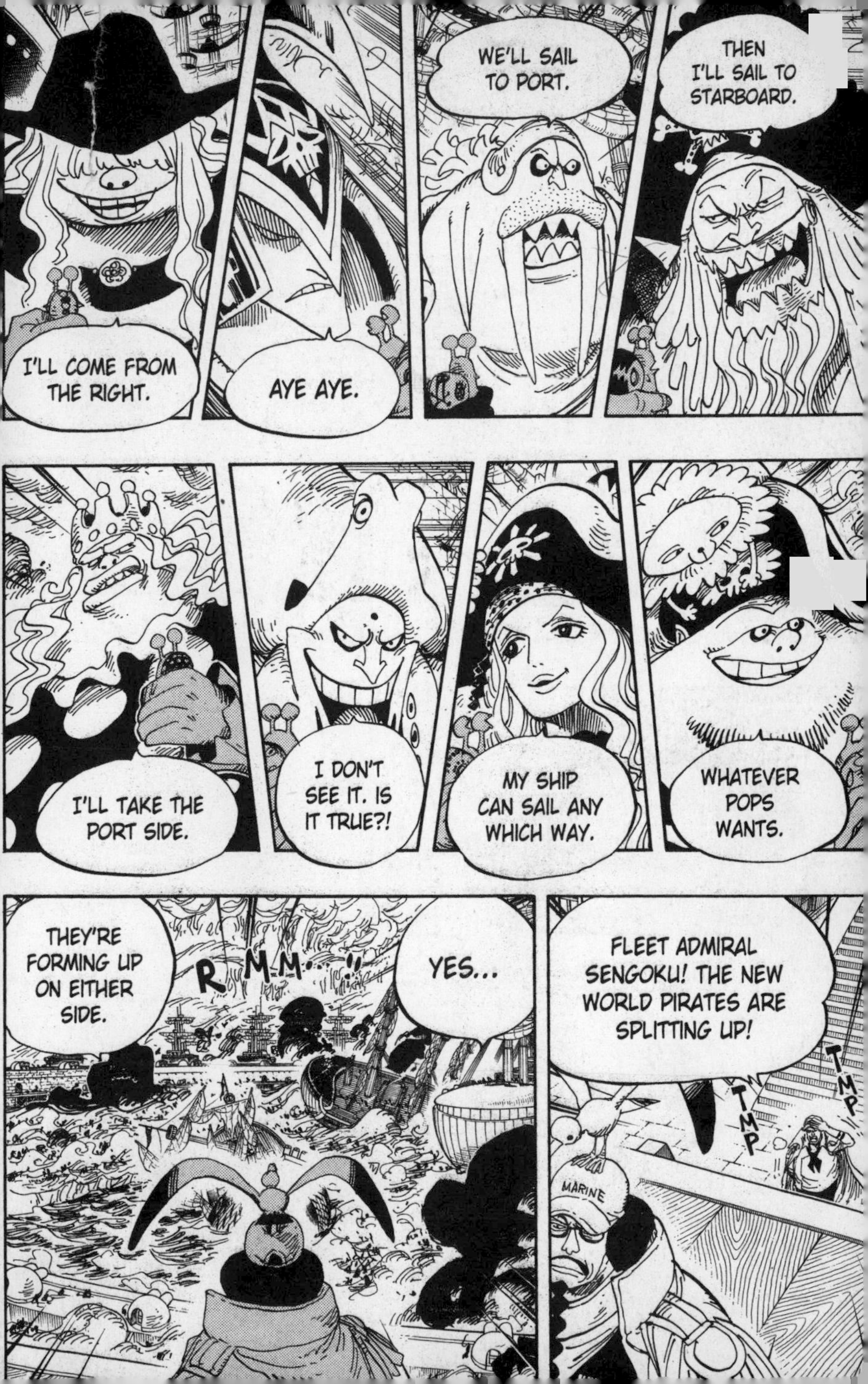
THEN I'LL SAIL TO STARBOARD.
WE'LL SAIL TO PORT.
AYE AYE.
I'LL COME FROM THE RIGHT.
WHATEVER POPS WANTS.
MY SHIP CAN SAIL ANY WHICH WAY.
I DON'T SEE IT. IS IT TRUE?!
I'LL TAKE THE PORT SIDE.
FLEET ADMIRAL SENGOKU! THE NEW WORLD PIRATES ARE SPLITTING UP!
TMP
TMP
MARINE
YES...
RMM...!!
THEY'RE FORMING UP ON EITHER SIDE.

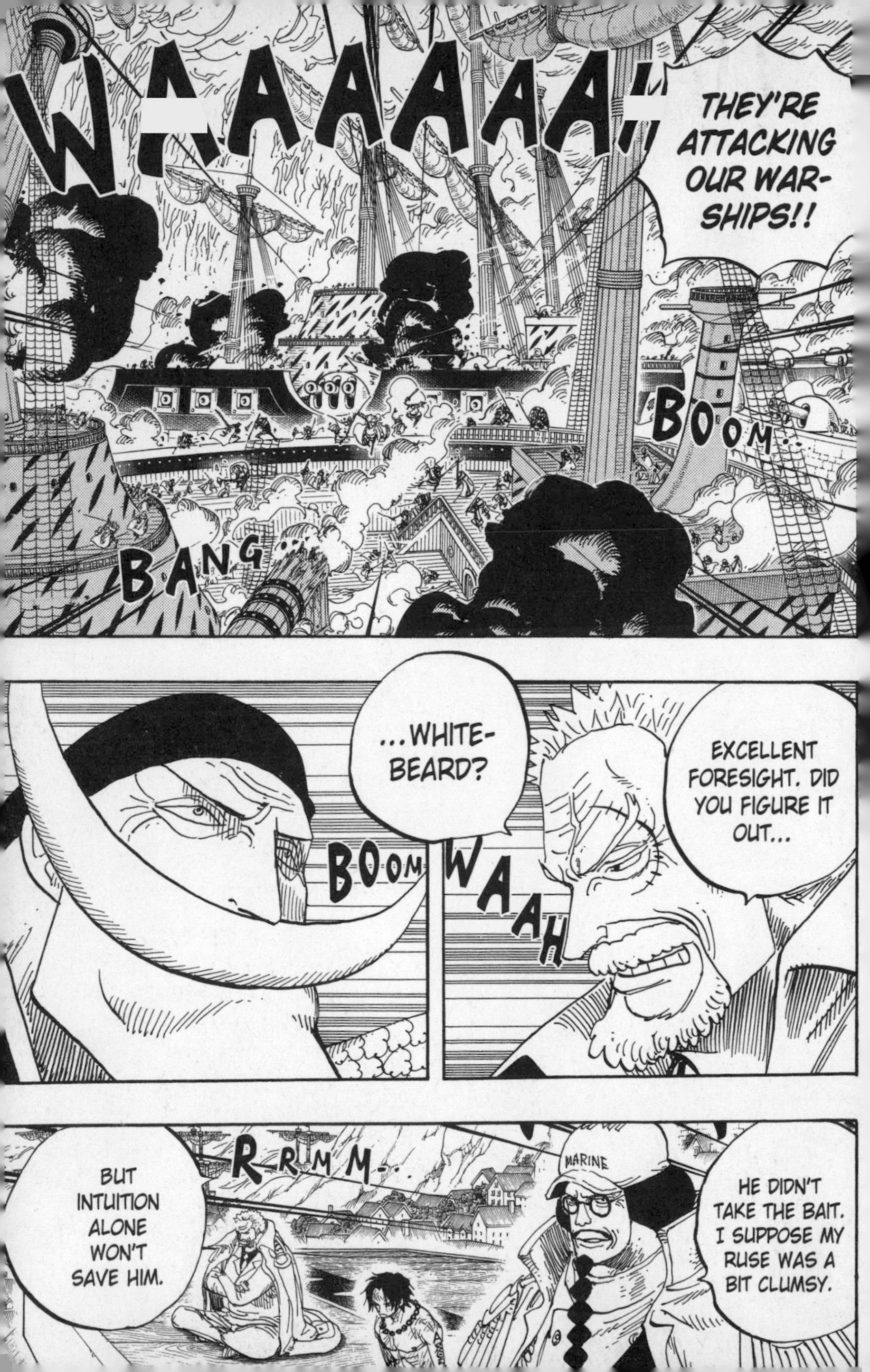
THEY'RE ATTACKING OUR WAR-SHIPS!!
WAAAAA!
BOOM...
BANG
EXCELLENT FORESIGHT. DID YOU FIGURE IT OUT...
WAAH
...WHITE-BEARD?
BOOM
HE DIDN'T TAKE THE BAIT. I SUPPOSE MY RUSE WAS A BIT CLUMSY.
MARINE
RRMM...
BUT INTUITION ALONE WON'T SAVE HIM.

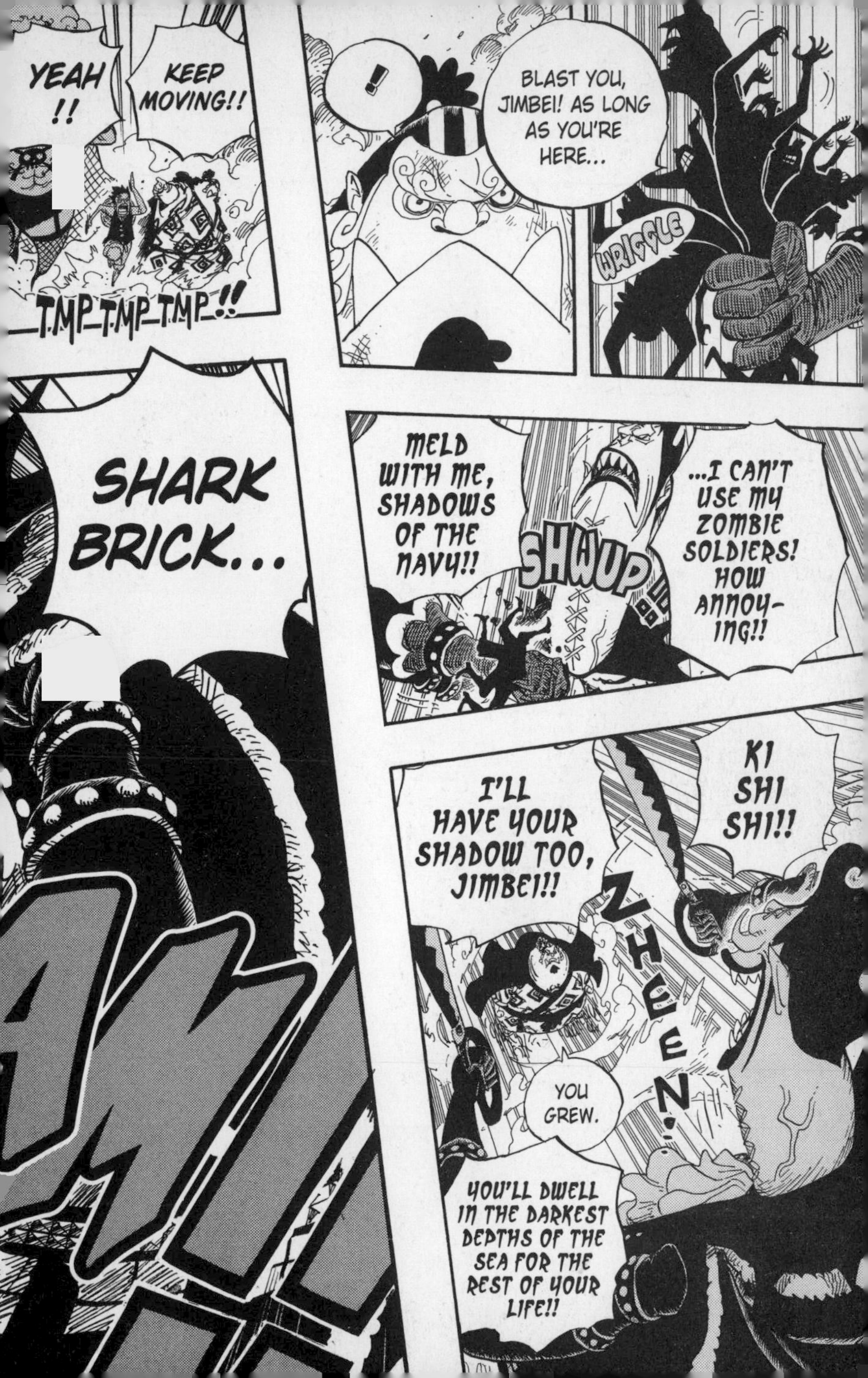
WRIGGLE
!
BLAST YOU, JIMBEI! AS LONG AS YOU'RE HERE...
KEEP MOVING!!
YEAH!!
T.MP T.MP T.MP!!
...I CAN'T USE MY ZOMBIE SOLDIERS! HOW ANNOY-ING!!
MELD WITH ME, SHADOWS OF THE NAVY!!
SHWUP
KI SHI SHI!!
I'LL HAVE YOUR SHADOW TOO, JIMBEI!!
ZHEEN!
YOU GREW.
YOU'LL DWELL IN THE DARKEST DEPTHS OF THE SEA FOR THE REST OF YOUR LIFE!!
SHARK BRICK...

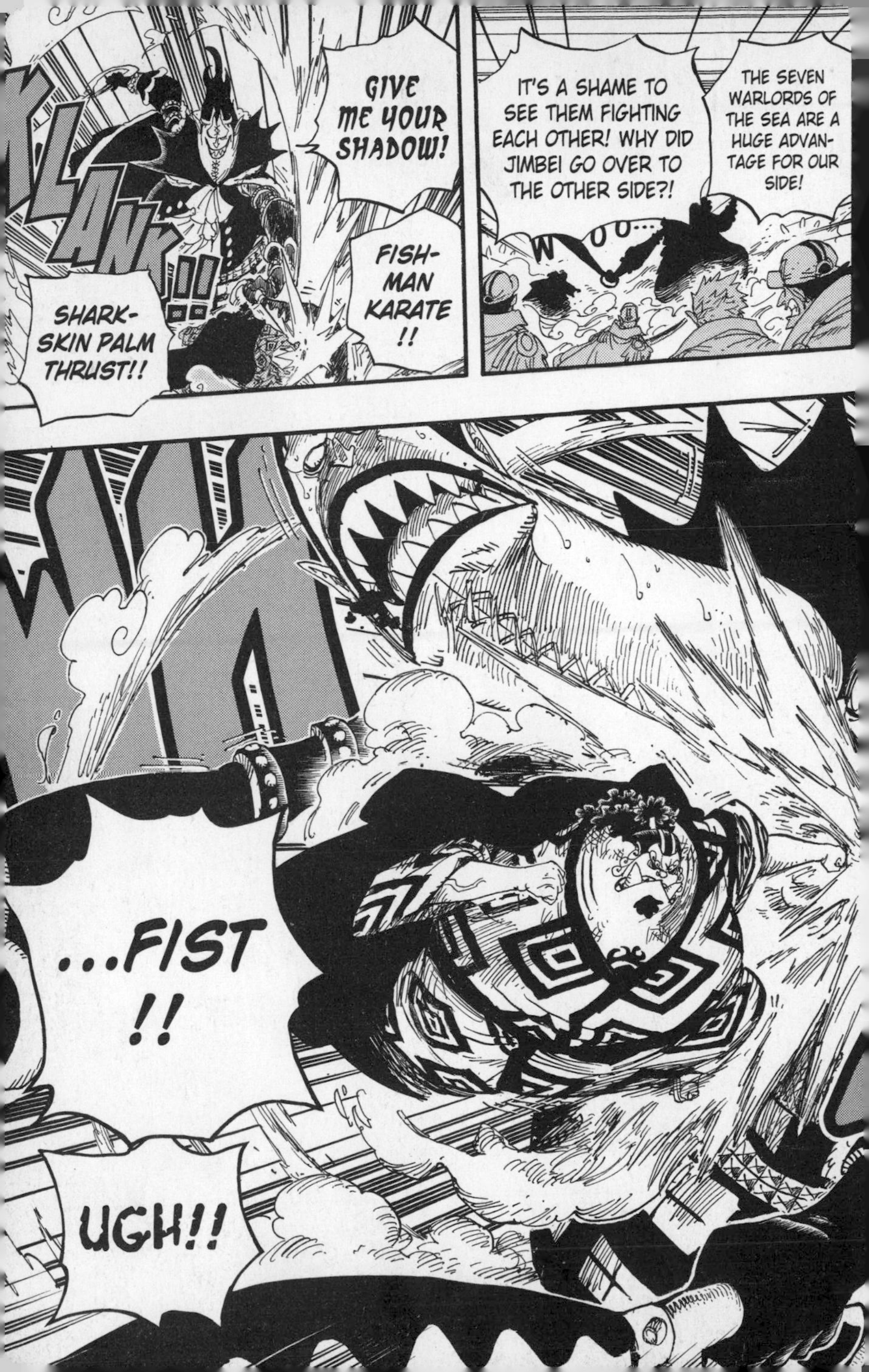
THE SEVEN WARLORDS OF THE SEA ARE A HUGE ADVANTAGE FOR OUR SIDE!
IT'S A SHAME TO SEE THEM FIGHTING EACH OTHER! WHY DID JIMBEI GO OVER TO THE OTHER SIDE?!
WOO...
GIVE ME YOUR SHADOW!
FISH-MAN KARATE!!
KLANK!!
SHARK-SKIN PALM THRUST!!
...FIST!!
UGH!!

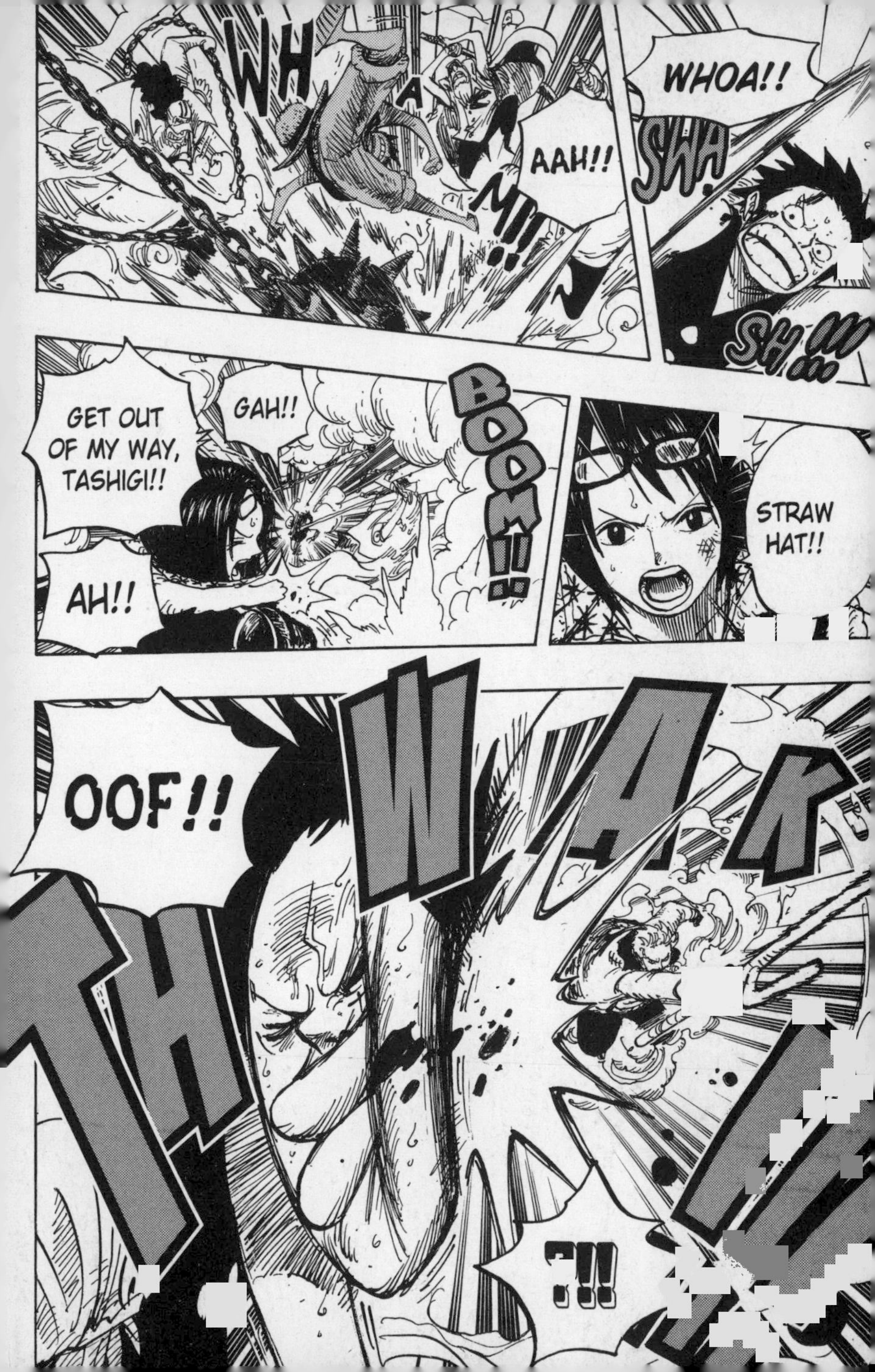
WHOA!!
SWA
SH...
WH
A
AAH!!
M!!
STRAW HAT!!
BOOM!!
GAH!!
GET OUT OF MY WAY, TASHIGI!!
AH!!
W
A
K
OOF!!
TH
?!!

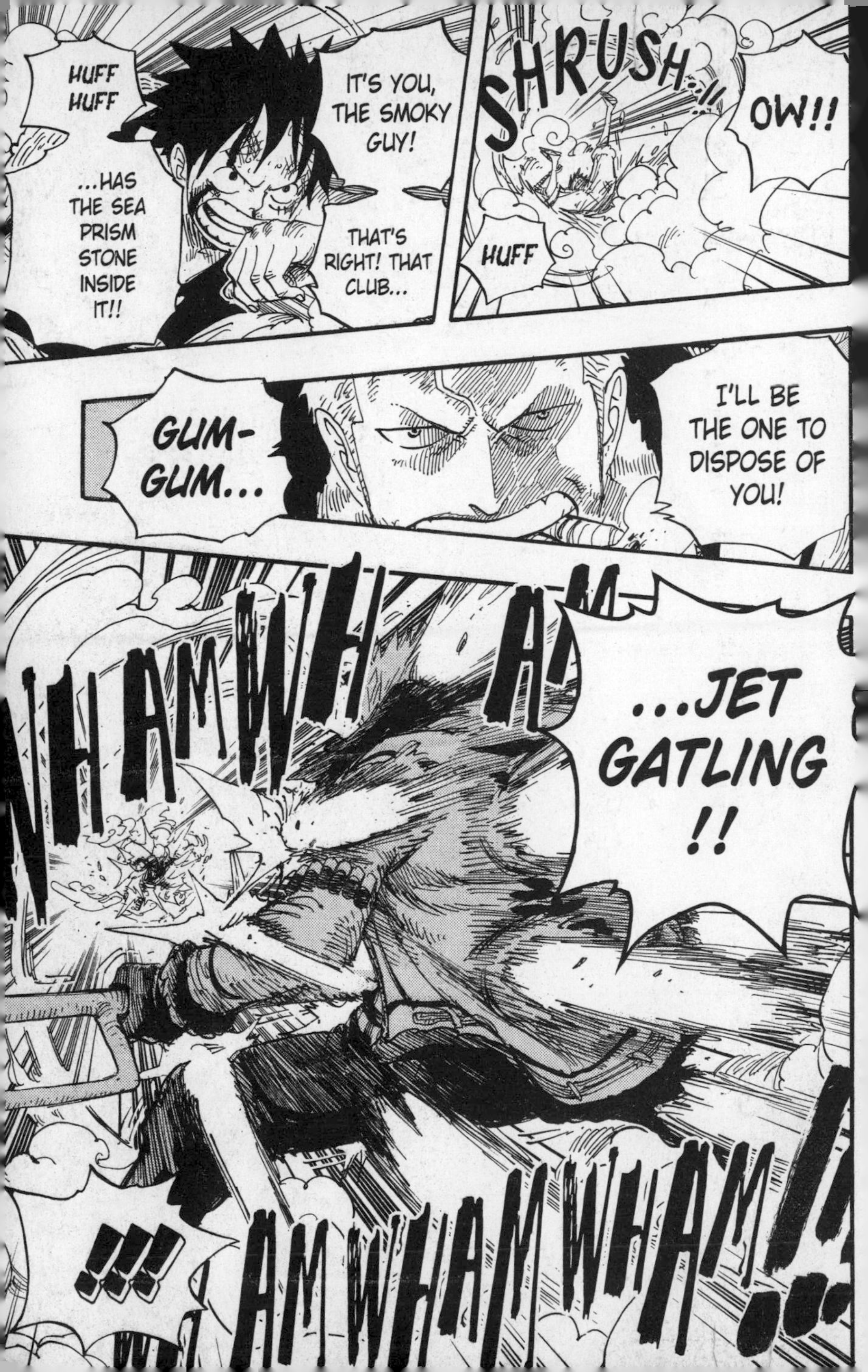
OW!!
SHRUSH...!!
HUFF
IT'S YOU, THE SMOKY GUY!
HUFF HUFF
THAT'S RIGHT! THAT CLUB...
...HAS THE SEA PRISM STONE INSIDE IT!!
I'LL BE THE ONE TO DISPOSE OF YOU!
GUM-GUM...
...JET GATLING!!
WHAM WHAM
AM WHAM WHAM!!

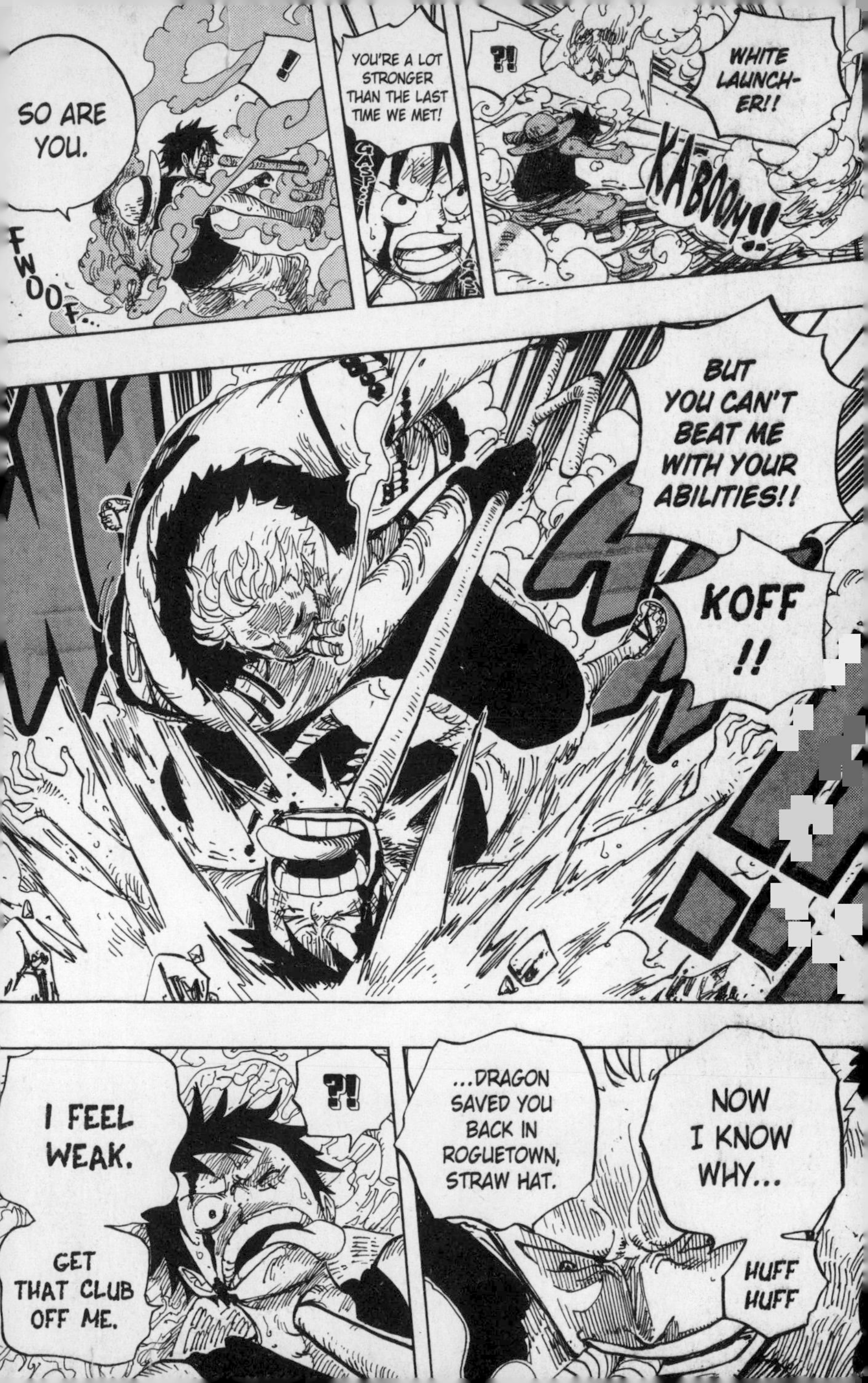
WHITE LAUNCH-ER!!
?!
KABOOM!!
YOU'RE A LOT STRONGER THAN THE LAST TIME WE MET!
!
SO ARE YOU.
FWOOF...
BUT YOU CAN'T BEAT ME WITH YOUR ABILITIES!!
KOFF !!
NOW I KNOW WHY...
...DRAGON SAVED YOU BACK IN ROGUETOWN, STRAW HAT.
HUFF HUFF
?!
I FEEL WEAK.
GET THAT CLUB OFF ME.

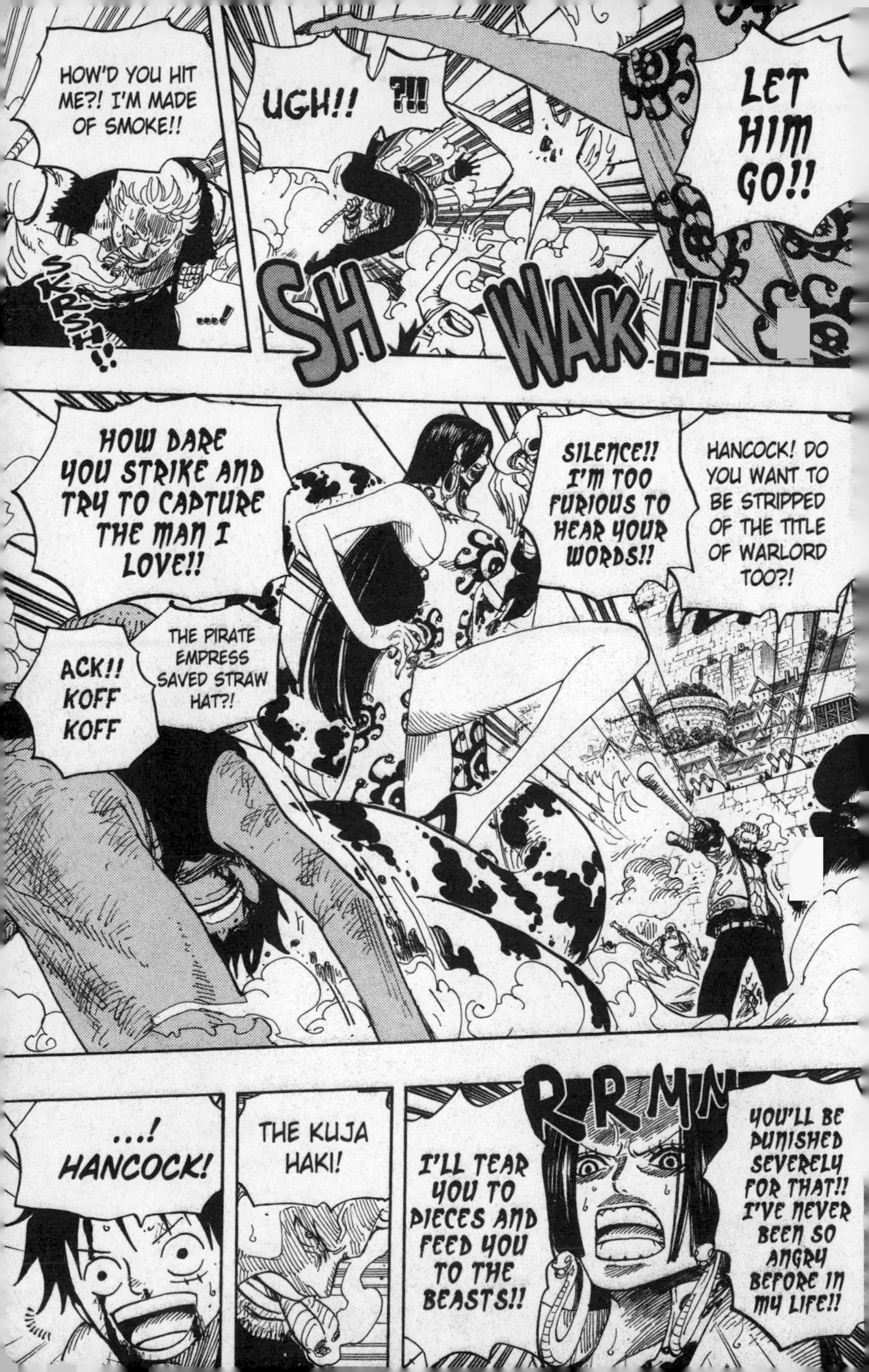
LET HIM GO!!
UGH!!
?!!
SH WAK!!
HOW'D YOU HIT ME?! I'M MADE OF SMOKE!!
SKRSH!!
...!
HANCOCK! DO YOU WANT TO BE STRIPPED OF THE TITLE OF WARLORD TOO?!
SILENCE!! I'M TOO FURIOUS TO HEAR YOUR WORDS!!
HOW DARE YOU STRIKE AND TRY TO CAPTURE THE MAN I LOVE!!
THE PIRATE EMPRESS SAVED STRAW HAT?!
ACK!! KOFF KOFF
RRMN
YOU'LL BE PUNISHED SEVERELY FOR THAT!! I'VE NEVER BEEN SO ANGRY BEFORE IN MY LIFE!!
I'LL TEAR YOU TO PIECES AND FEED YOU TO THE BEASTS!!
THE KUJA HAKI!
...! HANCOCK!

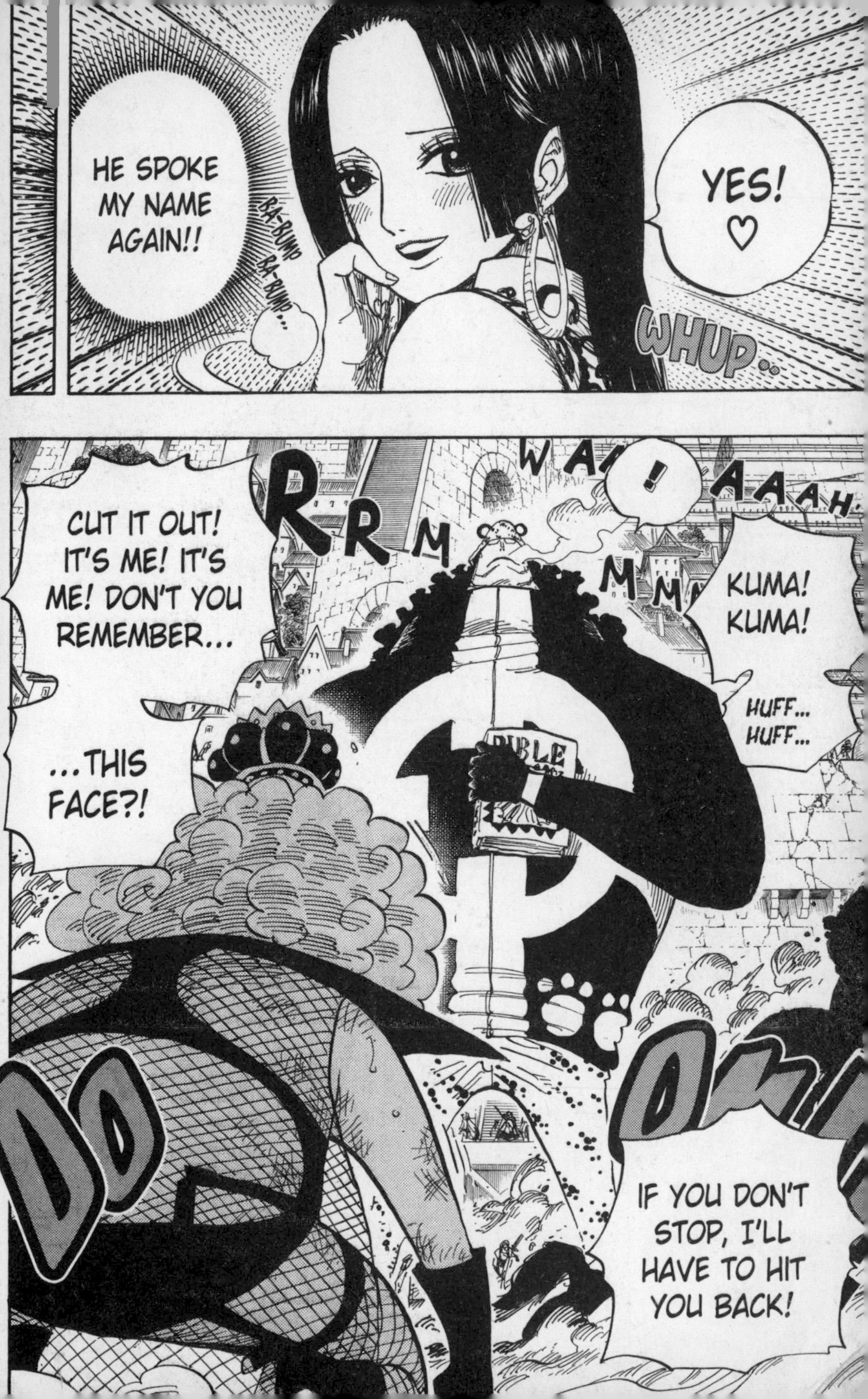
YES! ♥
WHUP..
HE SPOKE MY NAME AGAIN!!
BA-BUMP BA-BUMP...
WA AAAH
!
RRMMM
KUMA! KUMA!
HUFF... HUFF...
CUT IT OUT! IT'S ME! IT'S ME! DON'T YOU REMEMBER...
...THIS FACE?!
IF YOU DON'T STOP, I'LL HAVE TO HIT YOU BACK!
DO

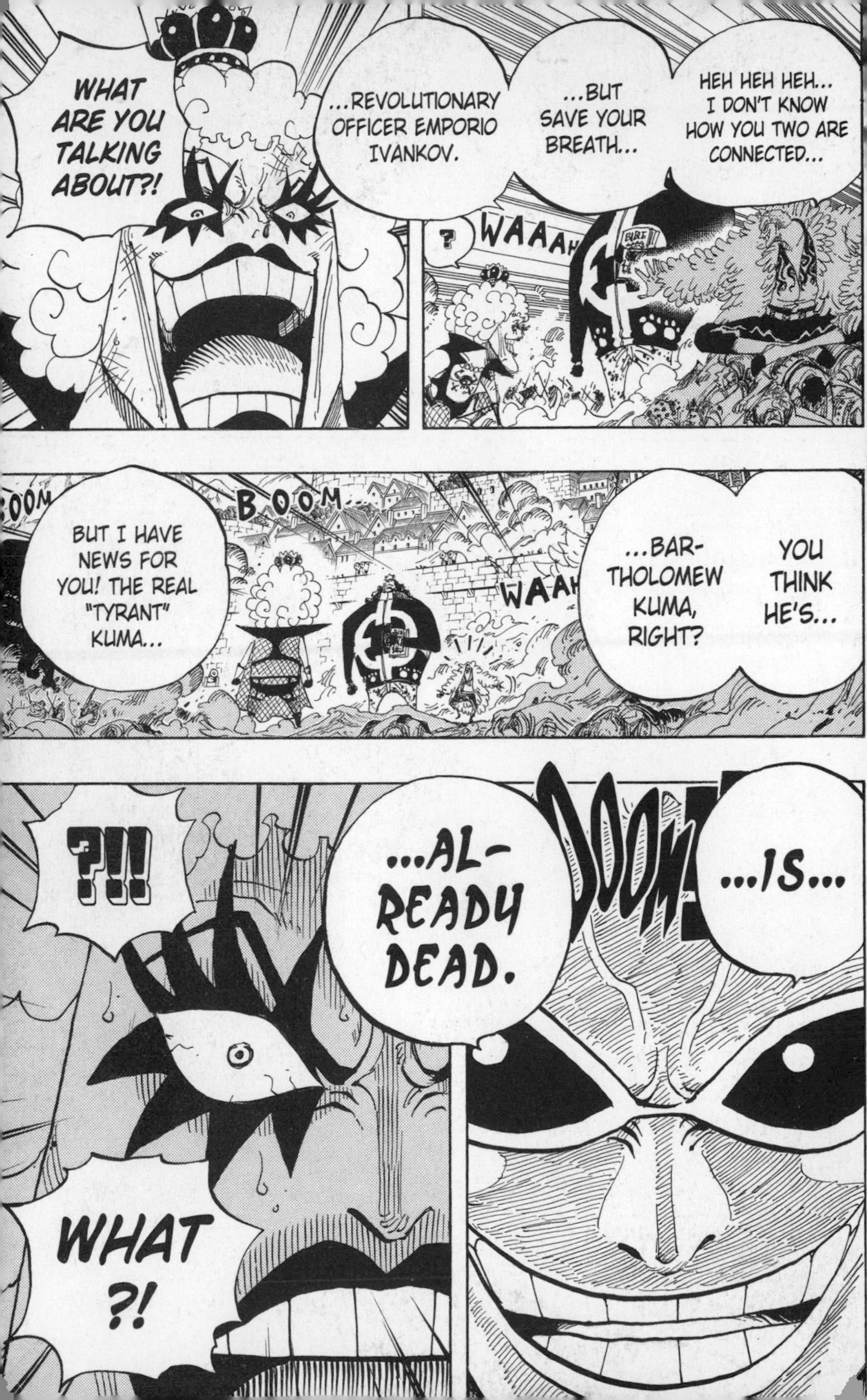
HEH HEH HEH... I DON'T KNOW HOW YOU TWO ARE CONNECTED...
...BUT SAVE YOUR BREATH...
...REVOLUTIONARY OFFICER EMPORIO IVANKOV.
?
WAAAH
WHAT ARE YOU TALKING ABOUT?!
YOU THINK HE'S...
...BAR-THOLOMEW KUMA, RIGHT?
WAAAH
BOOM
BUT I HAVE NEWS FOR YOU! THE REAL "TYRANT" KUMA...
OOM
...IS...
DOOM
...AL-READY DEAD.
?!!
WHAT ?!

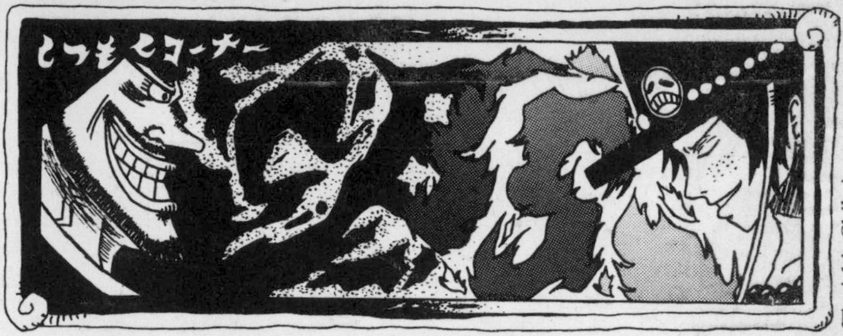

(Tanishi, Chiba)

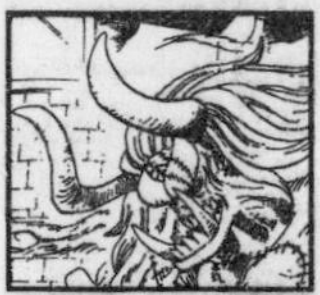

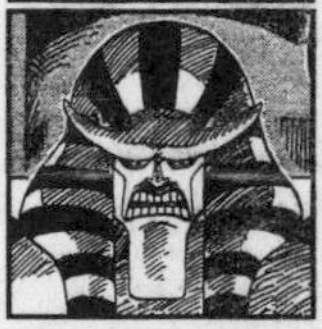

Q: We sometimes see people or giants with horns. Are horns like buckteeth in this world?

--Wozapomu

A: Yup. They're there. Sometimes you doubt if they even have the same physiology as other people. Well, just think of them as minor displays of personality. I want to keep drawing many more funny faces.

Q: When I was talking to my friends about *One Piece,* there's one thing I noticed. I realized that you never call Luffy and his crew the "Straw Hat Pirates" and never the "Luffy Pirates." You always call them the "Straw Hats" every single time. Is this a policy of yours?

--Polici

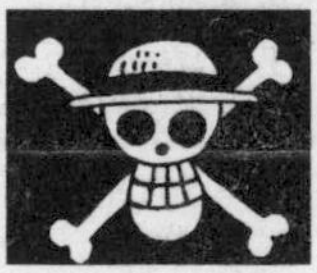

A: Oh! Here we go again. A great guy that sees through it all. You're right. You're exactly right. What the anime, games, or readers call them is really none of my concern. They can call them whatever's easiest for them. But for me, I've decided to always call them the "Straw Hats." I've never called them anything else. Well done.

Q: There's one mushroom on my body that just won't come off! Should I go to the Women Island to get it pulled… Hm?! I see that you got a mushroom on you too, Mr. Oda. Do you want to come with me?

--Shimizu Chagero

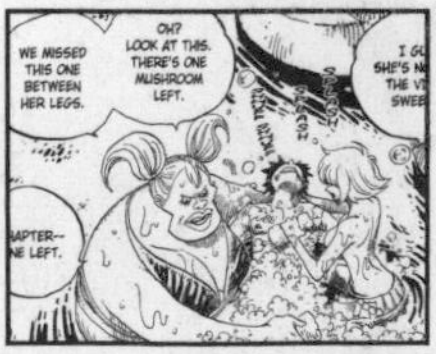
OH? LOOK AT THIS. THERE'S ONE MUSHROOM LEFT.
WE MISSED THIS ONE BETWEEN HER LEGS.

A: That's my wiener, Shimizu Chagero. Oh, excuse me for being so vulgar. I should censor it. That's my wie#@r, Chagero! My wie#@r! Now then. Starting from page 188 is the voice actor Question Corner!

Chapter 560:
PRISONERS OF IMPEL DOWN

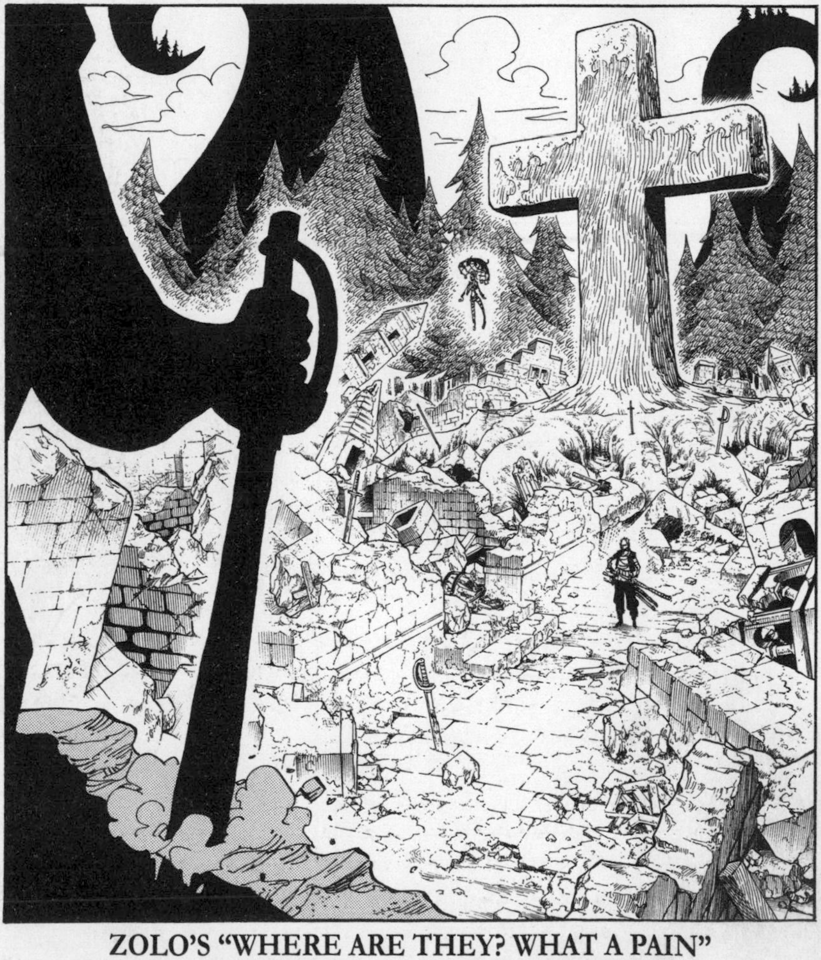

ZOLO'S "WHERE ARE THEY? WHAT A PAIN"
FINAL VOLUME: "CREEPING SHADOW"

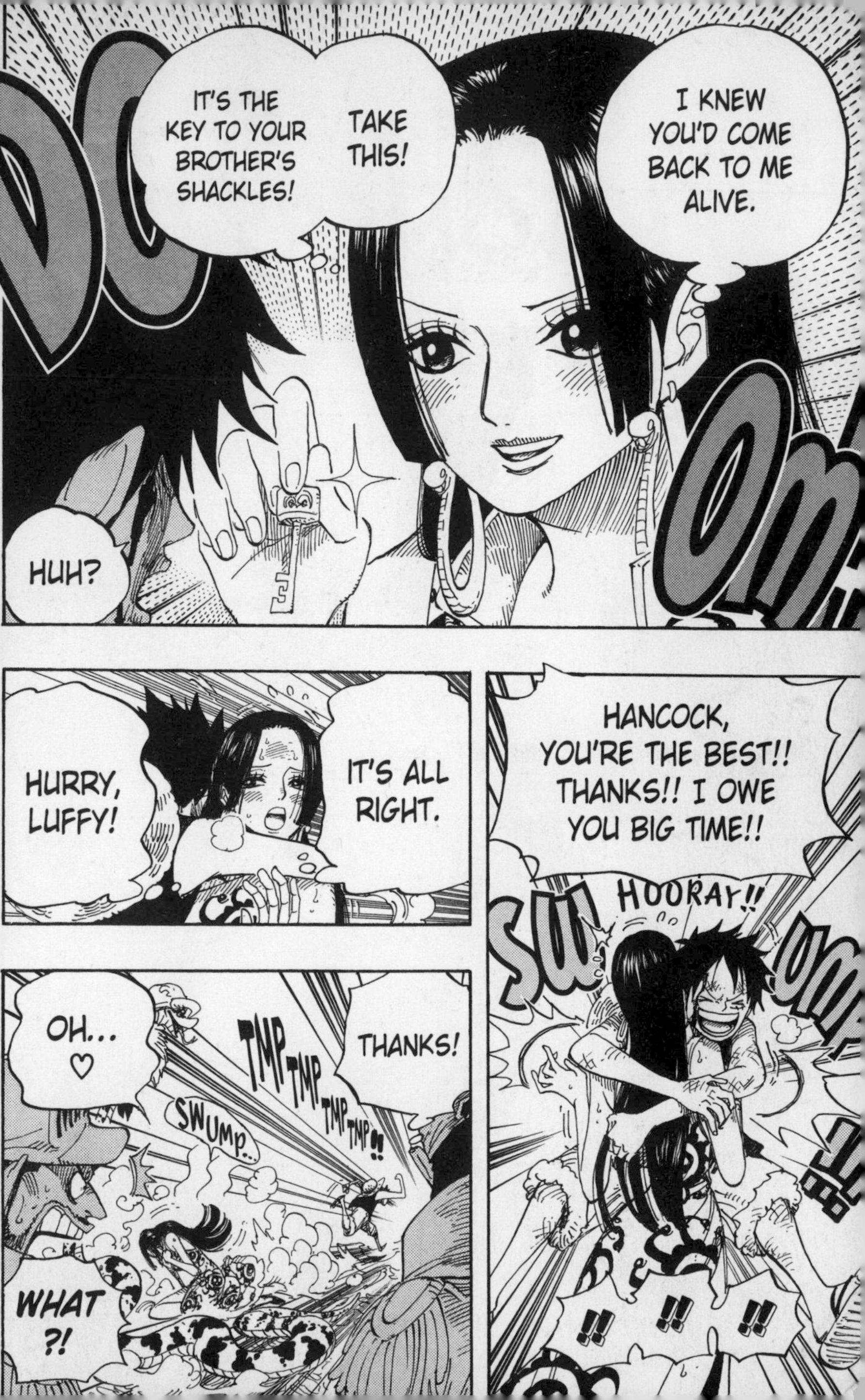
I KNEW YOU'D COME BACK TO ME ALIVE.
TAKE THIS!
IT'S THE KEY TO YOUR BROTHER'S SHACKLES!
HUH?
HANCOCK, YOU'RE THE BEST!! THANKS!! I OWE YOU BIG TIME!!
HOORAY!!
!!
!!
!!
IT'S ALL RIGHT.
HURRY, LUFFY!
THANKS!
TMP TMP TMP TMP!!
SWUMP...
OH... ♡
WHAT?!

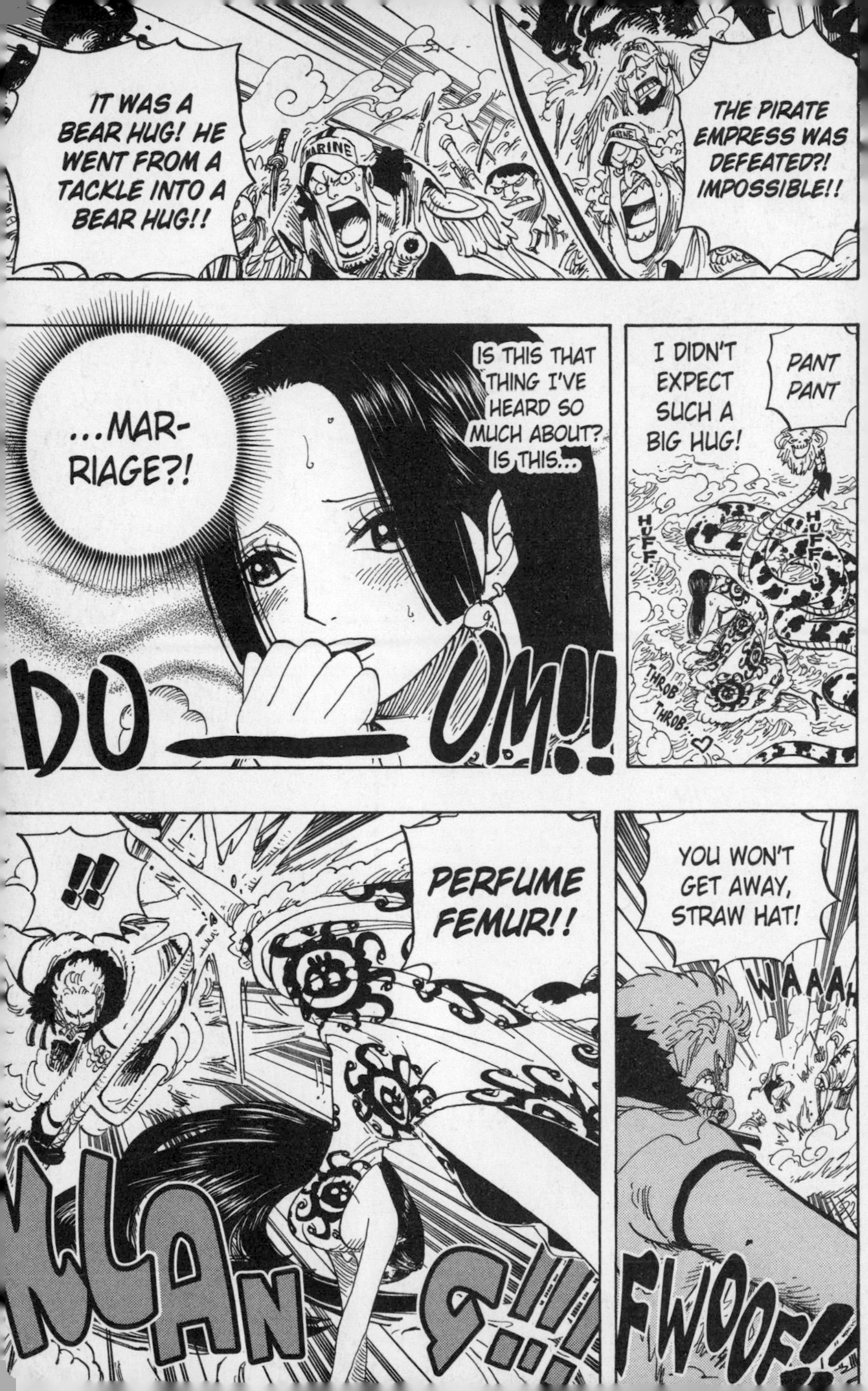
THE PIRATE EMPRESS WAS DEFEATED?! IMPOSSIBLE!!
IT WAS A BEAR HUG! HE WENT FROM A TACKLE INTO A BEAR HUG!!
PANT PANT
I DIDN'T EXPECT SUCH A BIG HUG!
HUFF HUFF...
HUFF...
THROB THROB...♡
IS THIS THAT THING I'VE HEARD SO MUCH ABOUT? IS THIS...
...MAR-RIAGE?!
DO—OM!!
YOU WON'T GET AWAY, STRAW HAT!
WAAAH
FWOOF!!
PERFUME FEMUR!!
!!

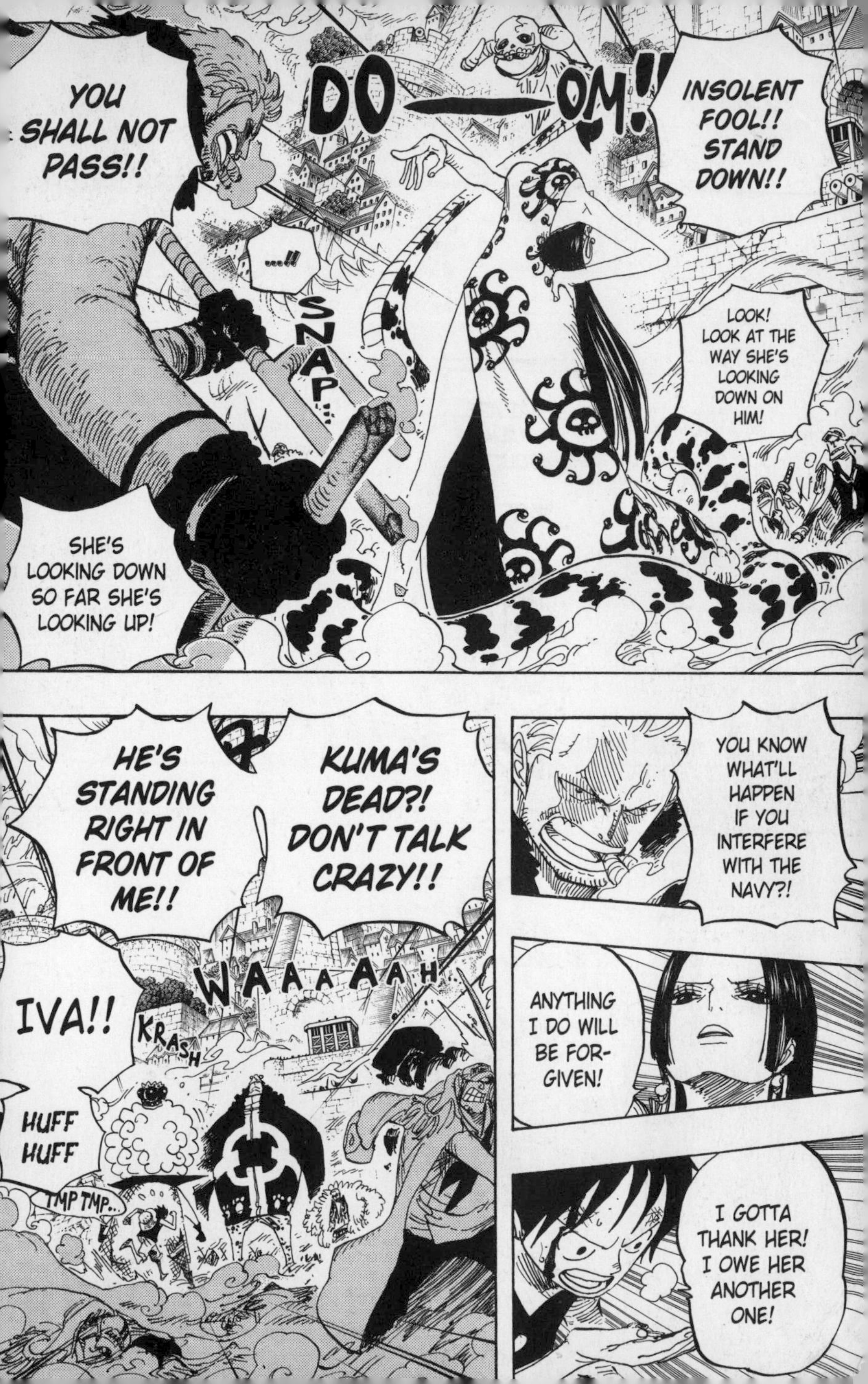
INSOLENT FOOL!! STAND DOWN!!
DO—OM!!
YOU SHALL NOT PASS!!
...!!
SNAP...
LOOK! LOOK AT THE WAY SHE'S LOOKING DOWN ON HIM!
SHE'S LOOKING DOWN SO FAR SHE'S LOOKING UP!
YOU KNOW WHAT'LL HAPPEN IF YOU INTERFERE WITH THE NAVY?!
ANYTHING I DO WILL BE FOR-GIVEN!
I GOTTA THANK HER! I OWE HER ANOTHER ONE!
KUMA'S DEAD?! DON'T TALK CRAZY!!
HE'S STANDING RIGHT IN FRONT OF ME!!
WAAAAAH...
IVA!!
KRASH
HUFF HUFF
TMP TMP...

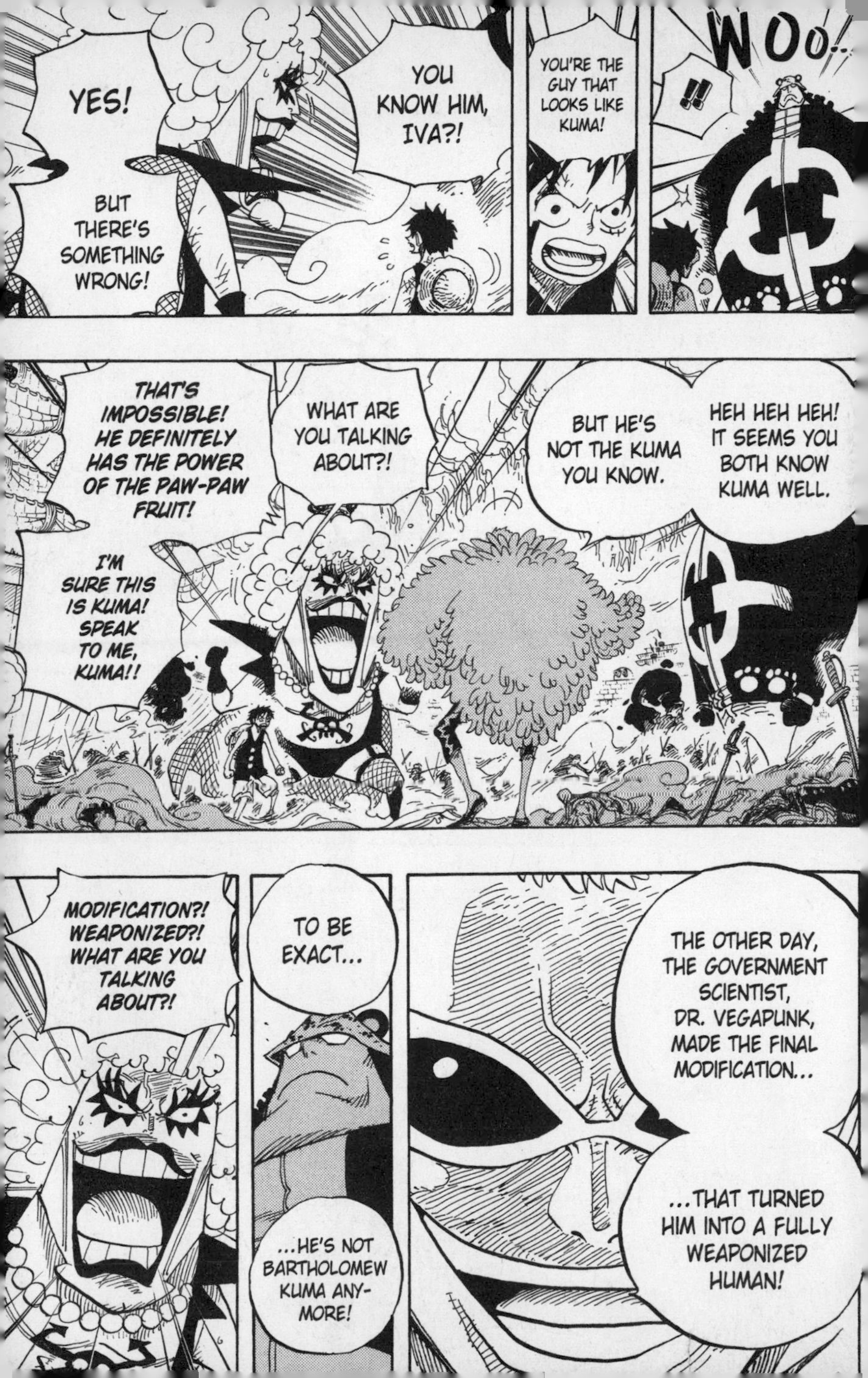
WOO!..
!!
YOU'RE THE GUY THAT LOOKS LIKE KUMA!
YOU KNOW HIM, IVA?!
YES!
BUT THERE'S SOMETHING WRONG!
HEH HEH HEH! IT SEEMS YOU BOTH KNOW KUMA WELL.
BUT HE'S NOT THE KUMA YOU KNOW.
WHAT ARE YOU TALKING ABOUT?!
THAT'S IMPOSSIBLE! HE DEFINITELY HAS THE POWER OF THE PAW-PAW FRUIT!
I'M SURE THIS IS KUMA! SPEAK TO ME, KUMA!!
THE OTHER DAY, THE GOVERNMENT SCIENTIST, DR. VEGAPUNK, MADE THE FINAL MODIFICATION...
...THAT TURNED HIM INTO A FULLY WEAPONIZED HUMAN!
TO BE EXACT...
...HE'S NOT BARTHOLOMEW KUMA ANY-MORE!
MODIFICATION?! WEAPONIZED?! WHAT ARE YOU TALKING ABOUT?!

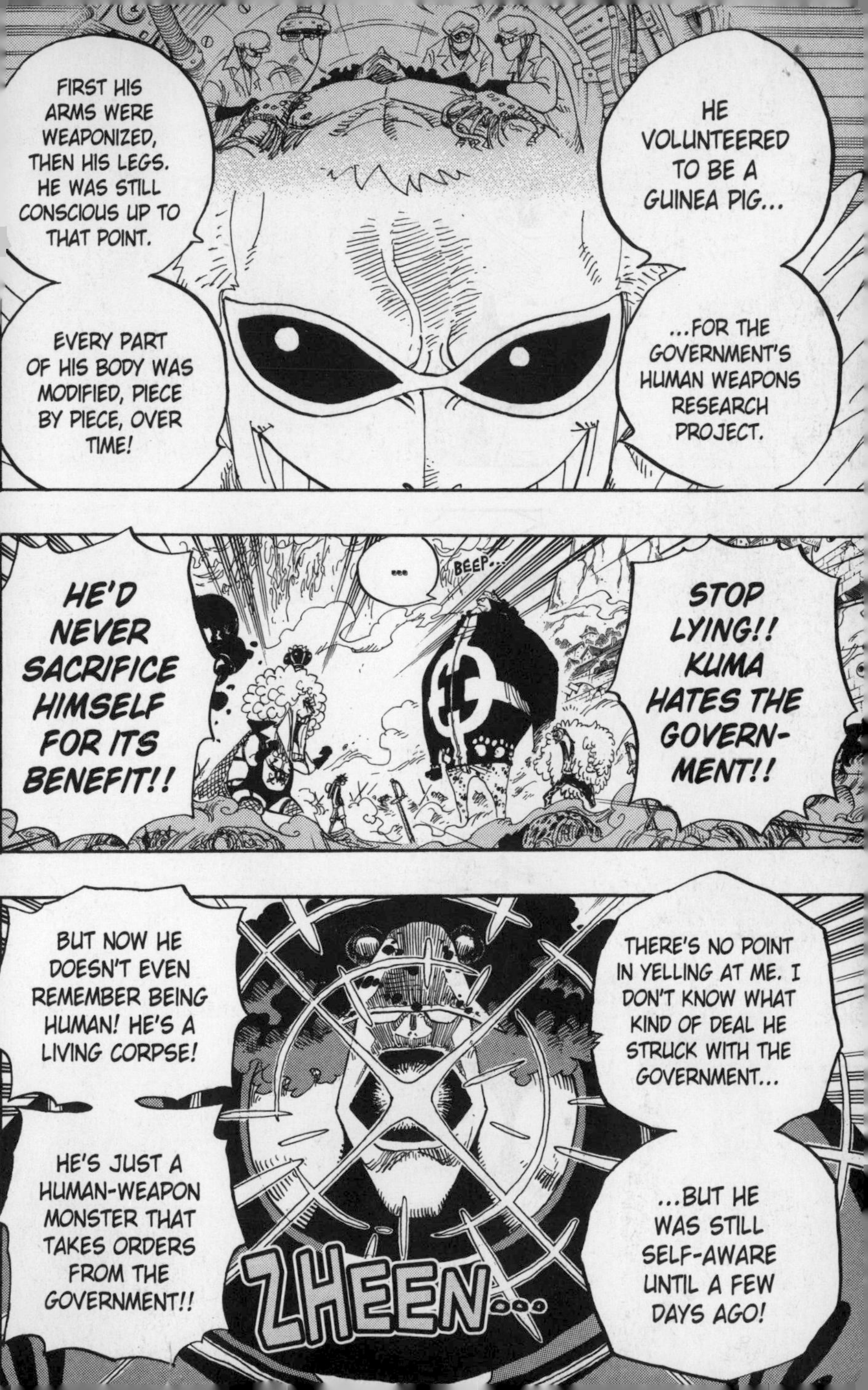
HE VOLUNTEERED TO BE A GUINEA PIG...
...FOR THE GOVERNMENT'S HUMAN WEAPONS RESEARCH PROJECT.
FIRST HIS ARMS WERE WEAPONIZED, THEN HIS LEGS. HE WAS STILL CONSCIOUS UP TO THAT POINT.
EVERY PART OF HIS BODY WAS MODIFIED, PIECE BY PIECE, OVER TIME!
STOP LYING!! KUMA HATES THE GOVERN-MENT!!
BEEP...
...
HE'D NEVER SACRIFICE HIMSELF FOR ITS BENEFIT!!
THERE'S NO POINT IN YELLING AT ME. I DON'T KNOW WHAT KIND OF DEAL HE STRUCK WITH THE GOVERNMENT...
...BUT HE WAS STILL SELF-AWARE UNTIL A FEW DAYS AGO!
BUT NOW HE DOESN'T EVEN REMEMBER BEING HUMAN! HE'S A LIVING CORPSE!
HE'S JUST A HUMAN-WEAPON MONSTER THAT TAKES ORDERS FROM THE GOVERNMENT!!
ZHEEN...

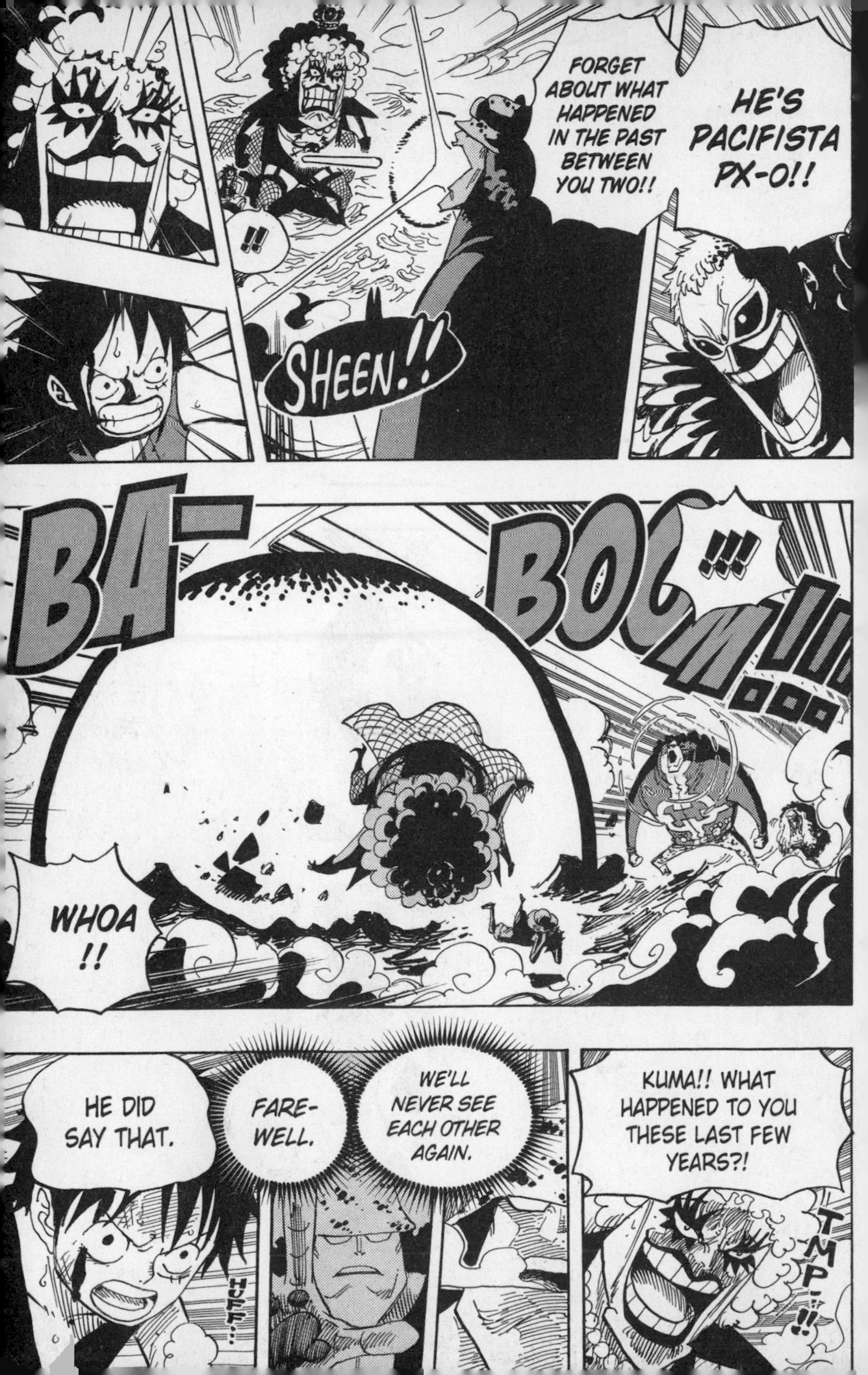
HE'S PACIFISTA PX-0!!
FORGET ABOUT WHAT HAPPENED IN THE PAST BETWEEN YOU TWO!!
SHEEN!!
!!
BA-BOOM!!!
WHOA !!
KUMA!! WHAT HAPPENED TO YOU THESE LAST FEW YEARS?!
TMP!!
WE'LL NEVER SEE EACH OTHER AGAIN.
FARE-WELL.
HUFF...
HE DID SAY THAT.

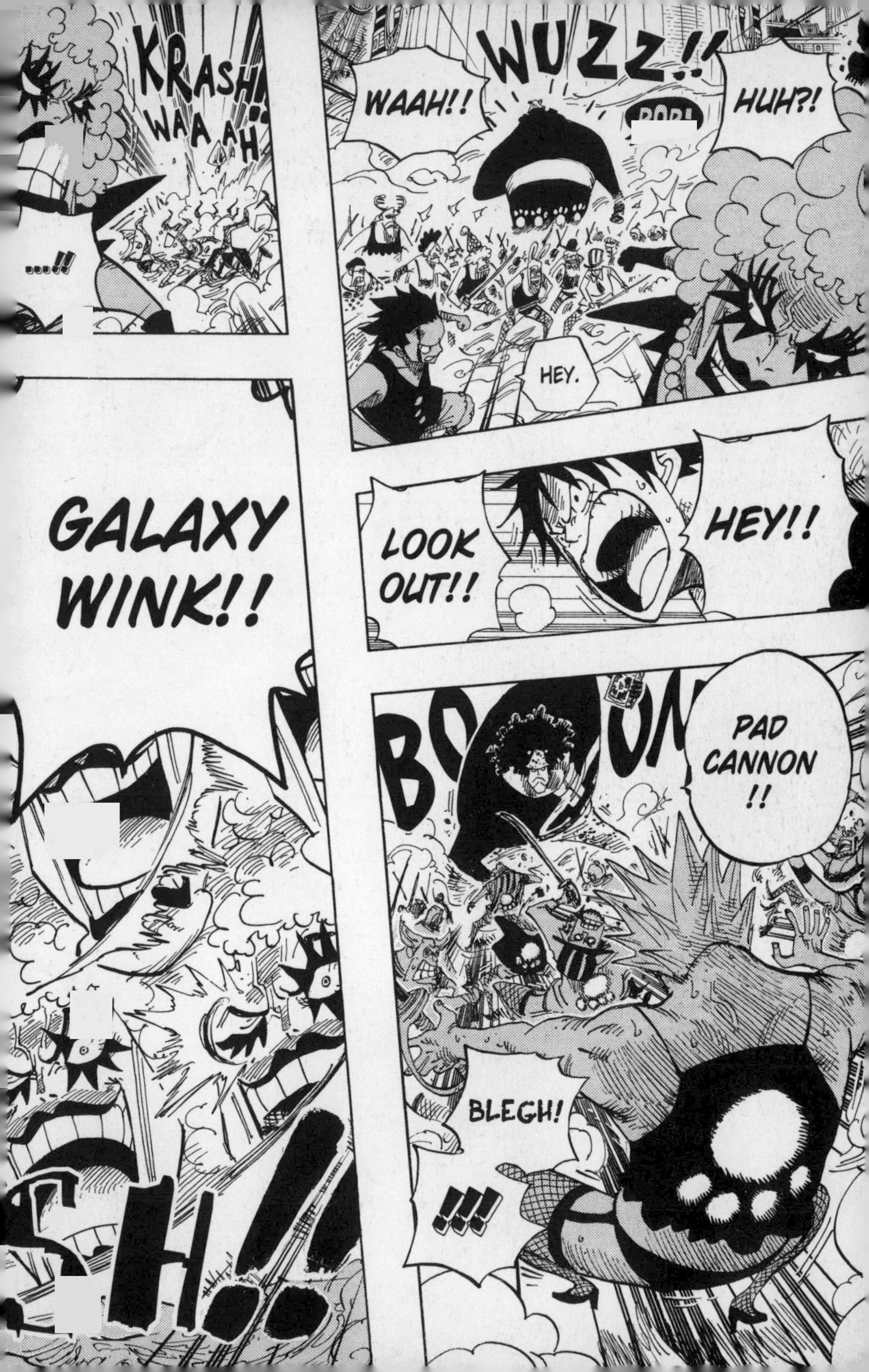
HUH?!
WUZZ!!
WAAH!!
HEY.
KRASH
WAAAH
...!!
HEY!!
LOOK OUT!!
PAD CANNON !!
BLEGH!
!!!
GALAXY WINK!!

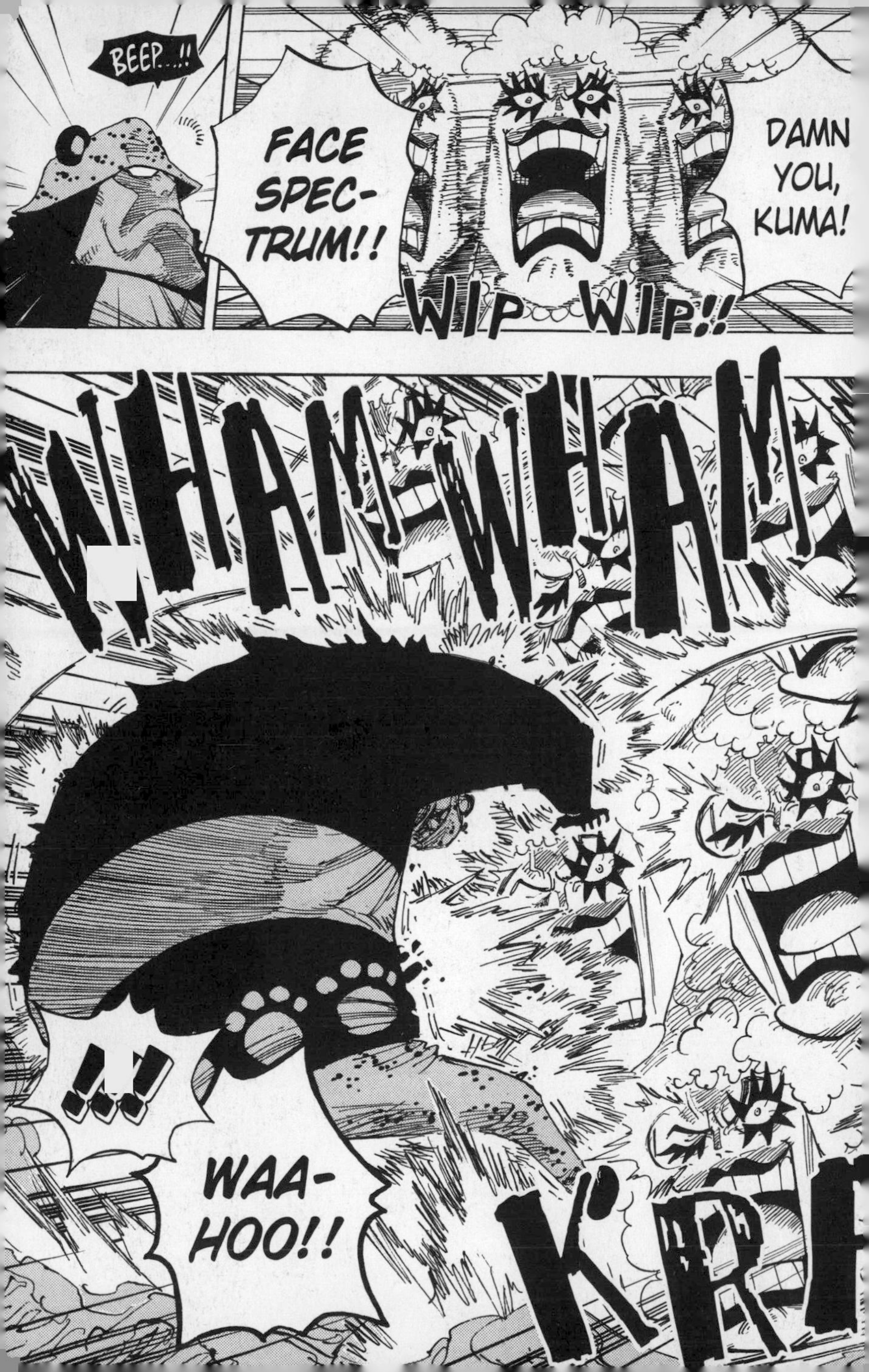
DAMN YOU, KUMA!
FACE SPEC-TRUM!!
WIP WIP!!
BEEP...!!
WHAM WHAM
WAA-HOO!!
!!

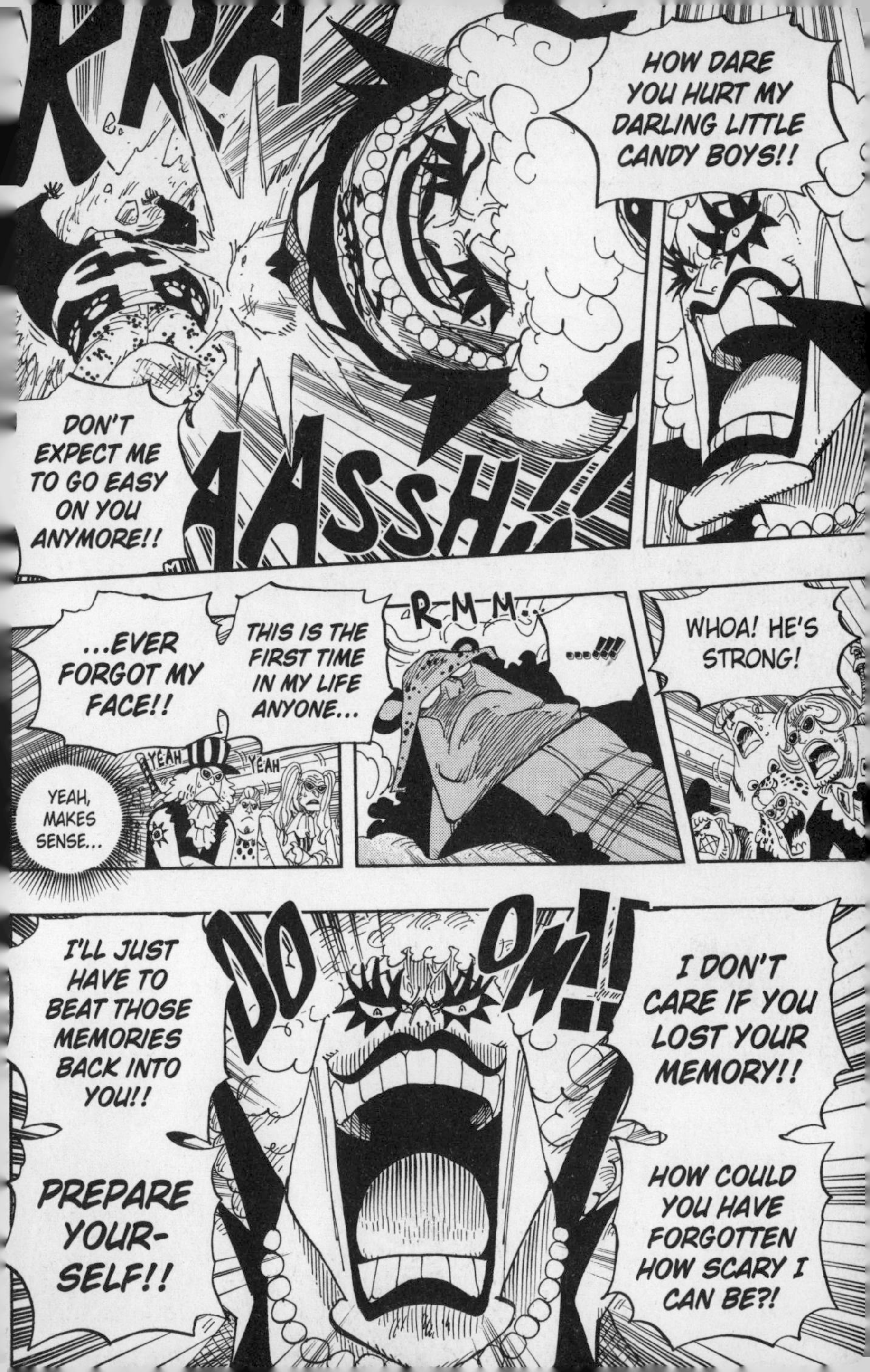
HOW DARE YOU HURT MY DARLING LITTLE CANDY BOYS!!
KRA
ASSH!!
DON'T EXPECT ME TO GO EASY ON YOU ANYMORE!!
WHOA! HE'S STRONG!
R-M-M...
...!!!
THIS IS THE FIRST TIME IN MY LIFE ANYONE...
...EVER FORGOT MY FACE!!
YEAH
YEAH
YEAH, MAKES SENSE...
I DON'T CARE IF YOU LOST YOUR MEMORY!!
DOOM!!
I'LL JUST HAVE TO BEAT THOSE MEMORIES BACK INTO YOU!!
HOW COULD YOU HAVE FORGOTTEN HOW SCARY I CAN BE?!
PREPARE YOURSELF!!

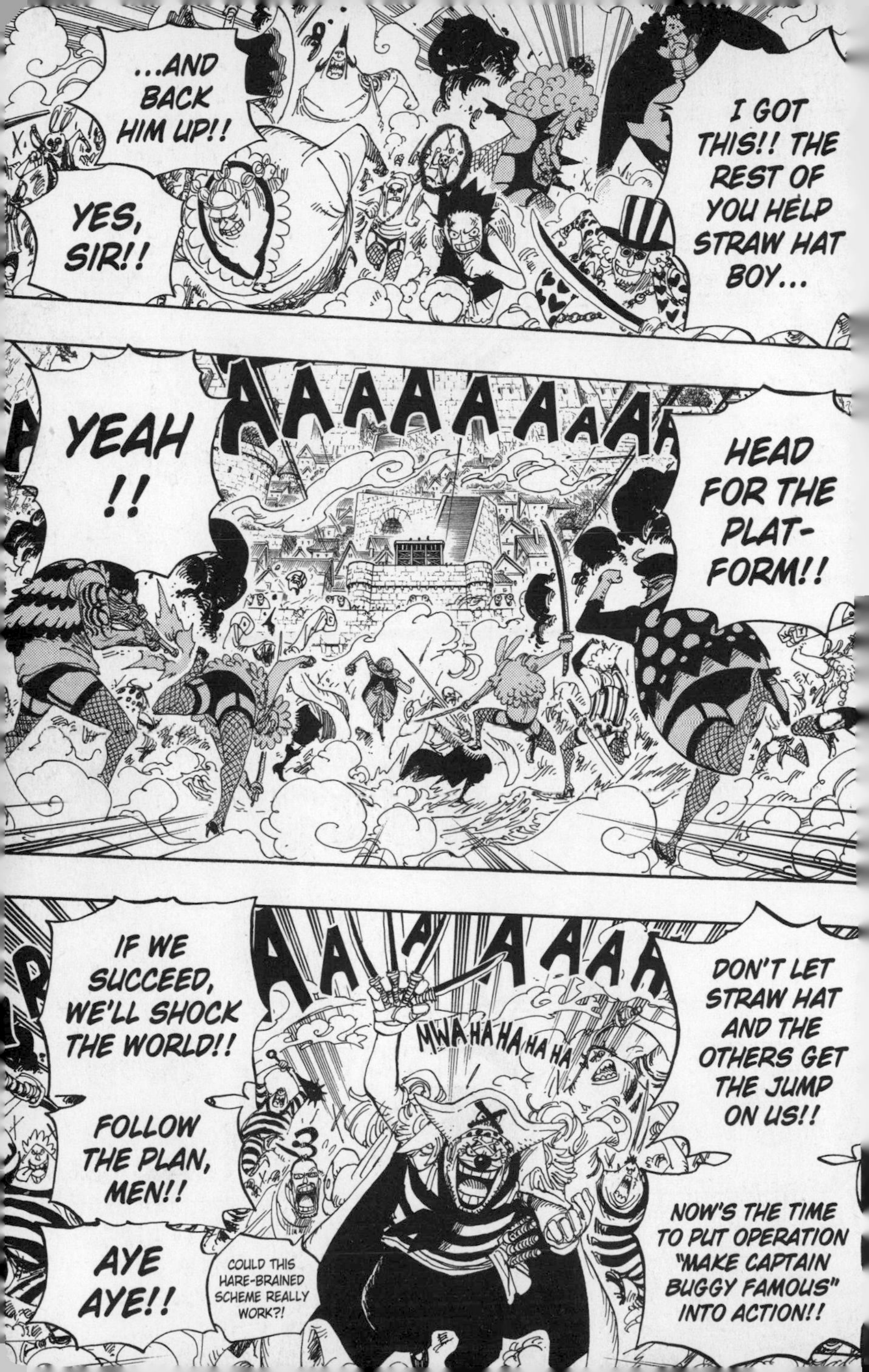
I GOT THIS!! THE REST OF YOU HELP STRAW HAT BOY...
...AND BACK HIM UP!!
YES, SIR!!
HEAD FOR THE PLAT-FORM!!
AAAAAAAAA
YEAH!!
DON'T LET STRAW HAT AND THE OTHERS GET THE JUMP ON US!!
NOW'S THE TIME TO PUT OPERATION "MAKE CAPTAIN BUGGY FAMOUS" INTO ACTION!!
MWAHAHAHAHAHA
AAAAAA
IF WE SUCCEED, WE'LL SHOCK THE WORLD!!
FOLLOW THE PLAN, MEN!!
COULD THIS HARE-BRAINED SCHEME REALLY WORK?!
AYE AYE!!

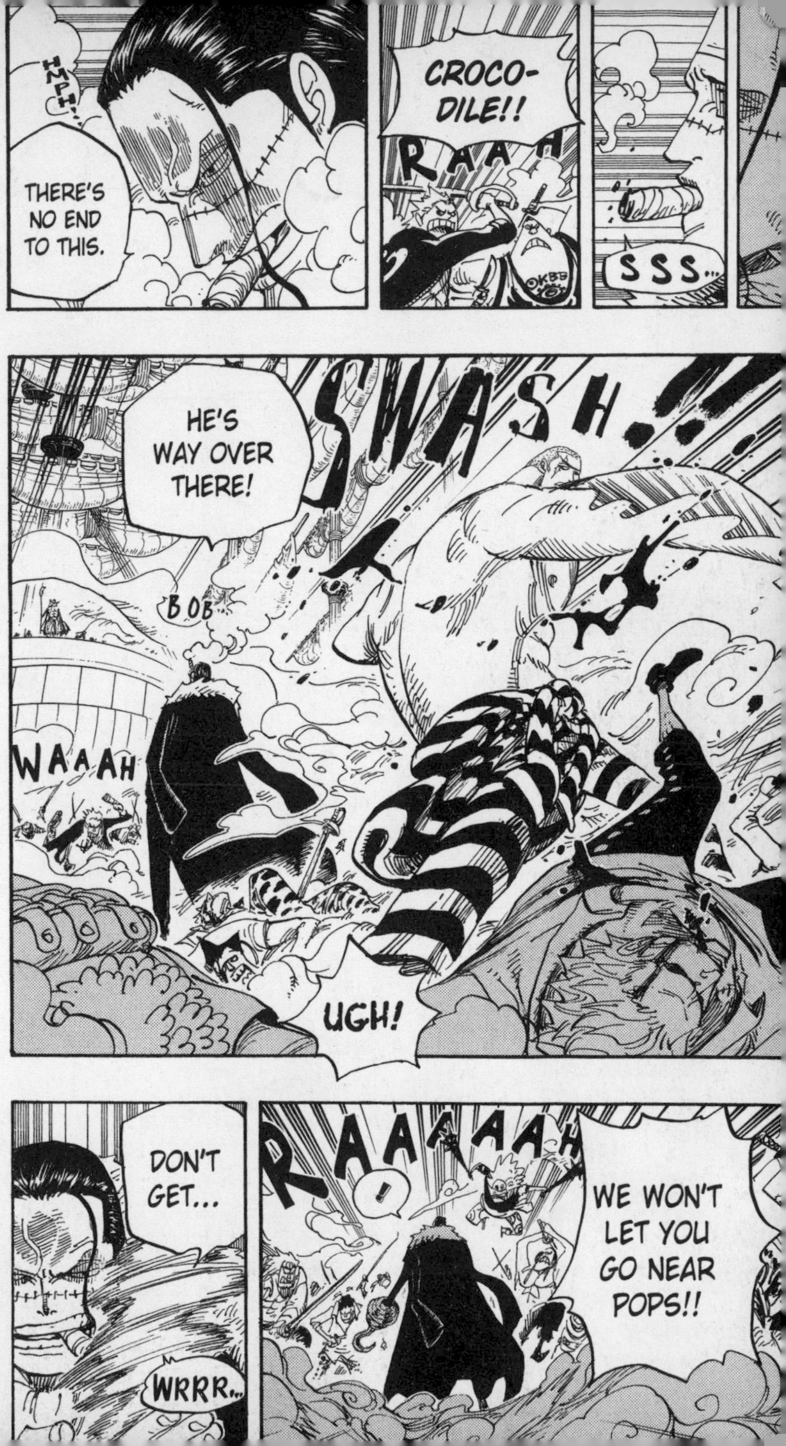
SSS...
CROCO-DILE!!
RAAAH
HMPH...
THERE'S NO END TO THIS.
SWASH!!!
HE'S WAY OVER THERE!
BOB
UGH!
WAAAH
WE WON'T LET YOU GO NEAR POPS!!
RAAAAAH
!
DON'T GET...
WRRR...

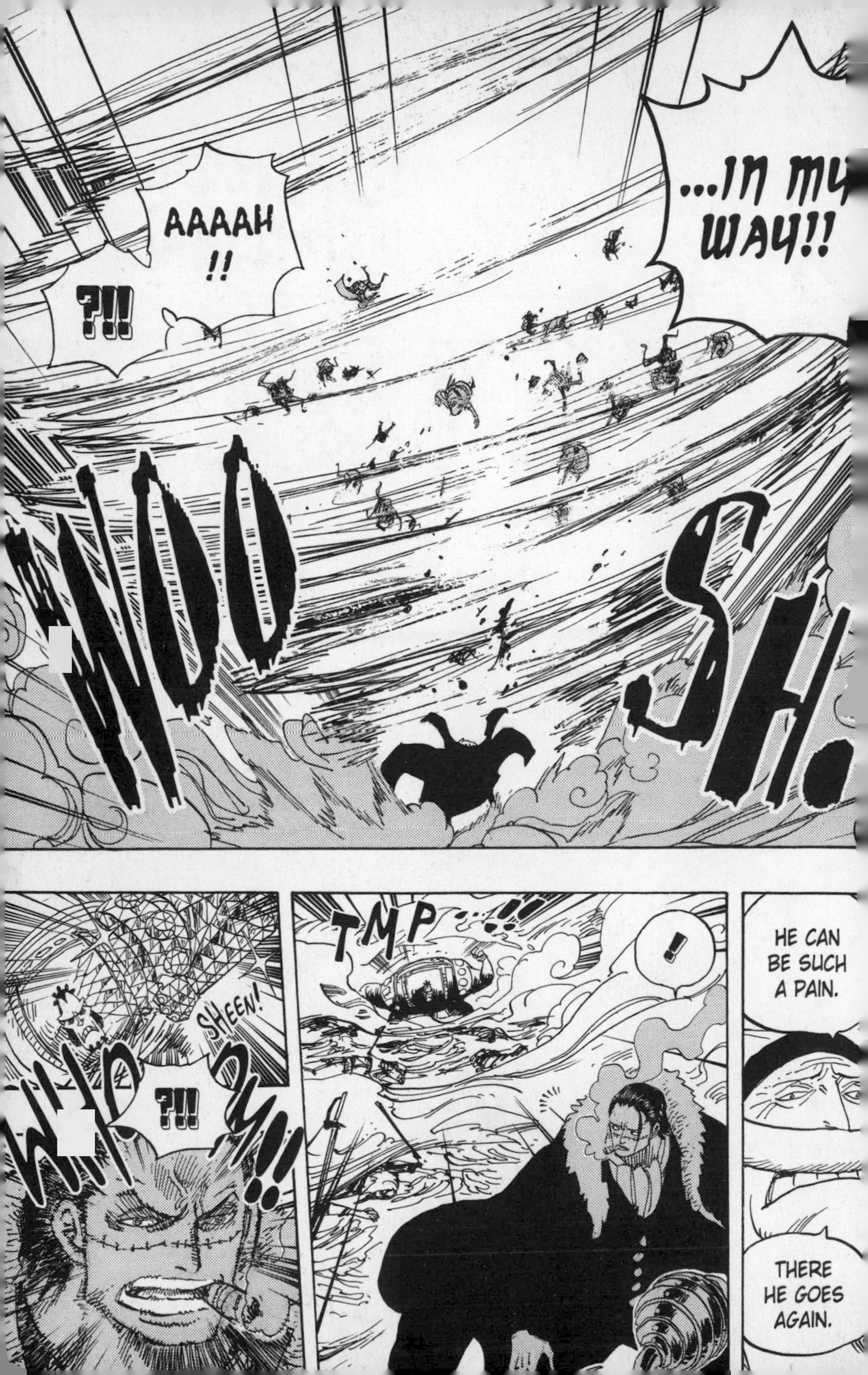

...IN MY WAY!!
AAAAH!!
?!!
HE CAN BE SUCH A PAIN.
THERE HE GOES AGAIN.
TMP
!!
!
SHEEN!
?!!

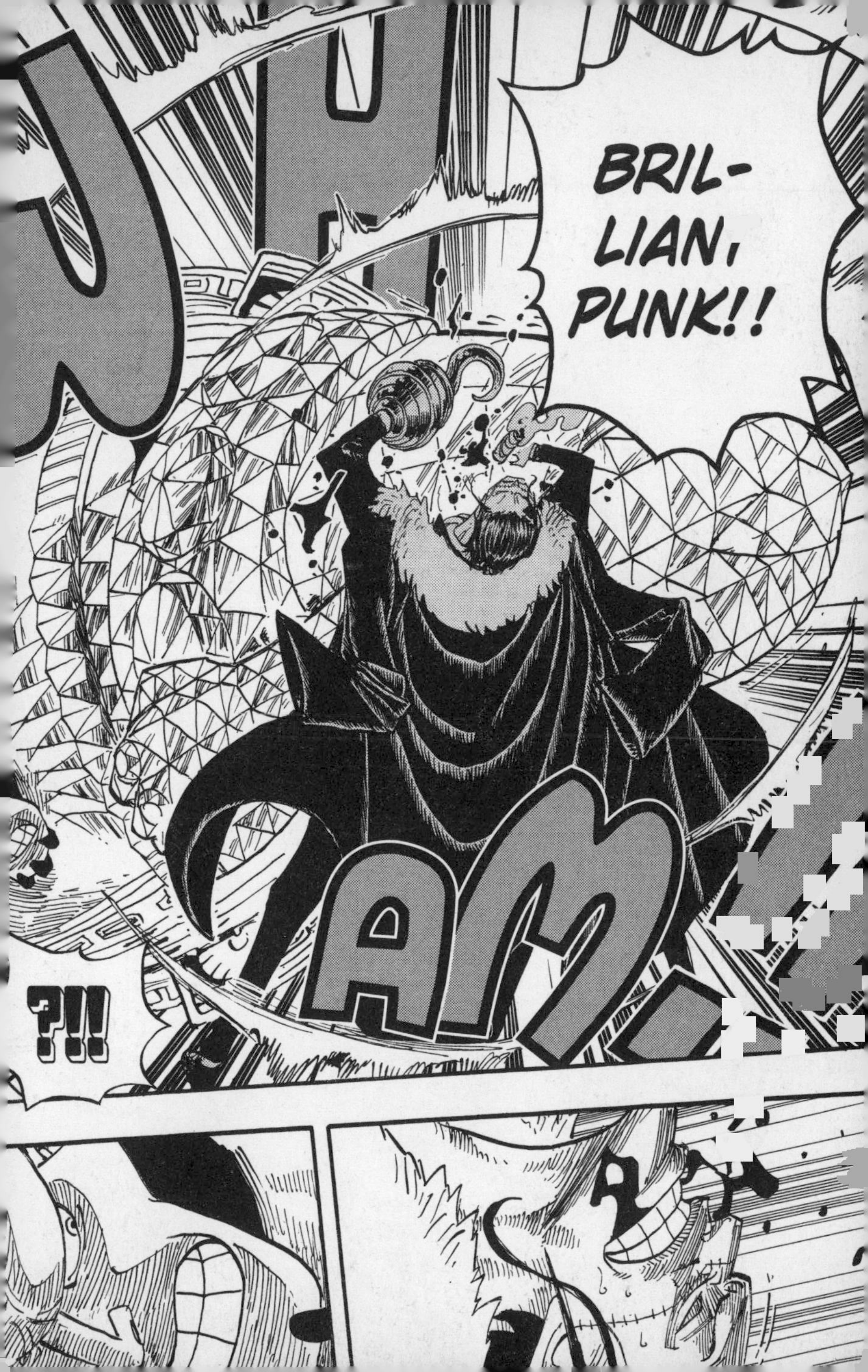
BRIL-
LIAN,
PUNK!!
?!!

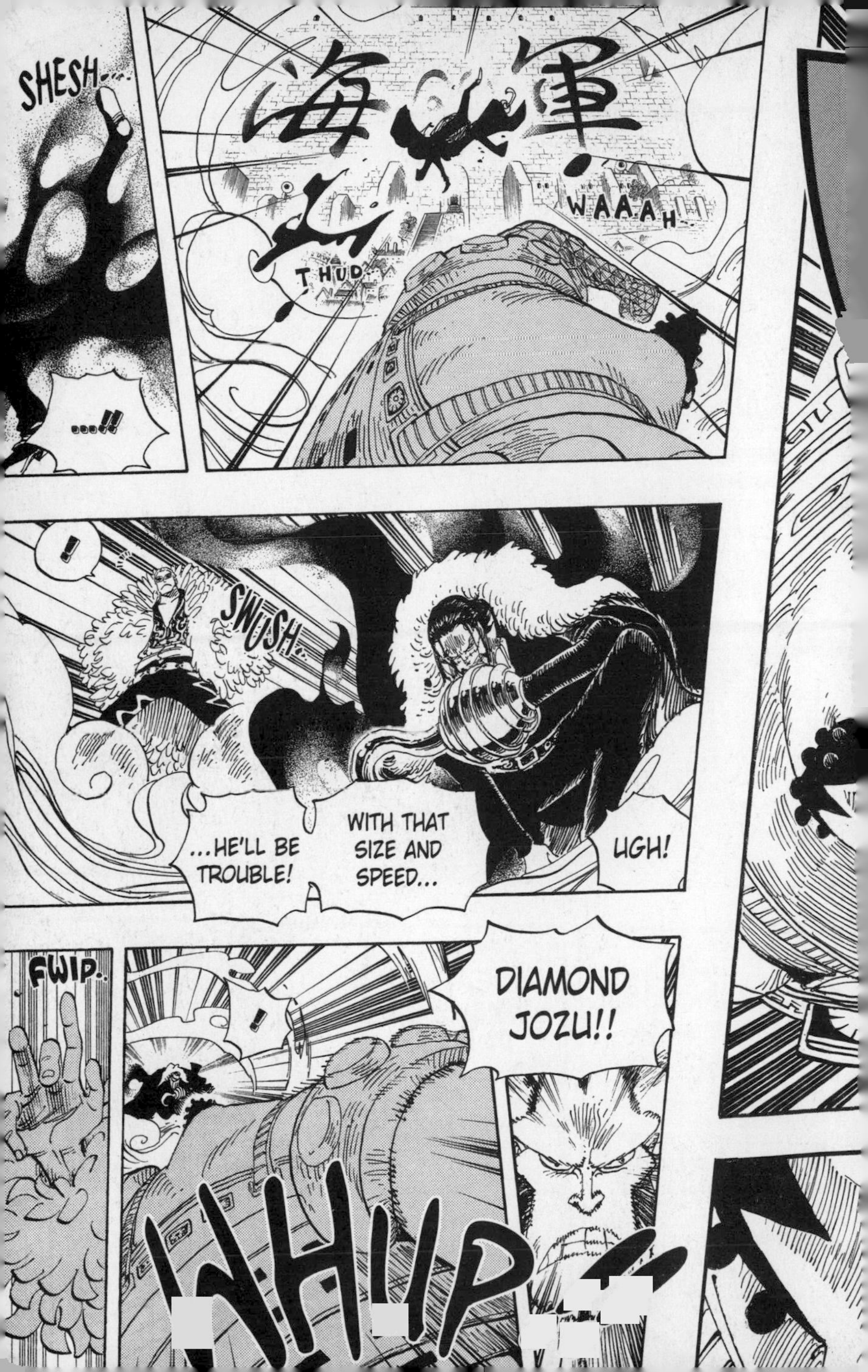
海軍
WAAAH!!
THUD
SHESH...
...!!
UGH!
WITH THAT SIZE AND SPEED...
...HE'LL BE TROUBLE!
!
SWUSH..
DIAMOND JOZU!!
WHUP
!
FWIP..

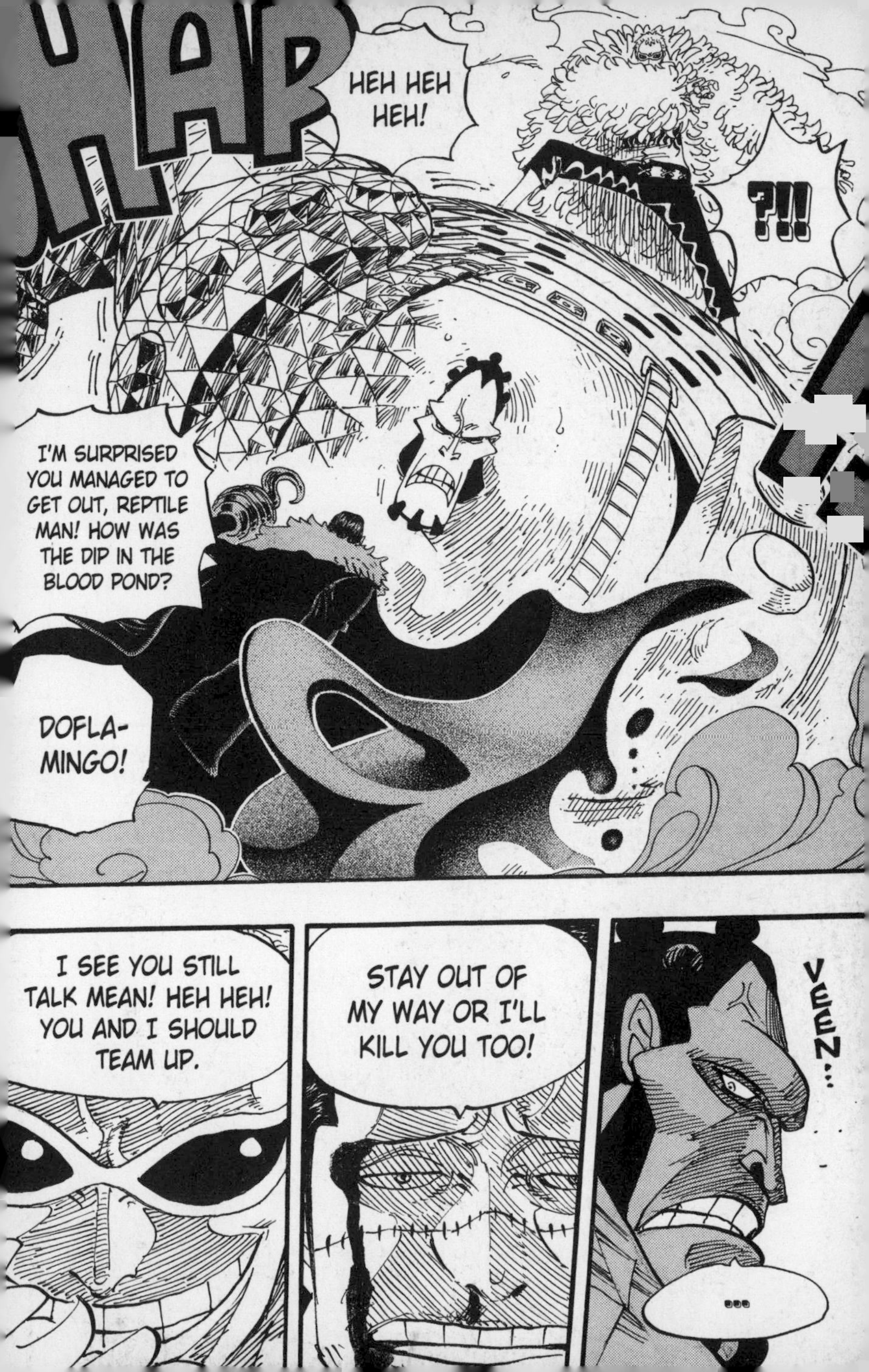
HEH HEH HEH!
?!!
HAP
I'M SURPRISED YOU MANAGED TO GET OUT, REPTILE MAN! HOW WAS THE DIP IN THE BLOOD POND?
DOFLA-MINGO!
VEEN...
...
STAY OUT OF MY WAY OR I'LL KILL YOU TOO!
I SEE YOU STILL TALK MEAN! HEH HEH! YOU AND I SHOULD TEAM UP.

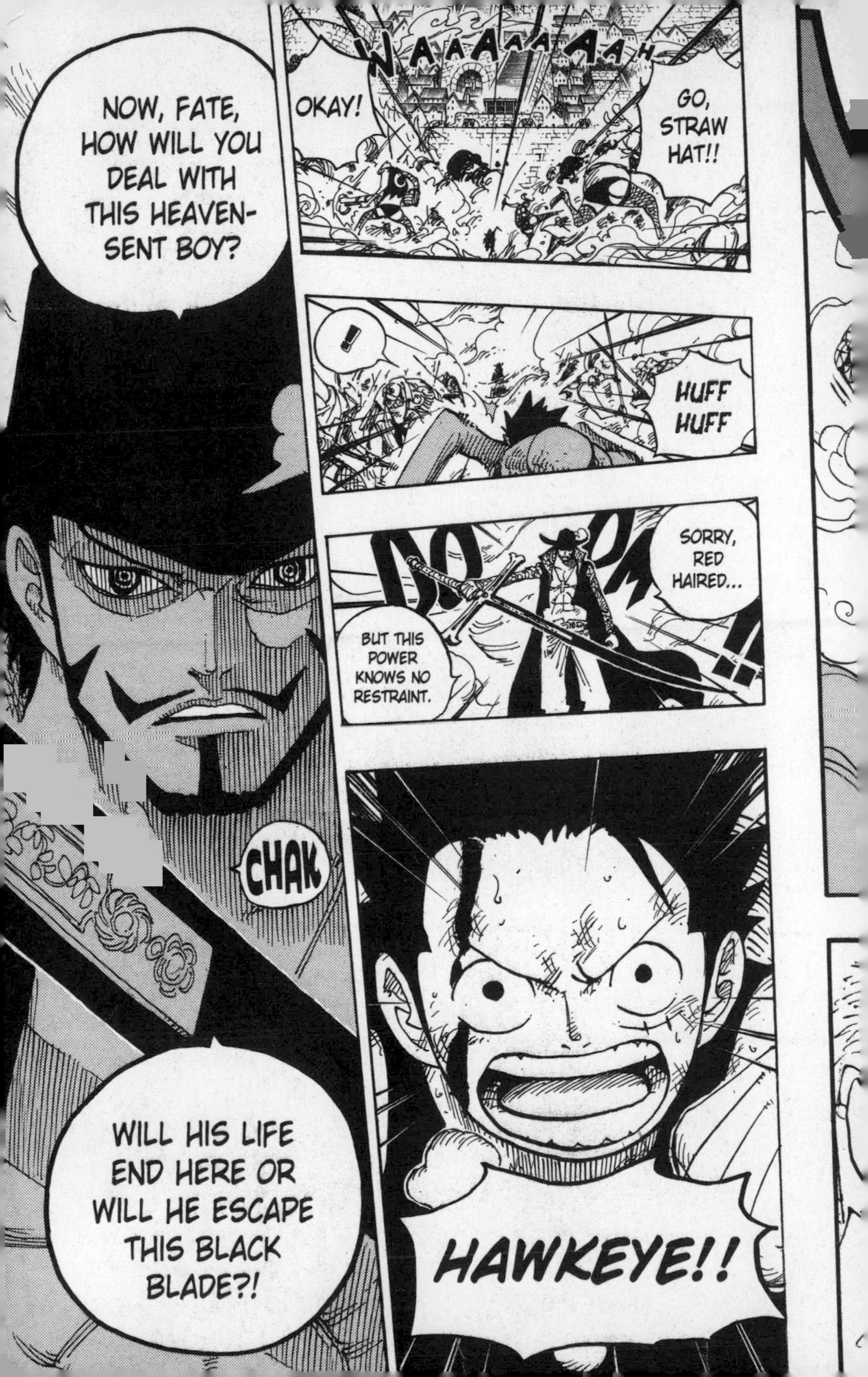
WAAAAAAAH
GO, STRAW HAT!!
OKAY!
!
HUFF HUFF
SORRY, RED HAIRED...
BUT THIS POWER KNOWS NO RESTRAINT.
HAWKEYE!!
NOW, FATE, HOW WILL YOU DEAL WITH THIS HEAVEN-SENT BOY?
CHAK
WILL HIS LIFE END HERE OR WILL HE ESCAPE THIS BLACK BLADE?!

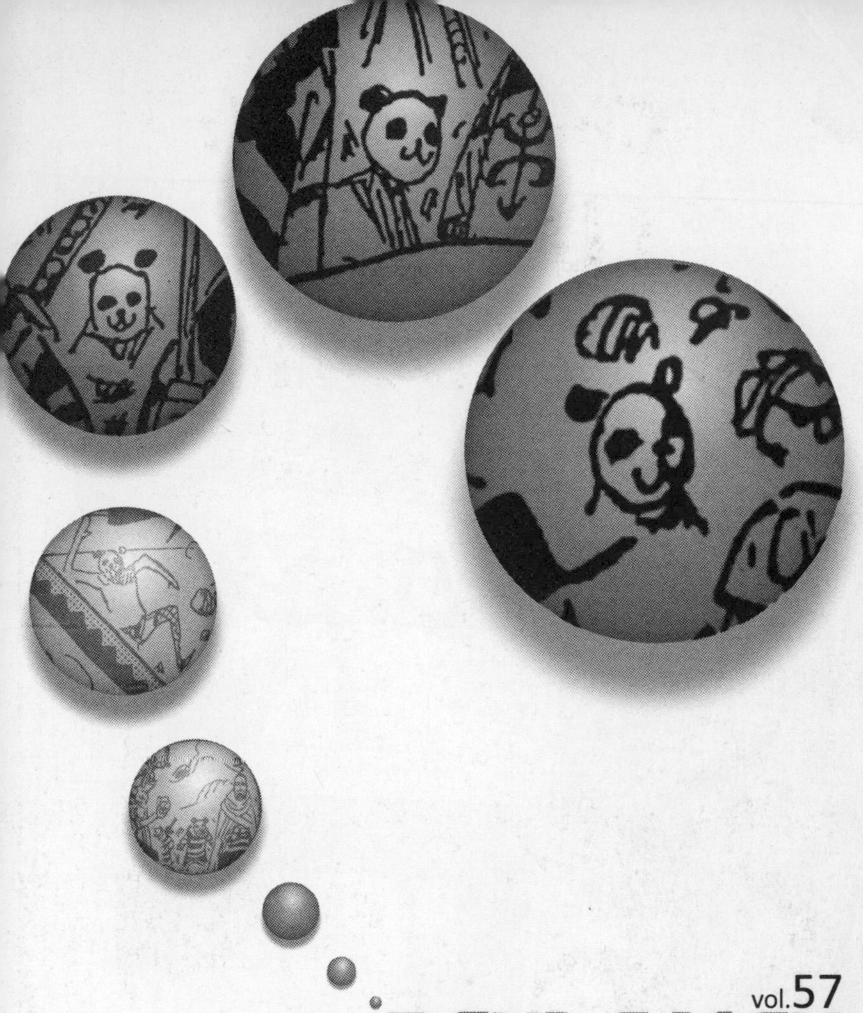

vol.57

PANDA MAN

Chapter 561: LUFFY VS. MIHAWK

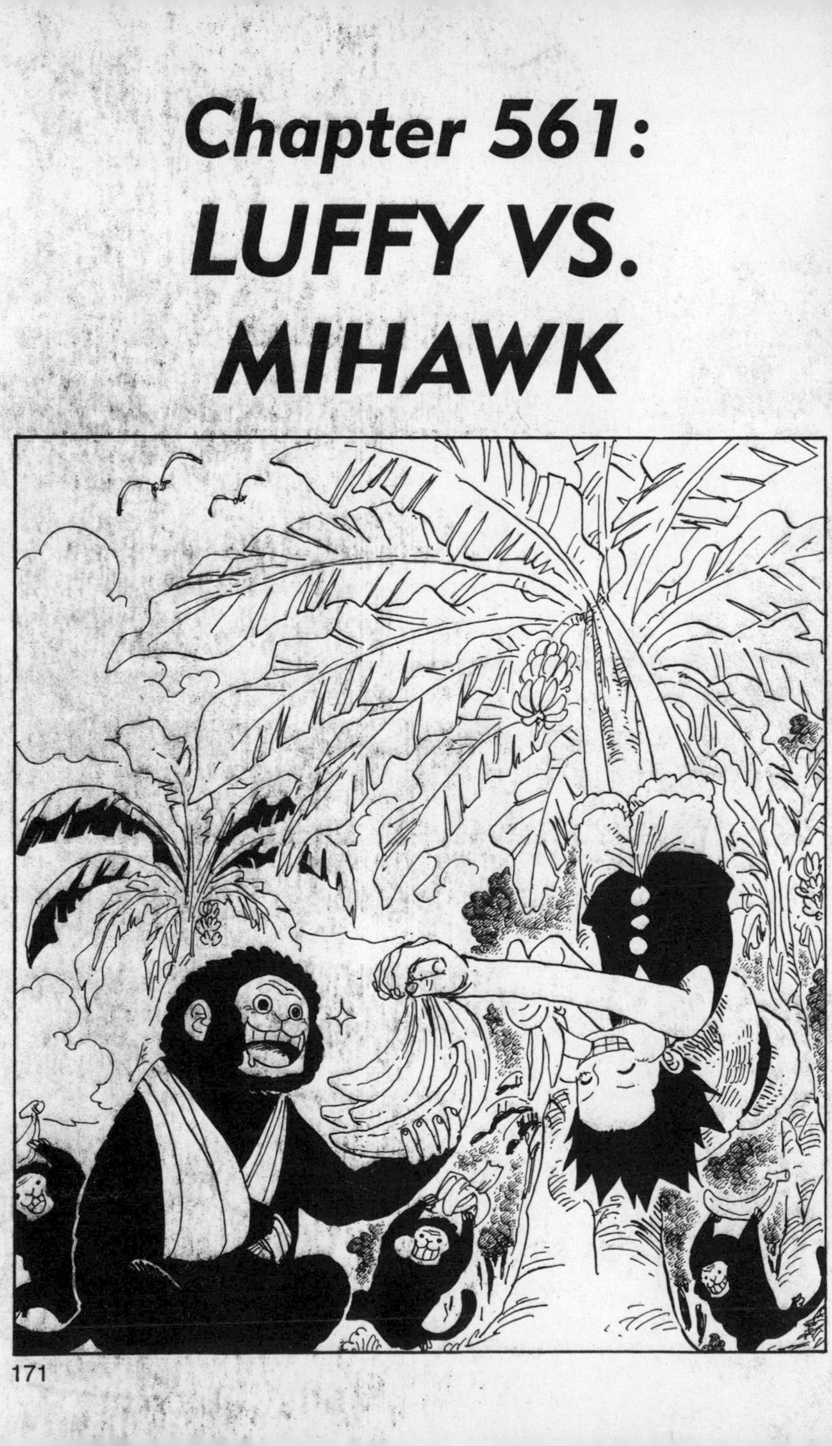

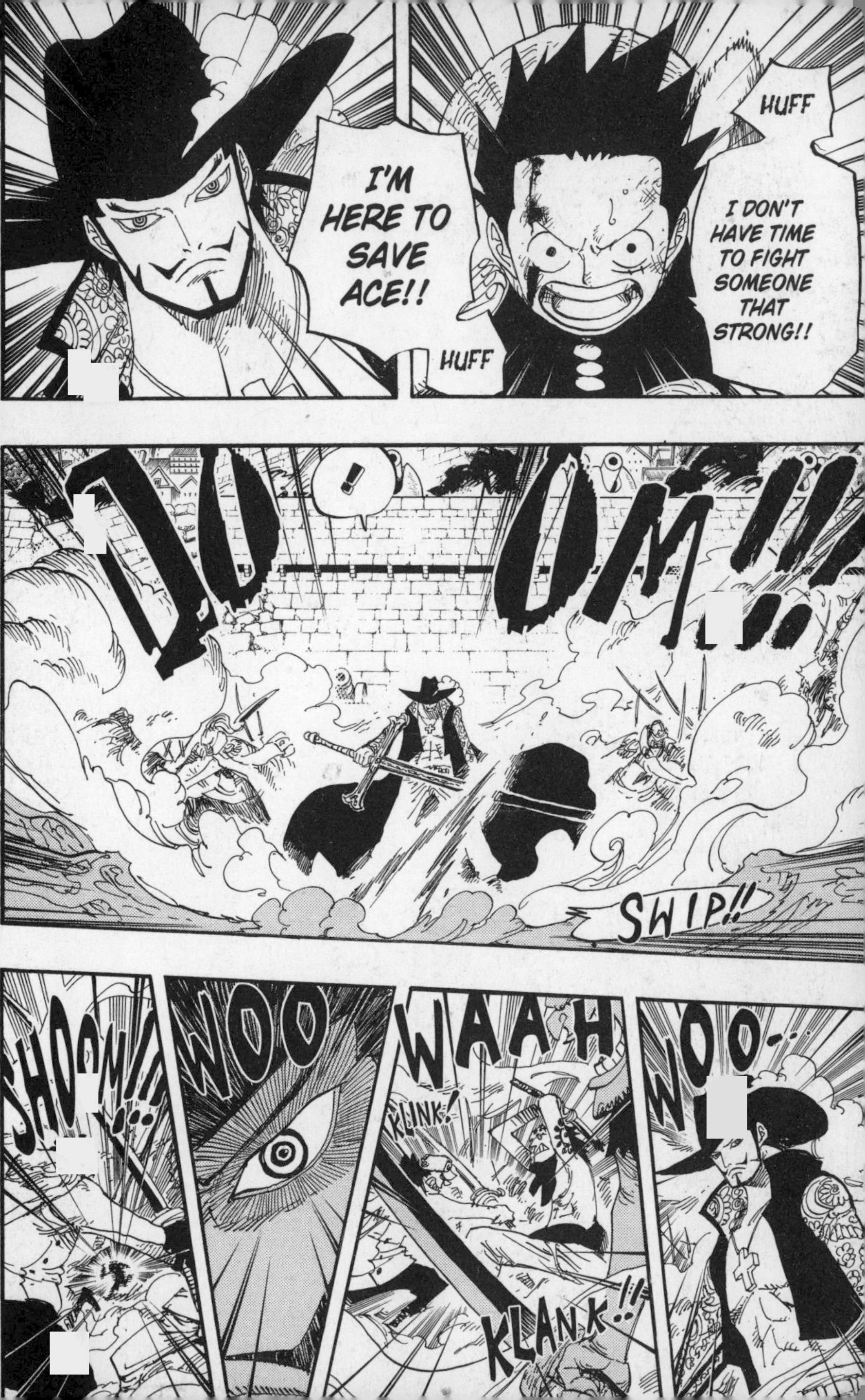
HUFF
I DON'T HAVE TIME TO FIGHT SOMEONE THAT STRONG!!
I'M HERE TO SAVE ACE!!
HUFF
!
DOOOM!!
SWIP!!
WOO-..
WAAH
KLINK!
KLANK!!
WOO
SHOOM!!

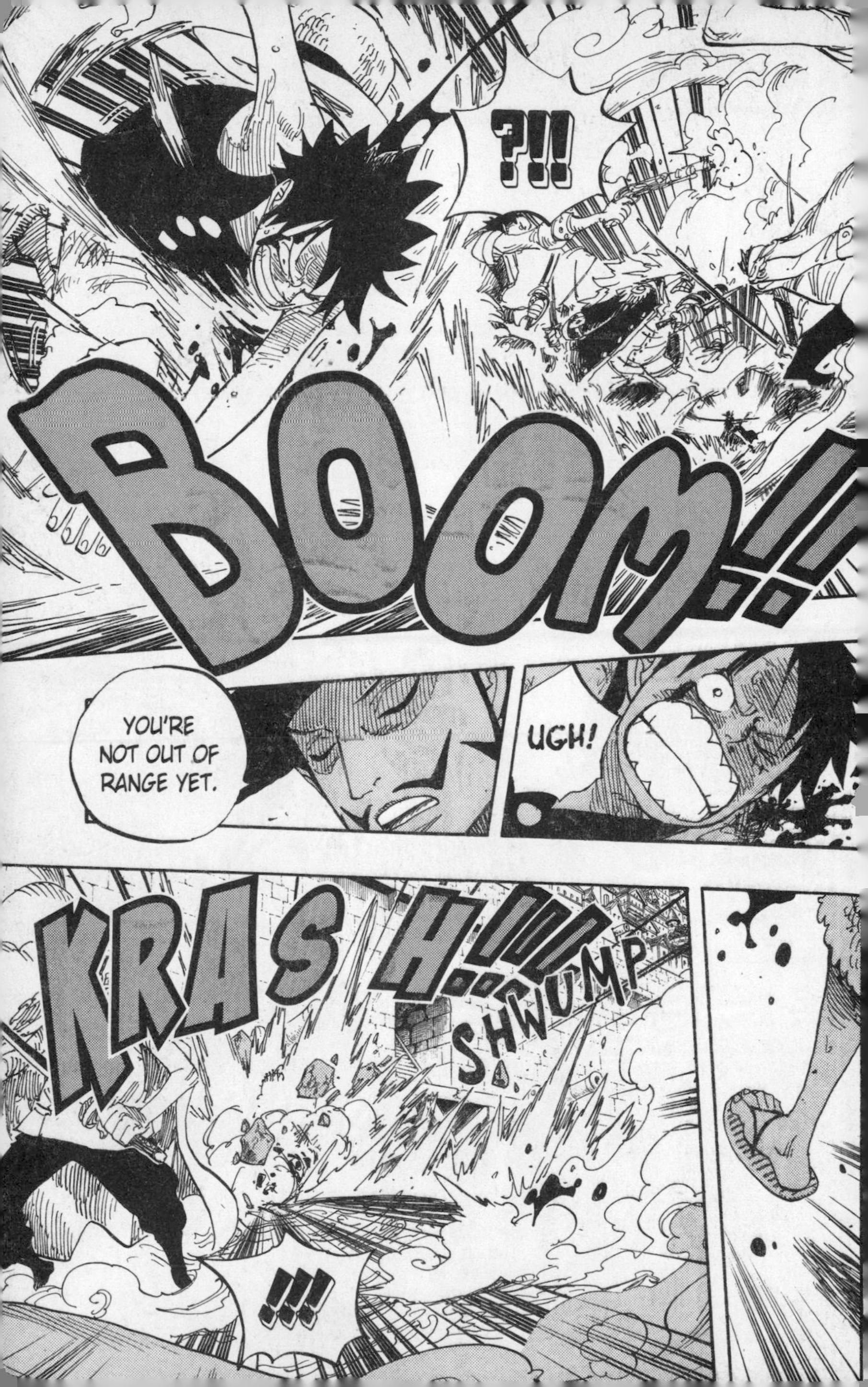
?!!
...
BOOM!!
UGH!
YOU'RE NOT OUT OF RANGE YET.
KRASH!!
SHWUMP
!!!

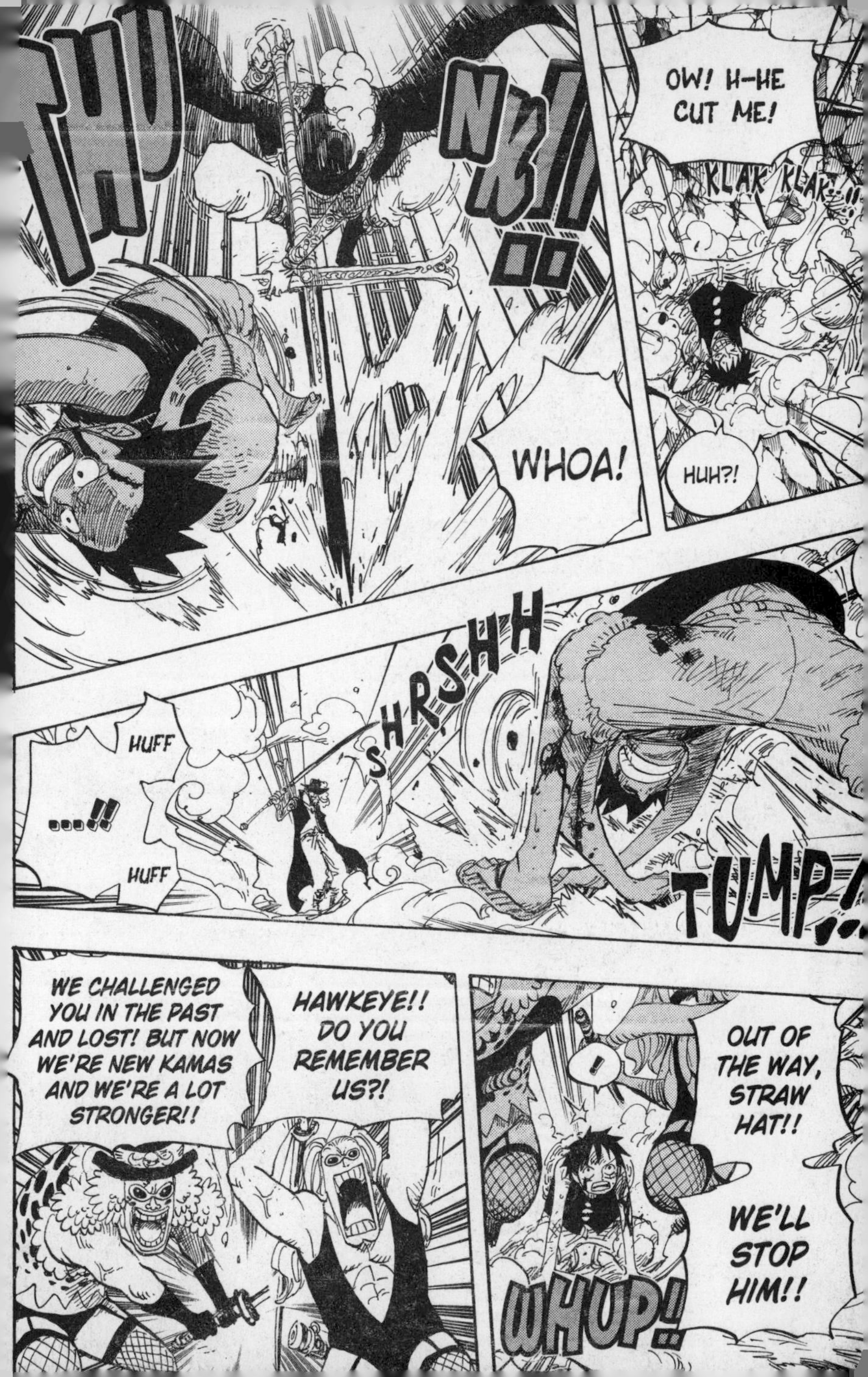
OW! H-HE CUT ME!
KLAK KLAK...!!
HUH?!
THUNK!!
WHOA!
TUMP!!
SHRSHH
HUFF
...!!
HUFF
!
OUT OF THE WAY, STRAW HAT!!
WE'LL STOP HIM!!
WHUP!
HAWKEYE!! DO YOU REMEMBER US?!
WE CHALLENGED YOU IN THE PAST AND LOST! BUT NOW WE'RE NEW KAMAS AND WE'RE A LOT STRONGER!!

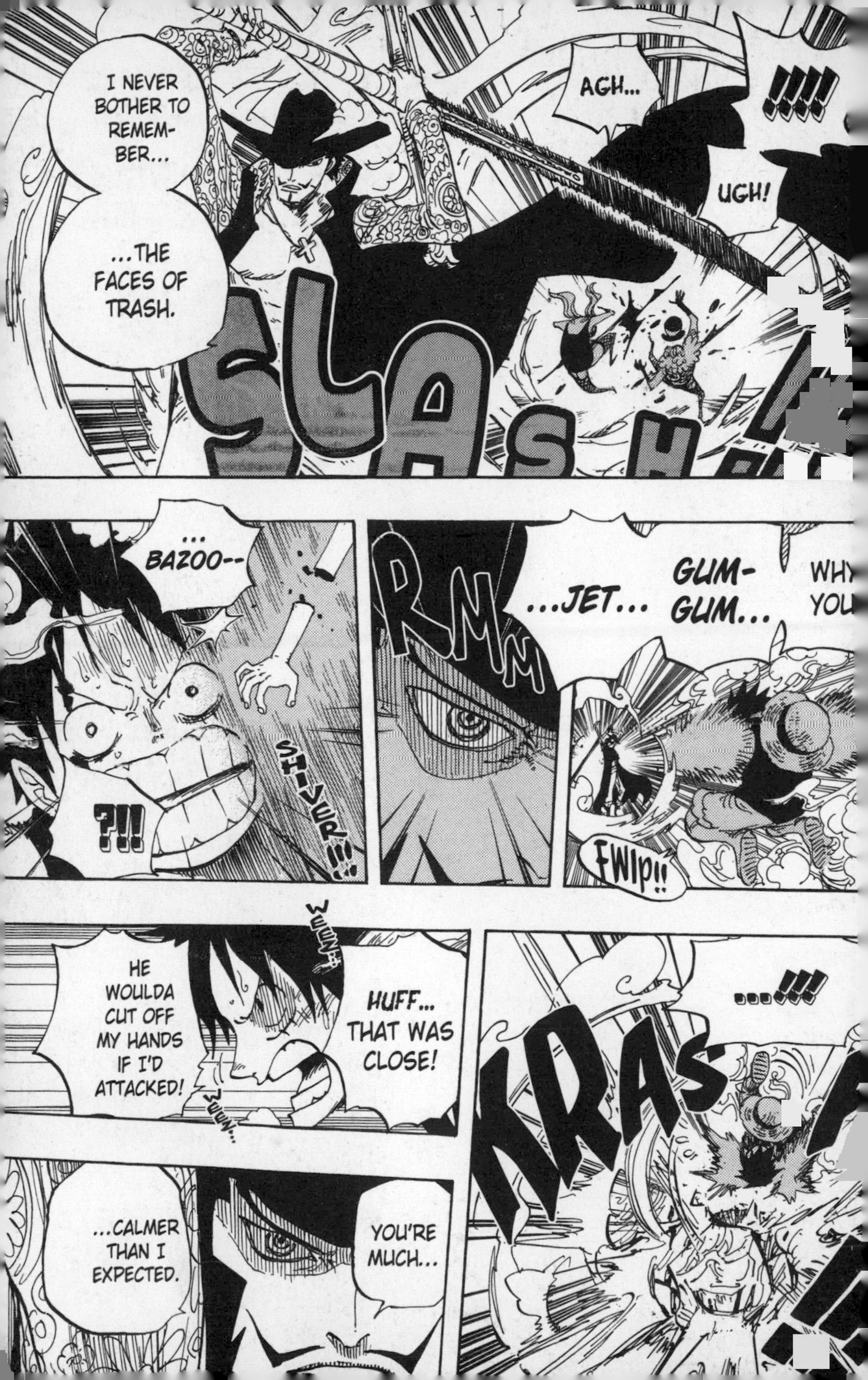
!!!!
AGH...
UGH!
I NEVER BOTHER TO REMEMBER...
...THE FACES OF TRASH.
SLASH
WHY YOU
GUM-GUM...
...JET...
FWIP!!
RMMM
...BAZOO--
?!!
SHIVER!!!
...!!!
KRAS
HUFF... THAT WAS CLOSE!
HE WOULDA CUT OFF MY HANDS IF I'D ATTACKED!
YOU'RE MUCH...
...CALMER THAN I EXPECTED.

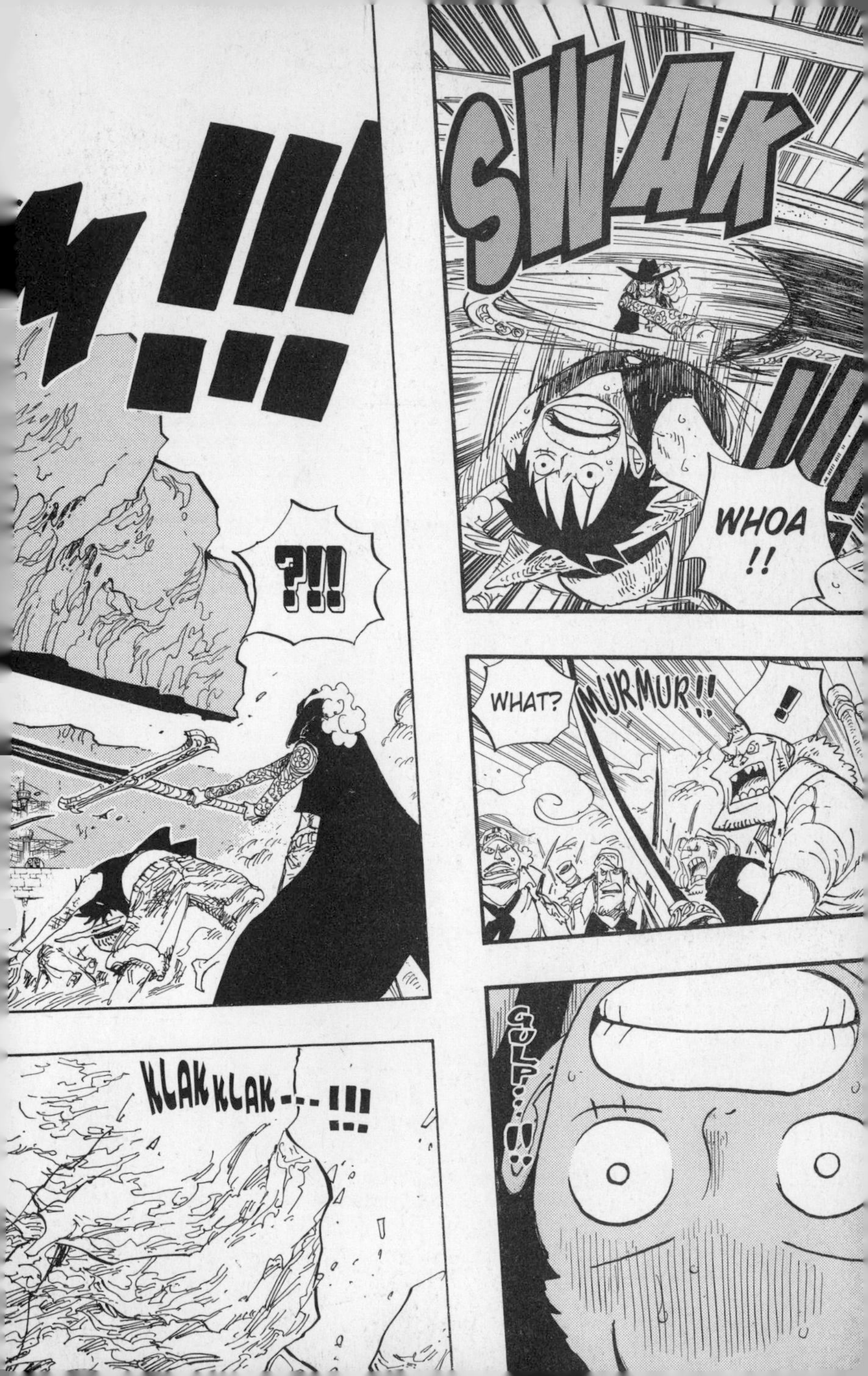
SWAK
WHOA !!
WHAT?
MURMUR!!
!
?!!
GULP...!!
KLAK KLAK...!!!

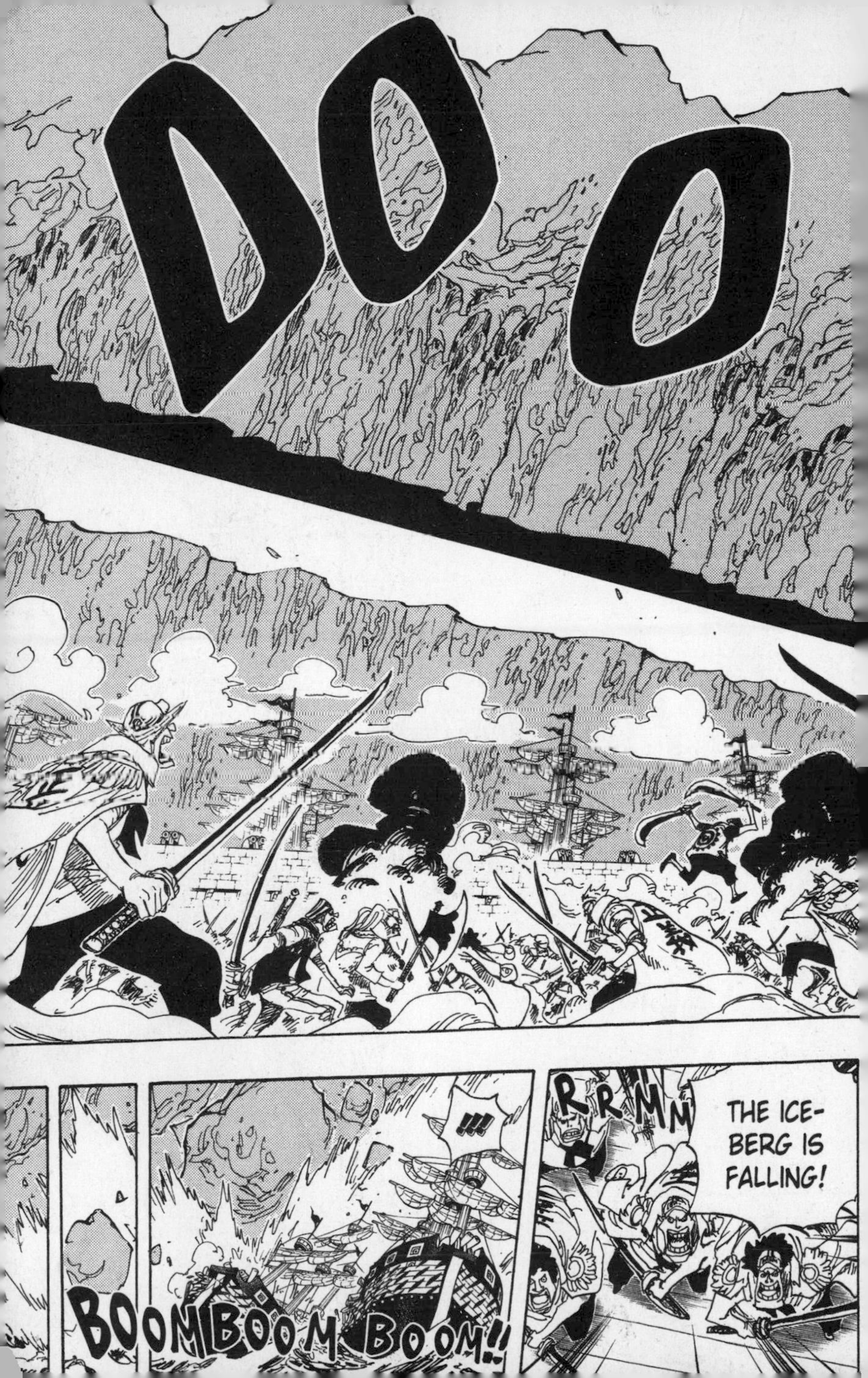
DOO
RRMN
THE ICE-BERG IS FALLING!
!!!
BOOM BOOM BOOM!!

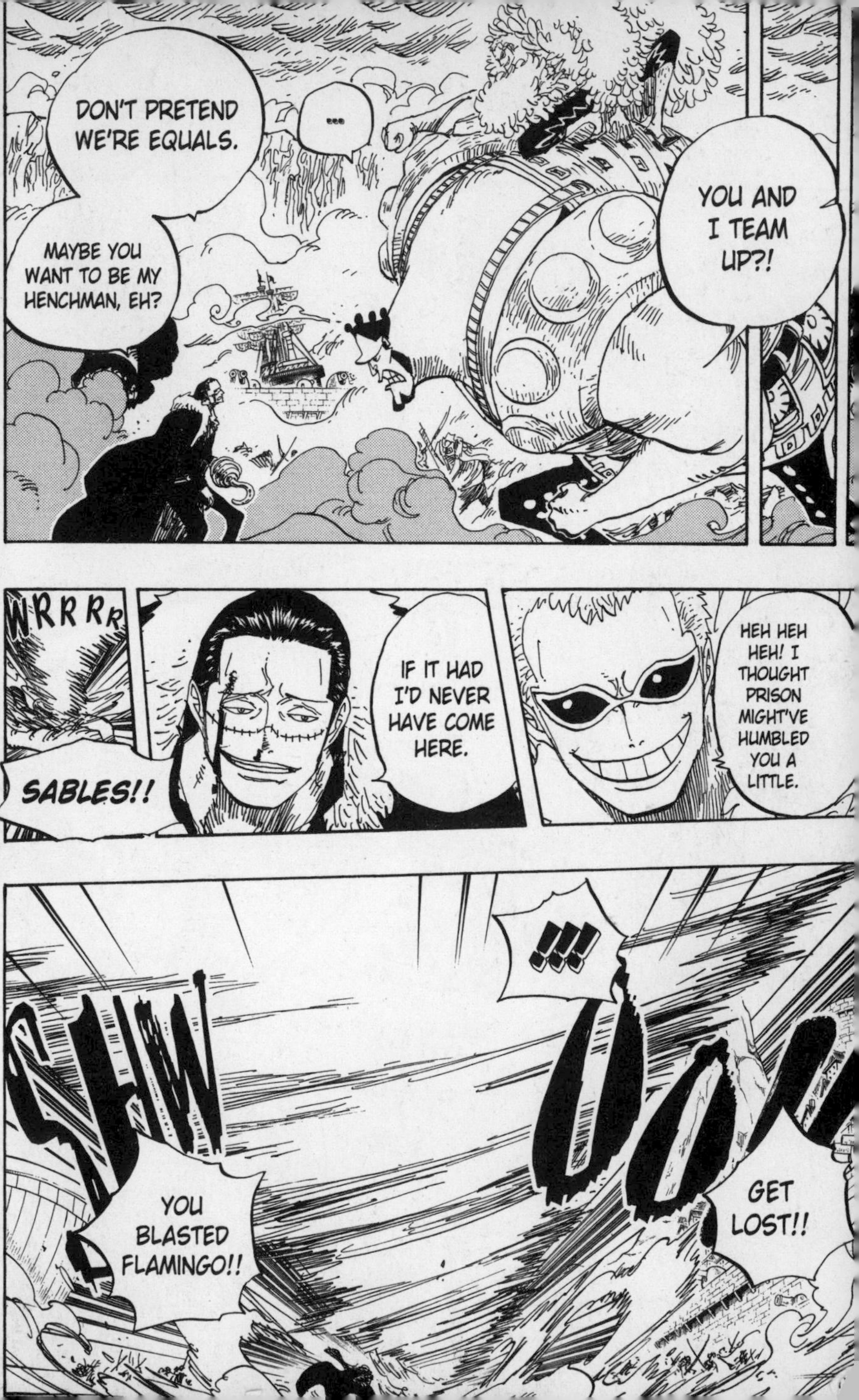
YOU AND I TEAM UP?!
...
DON'T PRETEND WE'RE EQUALS.
MAYBE YOU WANT TO BE MY HENCHMAN, EH?
HEH HEH HEH! I THOUGHT PRISON MIGHT'VE HUMBLED YOU A LITTLE.
IF IT HAD I'D NEVER HAVE COME HERE.
WRRRRR
SABLES!!
!!!
GET LOST!!
YOU BLASTED FLAMINGO!!

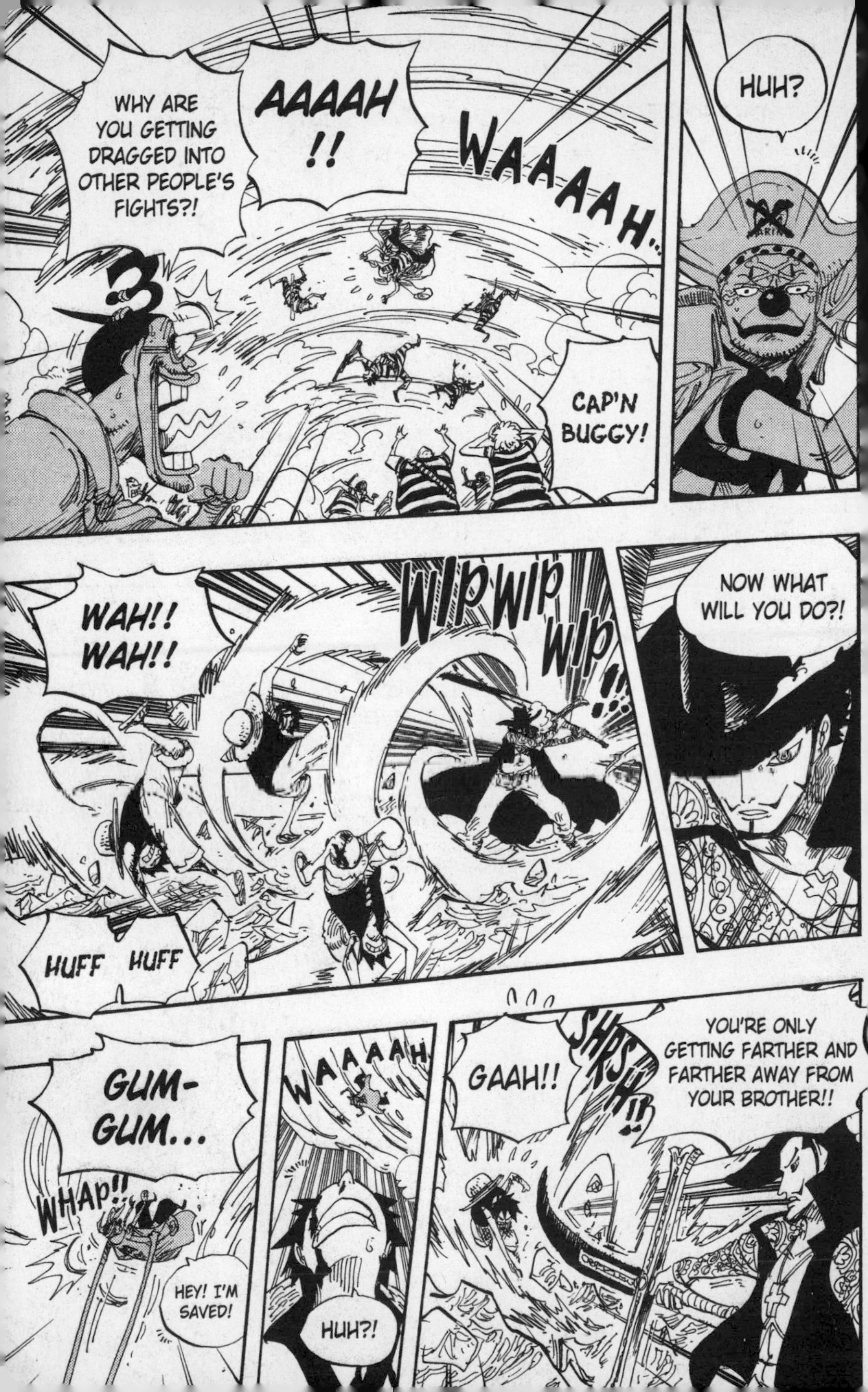
HUH?
WAAAAAH...
AAAAH!!
WHY ARE YOU GETTING DRAGGED INTO OTHER PEOPLE'S FIGHTS?!
CAP'N BUGGY!
NOW WHAT WILL YOU DO?!
WIP WIP WIP!!
WAH!! WAH!!
HUFF HUFF
YOU'RE ONLY GETTING FARTHER AND FARTHER AWAY FROM YOUR BROTHER!!
SHRSH!!
GAAH!!
WAAAAH
HUH?!
GUM-GUM...
WHAP!!
HEY! I'M SAVED!

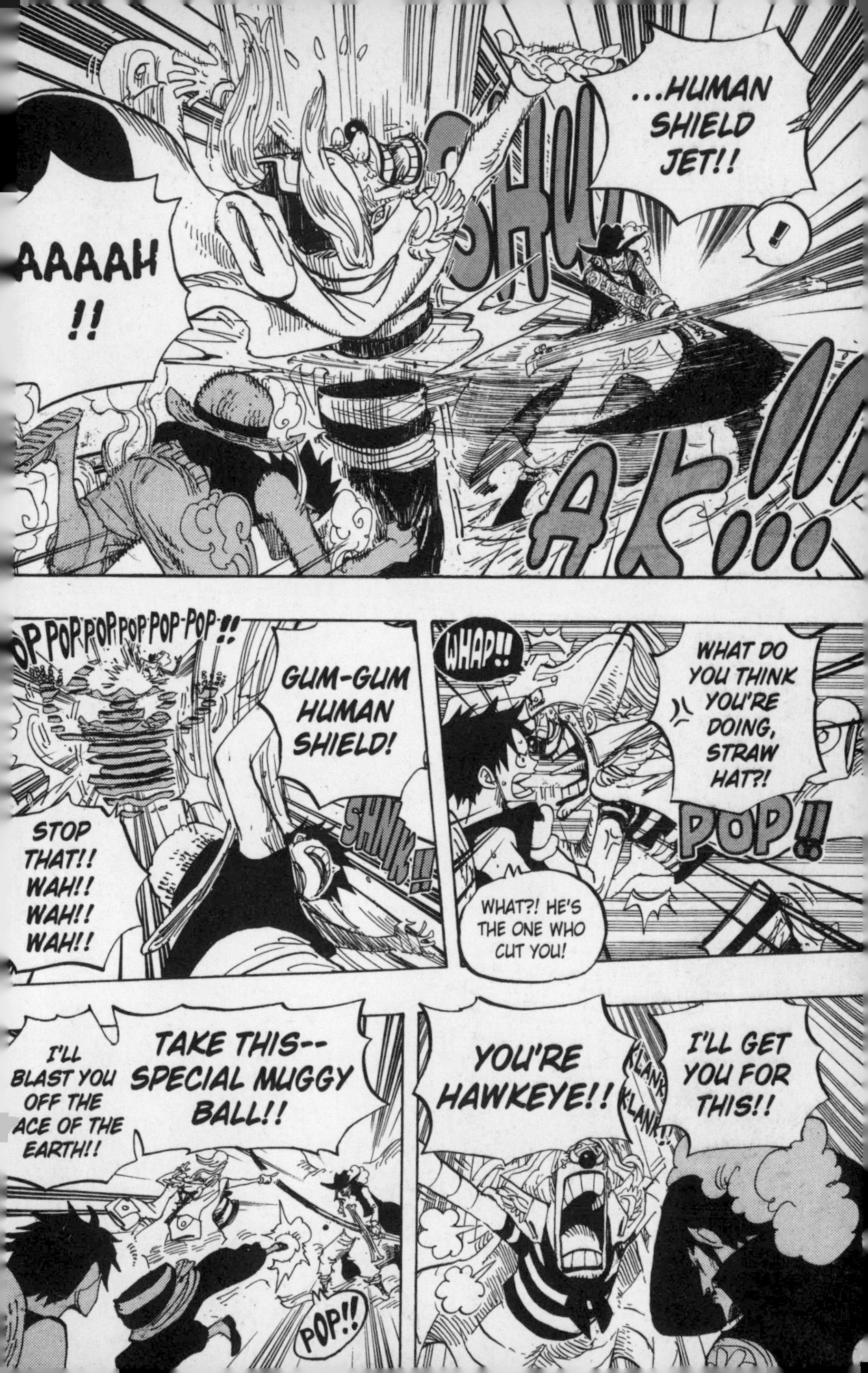
...HUMAN SHIELD JET!!
!
AAAAH !!
WHAP!!
WHAT DO YOU THINK YOU'RE DOING, STRAW HAT?!
POP!!
WHAT?! HE'S THE ONE WHO CUT YOU!
OP POP POP POP POP-POP!!
GUM-GUM HUMAN SHIELD!
SHNIK!!
STOP THAT!! WAH!! WAH!! WAH!!
I'LL GET YOU FOR THIS!!
YOU'RE HAWKEYE!!
KLANK KLANK!!
TAKE THIS-- SPECIAL MUGGY BALL!!
I'LL BLAST YOU OFF THE ACE OF THE EARTH!!
POP!!

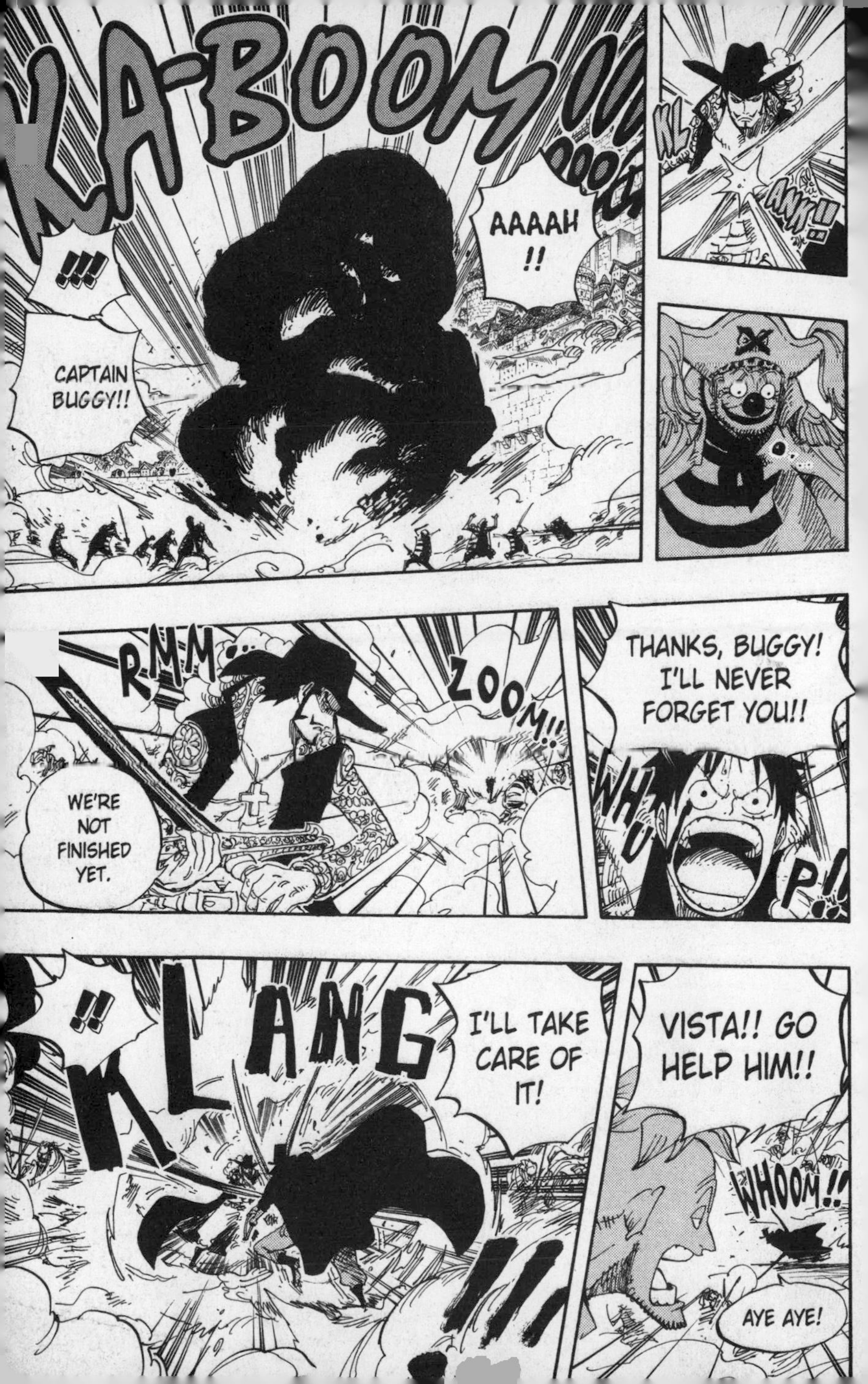
KL
ANK!!
KA-BOOM!!!
AAAAH!!
!!!
CAPTAIN BUGGY!!
THANKS, BUGGY! I'LL NEVER FORGET YOU!!
WHU
P!!
ZOOM!!
RMM..
WE'RE NOT FINISHED YET.
VISTA!! GO HELP HIM!!
WHOOM!!
AYE AYE!
I'LL TAKE CARE OF IT!
KLANG
!!

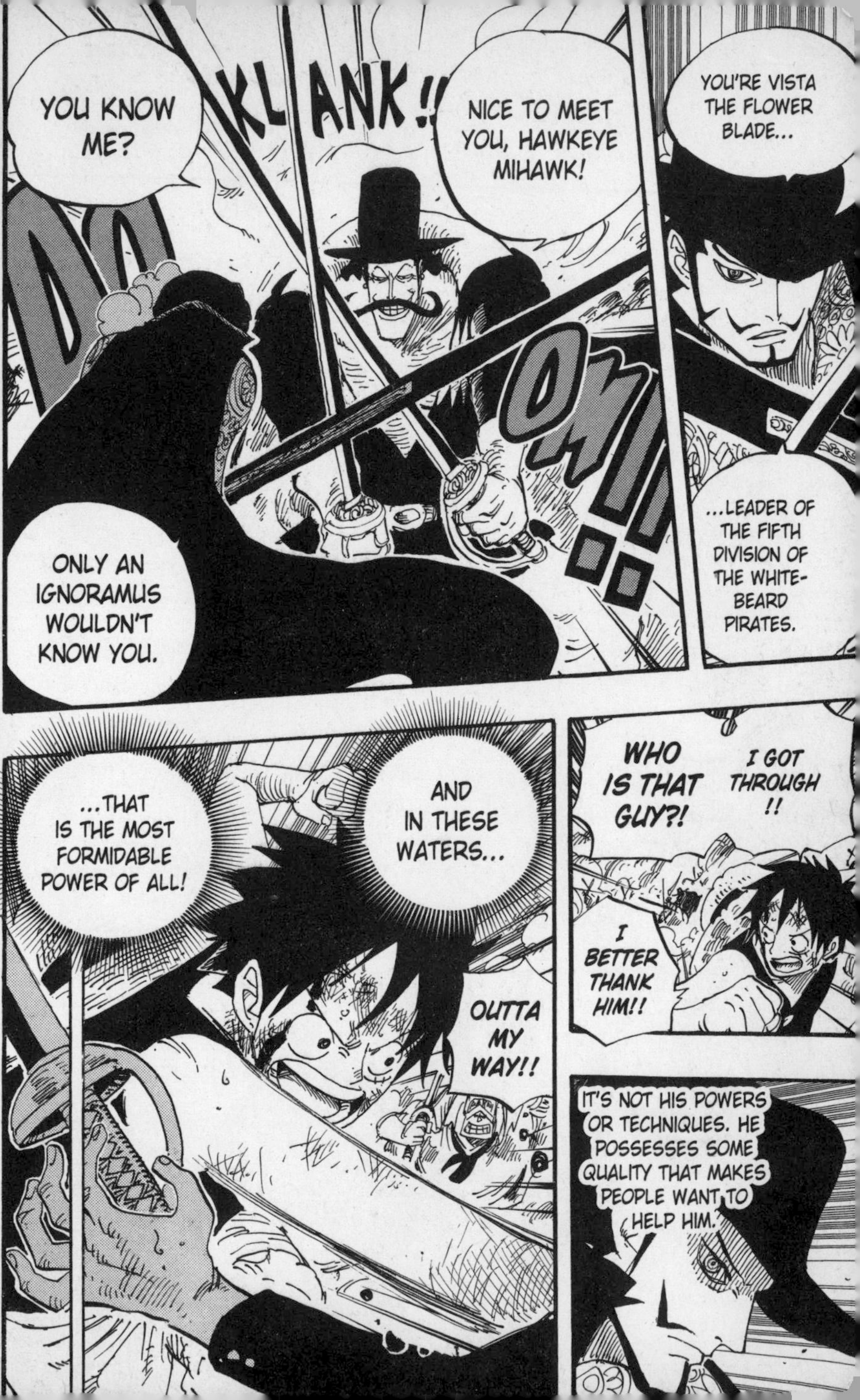
YOU'RE VISTA THE FLOWER BLADE...
...LEADER OF THE FIFTH DIVISION OF THE WHITE-BEARD PIRATES.
KLANK!!
NICE TO MEET YOU, HAWKEYE MIHAWK!
DOOM!!
YOU KNOW ME?
ONLY AN IGNORAMUS WOULDN'T KNOW YOU.
I GOT THROUGH!!
WHO IS THAT GUY?!
I BETTER THANK HIM!!
IT'S NOT HIS POWERS OR TECHNIQUES. HE POSSESSES SOME QUALITY THAT MAKES PEOPLE WANT TO HELP HIM.
AND IN THESE WATERS...
...THAT IS THE MOST FORMIDABLE POWER OF ALL!
OUTTA MY WAY!!

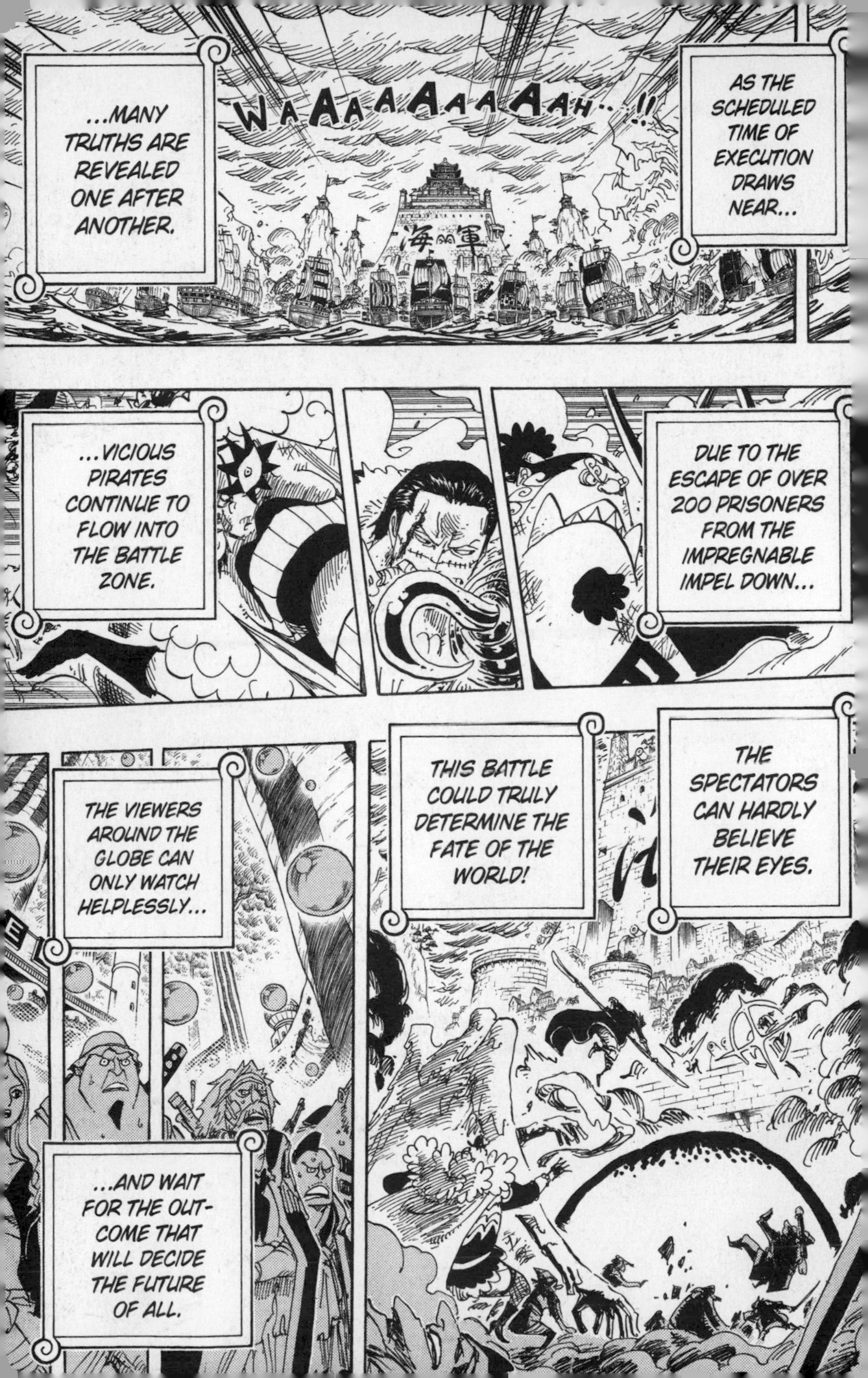
AS THE SCHEDULED TIME OF EXECUTION DRAWS NEAR...
WAAAAAAAAH...!!
...MANY TRUTHS ARE REVEALED ONE AFTER ANOTHER.
DUE TO THE ESCAPE OF OVER 200 PRISONERS FROM THE IMPREGNABLE IMPEL DOWN...
...VICIOUS PIRATES CONTINUE TO FLOW INTO THE BATTLE ZONE.
THE SPECTATORS CAN HARDLY BELIEVE THEIR EYES.
THIS BATTLE COULD TRULY DETERMINE THE FATE OF THE WORLD!
THE VIEWERS AROUND THE GLOBE CAN ONLY WATCH HELPLESSLY...
...AND WAIT FOR THE OUTCOME THAT WILL DECIDE THE FUTURE OF ALL.

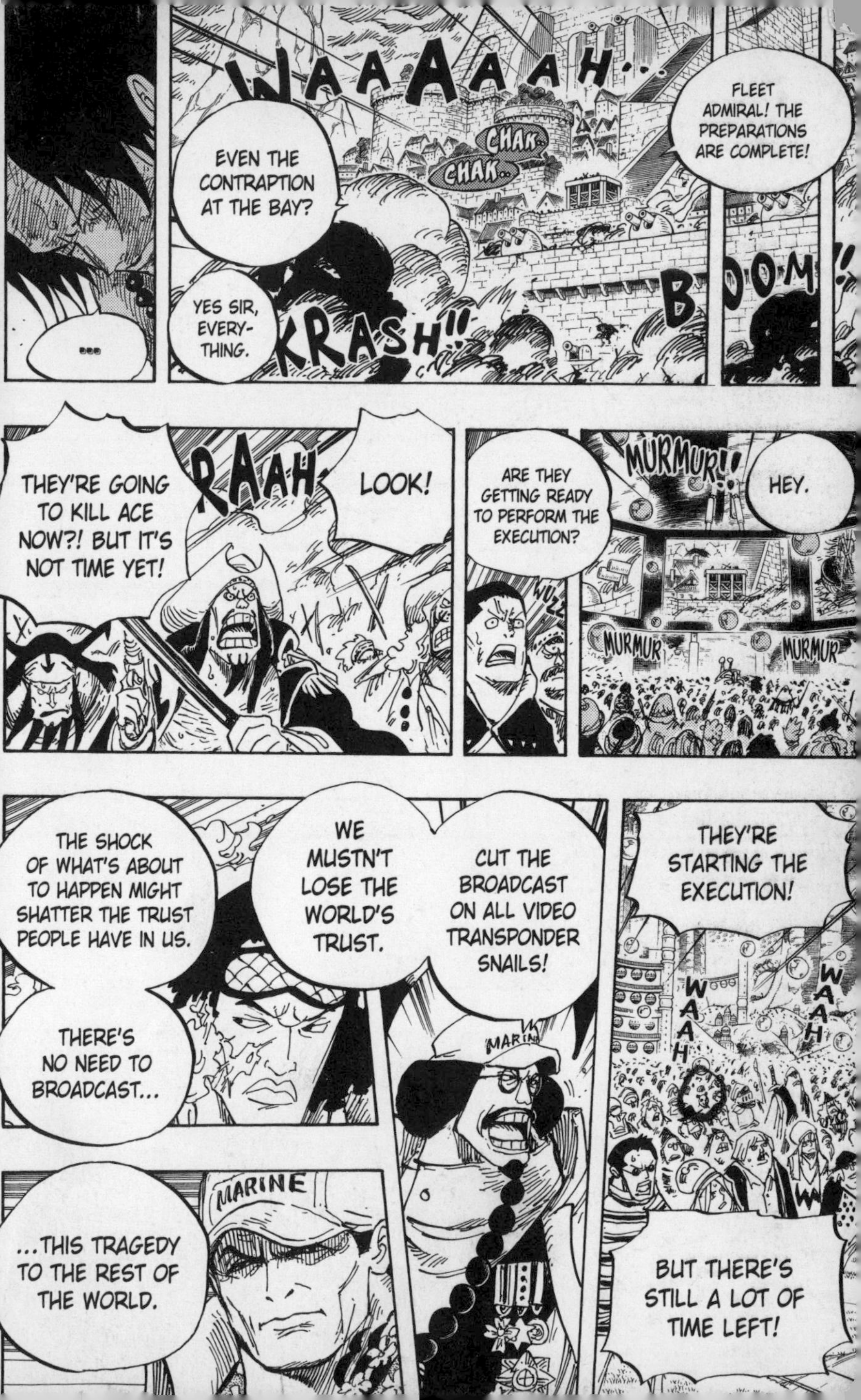
FLEET ADMIRAL! THE PREPARATIONS ARE COMPLETE!
WAAAAAH...
CHAK CHAK..
EVEN THE CONTRAPTION AT THE BAY?
YES SIR, EVERY-THING.
KRASH!!
BOOM!!
...
HEY.
MURMUR!!
MURMUR MURMUR
ARE THEY GETTING READY TO PERFORM THE EXECUTION?
WUZZ
LOOK!
RAAH
THEY'RE GOING TO KILL ACE NOW?! BUT IT'S NOT TIME YET!
THEY'RE STARTING THE EXECUTION!
WAAH WAAH
BUT THERE'S STILL A LOT OF TIME LEFT!
CUT THE BROADCAST ON ALL VIDEO TRANSPONDER SNAILS!
WE MUSTN'T LOSE THE WORLD'S TRUST.
MARINE
THE SHOCK OF WHAT'S ABOUT TO HAPPEN MIGHT SHATTER THE TRUST PEOPLE HAVE IN US.
THERE'S NO NEED TO BROADCAST...
MARINE
...THIS TRAGEDY TO THE REST OF THE WORLD.

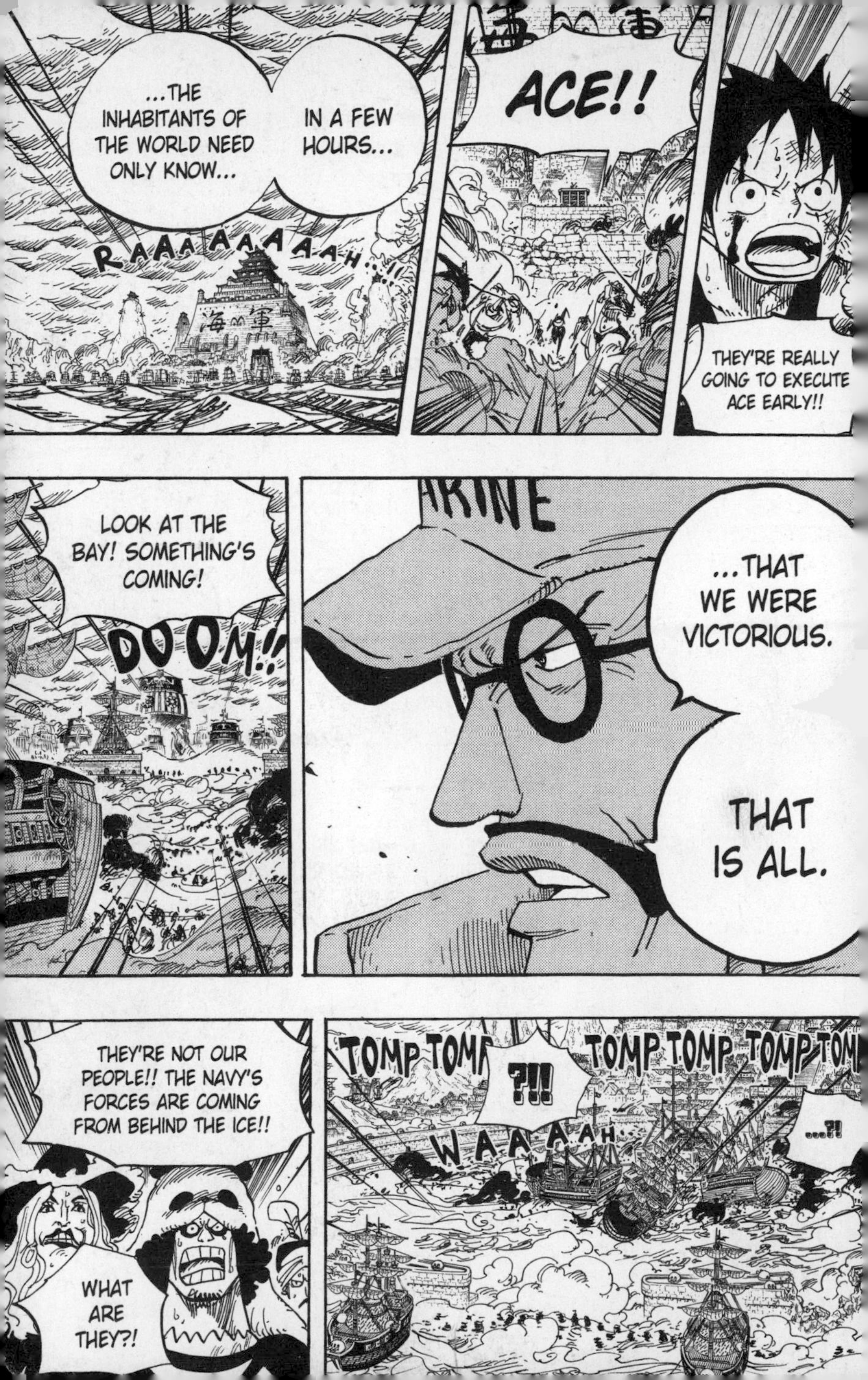
THEY'RE REALLY GOING TO EXECUTE ACE EARLY!!
ACE!!
IN A FEW HOURS...
...THE INHABITANTS OF THE WORLD NEED ONLY KNOW...
RAAAAAAAAAH...!!
...THAT WE WERE VICTORIOUS.
THAT IS ALL.
LOOK AT THE BAY! SOMETHING'S COMING!
DOOM!!
TOMP TOMP TOMP TOMP TOMP TOM
...?!
?!!
TOMP TOMP
WAAAAAH
THEY'RE NOT OUR PEOPLE!! THE NAVY'S FORCES ARE COMING FROM BEHIND THE ICE!!
WHAT ARE THEY?!

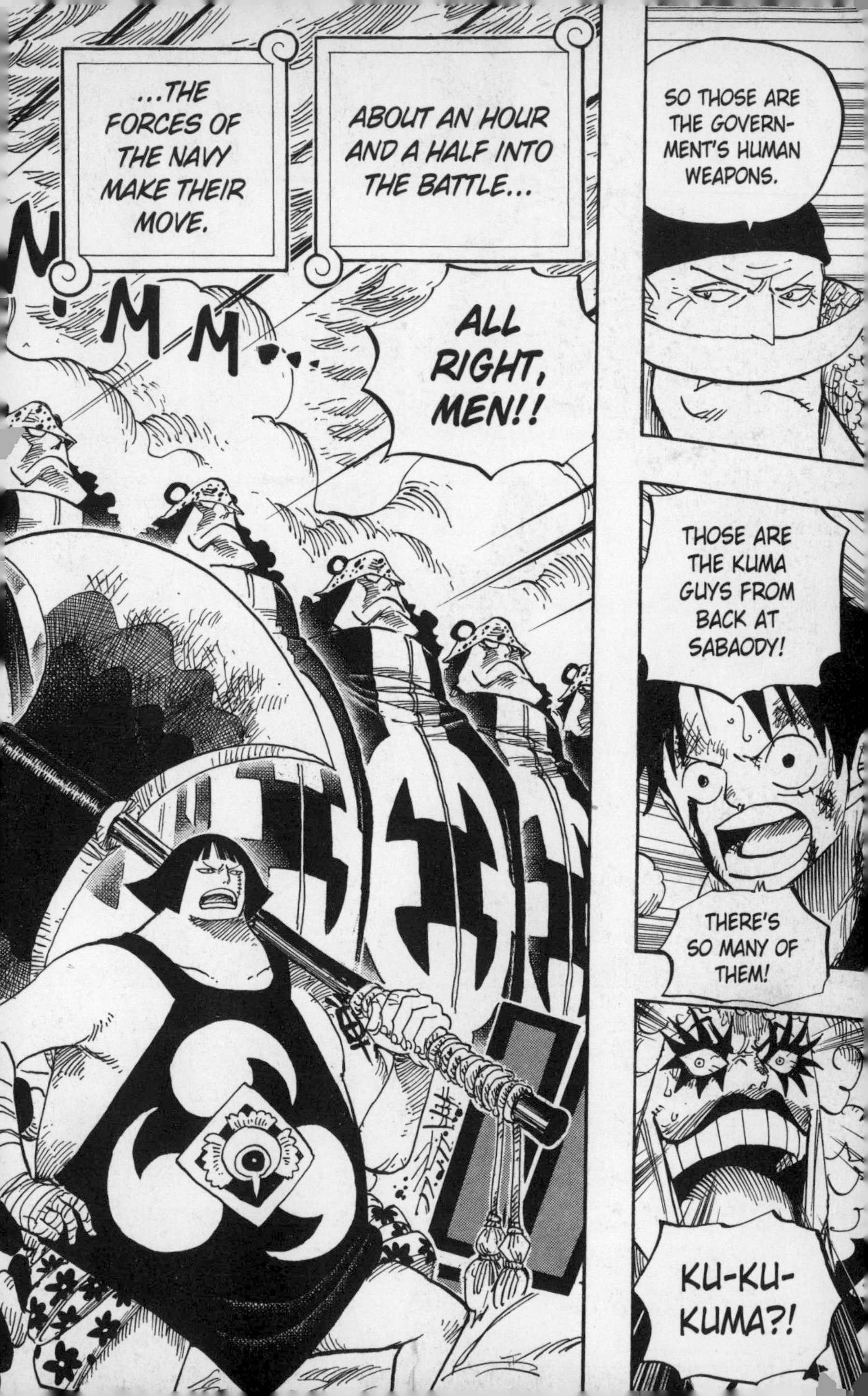
SO THOSE ARE THE GOVERN-MENT'S HUMAN WEAPONS.
THOSE ARE THE KUMA GUYS FROM BACK AT SABAODY!
THERE'S SO MANY OF THEM!
KU-KU-KUMA?!
ABOUT AN HOUR AND A HALF INTO THE BATTLE...
...THE FORCES OF THE NAVY MAKE THEIR MOVE.
NMM
ALL RIGHT, MEN!!

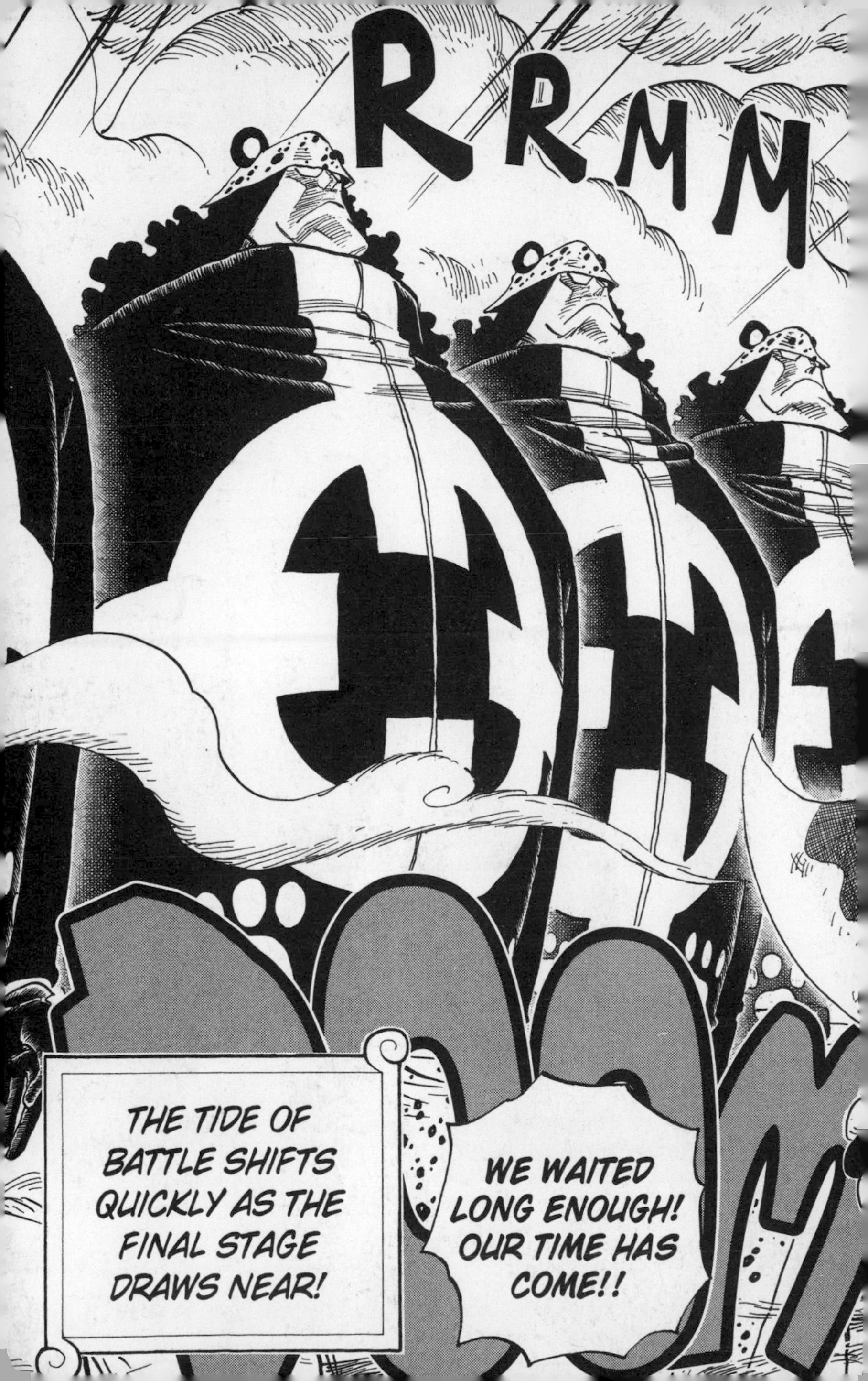
RRMM
WE WAITED LONG ENOUGH! OUR TIME HAS COME!!
THE TIDE OF BATTLE SHIFTS QUICKLY AS THE FINAL STAGE DRAWS NEAR!

THE VOICE OF SANJI, HIROAKI HIRATA!

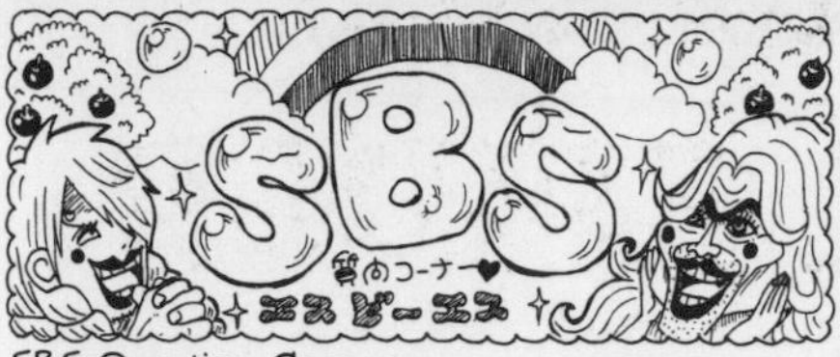
SBS
質問コーナー
エスビーエス
(Skull Yukichi, Iwate Prefecture)

SBS Question Corner

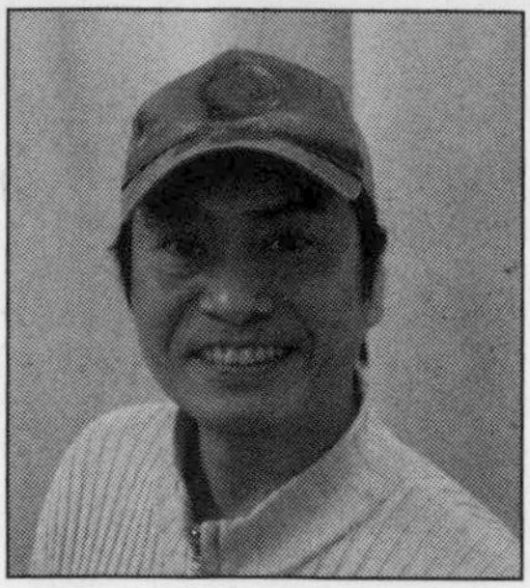

Hello, how do you do?! It's time for our fifth voice actor Question Corner! Who is it this time?! Yes! It's our favorite pervert cook! Sanji's voice! He's actually really good at cooking! And he's a real pervert too! If only he'd keep his mouth shut, people would think he's cool! Hiroaki Hirata in the house!

Oda (O): And now! To fulfill everyone's hopes! Here's Hirata!

Hirata (H): Yo! Here I am! It's finally my turn, isn't it?! Oh, hey! Beautiful ladies! Oh, Nami! Are you watching me? I'm doing the Question Corner right now—Hgeegh!

O: Wait, "Hgeegh"? What is that?

H: Uhh, didn't you write that line somewhere?!

O: Did I? I don't remember at all. Anyway, here are the postcards, so let's do the SBS Question Corner and...

H: Hold on just a second! Do the usual. I always read this part, you know? What happened to your usual questioning about what SBS stands for?

O: I'm done with that. You guys do nothing but try to poke fun at it anyway. Oh, Mr. Hirata's getting depressed... Okay, fine. Then do you know what SBS stands for?

H: What?! (Huge grin) Why would you ask me that all of a sudden? (Huge grin) Man, good question!

O: Whatever. You probably didn't think of anything. Just tell me now.

H: (W)hoops, (D)on't (K)now!

O: You really didn't think of anything! Not even one letter matched!

His Question Corner continues on page 206. ☞

PREVIEW FOR NEXT VOICE ACTOR'S SBS

The next two will feature these two!

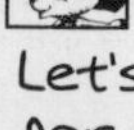 Chopper (Ikue Otani)

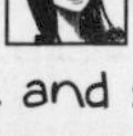 Robin (Yuriko Yamaguchi)

Let's try coming up with cute and strange questions for Chopper! Intelligent but easy questions for Robin!

Chapter 562: WHIRL SPIDER SQUARD

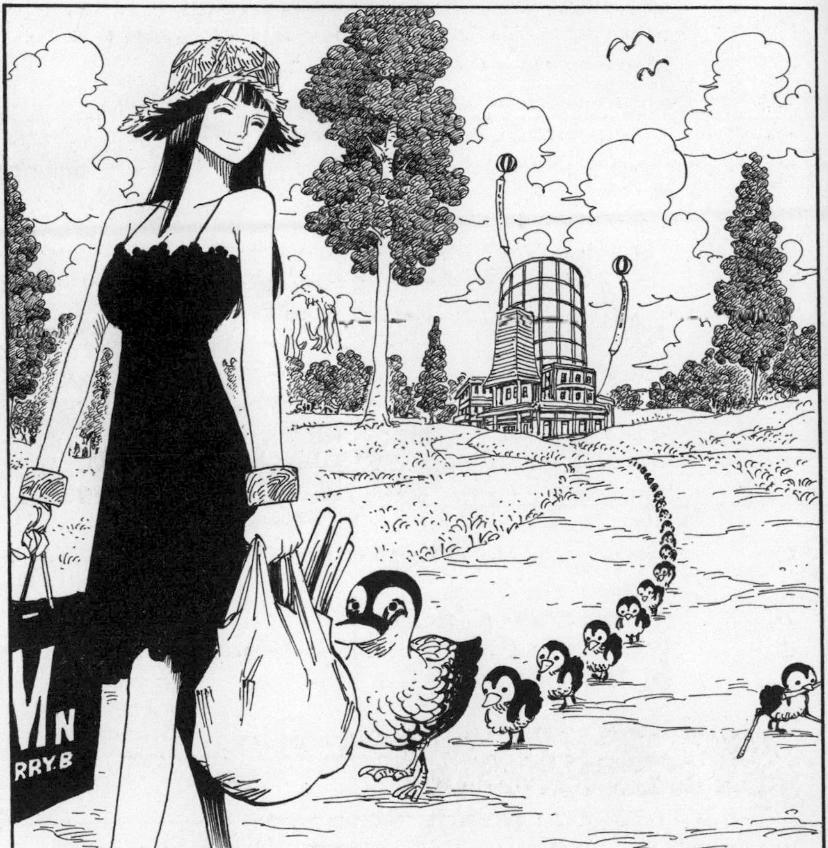
MN
RRY.B

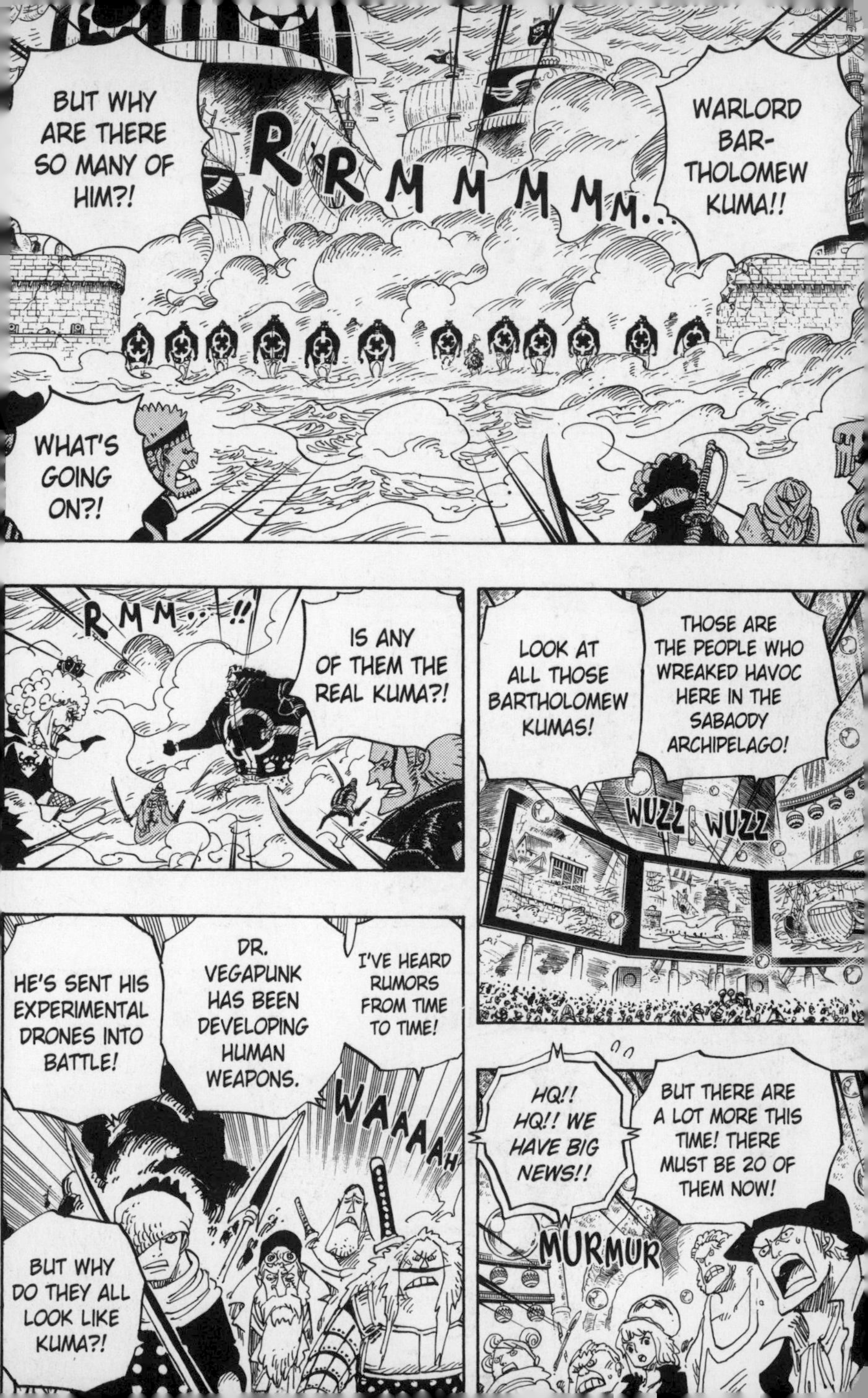
WARLORD BAR-THOLOMEW KUMA!!
RRMMMMMM...
BUT WHY ARE THERE SO MANY OF HIM?!
WHAT'S GOING ON?!
THOSE ARE THE PEOPLE WHO WREAKED HAVOC HERE IN THE SABAODY ARCHIPELAGO!
LOOK AT ALL THOSE BARTHOLOMEW KUMAS!
WUZZ WUZZ
IS ANY OF THEM THE REAL KUMA?!
RMM...!!
I'VE HEARD RUMORS FROM TIME TO TIME!
DR. VEGAPUNK HAS BEEN DEVELOPING HUMAN WEAPONS.
HE'S SENT HIS EXPERIMENTAL DRONES INTO BATTLE!
WAAAAAH
BUT WHY DO THEY ALL LOOK LIKE KUMA?!
BUT THERE ARE A LOT MORE THIS TIME! THERE MUST BE 20 OF THEM NOW!
HQ!! HQ!! WE HAVE BIG NEWS!!
MURMUR

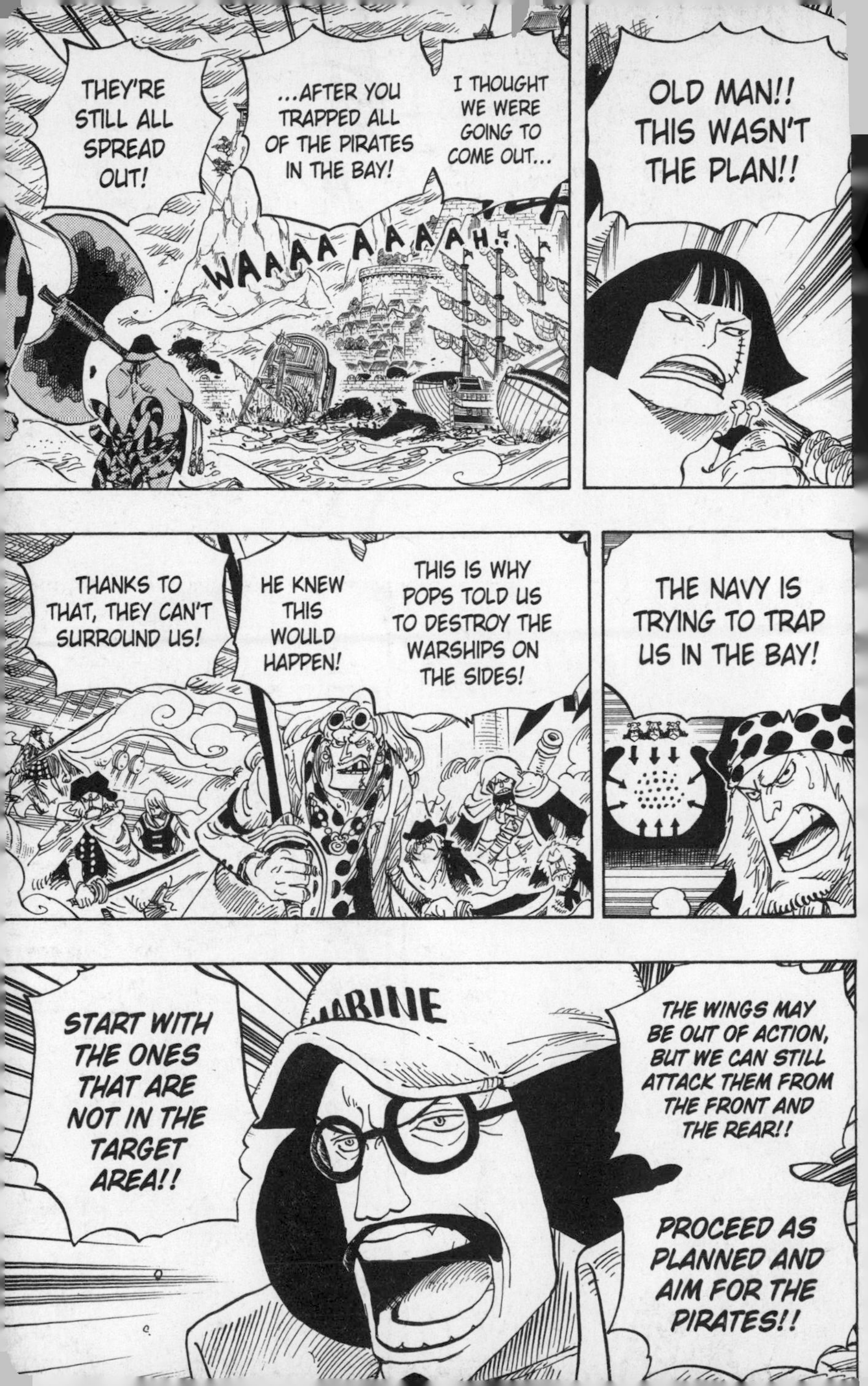
OLD MAN!! THIS WASN'T THE PLAN!!
I THOUGHT WE WERE GOING TO COME OUT...
...AFTER YOU TRAPPED ALL OF THE PIRATES IN THE BAY!
THEY'RE STILL ALL SPREAD OUT!
WAAAAAAAAAH!!
THE NAVY IS TRYING TO TRAP US IN THE BAY!
THIS IS WHY POPS TOLD US TO DESTROY THE WARSHIPS ON THE SIDES!
HE KNEW THIS WOULD HAPPEN!
THANKS TO THAT, THEY CAN'T SURROUND US!
THE WINGS MAY BE OUT OF ACTION, BUT WE CAN STILL ATTACK THEM FROM THE FRONT AND THE REAR!!
PROCEED AS PLANNED AND AIM FOR THE PIRATES!!
START WITH THE ONES THAT ARE NOT IN THE TARGET AREA!!

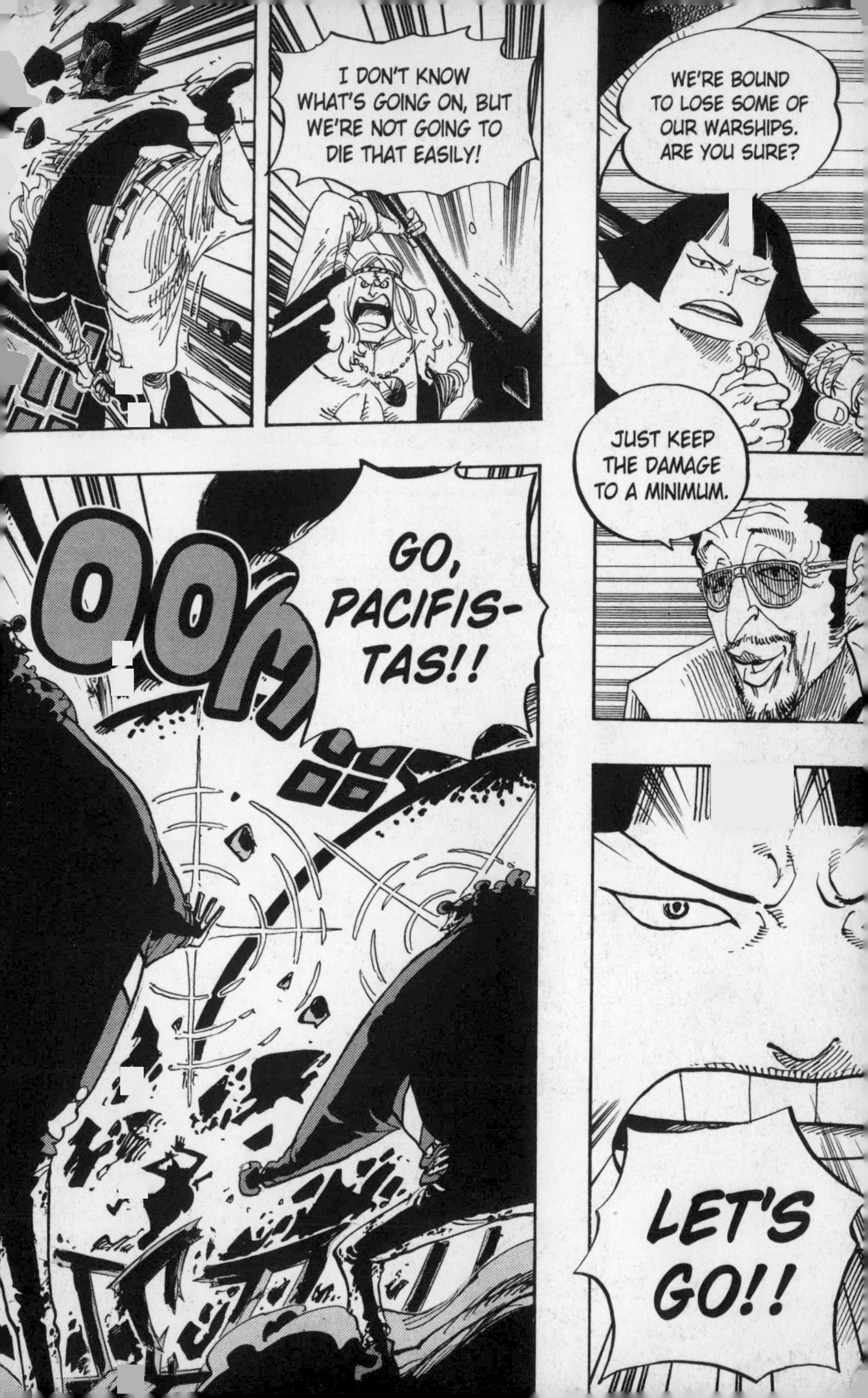
WE'RE BOUND TO LOSE SOME OF OUR WARSHIPS. ARE YOU SURE?
I DON'T KNOW WHAT'S GOING ON, BUT WE'RE NOT GOING TO DIE THAT EASILY!
JUST KEEP THE DAMAGE TO A MINIMUM.
LET'S GO!!
GO, PACIFIS-TAS!!
OOH

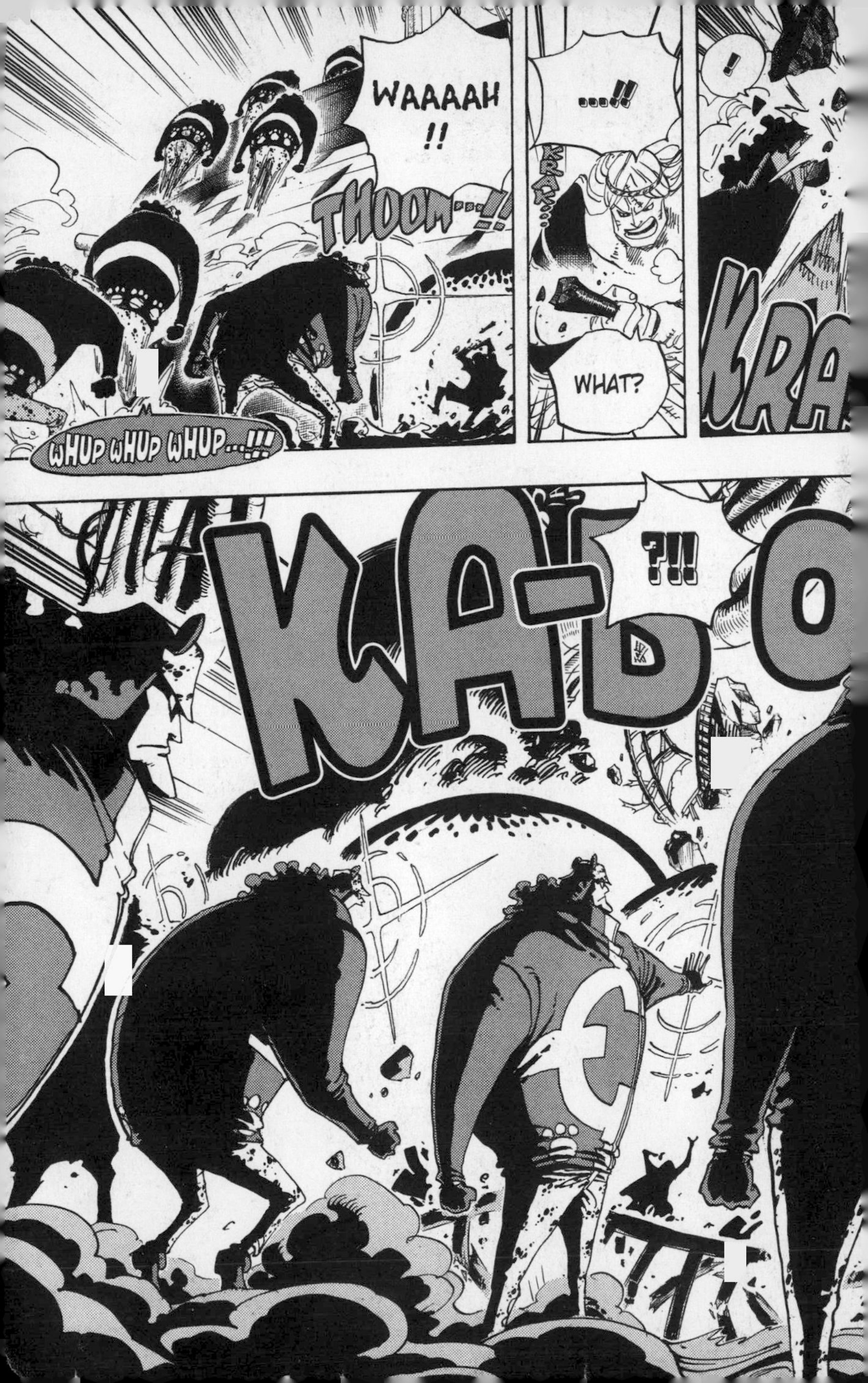
!
KRA
...!!
KRAK...
WHAT?
WAAAAH !!
THOOM...!!
WHUP WHUP WHUP...!!!
?!!
KA-BO

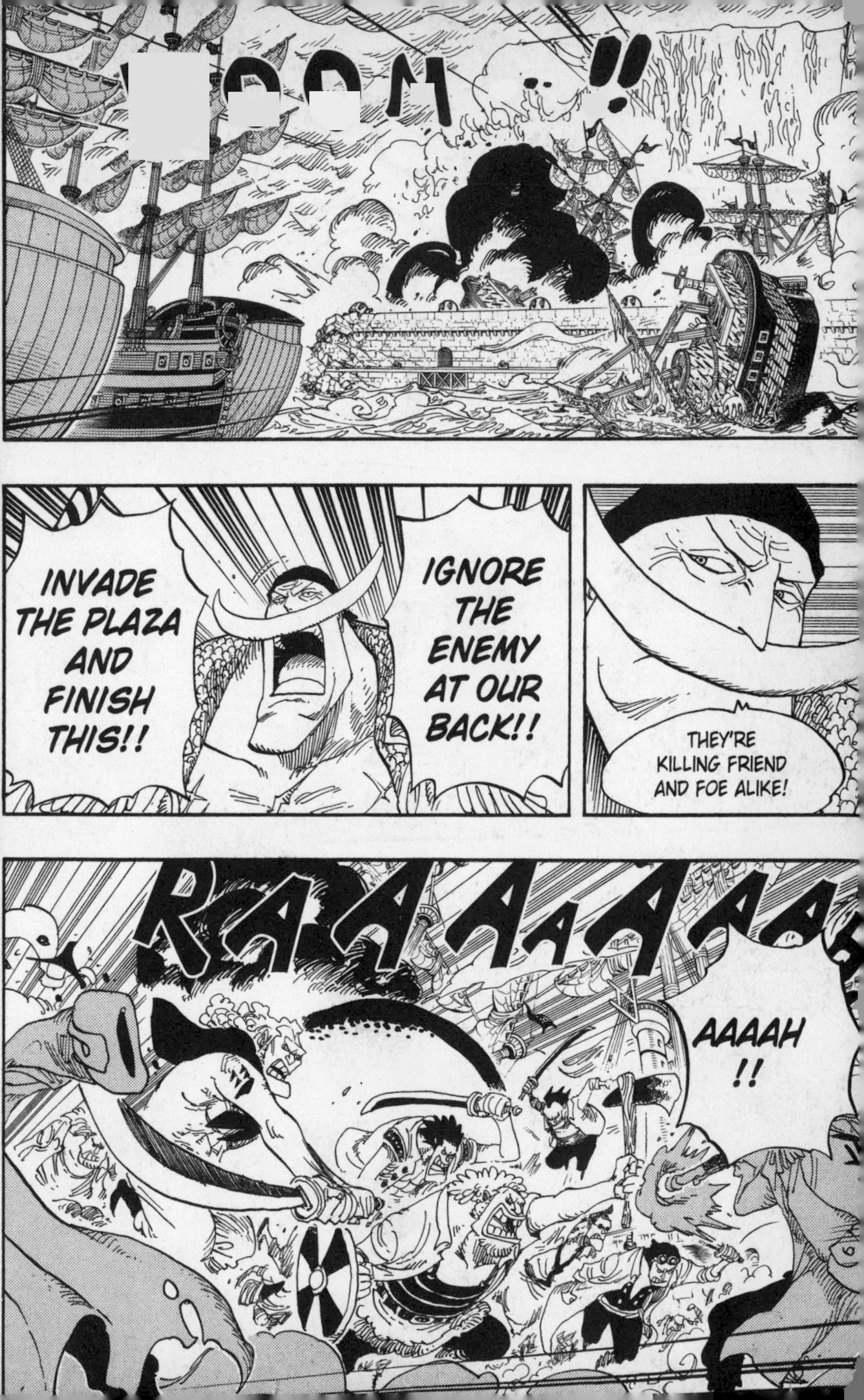
THEY'RE KILLING FRIEND AND FOE ALIKE!
IGNORE THE ENEMY AT OUR BACK!!
INVADE THE PLAZA AND FINISH THIS!!
RAAAAAAA
AAAAH !!

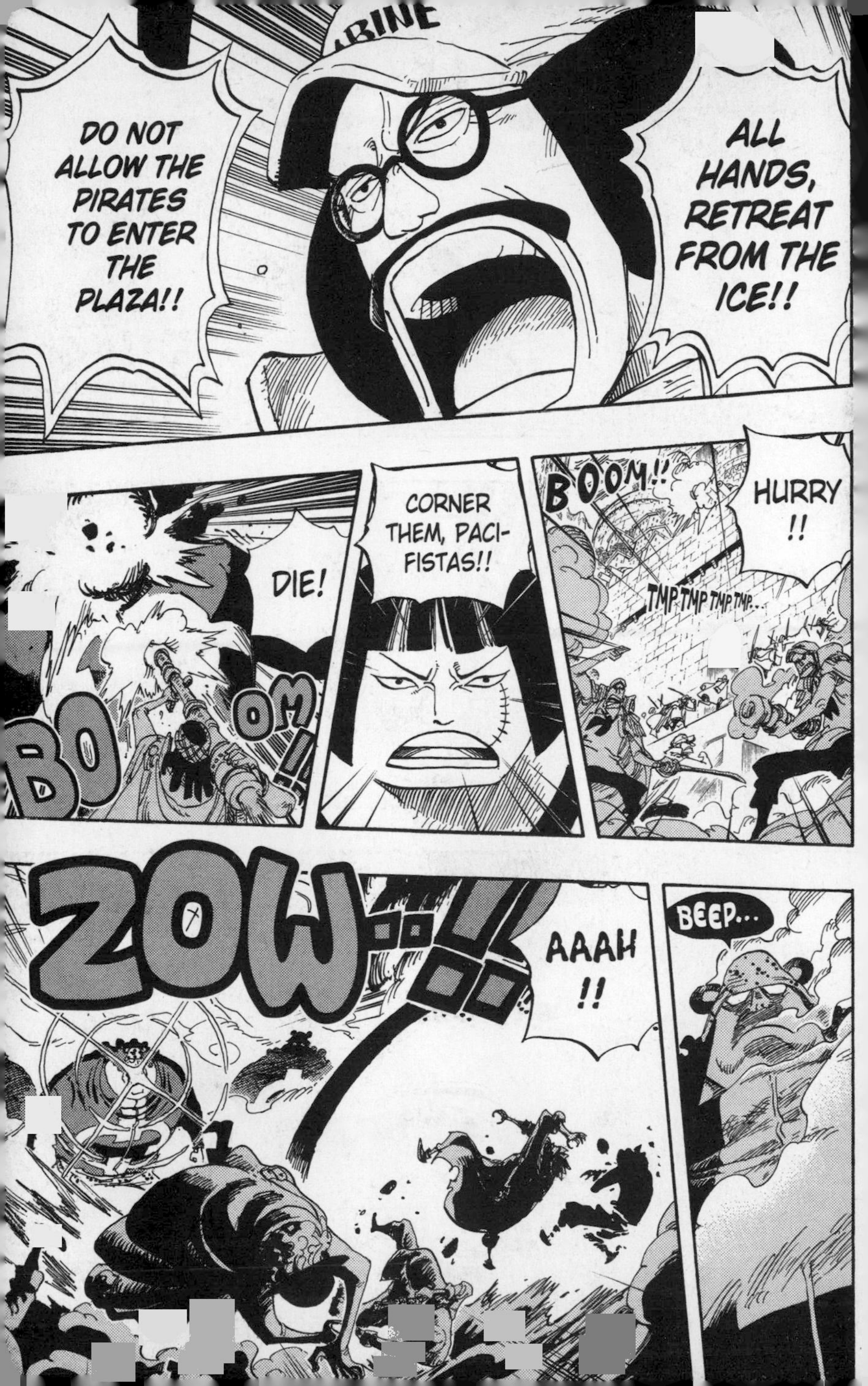
ALL HANDS, RETREAT FROM THE ICE!!
DO NOT ALLOW THE PIRATES TO ENTER THE PLAZA!!
HURRY !!
BOOM!!
TMP TMP TMP TMP...
CORNER THEM, PACI- FISTAS!!
DIE!
BOOM
BEEP...
AAAH !!
ZOW!!

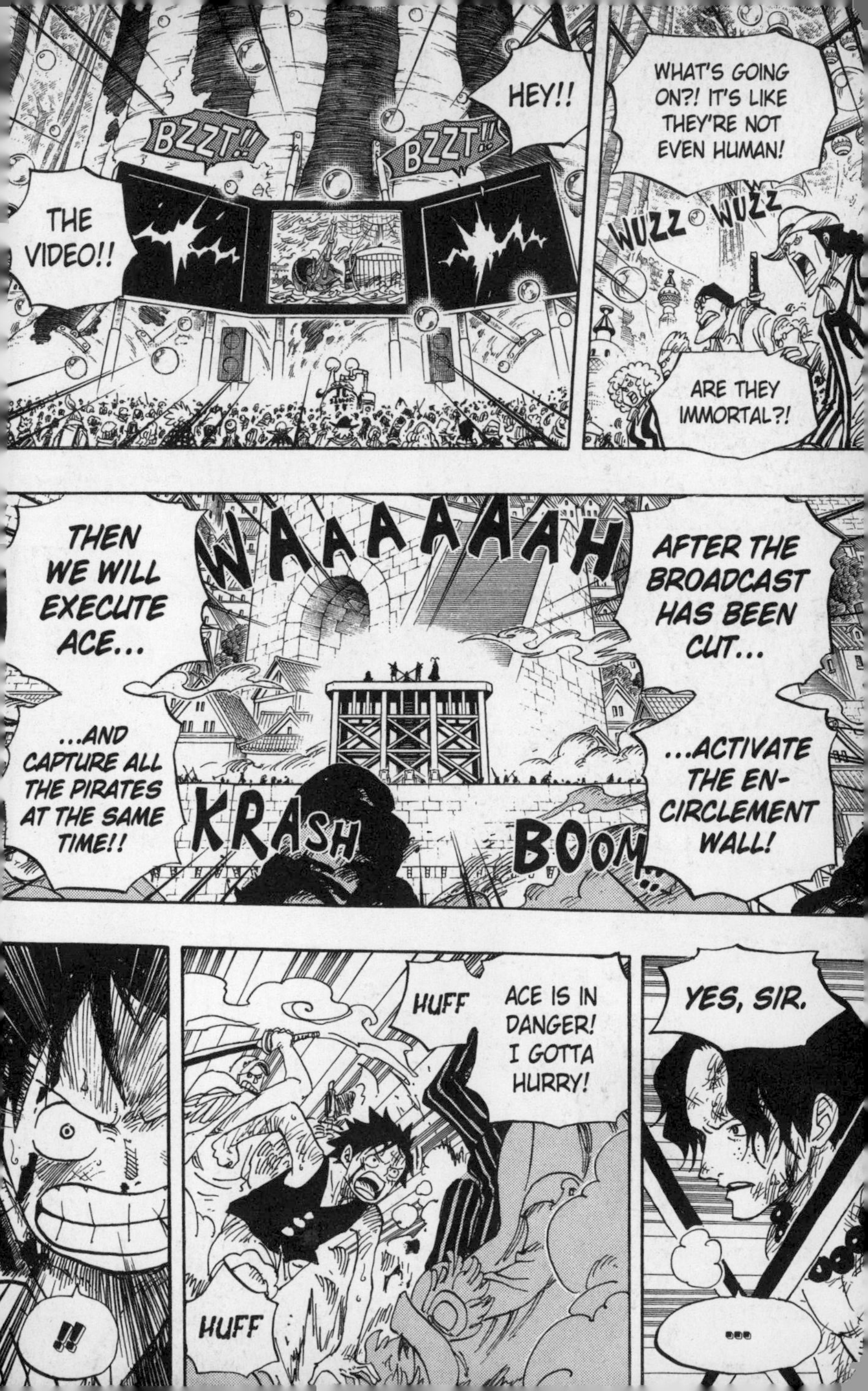

WHAT'S GOING ON?! IT'S LIKE THEY'RE NOT EVEN HUMAN!
WUZZ WUZZ
ARE THEY IMMORTAL?!
HEY!!
BZZT!!
BZZT!!
THE VIDEO!!
AFTER THE BROADCAST HAS BEEN CUT...
WAAAAAAH
THEN WE WILL EXECUTE ACE...
...ACTIVATE THE EN-CIRCLEMENT WALL!
BOOM..
KRASH
...AND CAPTURE ALL THE PIRATES AT THE SAME TIME!!
YES, SIR.
...
ACE IS IN DANGER! I GOTTA HURRY!
HUFF
HUFF
!!

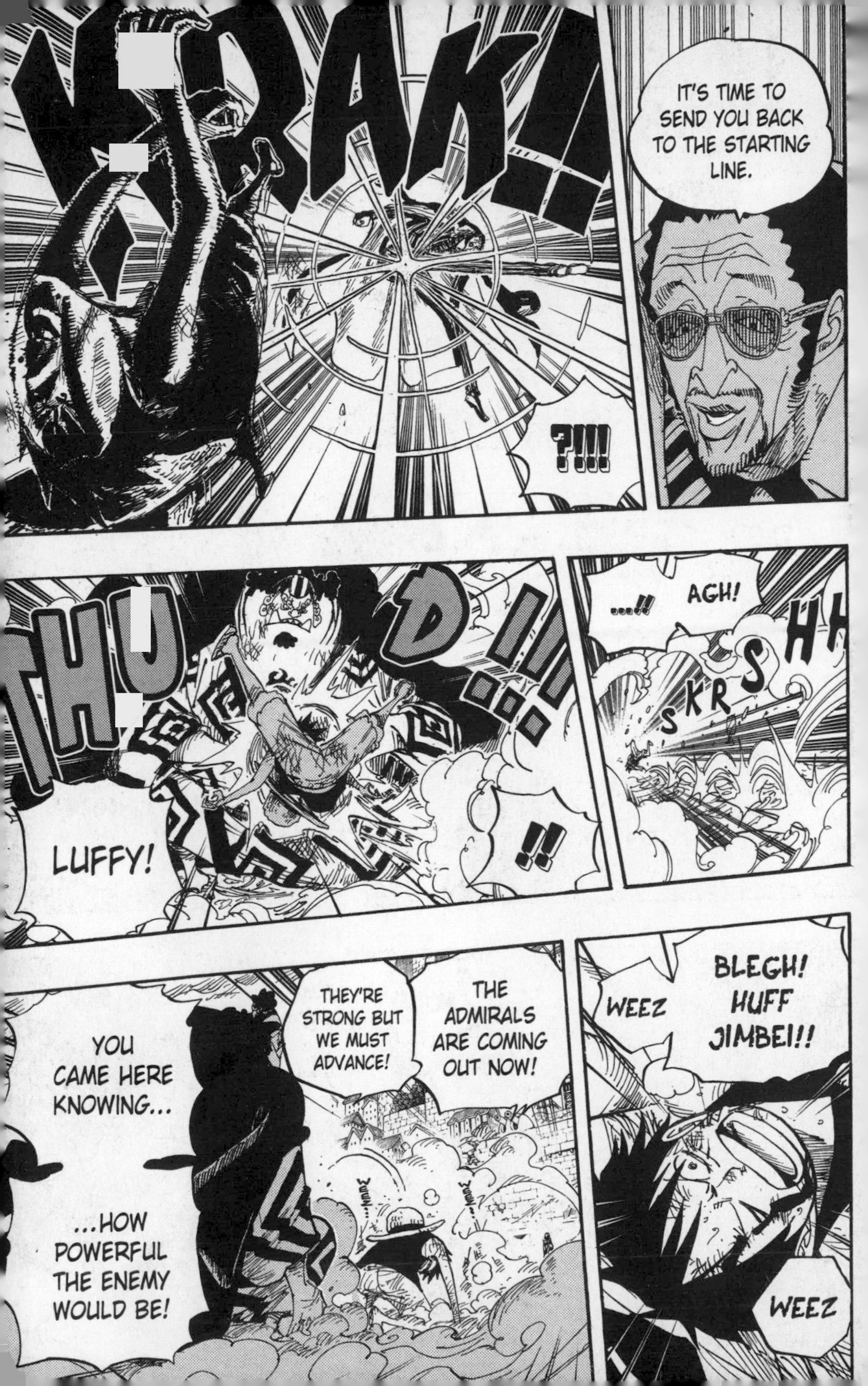
IT'S TIME TO SEND YOU BACK TO THE STARTING LINE.
KRAK!!
?!!!
...!!
AGH!
SKRSHH
THUD!!
LUFFY!
!!
BLEGH! HUFF JIMBEI!!
WEEZ
WEEZ
THE ADMIRALS ARE COMING OUT NOW!
THEY'RE STRONG BUT WE MUST ADVANCE!
YOU CAME HERE KNOWING...
...HOW POWERFUL THE ENEMY WOULD BE!

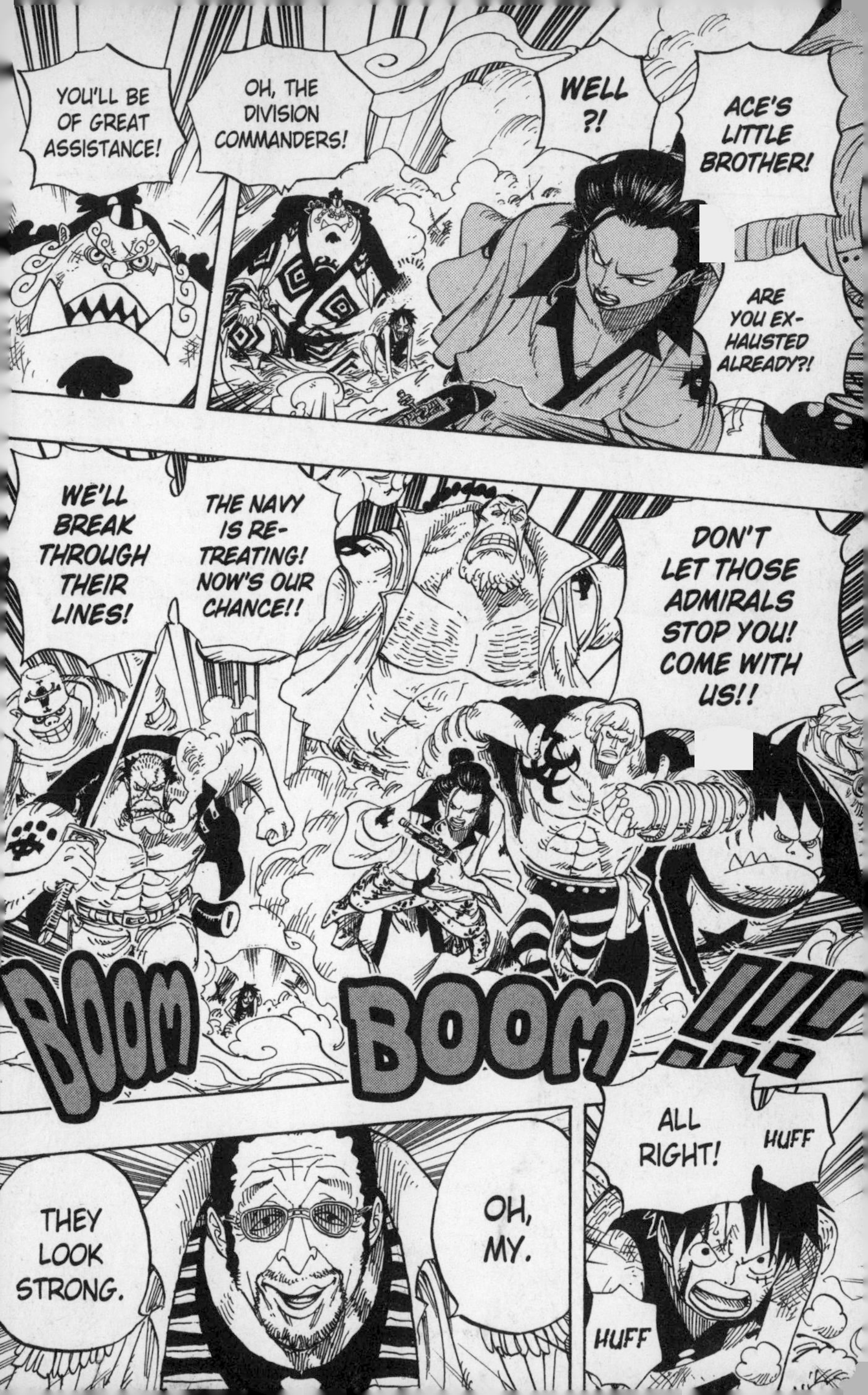
WELL ?!
ACE'S LITTLE BROTHER!
ARE YOU EXHAUSTED ALREADY?!
OH, THE DIVISION COMMANDERS!
YOU'LL BE OF GREAT ASSISTANCE!
DON'T LET THOSE ADMIRALS STOP YOU! COME WITH US!!
THE NAVY IS RETREATING! NOW'S OUR CHANCE!!
WE'LL BREAK THROUGH THEIR LINES!
BOOM BOOM!!!
ALL RIGHT!
HUFF
HUFF
OH, MY.
THEY LOOK STRONG.

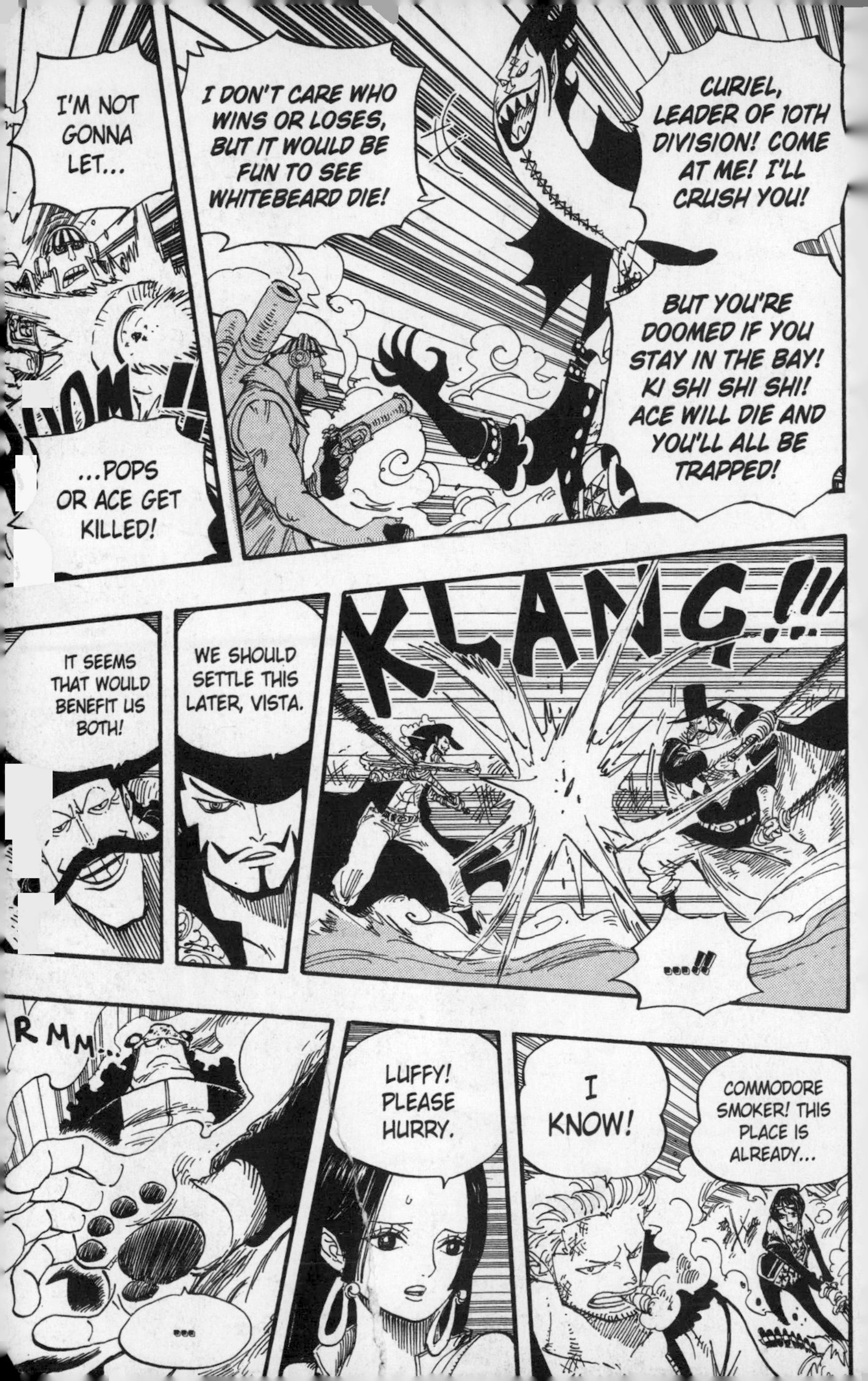
CURIEL, LEADER OF 10TH DIVISION! COME AT ME! I'LL CRUSH YOU!
I DON'T CARE WHO WINS OR LOSES, BUT IT WOULD BE FUN TO SEE WHITEBEARD DIE!
BUT YOU'RE DOOMED IF YOU STAY IN THE BAY! KI SHI SHI SHI! ACE WILL DIE AND YOU'LL ALL BE TRAPPED!
I'M NOT GONNA LET...
...POPS OR ACE GET KILLED!
KLANG!!!
...!!
WE SHOULD SETTLE THIS LATER, VISTA.
IT SEEMS THAT WOULD BENEFIT US BOTH!
COMMODORE SMOKER! THIS PLACE IS ALREADY...
I KNOW!
LUFFY! PLEASE HURRY.
RMM...
...

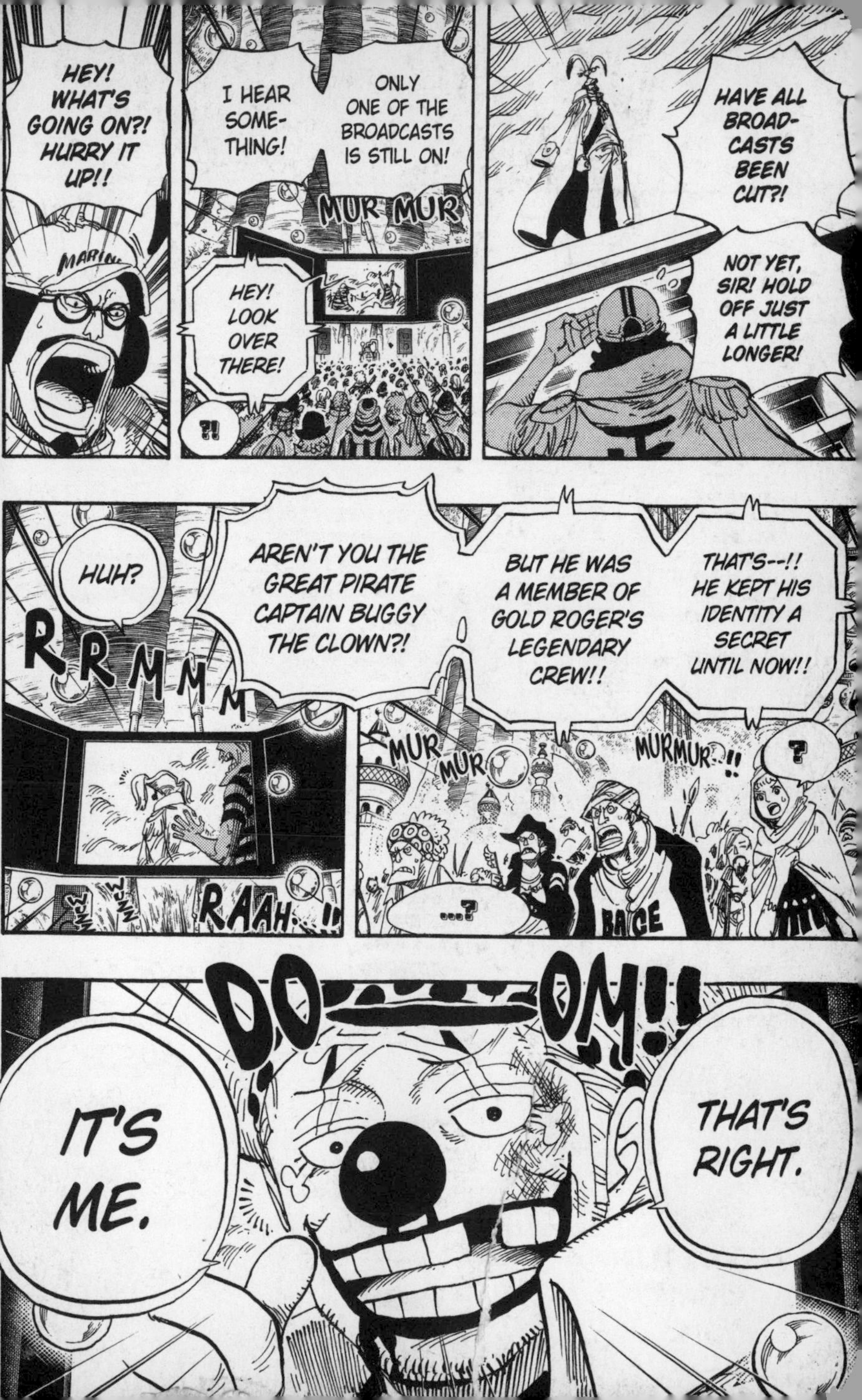
HAVE ALL BROADCASTS BEEN CUT?!
NOT YET, SIR! HOLD OFF JUST A LITTLE LONGER!
ONLY ONE OF THE BROADCASTS IS STILL ON!
I HEAR SOMETHING!
MUR MUR
HEY! LOOK OVER THERE!
?!
HEY! WHAT'S GOING ON?! HURRY IT UP!!
?
THAT'S--!! HE KEPT HIS IDENTITY A SECRET UNTIL NOW!!
MURMUR..!!
BUT HE WAS A MEMBER OF GOLD ROGER'S LEGENDARY CREW!!
MUR MUR
...?
AREN'T YOU THE GREAT PIRATE CAPTAIN BUGGY THE CLOWN?!
HUH?
RRMMMM
RAAH..!!
DO—OM!!
THAT'S RIGHT.
IT'S ME.

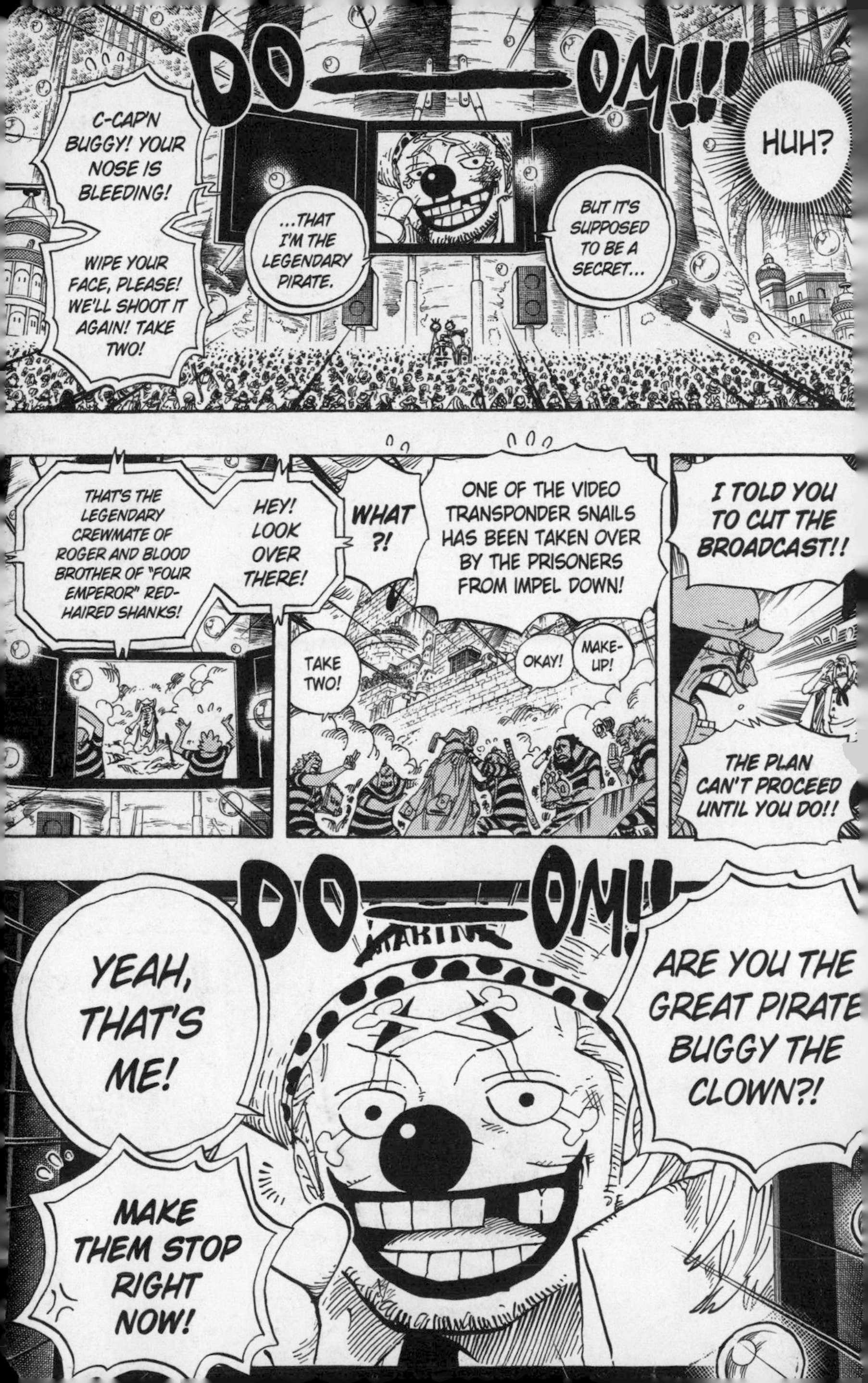
DO—OM!!!
HUH?
BUT IT'S SUPPOSED TO BE A SECRET...
...THAT I'M THE LEGENDARY PIRATE.
C-CAP'N BUGGY! YOUR NOSE IS BLEEDING!
WIPE YOUR FACE, PLEASE! WE'LL SHOOT IT AGAIN! TAKE TWO!
I TOLD YOU TO CUT THE BROADCAST!!
THE PLAN CAN'T PROCEED UNTIL YOU DO!!
ONE OF THE VIDEO TRANSPONDER SNAILS HAS BEEN TAKEN OVER BY THE PRISONERS FROM IMPEL DOWN!
WHAT ?!
MAKE-UP!
OKAY!
TAKE TWO!
HEY! LOOK OVER THERE!
THAT'S THE LEGENDARY CREWMATE OF ROGER AND BLOOD BROTHER OF "FOUR EMPEROR" RED-HAIRED SHANKS!
DO—OM!!
ARE YOU THE GREAT PIRATE BUGGY THE CLOWN?!
YEAH, THAT'S ME!
MAKE THEM STOP RIGHT NOW!

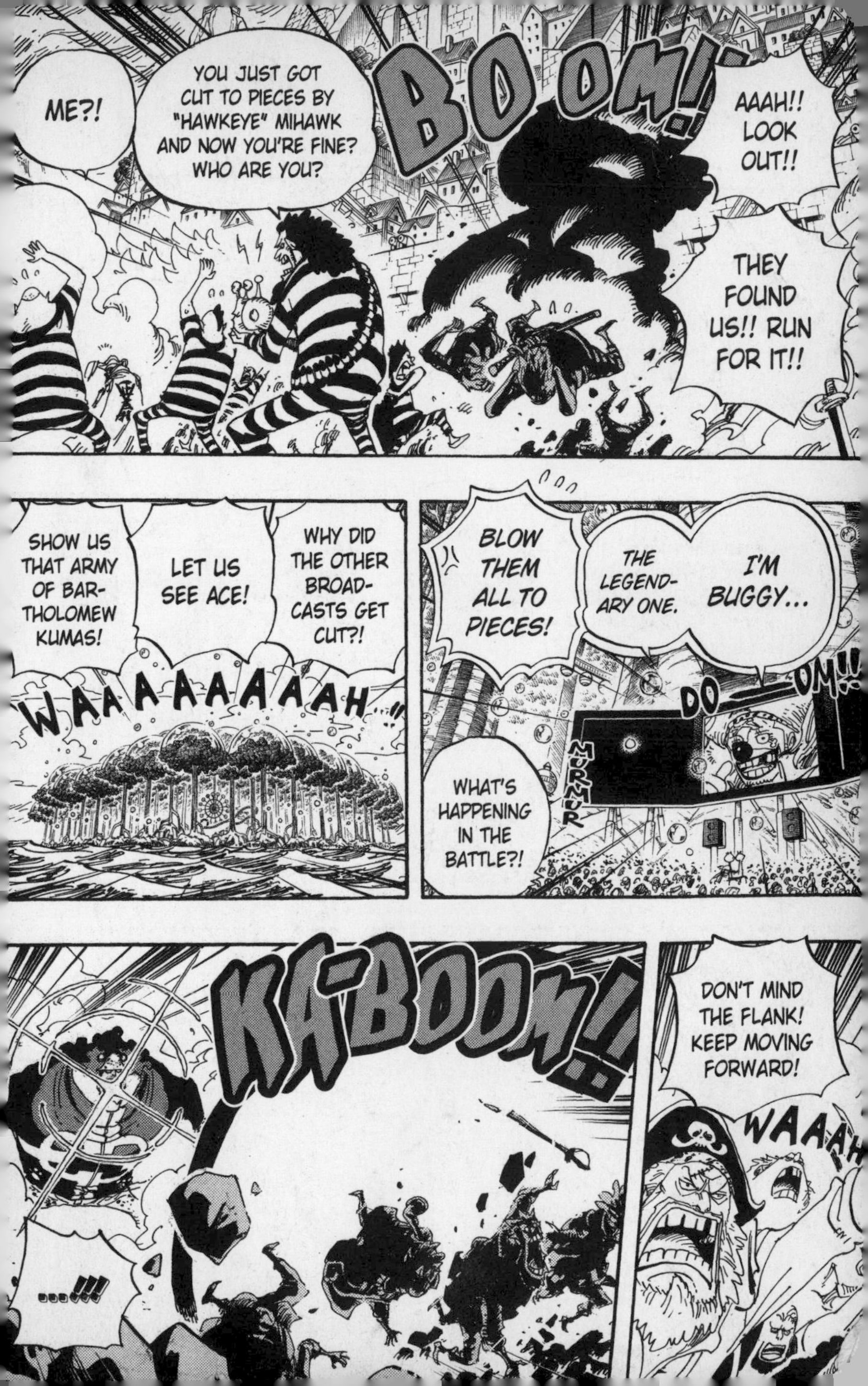
AAAH!! LOOK OUT!!
BOOM!!
THEY FOUND US!! RUN FOR IT!!
YOU JUST GOT CUT TO PIECES BY "HAWKEYE" MIHAWK AND NOW YOU'RE FINE? WHO ARE YOU?
ME?!
I'M BUGGY...
THE LEGEND-ARY ONE.
BLOW THEM ALL TO PIECES!
DO—OM!!
MURMUR
WHAT'S HAPPENING IN THE BATTLE?!
WHY DID THE OTHER BROAD-CASTS GET CUT?!
LET US SEE ACE!
SHOW US THAT ARMY OF BAR-THOLOMEW KUMAS!
WAAAAAAAAAH
DON'T MIND THE FLANK! KEEP MOVING FORWARD!
WAAAH
KA-BOOM!!
...!!!

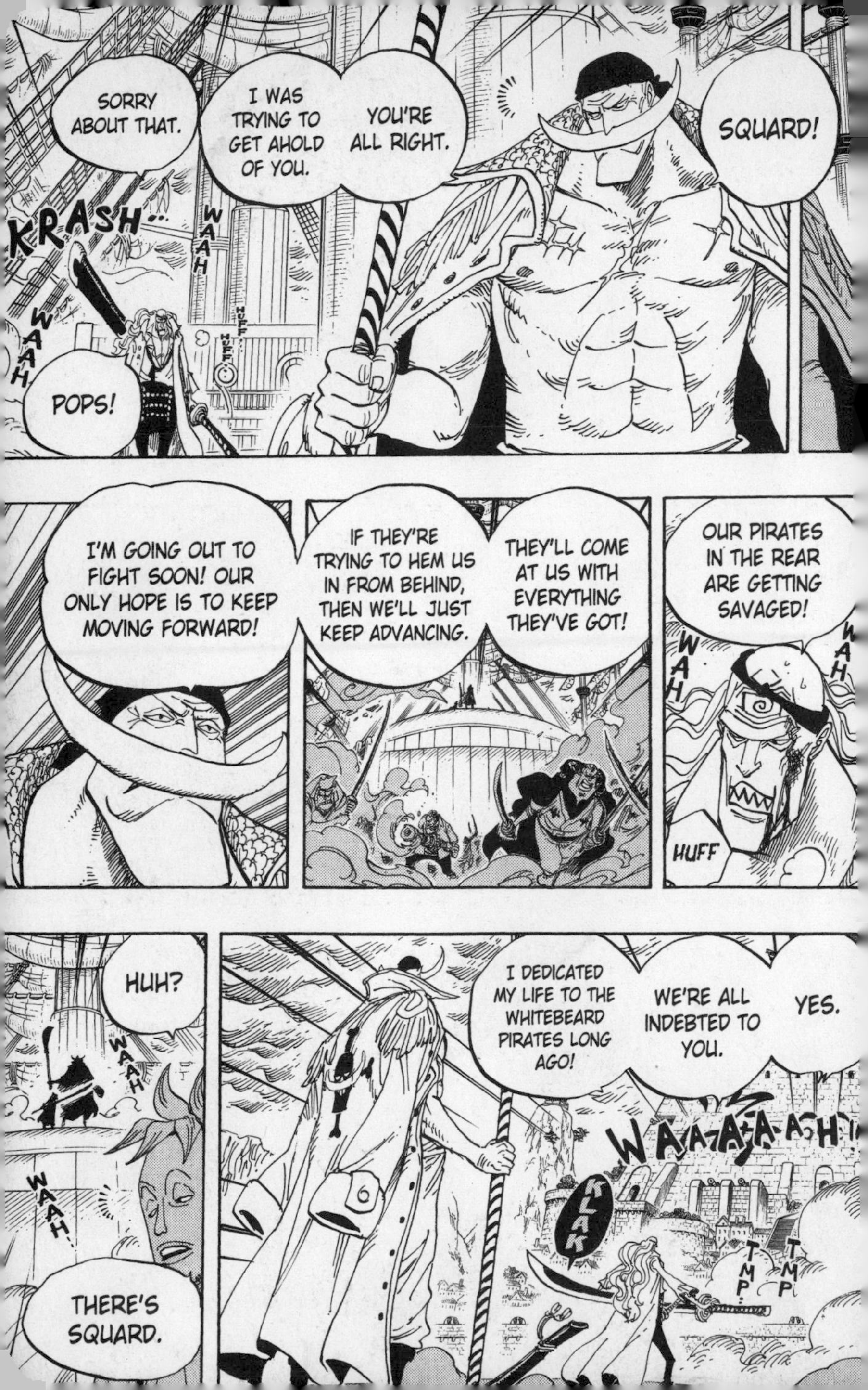
SQUARD!
YOU'RE ALL RIGHT.
I WAS TRYING TO GET AHOLD OF YOU.
SORRY ABOUT THAT.
KRASH..
WAAH
HUFF HUFF
WAAH
POPS!
OUR PIRATES IN THE REAR ARE GETTING SAVAGED!
WAAH
WAAH
HUFF
THEY'LL COME AT US WITH EVERYTHING THEY'VE GOT!
IF THEY'RE TRYING TO HEM US IN FROM BEHIND, THEN WE'LL JUST KEEP ADVANCING.
I'M GOING OUT TO FIGHT SOON! OUR ONLY HOPE IS TO KEEP MOVING FORWARD!
YES.
WE'RE ALL INDEBTED TO YOU.
I DEDICATED MY LIFE TO THE WHITEBEARD PIRATES LONG AGO!
WAAAAAH!
KLAK
TMP
TMP
HUH?
WAAH
WAAH
THERE'S SQUARD.

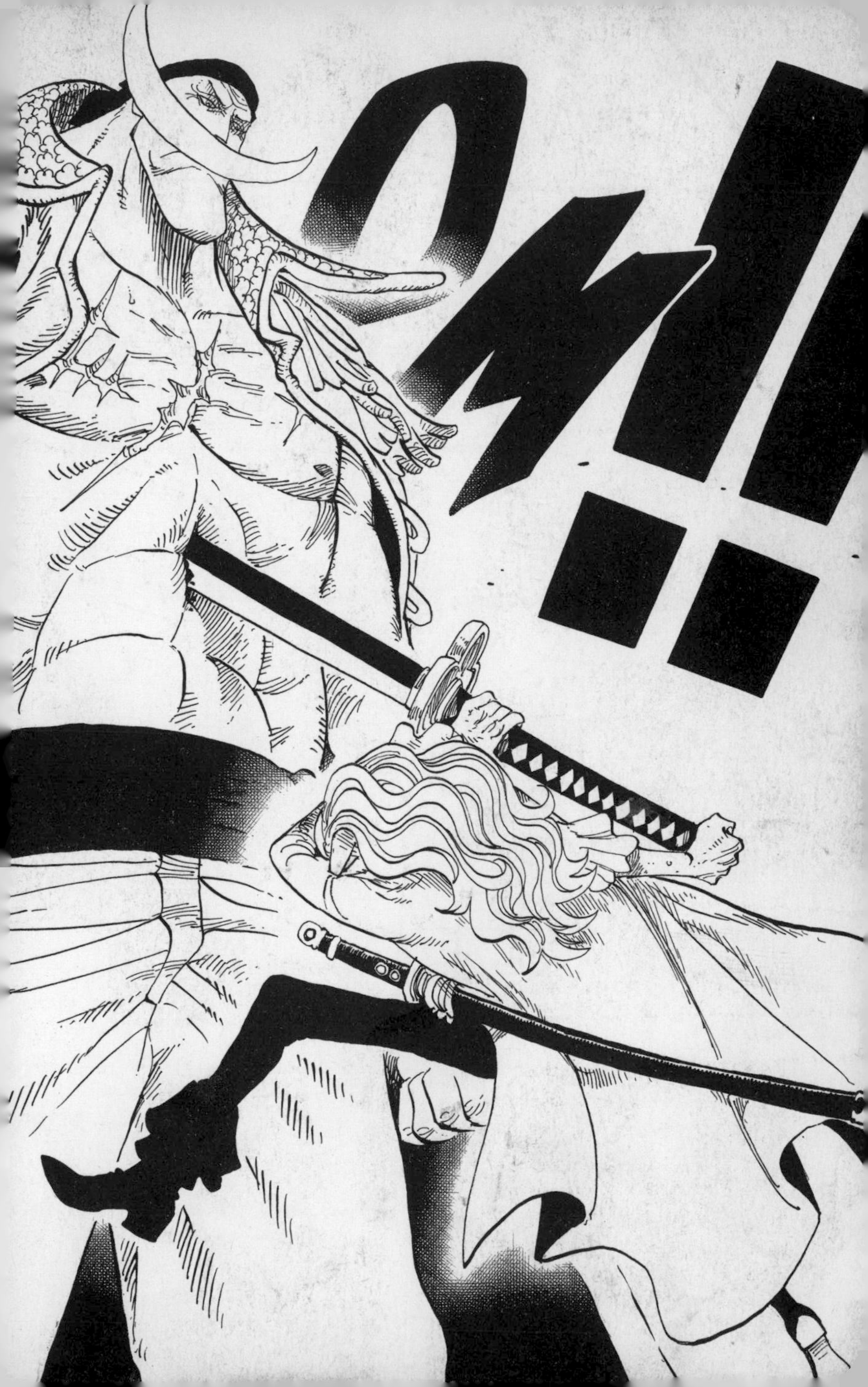
ON!!

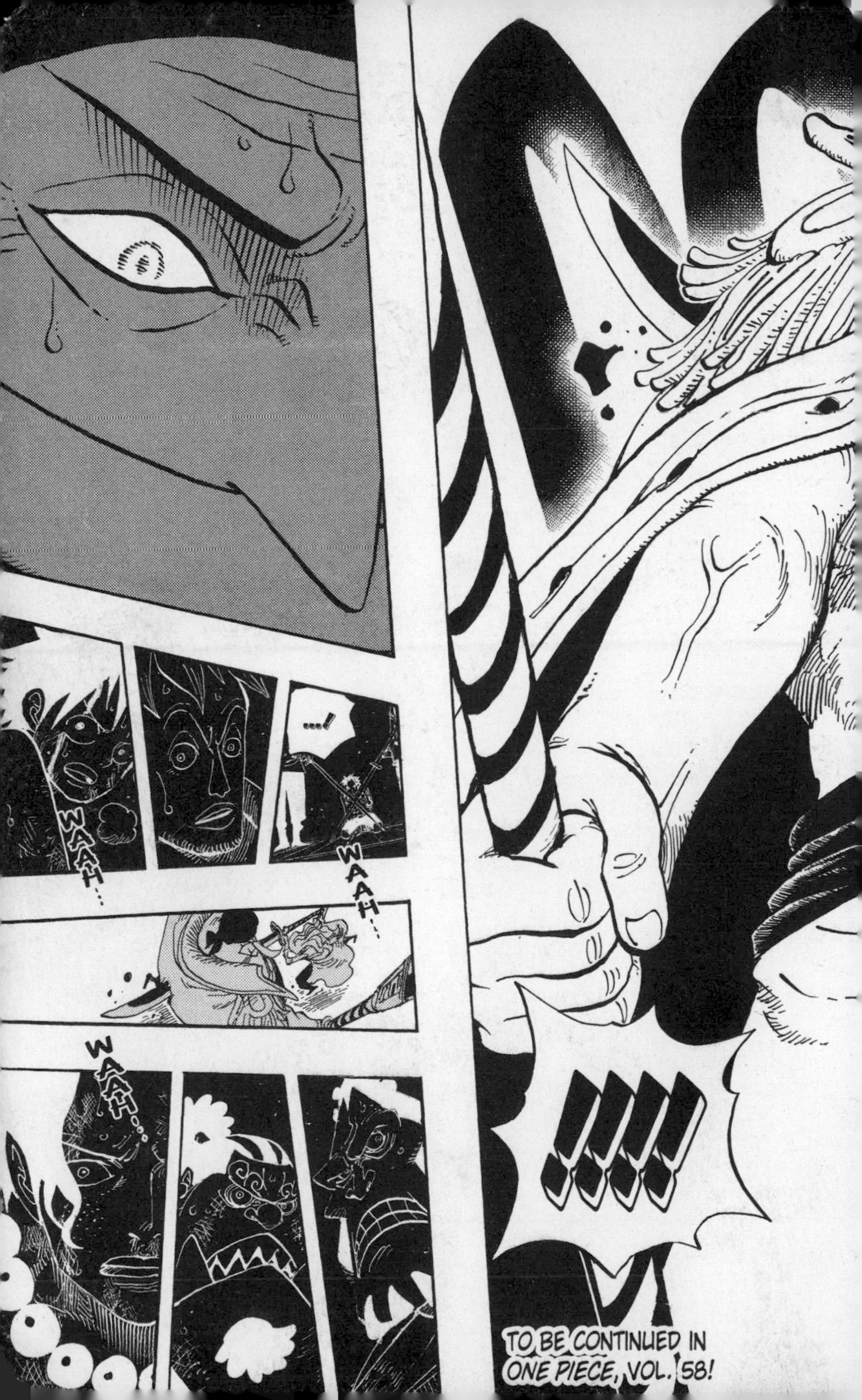
!!!!!
...!
WAAH...
WAAH...
WAAH...

TO BE CONTINUED IN ONE PIECE, VOL. 58!

OUR FIRST-RATE COOK, HIROAKI HIRATA!

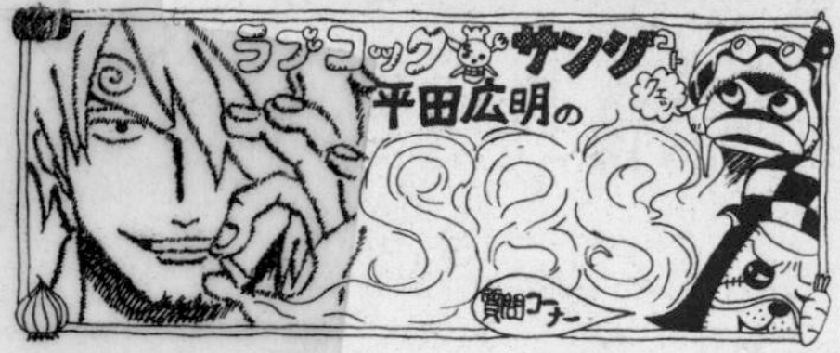
平田広明の
SBS

(Monkey B. Lily, Chiba)

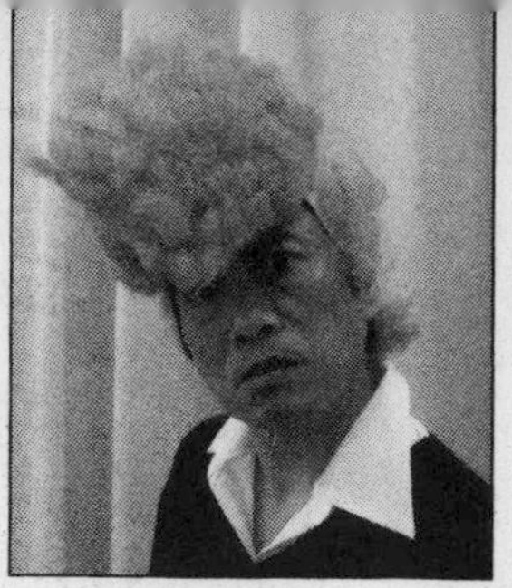

Reader (Q): Mr. Hirata, I think you have already been fused in body and mind with Sanji, but what really is going on with Sanji's mystical left eye? Can you draw it out?

--My Top Measurement is 92cm ♡

Hirata (H):

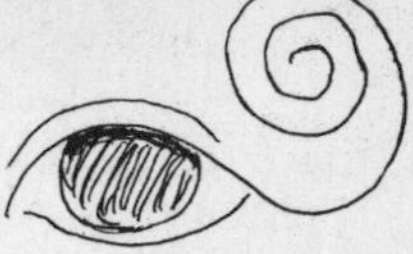

Q: Is there anything that's curly on you?

--Tamaki

H: My wie@#r.

Q: Sanji is a great cook, but I also heard that you can do some cooking yourself! Is it true that you're good at making peperoncino? What other dishes are you good at making? ♡

--Udonya

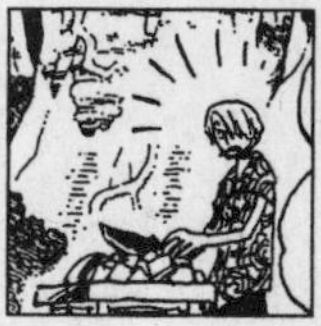

H: The peperoncino that I make is super spicy. There were about three younger members of my theatrical troupe that fell victim to it. Too bad for them. Oh, and I'm good at making curry and dumplings too. ♪

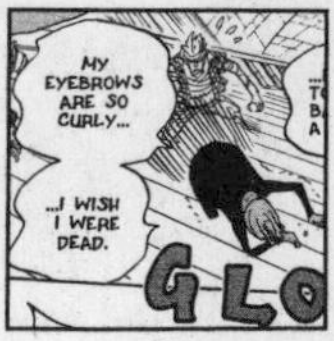
MY EYEBROWS ARE SO CURLY...
...I WISH I WERE DEAD.

Q: What is...love? ♡

--Jan Jack Man

H: Sweet trials and tribulations.

Q: Are you perverted like Sanji? How do you treat the other people you act with? But before that... Take this! Negative Hollow!

-Courage Hero

H: I'm so sorry... Out of everyone, the only one I couldn't make perverted advances on was Mayumi (Luffy's voice actress).

Q: Marry me! I'm so much cuter than Nami or Robin! I'd do anything for Sanji's voice actor! ♡

--Dilka

H: Hmm. Too bad. You were just a bit too late!

Q: Do you know "Zolo"?

--How Do You Like Married Women? ♡

H: Sorry. I don't know too much about foreign languages. Does it mean "fart?"

Q: Hello, Mr. Hirata. I heard from Mr. Nakai (Zolo's voice actor) that you're a mature adult that would never go peeping in a women's bath. You really would, right?

--Twirly Beam

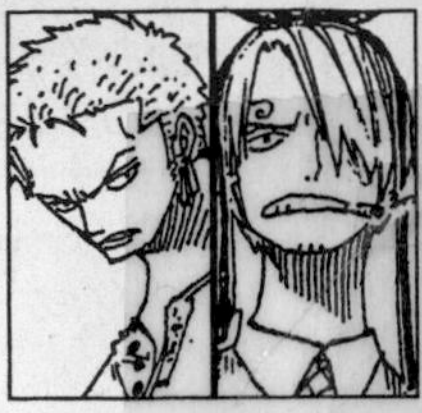

H: Shhhhh! Be quiet! I'm in the women's bath right now!

Q: Look! There's a MAN with the perfect feminine body (but with balls) an a WOMAN with the face of a middle-aged man right in front of you! Which one will you choose? As a man, you'll pick THAT one, right?! Huh?! That one?! That one?!

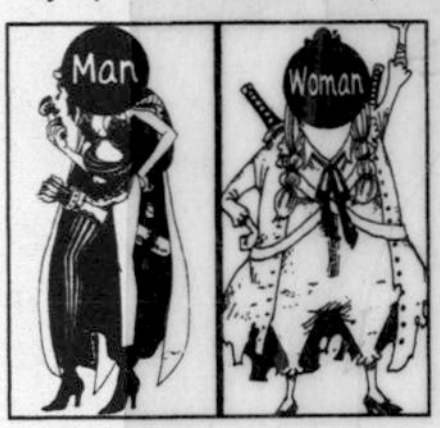
Man
Woman

H: Hmm... Yes, THAT one too.

Q: If you hadn't become a voice actor, what would you have become?

--Love Your Last Line Said to Zeff

H: A train driver. Either that or a manga creator that also works as a voice actor!

Q: Bro! Wait! Phew. Glad I caught up with you... *weez* *weez* Here's the smutty mag that you lent me. Bye! ♪

--Yuccho

H: Took you long enough! I borrowed this from someone else too! Hey, Nakai! Sorry I didn't return this to you earlier.

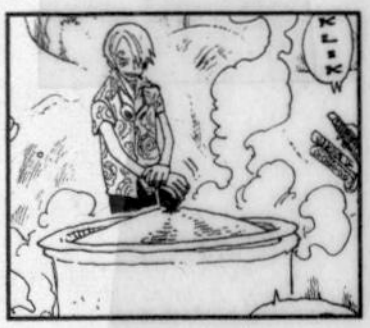

Q: Let's have a cooking battle with Mr. Hiroaki Hirata! I got a roach and rat stew! Want some?

--Prince Dirty

H: What? Then I have stew made with soup stock from Cho-san's (Brook) bones along with Yao (Franky), Nakai (Zolo), and Kappei (Usopp). It smells like booze and farts and it'll cost you 8,000 yen!

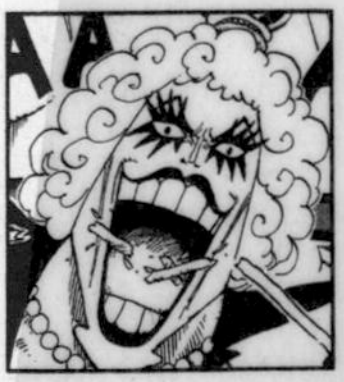

Q: Mr. Hirata! I love you! You have to take responsibility for stealing my heart!♡ "Emporio Female Hormone!" (You can tell me in secret if your boobs are big or small.♡)

--Death Wink Kikui

H: No! Stop! It's embarrassing! I got a big gut! A big gut!

Oda: Thank you, Mr. Hirata. Now I think it's time that we wrap this up and... Ahhhhhhhh! Scary!

H: Ahhhhhhhh!

Oda: Ahhhhhhh! See you next volume!

COMING NEXT VOLUME:

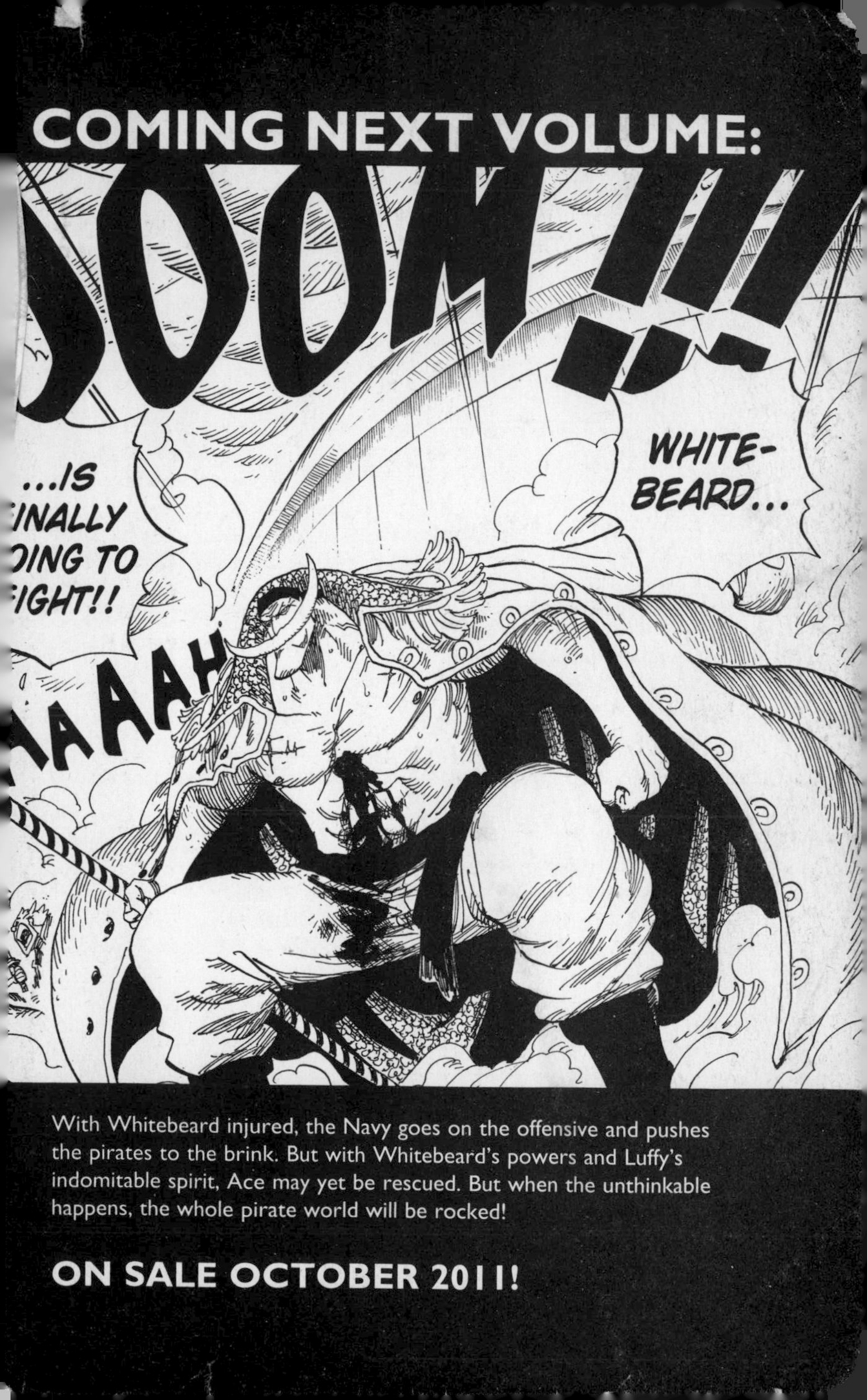

DOOM!!!
WHITE-BEARD...
...IS
INALLY
OING TO
IGHT!!
AAAAH

With Whitebeard injured, the Navy goes on the offensive and pushes the pirates to the brink. But with Whitebeard's powers and Luffy's indomitable spirit, Ace may yet be rescued. But when the unthinkable happens, the whole pirate world will be rocked!

ON SALE OCTOBER 2011!